CIMA

PRACTICE & REVISION KIT

MANAGEMENT

PAPER P2

PERFORMANCE MANAGEMENT

This Kit is for CIMA's exams in 2012.

In this Kit we:

- Discuss the **best strategies** for revising and taking your P2 exam

- Show you how to be well prepared for the **2012 exams**

- Give you **lots of great guidance** on tackling questions

- Demonstrate how you can **build your own exams**

- Provide you with **three** mock exams

FOR EXAMS IN 2012

BPP
LEARNING MEDIA

Third edition January 2012
(First edition January 2010)

ISBN 9781 4453 8094 0
(Previous ISBN 9780 7517 9460 1)

e-ISBN 9781 4453 7650 9

British Library Cataloguing-in-Publication Data
A catalogue record for this book
is available from the British Library

Published by

BPP Learning Media Ltd
BPP House, Aldine Place
London W12 8AA

www.bpp.com/learningmedia

Printed in the United Kingdom

Your learning materials, published by BPP
Learning Media Ltd, are printed on paper sourced
from sustainable, managed forests.

We are grateful to the Chartered Institute of
Management Accountants for permission to
reproduce past examination questions. The
answers to past examination questions have been
prepared by BPP Learning Media Ltd.

Contents

Question index

The headings in this checklist/index indicate the main topics of questions, but questions often cover several different topics.

Questions set under the old syllabus's *Management Accounting – Performance Management (IMPM) and Management Accounting – Decision Making (IDEC)* exams and the last syllabus's *Management Accounting – Decision Management (MADM)* and *Management Accounting – Performance Evaluation* exams are included because their style and content are similar to those that appear in the Paper P2 exam.

Mock exam 1

Questions 108-114

Mock exam 2 (September 2011 resit examination)

Questions 115-121

Mock exam 3 (November 2011 examination)

Questions 122-128

Planning your question practice

Our guidance from page xvii shows you how to organise your question practice, either by attempting questions from each syllabus area or by **building your own exams** – tackling questions as a series of practice exams.

Topic index

Listed below are the key Paper P2 syllabus topics and the numbers of the questions in this Kit covering those topics.

If you need to concentrate your practice and revision on certain topics or if you want to attempt all available questions that refer to a particular subject you will find this index useful.

Using your BPP Learning Media Practice and Revision Kit

Tackling revision and the exam

You can significantly improve your chances of passing by tackling revision and the exam in the right ways. Our advice is based on feedback from CIMA. We focus on Paper P2; we discuss revising the syllabus, what to do (and what not to do) in the exam, how to approach different types of question and ways of obtaining easy marks.

Selecting questions

We provide signposts to help you plan your revision.

- A full **question index**

- A **topic index**, listing all the questions that cover key topics, so that you can locate the questions that provide practice on these topics, and see the different ways in which they might be examined

- **BPP's question plan**, highlighting the most important questions

- **Build your own exams**, showing you how you can practise questions in a series of exams

Making the most of question practice

We realise that you need more than questions and model answers to get the most from your question practice.

- Our **Top tips** provide essential advice on tackling questions and presenting answers

- We show you how you can pick up **Easy marks** on questions, as picking up all readily available marks can make the difference between passing and failing

- We include **marking guides** to show you what the examiner rewards

- We refer to the **BPP 2011 Study Text** (for 2012 exams) for detailed coverage of the topics covered in each question

Attempting mock exams

There are three mock exams that provide practice at coping with the pressures of the exam day. We strongly recommend that you attempt them under exam conditions, as they reflect the question styles and syllabus coverage of the exam. To help you get the most out of doing these exams, we provide guidance on how you should have approached the whole exam.

Our other products

BPP Learning Media also offers these products for practising and revising for the P2 exam:

Passcards	Summarising what you should know in visual, easy to remember, form
Success CDs	Covering the vital elements of the P2 syllabus in less than 90 minutes and also containing exam hints to help you fine tune your strategy
i-Pass	Providing computer-based testing in a variety of formats, ideal for self-assessment
Interactive Passcards	Allowing you to learn actively with a clear visual format summarising what you must know

You can purchase these products by visiting www.bpp.com/learningmedia

Revising P2

The P2 exam

This will be a time-pressured exam that combines calculations with discussion. It is very important that you do not concentrate completely on the calculations at the expense of fully understanding the management issues involved.

Topics to revise

You need to be comfortable with **all areas of the syllabus** as all questions are compulsory. Question spotting will **not work** on this paper!

Pricing and product decisions

- Calculation and interpretation of relevant costs and revenues
- Short-term decisions, including acceptance/rejection of contracts, make or buy decisions
- Allocation of joint costs and treatment of by-products
- Working with limiting factors, including the graphical and simplex methods of linear programming (use and interpretation of shadow prices, formulation of initial tableau, interpretation of final simplex tableau)
- Multi-product CVP analysis, including breakeven and P/V charts, contribution/sales ratio and margin of safety
- Pricing decisions and pricing strategies, including premium pricing, market skimming, penetration pricing and product differentiation

Cost planning and analysis for competitive advantage

- Evaluation of techniques for analysing and managing costs for competitive advantage (including JIT, value analysis, TQM, learning curves, value chain, ABC and life cycle costing)

Budgeting and management control

- Explanation of the principles underlying the use of budgets in control. This includes controllable and uncontrollable costs, responsibility accounting and the concepts of feedback and feed-forward control.
- The use of flexible budgets for control purposes
- Calculation and interpretation of variances (this is assumed knowledge from P1)
- Discussion and application of the balanced scorecard
- Critique of budgeting as a control mechanism, including the consideration of 'Beyond Budgeting' techniques

Control and performance measurement of responsibility centres

- Calculation and interpretation of divisional performance measures such as return on investment (ROI), residual income (RI) and economic value added (EVA)
- Discussion of the use of profit centres, cost centres, revenue centres and investment centres in devising organisational structure
- Calculation of appropriate transfer prices in different situations, including perfect, imperfect and no market for the goods being transferred
- Discussion of the implications of different transfer prices for divisional decision-making and divisional and group profitability
- Discussion of how different transfer pricing policies can affect divisional autonomy and the motivation of divisional management

Question practice

Question practice under timed conditions is essential, so that you can get used to the pressures of answering exam questions in **limited time** and practise not only the key techniques but allocating your time between different requirements in each question. It's particularly important to do questions from both sections of the paper in full to see how the numerical and written elements balance in longer questions.

Passing the P2 exam

Displaying the right qualities

You will be expected to display the following qualities.

Qualities required	
Business awareness	You are expected to read the business press. This awareness will enable you to apply your knowledge in context when answering questions.
Time management skills	You need to attempt all parts of all questions. So you must work out before you start the exam how much time you will spend on each question. Stick to this!
Flexible thinking	Questions often won't state what technique(s) you should be using. You need to select the appropriate technique yourself.
Evaluation of past and future performance using information provided	You will need to perform calculations that directly evaluate the scenario presented and based on these give advice.
Show strategic awareness	Although this is a Management level paper, the questions will be starting to test your wider awareness of the environment and strategic issues that a company faces. For instance, questions on pricing policy or externally-oriented management accounting techniques will require a strategic view.

Avoiding weaknesses

You will enhance your chances significantly if you ensure you avoid these mistakes:

- Lacking basic management accounting knowledge, for instance, correctly identifying fixed and variable costs
- Syllabus spotting leading to gaps in knowledge
- Not answering requirements stated in questions
- Not using the scenario in written questions and not answering the question in the context of that scenario
- Failing to learn topics in enough detail to answer longer questions
- Brain dumping all that is known about a topic (no credit is given for this)
- Failing to answer sufficient questions because of poor time management
- Not showing clear workings to enable method marks to be awarded

Using the reading time

We recommend you spend at least part of the reading time reading the requirements of the questions. By doing this you can start to plan the order in which you might answer the questions. Jot down some ideas on how you plan to answer the questions. If you collect your thoughts at this early stage you are less likely to forget key facts later on.

Choosing which questions to answer first

Choosing which questions to answer first is a matter of preference. You should practise different methods during your revision to decide which one suits you best. Remember that all questions are compulsory in this paper so you will have to answer them all eventually! Make use of your reading time (see above) to pick out the questions you are likely to be most confident with. If you start with a question you feel you can answer well, it will give you a boost quite early on in the exam. Make sure you don't spend too long on such questions though – you still have to answer all seven questions!

Numerical questions

You are likely to see calculation questions covering:

- Relevant costing
- Transfer pricing
- Divisional performance measures
- Learning curves and learning rates
- Variances
- Management accounting techniques such as ABC
- Linear programming

Even if you do make a mistake on the numbers, you will gain credit for the correct approach on these questions. A brief narrative explaining your approach to tricky calculations will help the marker.

You can expect to come across some very difficult things in the questions. You must learn to move on and do as much of the question as possible.

Present your numbers neatly in a table format with key numbers underlined and clear workings.

Discussion questions

You will not only be expected to calculate numbers, you will also be expected to discuss their meaning and implications for the business as a whole. Even if your numbers are incorrect, you will still get marks for relevant comments about the figures you have calculated. Make sure you don't miss out the discussion parts of questions in your revision as discussion marks make up a substantial proportion of the total marks available.

In Section A, you should expect questions that are solely based on discussion therefore you should make sure you practise such questions as much as possible. Remember to pay attention to the verbs used (a list of the verbs CIMA use in their exam questions is provided in this Practice and Revision Kit). Be familiar with what is expected of you from each of these verbs and apply these skills when answering the questions. You will get few, if any, marks if you are asked to 'discuss' an issue and you only 'explain' it.

If you are given a scenario in a discussion question, make sure your answer relates to this scenario. Do not be tempted to simply write all you know about a topic. Markers have seen all this before and it becomes obvious very quickly if you do not really know what you are talking about. If you can think of relevant real life examples of issues (you are provided with numerous short case studies in your BPP Learning Media Study Text), don't be afraid to include them as this shows that you can apply the theory to practical situations.

Remember that the marking schemes for discussion questions will be fairly general, and you will gain credit for all relevant points.

Gaining the easy marks

Suggestions of where to pick up easy marks have been given at the beginning of the answers to numerous questions in the Answer Bank. You could argue that most marks are easy if you are familiar with the topic but there are ways in which you can secure marks for very little effort. A simple thing like writing your answer in report format when the question requires it brings very easy marks. Other ways of gaining marks (or avoiding losing them!) include

- Setting out calculations clearly and providing explanations for calculations when required

- Clearly labelling the points you make in discussions so that the marker can identify them all rather than getting lost in the detail

- Making your answer relevant to the scenario (if there is one) rather than just writing everything you know about the topic

The most obvious way of gaining easy marks is to answer the question set rather than the one you hoped might come up!

The exam paper

Format of the paper

		Number of marks
Section A:	5 compulsory questions of 10 marks each	50
Section B:	2 compulsory questions of 25 marks each	50
		100

Time allowed: 3 hours, plus 20 minutes reading time.

Breadth of question coverage

Questions in *both* sections of the paper may cover more than one syllabus area.

Knowledge from other syllabuses

You are expected to have knowledge from previous papers, particularly Paper P1 – *Performance Operations*.

November 2011

This exam is Mock exam 3 in this Kit.

Section A

1   Learning curve; CVP analysis

2   Kaizen costing and standard costing

3   Value analysis and function analysis

4   Feedback and feedforward control

5   Balanced scorecard; performance measures

Section B

6   Relevant costing; transfer pricing

7   Divisional performance; costs of quality

September 2011 (resit exam)

This exam is Mock exam 2 in this Kit.

Section A

1   Optimum price and quantity

2   Customer life cycle costing

3   Kaizen costing

4   Variances; material mix and yield

5   Balanced scorecard; NFPIs

Section B

6   Profitability statements; breakeven; value analysis

7   Transfer pricing; NPV

May 2011

Section A

1 Optimal pricing

2 Product life cycle

3 Target costing; Kaizen costing

4 Variance analysis; planning and operational variances

5 Non-financial performance measures

Section B

6 Relevant costing

7 Divisionalised performance; transfer pricing; investment appraisal

March 2011 (resit exam)

Section A

1 The learning curve

2 Just-in-time production

3 Participative budgeting

4 Variance analysis; reconciliation statement

5 Total quality management

Section B

6 Short-term decisions; linear programming

7 Divisional performance; transfer pricing

November 2010

Section A

1 Learning curve; planning and operational variances

2 Costs of quality

3 Total quality management; JIT

4 Budgeting systems; rolling budgets

5 Activity-based costing (ABC)

Section B

6 Limiting factor analysis; linear programming – the simplex method

7 Measuring performance in divisionalised businesses

September 2010 (resit exam)

Section A

1   Multi-product breakeven analysis

2   Kaizen; costs of quality

3   Customer profitability analysis

4   Participative budgeting; motivation

5   Learning curve; target costing; variance analysis

Section B

6   Pricing strategies; product life cycle

7   Performance measures; FPIs

May 2010

Section A

1   Learning curve; budgets; variances

2   Product life cycle

3   Inventory holding; JIT

4   Budgeting systems; FPIs and NFPIs

5   Divisional performance statement; ABC

Section B

6   Limiting factor analysis; linear programming – the graphical method

7   ROI; NPV

Specimen paper

Section A

1   Gain sharing; value chain

2   Learning curve; variances

3   Budget systems; motivation

4   Pareto analysis; ABC

5   Target costs; pricing decisions

Section B

6   Relevant costing

7   Performance measurement; transfer pricing

What the examiner means

The table below has been prepared by CIMA to help you interpret exam questions.

Learning objective	Verbs used	Definition	Examples in the Kit
1 Knowledge			
What you are expected to know	• List	• Make a list of	
	• State	• Express, fully or clearly, the details of/facts of	9(a)
	• Define	• Give the exact meaning of	
2 Comprehension			
What you are expected to understand	• Describe	• Communicate the key features of	
	• Distinguish	• Highlight the differences between	
	• Explain	• Make clear or intelligible/state the meaning or purpose of	52(b)
	• Identify	• Recognise, establish or select after consideration	30(b)
	• Illustrate	• Use an example to describe or explain something	
3 Application			
How you are expected to apply your knowledge	• Apply	• Put to practical use	
	• Calculate/compute	• Ascertain or reckon mathematically	16(b)
	• Demonstrate	• Prove the certainty or exhibit by practical means	
	• Prepare	• Make or get ready for use	4(a)
	• Reconcile	• Make or prove consistent/ compatible	
	• Solve	• Find an answer to	
	• Tabulate	• Arrange in a table	
4 Analysis			
How you are expected to analyse the detail of what you have learned	• Analyse	• Examine in detail the structure of	
	• Categorise	• Place into a defined class or division	
	• Compare and contrast	• Show the similarities and/or differences between	43(c)(i)
	• Construct	• Build up or complete	
	• Discuss	• Examine in detail by argument	91(c)
	• Interpret	• Translate into intelligible or familiar terms	
	• Prioritise	• Place in order of priority or sequence for action	
	• Produce	• Create or bring into existence	5(a)(iii)
5 Evaluation			
How you are expected to use your learning to evaluate, make decisions or recommendations	• Advise	• Counsel, inform or notify	
	• Evaluate	• Appraise or assess the value of	1(b)
	• Recommend	• Propose a course of action	106(c)

Planning your question practice

We have already stressed that question practice should be right at the centre of your revision. Whilst you will spend some time looking at your notes and the Paper P2 Passcards, you should spend the majority of your revision time practising questions.

We recommend two ways in which you can practise questions.

- Use **BPP Learning Media's question plan** to work systematically through the syllabus and attempt key and other questions on a section-by-section basis

- **Build your own exams** – attempt the questions as a series of practice exams

These ways are suggestions and simply following them is no guarantee of success. You or your college may prefer an alternative but equally valid approach.

BPP's question plan

The plan below requires you to devote a **minimum of 45 hours** to revision of Paper P2. Any time you can spend over and above this should only increase your chances of success.

 Review your notes and the chapter summaries in the Paper P2 **Passcards** for each section of the syllabus.

 Answer the key questions for that section. These questions have boxes round the question number in the table below and you should answer them in full. Even if you are short of time you must attempt these questions if you want to pass the exam. You should complete your answers without referring to our solutions.

 Attempt the other questions in that section. For some questions we have suggested that you prepare **answer plans or do the calculations** rather than full solutions. Planning an answer means that you should spend about 40% of the time allowance for the questions brainstorming the question and drawing up a list of points to be included in the answer.

 Attempt Mock exams 1, 2 and 3 under strict exam conditions.

Syllabus section	2011 Passcards chapters	Questions in this Kit	Comments	Done ☑
Relevant costs and short-term decisions	1A, 1B	1	Answer in full. This past exam question covers joint products and dealing with joint costs. Part (b) requires some evaluation.	☐
		3	Answer in full. Another past exam question that tests the further processing decision relating to joint products.	☐
		4	Answer in full. This question from May 2011 gives you the opportunity to put your knowledge of relevant costing into practise, not just in identifying the relevant costs but also in preparing a statement for management.	☐
		5	Answer in full. This question from the specimen paper tests relevant costing and non-financial matters in decision-making	☐
Limiting factor analysis	2	9	Answer in full. This question links limiting factors to throughput and simplex.	☐
		13	Answer in full. This question from the March 2011 resit exam tests a number of areas related to limiting factors and how to deal with them.	☐
Linear programming	3, 4	10	Answer in full. A good practice question for formulating a linear programming model.	☐
		14	Answer in full. This question from November 2010 looks at single limiting factors, defining constraints and interpreting a simplex model.	☐
		15	Answer in full. A simplex linear programming question that gives you practice in formulating the initial tableau and interpreting the final tableau.	☐
		16	Answer in full. This past exam question mixes limiting factors and graphical linear programming.	☐
Multi-product CVP analysis	5	19	Answer in full. This question from the September 2010 resit exam tests a number of CVP techniques.	☐
		20	Attempt the calculations in (b) as practice.	☐
		22	Answer in full. Another excellent question that covers a wide spectrum of CVP issues.	☐

Syllabus section	2011 Passcards chapters	Questions in this Kit	Comments	Done ✓
Pricing decisions and pricing strategies	6	23	Worth trying each stand-alone section of this question to practise calculating optimal prices.	☐
		24	Write an answer plan. This scenario-based question tests your knowledge of absorption and marginal cost pricing and the concept of contribution.	☐
		27	Answer in full. This question from May 2011 tests optimal pricing.	☐
		31	Answer in full. This question from the September 2010 resit exam tests your knowledge of pricing strategies, the product life cycle and the demand curve. Scenario based.	☐
Cost planning	7	33	Answer in full. A good question that tests your knowledge of cost reduction and value analysis.	☐
		34	Answer in full. This question from May 2011 tests your knowledge of target costing and Kaizen costing.	☐
		38	Answer in full. This question from May 2010 tests your knowledge of variances and the learning curve.	☐
		40	Answer in full. This learning curve question tests both discursive and numerical elements.	☐
		42	Answer in full. This question tests several cost planning techniques and pricing policies.	☐
Cost analysis	8	47	Answer in full. A question from the specimen paper on Pareto analysis and ABC.	☐
		51	Answer in full. This question provides good coverage of traditional methods of pricing and the ABC approach.	☐
		52	Answer in full. This question covers both limiting factor analysis and ABC.	☐
		53	Answer in full. This is a good question that tests your knowledge and understanding of direct product profitability.	☐

Syllabus section	2011 Passcards chapters	Questions in this Kit	Comments	Done ☑
Cost management techniques	9A, 9B	54	Write an answer plan. This question covers business process re-engineering.	☐
		56	Answer in full. This question from November 2010 focuses on costs of quality.	☐
		57	Answer in full. This question from November 2010 focuses on JIT and TQM.	☐
		63	Answer in full. This question looks at the implications of changing cost structures on inventory valuation and short-term decision-making.	☐
		67	Write an answer plan. This question from the specimen paper covers the value chain and gain sharing.	☐
		71	Answer in full. This question covers various aspects of JIT, both discursive and numerical.	☐
		72	Answer in full. A good question to practise throughput accounting techniques.	☐
Budgeting and management control	10, 11	74	Answer in full. This is a good preparatory question to get you thinking about budgetary issues.	☐
		76	Answer in full. This question from May 2011 tests non-financial performance measures and non-controllable costs.	☐
		77	Answer in full. This question from the March 2011 resit exam focuses on the behavioural aspects of budgeting.	☐
		81	Answer in full. A question from the specimen paper on feedback and feedforward control systems and participative budgeting.	☐
		88	Answer in full. This question from the March 2011 resit exam requires you to produce a statement that reconciles budgeted and actual profit.	☐
		90	Answer in full. This is a good question that tests your knowledge of variances and budgeting systems.	☐

Syllabus section	2011 Passcards chapters	Questions in this Kit	Comments	Done ☑
Control and performance measurement of responsibility centres	12, 13	93	Answer in full. This question focuses on behavioural aspects of transfer pricing policies and appropriate policies to use in a given scenario.	☐
		94, 95	Write answer plans. These questions are good preparatory questions on transfer pricing.	☐
	12, 13	96	Answer in full. This question from November 2010 focuses on divisional performance, RI and ROI.	☐
		98, 99	Write answer plans. These are good preparatory questions on performance measures for responsibility centres.	☐
		101	Answer in full. This question from May 2011 tests your knowledge of transfer pricing and investment appraisal.	☐
		104	Answer in full. This question from the specimen paper is a mixture of performance measures and transfer pricing elements.	☐
		107	Answer in full. This question tests transfer pricing and contains a number of computational and discursive requirements.	☐

Build your own exams

Having revised your notes and the BPP Passcards, you can attempt the questions in the Kit as a series of practice exams, making them up yourself or using the mock exams that we have listed below.

	Practice exams					
	1	2	3	4	5	6
Section A						
1	35	19	60	26	19	24
2	68	40	28	46	94	41
3	93	3	10	33	30	59
4	20	99	66	1	38	2
5	39	29	80	70	68	99
Section B						
6	6	52	50	15	86	18
7	105	72	104	106	9	71

Whichever practice exams you use, you must attempt **Mock exams 1, 2 and 3** at the end of your revision.

QUESTIONS

2

SECTION A – PRICING AND PRODUCT DECISIONS

Questions 1 to 32 cover pricing and product decisions, the subject of Part A of the BPP Study Text for Paper P2.

1   Z Ltd (MADM, 5/05)   18 mins

Z Ltd manufactures three joint products (M, N and P) from the same common process. The following process account relates to the common process last month and is typical of the monthly results of operating this process:

COMMON PROCESS ACCOUNT

	Litres	$		Litres	$
Opening work in process	1,000	5,320	Normal loss	10,000	20,000
Materials	100,000	250,000	Output M	25,000	141,875
Conversion costs:			Output N	15,000	85,125
Variable		100,000	Output P	45,000	255,375
Fixed		180,000	Closing work in process	800	3,533
			Abnormal loss	5,200	29,412
	101,000	535,320		101,000	535,320

Each one of the products can be sold immediately after the common process, but each one of them can be further processed individually before being sold. The following further processing costs and selling prices per litre are expected:

Product	Selling price after common process $/litre	Selling price after further processing $/litre	Further variable processing cost $/litre
M	6.25	8.40	1.75
N	5.20	6.45	0.95
P	6.80	7.45	0.85

Required

(a)   State the method used to apportion the common costs between the products M, N and P and comment on its acceptability. Explain why it is necessary to apportion the common costs between each of the products.

(5 marks)

(b)   Evaluate the viability of the common process, and determine the optimal processing plan for each of the three products, showing appropriate calculations.

(5 marks)

(Total = 10 marks)

2   Exe (MADM, Pilot paper, amended)   18 mins

You have received a request from EXE to provide a quotation for the manufacture of a specialised piece of equipment. This would be a one-off order, in excess of normal budgeted production. The following cost estimate has already been prepared:

		Note	$
Direct materials:			
Steel	10m² @ $5.00 per m²	1	50
Brass fittings		2	20
Direct labour:			
Skilled	25 hours @ $8.00 per hour	3	200
Semi-skilled	10 hours @ $5.00 per hour	4	50
Overhead	35 hours @ $10.00 per hour	5	350
Estimating time		6	100
			770
Administration overhead @ 20% of production cost		7	154
			924
Profit @ 25% of total cost		8	231
Selling price			1,155

Notes

1   The steel is regularly used, and has a current stock value of $5.00 per square metre. There are currently 100 square metres in stock. The steel is readily available at a price of $5.50 per square metre.

2   The brass fittings would have to be bought specifically for this job: a supplier has quoted the price of $20 for the fittings required.

3   The skilled labour is currently employed by your company and paid at a rate of $8.00 per hour. If this job were undertaken it would be necessary either to work 25 hours' overtime, which would be paid at time plus one half, OR in order to carry out the work in normal time, reduce production of another product that earns a contribution of $13.00 per hour.

4   The semi-skilled labour currently has sufficient paid idle time to be able to complete this work.

5   The overhead absorption rate includes power costs which are directly related to machine usage. If this job were undertaken, it is estimated that the machine time required would be ten hours. The machines incur power costs of $0.75 per hour. There are no other overhead costs that can be specifically identified with this job.

6   The cost of the estimating time is that attributed to the four hours taken by the engineers to analyse the drawings and determine the cost estimate given above.

7   It is company policy to add 20% to the production cost as an allowance for administration costs associated with the jobs accepted.

8   This is the standard profit added by your company as part of its pricing policy.

Required

Prepare on a relevant cost basis, the lowest cost estimate that could be used as the basis for a quotation. Explain briefly your reasons for using *each* of the values in your estimate. **(10 marks)**

3   Z (MADM, 5/07)   18 mins

Z is one of a number of companies that produce three products for an external market. The three products, R, S and T may be bought or sold in this market.

The common process account of Z for March 20X7 is shown below:

	Kg	$		Kg	$
Inputs					
Material A	1,000	3,500	Normal loss	500	0
Material B	2,000	2,000	Outputs:		
Material C	1,500	3,000	Product R	800	3,500
Direct labour		6,000	Product S	2,000	8,750
Variable overhead		2,000	Product T	1,200	5,250
Fixed cost		1,000			
Totals	4,500	17,500		4,500	17,500

Z can sell products R, S or T after this common process or they can be individually further processed and sold as RZ, SZ and TZ respectively. The market prices for the products at the intermediate stage and after further processing are:

Market prices per kg:

	$
R	3.00
S	5.00
T	3.50
RZ	6.00
SZ	5.75
TZ	6.75

The specific costs of the three individual further processes are:

Process R to RZ	variable cost of $1·40 per kg, no fixed costs
Process S to SZ	variable cost of $0·90 per kg, no fixed costs
Process T to TZ	variable cost of $1·00 per kg, fixed cost of $600 per month

Required

(a) Produce calculations to determine whether any of the intermediate products should be further processed before being sold. Clearly state your recommendations together with any relevant assumptions that you have made. **(3 marks)**

(b) Produce calculations to assess the viability of the common process:

(i) Assuming that there is an external market for products R,S and T

(ii) Assuming that there is **not** an external market for products R,S and T. State clearly your recommendations **(7 marks)**

(Total = 10 marks)

4 Hotel (5/11)   45 mins

The management of a hotel is planning for the next year. The hotel has 100 bedrooms. The price of a room night includes breakfast for the guests. Other services (a snack service and a bar and restaurant) are available but are not included in the price of the room night. These additional services are provided to hotel guests only.

For planning purposes the hotel divides the year (based on 360 days) into three seasons: peak, mid and low.

Details of the hotel and its services and forecasts for the next year are given below.

1 <u>Seasons, room charges, room occupancy, guests per room and room revenue</u>

The hotel charges a price per room per night (including breakfast) irrespective of the number of guests per room. The price charged is different in each of the seasons.

Season	Peak	Mid	Low
Number of days	90	120	150
Price charged per room per night ($)	100.00	80.00	55.00
Hotel room occupancy %	95	75	50
Average number of guests per room	1.8	1.5	1.2
Total room revenue ($)	855,000	720,000	412,500

2 <u>Guest related costs</u>

The hotel incurs some costs, including providing breakfast, that are directly related to the number of guests in the hotel. These are $12 per guest per night in all seasons.

3 <u>Room related costs</u>

The hotel incurs some costs that are directly related to the number of rooms occupied. These include cleaning and laundry costs of $5 per occupied room per night regardless of season. There are also power and lighting costs of $3 in the peak season, $4 in the mid season and $6 in the low season per occupied room per night.

4 <u>Hot snacks</u>

The hotel offers a 24 hour hot snacks service to the guests. Past records show that this service has been used by 30% of its guests in the mid and low seasons but only 10% in the peak season. It is forecast that the average spend per guest per night will be $10. The hotel earns a 30% gross contribution from this income.

The hotel employs a cook on a salary of $20,000 per year to provide this service. All of the costs for the hot snacks service, except for the cook's salary, are variable. The cook could be made redundant with no redundancy costs.

5 <u>Restaurant & Bar</u>

Past records show that the usage of the restaurant and bar is seasonal. The restaurant and bar are particularly popular with the hotel's business guests. The forecast usage is shown below.

Season	Daily demand
Peak	30% of hotel guests spend an average of $15 each
Mid	50% of hotel guests spend an average of $20 each
Low	70% of hotel guests spend an average of $30 each

The hotel earns a 25% gross contribution from this income and employs two chefs on a combined salary of $54,000 per year to provide this facility. All of the costs in the restaurant and bar, except for the salaries of the chefs, are variable.

The two chefs could be made redundant with no redundancy costs.

6 General hotel costs

These include the costs of reception staff, the heating and lighting of the common areas and other facility related costs. The forecast costs for next year are:

Peak season $300,000
Mid season $400,000
Low season $500,000

These costs could be reduced by 75% if the hotel were to close temporarily for one or more seasons of the year.

There are also some costs that are incurred by the hotel and can only be avoided by its permanent closure. These are estimated to $200,000 for next year.

Required

(a) Prepare, in an appropriate format, a columnar statement that will help the managers of the hotel to plan for next year. Your statement should show the hotel's activities by season and in total. **(18 marks)**

(b)

(i) Identify, based on your statement, the actions that the managers could take to maximise the profit of the hotel for next year. **(3 marks)**

(ii) Explain TWO factors that the managers should consider before implementing the actions you identified in (b)(i). **(4 marks)**

(Total = 25 marks)

5 M Group (Specimen paper)   45 mins

M is the holding company of a number of companies within the engineering sector. One of these subsidiaries is PQR which specialises in building machines for manufacturing companies. PQR uses absorption costing as the basis of its routine accounting system for profit reporting.

PQR is currently operating at 90% of its available capacity, and has been invited by an external manufacturing company, to tender for the manufacture of a bespoke machine. If PQR's tender is accepted by the manufacturing company then it is likely that another company within the M group will be able to obtain work in the future servicing the machine. As a result, the Board of Directors of M are keen to win the tender for the machine and are prepared to accept a price from the manufacturing company that is based on the relevant costs of building the machine.

An engineer from PQR has already met with the manufacturing company to determine the specification of the machine and he has worked with a non-qualified accountant from PQR to determine the following cost estimate for the machine.

	Note	$
Engineering specification	1	1,500
Direct material A	2	61,000
Direct Material B	3	2,500
Components	4	6,000
Direct Labour	5	12,500
Supervision	6	350
Machine hire	7	2,500
Overhead costs	8	5,500
Total		91,850

Notes

1   The engineer that would be in charge of the project to build the machine has already met with the manufacturing company, and subsequently prepared the specification for the machine. This has taken three days of his time and his salary and related costs are $500 per day. The meeting with the manufacturing company only took place because of this potential work; no other matters were discussed at the meeting.

2   The machine would require 10,000 square metres of Material A. This material is regularly used by PQR. There is currently 15,000 square metres in inventory, 10,000 square metres were bought for $6 per square metre and the remainder were bought for $6·30 per square metre. PQR uses the weighted average basis to value its inventory. The current market price of Material A is $7 per square metre, and the inventory could be sold for $6·50 per square metre.

3   The machine would also require 250 metre lengths of Material B. This is not a material that is regularly used by PQR and it would have to be purchased specifically for this work. The current market price is $10 per metre length, but the sole supplier of this material has a minimum order size of 300 metre lengths. PQR does not foresee any future use of any unused lengths of Material B, and expects that the net revenue from its sale would be negligible.

4   The machine would require 500 components. The components could be produced by HK, another company within the M group. The direct costs to HK of producing each component is $8, and normal transfer pricing policy within the M group is to add a 50% mark up to the direct cost to determine the transfer price. HK has unused capacity which would allow them to produce 350 components, but thereafter any more components could only be produced by reducing the volume of other components that are currently sold to the external market. These other components, although different, require the same machine time per unit as those required by PQR, have a direct cost of $6 per component and currently are sold for $9 each. Alternatively PQR can buy the components from the external market for $14 each.

5   The machine will require 1000 hours of skilled labour. The current market rate for engineers with the appropriate skills is $15 per hour. PQR currently employs engineers that have the necessary skills at a cost of $12.50 per hour, but they do not have any spare capacity. They could be transferred from their existing duties if temporary replacements were to be engaged at a cost of $14 per hour.

6   The project would be supervised by a senior engineer who currently works 150 hours per month and is paid an annual salary of $42,000. The project is expected to take a total of one month to complete, and if it goes ahead is likely to take up 10% of the supervisor's time during that month. If necessary the supervisor will work overtime which is unpaid.

7   It will be necessary to hire a specialist machine for part of the project. In total the project will require the machine for 5 days but it is difficult to predict exactly which five days the machine will be required within the overall project time of one month. One option is to hire the machine for the entire month at a cost of $5,000 and then sub-hire the machine for $150 per day when it is not required by PQR. PQR expects that it would be able to sub-hire the machine for 20 days. Alternatively PQR could hire the machine on the days it requires and its availability would be guaranteed at a cost of $500 per day.

8   PQR's fixed production overhead cost budget for the year totals $200,000 and is absorbed into its project costs using a skilled direct labour hour absorption rate, based on normal operating capacity of 80%. PQR's capacity budget for the year is a total of 50,000 skilled direct labour hours. PQR's latest annual forecast is for overhead costs to total $220,000, and for capacity to be as originally budgeted.

Required

(a)   You are employed as assistant Management Accountant of the M group. For each of the resource items identified you are to:

(i)   discuss the basis of the valuation provided for each item

(ii)   discuss whether or not you agree with the valuation provided in the context of the proposed tender

(iii)   prepare a revised schedule of relevant costs for the tender document on behalf of the M group.

(15 marks)

(b)   Assume that PQR successfully wins the bid to build the machine for a selling price of $100,000 and that the costs incurred are as expected. Discuss the conflict that will arise between the profit expected from the project by the Board of M on a relevant cost basis and the project profit that will be reported to them by PQR using its routine accounting practices. Use at least two specific examples from the bid to explain the conflict that you discuss.   **(5 marks)**

(c)   Discuss two non-financial matters that you consider relevant to this decision.   **(5 marks)**

(Total = 25 marks)

6   H (MADM, 5/07)   45 mins

H, a printing company, uses traditional absorption costing to report its monthly profits.

It is seeking to increase its business by winning work from new customers. It now has the opportunity to prepare a quotation for a large organisation that currently requires a new catalogue of its services.

A technical report on the resource requirements for the catalogues has been completed at a cost of $1,000 and its details are summarised below:

Production period

It is expected that the total time required to print and despatch the catalogue will be one week.

Material A

10,000 sheets of special printing paper will be required. This is a paper that is in regular use by H and the company has 3,400 sheets in inventory. These originally cost $1·40 per sheet but the current market price is $1·50 per sheet. The resale price of the sheets held in inventory is $1·20 per sheet.

Material B

This is a special ink that H will need to purchase at a cost of $8 per litre. 200 litres will be required for this catalogue but the supplier has a minimum order size of 250 litres. H does not foresee any other use for this ink, but will hold the surplus in inventory. H's inventory policy is to review slow moving items regularly. The cost of any inventory item that has not been used for more than 6 months is accounted for as an expense of the period in which that review occurs.

Direct labour

Sufficient people are already employed by H to print the catalogue, but some of the printing will require overtime working due to the availability of a particular machine that is used on other work. The employees are normally paid $8 per hour, the order will require 150 hours of work and 50 of these hours will be in excess of the employees' normal working week. A rate of $10 per hour is paid for these overtime hours. Employees are paid using an hourly rate with a guaranteed minimum wage for their normal working week.

Supervision

An existing supervisor will take responsibility for the catalogue in addition to her existing duties. She is not currently fully employed and receives a salary of $500 per week.

Machinery

Two different types of machine will be required:

Machine A will print the catalogues. This is expected to take 20 hours of machine time. The running cost of machine A is $5 per hour. There is currently 30 hours of unused time on machine A per week that is being sold to other printers for $12 per hour.

Machine B will be used to cut and bind the catalogues. This machine is being used to full capacity in the normal working week and this is why there is a need to work overtime. The catalogue will require 25 machine hours and these have a running cost of $4 per hour.

Despatch

There will be a delivery cost of $400 to transport the catalogues to the customer.

Fixed overhead costs

H uses a traditional absorption costing system to attribute fixed overhead costs to its work. The absorption rate that it uses is $20 per direct labour hour.

Profit mark-up

H applies a 30% mark-up to its costs to determine its selling prices.

Required

(a)   In order to assist the management of H in preparing its quotation, prepare a schedule showing the relevant costs for the production of the catalogues. State clearly your reason for including or excluding each value that has been provided in the above scenario.   **(15 marks)**

(b)   Explain how the use of relevant costs as the basis of setting a selling price may be appropriate for short-term pricing decisions but may be inappropriate for long-term pricing decisions. Your answer should also discuss the conflict between reporting profitability within a traditional absorption costing system and the use of relevant cost based pricing.   **(10 marks)**

(Total = 25 marks)

7 Engineering company with limiting factors (MADM, 5/08) 45 mins

An engineering company manufactures a number of products and components, using a team of highly skilled workers and a variety of different metals.

The current supplier has announced that the amount of M1, one of the materials it currently supplies, will be limited to 1,000 square metres in total for the next three-month period because there will be insufficient M1 to satisfy demand.

The only items manufactured using M1 and their production costs and selling prices (where applicable) are shown below.

	Product P4 $/unit	Product P6 $/unit	Component C3 $/unit	Component C5 $/unit
Selling price	125	175	n/a	n/a
Direct materials:				
M1*	15	10	5	10
M2	10	20	15	20
Direct labour	20	30	16	10
Variable overhead	10	15	8	5
Fixed overhead**	20	30	16	10
Total cost	75	105	60	55

*   Material M1 is expected to be limited in supply during the next three months. These costs are based on M1 continuing to be available at a price of $20 per square metre.

**   Fixed overhead is absorbed on the basis of direct labour cost.

Products P4 and P6 are sold externally. Components C3 and C5 are used in other products made by the company. These other products do not require any further amounts of material M1.

The estimated total demand for these products and components during the next three months is as follows.

	Units
P4	2,000
P6	1,500
C3	500
C5	1,000

Components C3 and C5 are essential components. They would have to be bought in if they could not be made internally. They can be purchased from external suppliers for $75 and $95 per unit respectively The bought in components are of the same quality as those manufactured by the company. The product they are used in have sufficient margins to remain financially worthwhile if C3 and C5 are bought in at these prices.

Required

(a) Prepare calculations to show the most profitable course of action for the company for the next three months, assuming that there are no other suppliers of material M1, and advise the company on **three** other factors that it should consider before making its decision. **(14 marks)**

(b) Calculate the maximum prices that the company should pay to obtain further supplies of material M1 from an alternative supplier and the quantities of material M1 to which each of these prices apply.

(6 marks)

(c) The company has now become aware of a contract that it has already accepted, for the immediate delivery of 500 units of P4 at a selling price of $125 per unit. This contract has a financial penalty clause for non-delivery. This contract is in addition to the 2,000 units of estimated demand for P4 stated previously. Assume that there is no alternative supplier of material M1.

Calculate the minimum financial penalty that would change your recommendation. **(5 marks)**

(Total = 25 marks)

8 Engineering project (MADM, 5/09)   45 mins

A company has been asked to provide a quotation for an engineering project that will take one year to complete. An analysis of the project has already been completed and the following resource requirements have been identified:

(1) A specialised machine will be required for a total of 10 weeks. Two of these weeks are at the start of the project and three of them are at the end. The machine could be hired in from a reputable supplier, who would guarantee its availability when it is required, for $4,000 per week. Alternatively it could be purchased at a cost of $250,000. If it were purchased it could be sold in one year's time for $150,000. If the machine were purchased it could be hired out to other companies for $2,500 per week and it is believed that it would be hired out for a total of 30 weeks.

(2) The machinery has a running cost of $720 per week. This cost is incurred by the user of the machine.

(3) It is company policy to depreciate non-current assets by 25% per year on a reducing balance basis.

(4) Skilled labour would be required for a total of 9,000 hours during the year. The labour required could be recruited at an hourly rate of $12. Alternatively some of the employees currently working on other projects within the company could be transferred to this project. Their hourly rate is $10 per hour. If these existing employees were to be transferred to this project then they would need to be replaced on their existing project work. Replacements for their existing project work would cost $11 per hour.

(5) Unskilled labour would be required for a total of 12,000 hours during the year. These employees would need to be recruited on a one year contract at a cost of $8 per hour.

(6) The project would need to be supervised and it is estimated that there would be a total of 500 hours of supervision required during the year. One of the existing supervisors could undertake this work, but if he did so he would have to work a total of 300 hours overtime during the year to carry out the supervision on this project as well as his existing duties. The supervisor earns a salary of $50,000 per year for working 2,000 hours and is not paid for overtime work. If this project goes ahead the supervisor will be paid a bonus of $500, which would not be paid if the project is not undertaken.

(7) The direct materials required for the project are as follows:

Material A

The total amount required for the project would have to be purchased at a cost of $15,000.

Material B

The total amount required would be 10,000 square metres. The company purchased 25,000 square metres of this material for a project two years ago at a total cost of $100,000. The earlier project used 20,000 square metres of the material and the remainder is currently held in inventory. The company does not foresee any other use for this material in the future and could sell it for $2 per square metre. The current purchase price of the material is $5 per square metre.

(8)   The company has already incurred expenditure of $25,000 in analysing the resource requirements of the project.

(9)   It is company policy to attribute overhead costs to projects using an absorption rate of 40% of prime costs.

(10)   It is company policy to add a 25% profit mark-up to total costs when setting its prices.

Required

(a)   Prepare a statement that shows the relevant cost of the project. For each of the resources indicated in notes (1) to (10) you must clearly explain the reason for the cost value that you have used.   **(20 marks)**

(b)   Assume that the company used your calculations as the basis of the quotation and then added $125,000 for profit. Also assume that all costs incurred were the same as forecast.

Explain why the financial profit reports at the end of the year would not show a profit of $125,000 for the engineering project.   **(5 marks)**

(Total = 25 marks)

9   QP plc (MADM, 11/05)   45 mins

QP plc is a food processing company that produces pre-prepared meals for sale to consumers through a number of different supermarkets. The company specialises in three particular pre-prepared meals and has invested significantly in modern manufacturing processes to ensure a high quality product. The company is very aware of the importance of training and retaining high quality staff in all areas of the company and, in order to ensure their production employees' commitment to the company, the employees are guaranteed a weekly salary that is equivalent to their normal working hours paid at their normal hourly rate of £7 per hour.

The meals are produced in batches of 100 units. Costs and selling prices per batch are as follows.
QP plc has adopted throughput accounting for its short-term decisions.

Meal	TR	PN	BE
	£/batch	£/batch	£/batch
Selling price	340	450	270
Ingredient K (£5/kg)	150	120	90
Ingredient L (£10/kg)	70	90	40
Ingredient M (£15/kg)	30	75	45
Labour (£7/hour)	21	28	42
Factory costs absorbed	20	80	40

Required

(a)   State the principles of throughput accounting and the effects of using it for short-term decision making.
    (6 marks)

(b)   QP plc is preparing its production plans for the next three months and has estimated the maximum demand from its customers to be as follows.

	Batches
TR	500
PN	400
BE	350

These demand maximums are amended figures because a customer has just delayed its request for a large order and QP plc has unusually got some spare capacity over the next three months. However, these demand maximums do include a contract for the delivery of 50 batches of each to an important customer. If this minimum contract is not satisfied then QP plc will have to pay a substantial financial penalty for non-delivery.

The production director is concerned at hearing news that two of the ingredients used are expected to be in short supply for the next three months. QP plc does not hold inventory of these ingredients and although there are no supply problems for ingredient K, the supplies of ingredients L and M are expected to be limited to.

	Kilos
Ingredient L	7,000
Ingredient M	3,000

The production director has researched the problem and found that ingredient V can be used as a direct substitute for ingredient M. It also costs the same as ingredient M. There is an unlimited supply of ingredient V.

Required

Prepare calculations to determine the production mix that will maximise the profit of QP plc during the next three months. **(10 marks)**

(c) The World Health Organisation has now announced that ingredient V contains dangerously high levels of a chemical that can cause life-threatening illnesses. As a consequence it can no longer be used in the production of food.

As a result, the production director has determined the optimal solution to the company's production mix problem using linear programming. This is set out below.

Objective function value	110,714
TR value	500
PN value	357
BE value	71
TR slack value	0
PN slack value	43
BE slack value	279
L value	3
M value	28

Required

Explain the meaning of each of the values contained in the above solution. **(9 marks)**

(Total = 25 marks)

The following scenario relates to questions 10 and 11

A chemical manufacturer is developing three fertiliser compounds for the agricultural industry. The product codes for the three products are X1, X2 and X3 and the relevant information is summarised below.

	Chemical constituents: percentage make-up per tonne			
	Nitrate	Phosphate	Potash	Filler
X1	10	10	20	60
X2	10	20	10	60
X3	20	10	10	60

Input prices per tonne £	
Nitrate	150
Phosphate	60
Potash	120
Filler	10

Maximum available input per month Tonnes	
Nitrate	1,200
Phosphate	2,000
Potash	2,200
Filler	No limit

The fertilisers will be sold in bulk and managers have proposed the following prices per tonne.

X1   £83
X2   £81
X3   £81

The manufacturing costs of each type of fertiliser, excluding materials, are £11 per tonne.

10   Fertiliser 1   18 mins

Formulate the above data into a linear programming model so that the company may maximise contribution. Include slack variables.

(10 marks)

11   Fertiliser 2   18 mins

Interpret the spreadsheet package output of the simplex solution given below.

Objective (Z)		284,000
Variable	*Value*	*Relative loss*
X1	4,000	0
X2	8,000	0
X3	0	22
Constraint	*Slack/surplus*	*Worth*
X4	0	170
X5	0	40
X6	600	0

(10 marks)

12   Company C (MADM, 11/09)   45 mins

Company C manufactures two products. The budgeted selling price and cost per unit are as follows.

Product	X	Y
	$/unit	$/unit
Selling price	86	74
Direct labour ($8 per hour)	16	12
Direct material A ($3 per kg)	12	15
Direct material B ($4 per kg)	12	8
Other variable costs	20	15
Fixed overhead absorbed	12	12
Profit	14	12

Demand for the products is seasonal. In order to ensure that the production facilities are not idle at various times during the year the company has signed a contract with company D to supply them with the products as "own label" goods.

Company D Contract

The company is to supply Company D with 500 units of product X and 300 units of product Y in each of November and December 20X9 for $73 and $62 per unit respectively. If Company C fails to honour this contract in full in each of these months then there is a significant financial penalty for each month of their failure.

November 20X9

The total number of direct labour hours available to produce products X and Y in November 20X9 is limited to 4,000 hours, but all of the other production resources are readily available in November 20X9.

In addition to the contract with Company D, the demand for products X and Y in November 20X9 is 1,000 units and 800 units respectively.

December 20X9

In December there will be 5,450 direct labour hours available to produce products X and Y and the supply of materials will also be limited. Only 11,000 kgs of material A and 6,100 kgs of material B will be available.

In addition to the contract with Company D, the demand for products X and Y in December 20X9 is 1,300 units and 1,400 units respectively.

Inventory

Company C does not hold inventories of materials or finished goods.

Required

(a)   Prepare calculations to determine the production plan that will maximise the profits of Company C in November 20X9.   **(5 marks)**

(b)   **For December 20X9 only:**

   (i)   Use graphical linear programming to calculate the optimal production plan for the month.
                                                                                                                (10 marks)

   (ii)   Calculate the value of the monthly financial penalty at which the company would be indifferent between supplying products X and Y under the Company D contract or selling them in the general market.   **(5 marks)**

   (iii) Calculate the maximum price per kg that should be paid to an alternative supplier to obtain additional material B.   **(5 marks)**

(Total = 25 marks)

13   WZ manufacturing (3/11)   45 mins

WZ is a manufacturing company with two factories. The company's West factory currently produces a number of products. Four of these products use differing quantities of the same resources. Details of these four products and their resource requirements are as follows:

Product	J	K	L	M
	$/unit	$/unit	$/unit	$/unit
Selling price	56	40	78	96
Direct labour ($8 per hour)	20	16	24	20
Direct material A ($3 per litre)	6	3	0	9
Direct material B ($5 per kg)	10	0	15	20
Variable overhead (see note 1)				
Labour related	1.25	1	1.50	1.25
Machine related	1.25	2	0.75	1
Total variable cost	38.50	22	41.25	51.25
Other data:				
Machine hours per unit	5	8	3	4
Maximum demand per week	1,000	3,500	2,800	4,500

Notes

1   An analysis of the variable overhead shows that some of it is caused by the number of labour hours and the remainder is caused by the number of machine hours.

2   Currently WZ purchases a component P from an external supplier for $35 per component. A single unit of this component is used in producing N the company's only other product. Product N is produced in WZ's other factory and does not use any of the resources identified above. Product N currently yields a positive contribution. WZ could manufacture the component in its West factory, but to do so would require: 1 hour of direct labour, 0.5 machine hours, and 2 kgs of direct material B. WZ purchases 500 components per week. WZ could not produce the component in its other factory.

3 The purchasing director has recently advised you that the availability of direct materials A and B is to be restricted to 21,000 litres and 24,000 kgs per week respectively. This restriction is unlikely to change for at least 10 weeks. No restrictions are expected on any other resources.

4 WZ does not hold inventory of either finished goods or raw materials.

5 WZ has already signed a contract, which must be fulfilled, to deliver the following units of its products each week for the next 10 weeks:

Product	Contract units
J	100
K	200
L	150
M	250

These quantities are in addition to the maximum demand identified above.

Required

(a) Calculate whether WZ should continue to purchase the component P or whether it should manufacture it internally during the next 10 weeks. **(11 marks)**

(b) Prepare a statement to show the optimum weekly usage of the West factory's available resources.

Note: You are NOT required to use linear programming. **(3 marks)**

(c)

    (i) Assuming no other changes, calculate the purchase price of the component P at which your advice in part (a) above would change. **(4 marks)**

    (ii) Explain TWO non-financial factors that should be considered before deciding whether or not to manufacture the component internally. **(4 marks)**

(d) If you were to solve part (b) above using linear programming state the following:

- The objective function
- The inequality for the material A constraint
- The inequality for the material B constraint **(3 marks)**

(Total = 25 marks)

14 LM (11/10)   45 mins

LM produces two products from different quantities of the same resources using a just-in-time (JIT) production system. The selling price and resource requirements of each of these two products are as follows:

Product	L	M
Unit selling price ($)	70	90
Variable costs per unit:		
Direct labour ($7 per hour)	28	14
Direct material ($5 per kg)	10	45
Machine hours ($10 per hour)	10	20
Fixed overheads absorbed	12	6
Profit per unit	10	5

Fixed overheads are absorbed at the rate of $3 per direct labour hour.

Market research shows that the maximum demand for products L and M during December 20X0 will be 400 units and 700 units respectively.

At a recent meeting of the purchasing and production managers to discuss the company's production plans for December 20X0, the following resource availability for December 20X0 was identified:

Direct labour	3,500 hours
Direct material	6,000 kg
Machine hours	2,000 hours

Required

(a) Prepare calculations to show, from a financial perspective, the optimum production plan for December 20X0 and the contribution that would result from adopting your plan. **(6 marks)**

(b) You have now presented your optimum plan to the purchasing and production managers of LM. During the presentation, the following additional information became available:

   (i) The company has agreed to an order for 250 units of product M for a selling price of $90 per unit from a new overseas customer. This order is in addition to the maximum demand that was previously predicted and must be produced and delivered in December 20X0;

   (ii) The originally predicted resource restrictions were optimistic. The managers now agree that the availability of all resources will be 20% lower than their original predictions.

   Required

   Construct the revised resource constraints and the objective function to be used to identify, given the additional information above, the revised optimum production plan for December 20X0. **(6 marks)**

(c) The resource constraints and objective function requested in part (b) above have now been processed in a simplex linear programming model and the following solution has been printed:

Product L	400	Product L other value	**0**
Product M	194	Product M other value	**506**
Direct labour	312		
Direct material ($)	**1.22**		
Machine hours	312		
Contribution ($)	**10,934.00**		

Required

Analyse the meaning of each of the above eight values in the solution to the problem. Your answer should include a proof of the five individual values highlighted in **bold**. **(13 marks)**
(Total = 25 marks)

15 Staff uniforms (IMPM, 11/03) 45 mins

W plc provides two cleaning services for staff uniforms to hotels and similar businesses. One of the services is a laundry service and the other is a dry cleaning service. Both of the services use the same resources, but in different quantities. Details of the expected resource requirements, revenues and costs of each service are shown below.

		Laundry $ per service	Dry cleaning $ per service
Selling price		7.00	12.00
Cleaning materials	($10.00 per litre)	2.00	3.00
Direct labour	($6.00 per hour)	1.20	2.00
Variable machine cost	($3.00 per hour)	0.50	1.50
Fixed costs *		1.15	2.25
Profit		2.15	3.25

* The fixed costs per service were based on meeting the budget demand for December 20X3.

W plc has already prepared its budget for December based on sales and operational activities of 8,000 laundry services and 10,500 dry cleaning services, but it is now revising its plans because of forecast resource problems.

The maximum resources expected to be available in December 20X3 are

Cleaning materials	5,000 litres
Direct labour hours	6,000 hours
Machine hours	5,000 hours

W plc has one particular contract which it entered into six months ago with a local hotel to guarantee 1,200 laundry services and 2,000 dry cleaning services every month. If W plc does not honour this contract it has to pay substantial financial penalties to the local hotel.

Required

(a)   Calculate the mix of services that should be provided by W plc so as to maximise its profit for
        December 20X3.   **(9 marks)**

(b)   The sales director has reviewed the selling prices being used by W plc and has provided the following
        further information.

   (1)   If the price for laundry were to be reduced to $5.60 per service, this would increase the demand to
         14,000 services.

   (2)   If the price for dry cleaning were to be increased to $13.20 per service, this would reduce the
         demand to 9,975 services.

   Required

   Assuming that such selling price changes would apply to **all sales** and that the resource limitations
   continue to apply, and that a graphical linear programming solution is to be used to maximise profit:

   (i)   State the constraints and objective function.   **(6 marks)**

   (ii)   Use a graphical linear programming solution to advise W plc whether it should revise its selling
          prices.   **(10 marks)**

                                                                                    (Total = 25 marks)

16   RT (5/10)   45 mins

RT produces two products from different quantities of the same resources using a just-in-time (JIT) production
system. The selling price and resource requirements of each of the products are shown below.

Product	R	T
Unit selling price ($)	130	160
Resources per unit:		
Direct labour ($8 per hour)	3 hours	5 hours
Material A ($3 per kg)	5 kgs	4 kgs
Material B ($7 per litre)	2 litres	1 litre
Machine hours ($10 per hour)	3 hours	4 hours

Market research shows that the maximum demand for products R and T during June 20X0 is 500 units and 800
units respectively. This does not include an order that RT has agreed with a commercial customer for the supply
of 250 units of R and 350 units of T at selling prices of $100 and $135 per unit respectively. Although the
customer will accept part of the order, failure by RT to deliver the order in full by the end of June will cause RT
to incur a $10,000 financial penalty.

At a recent meeting of the purchasing and production managers to discuss the production plans of RT for June,
the following resource restrictions for June were identified.

Direct labour hours	7,500 hours
Material A	8,500 kgs
Material B	3,000 litres
Machine hours	7,500 hours

Required

(a)   Assuming that RT completes the order with the commercial customer, prepare calculations to show, from
        a financial perspective, the optimum production plan for June 20X0 and the contribution that would
        result from adopting this plan.   **(6 marks)**

(b)   Prepare calculations to show, from a financial perspective, whether RT should complete the order from
        the commercial customer.   **(3 marks)**

You have now presented your optimum production plan to the purchasing and production managers of
RT. During your presentation it became clear that the predicted resource restrictions were rather
optimistic. In fact the managers agreed that the availability of all of the resources could be as much as
10% lower than their original predictions.

(c) Assuming that RT completes the order with the commercial customer, and using graphical linear programming, prepare a graph to show the optimum production plan for RT for June 20X0 on the basis that the availability of all resources is 10% lower than originally predicted. **(11 marks)**

(d) Discuss how the graph in your solution to (c) above can be used to help to determine the optimum production plan for June 20X0 if the actual resource availability lies somewhere between the managers' optimistic and pessimistic predictions. **(5 marks)**

(Total = 25 marks)

17 HT plc   45 mins

(a) HT plc produces and sells three products, HT01, HT02 and HT03.

The following details of prices and product costs have been extracted from HT plc's cost accounting records.

	HT01 £	HT02 £	HT03 £
Prices per unit	150	200	220
Costs per unit			
Direct labour at £4/hr	100	120	132
Direct material at £20/kg	20	40	40

Direct labour is regarded as a variable production cost.

A regression analysis had been carried out in order to estimate the relationship between overhead costs and production of the three products. Expressed in weekly terms the results of the analysis show the following.

$y = 4{,}000 + 0.5x_1 + 0.7x_2 + 0.8x_3$

Where y = total overhead cost per week
       x_1 = HT01, weekly direct labour hours
       x_2 = HT02, weekly direct labour hours
       x_3 = HT03, weekly direct labour hours

The company operates a 46-week year.

Required

Compute the total variable product costs for each of HT01, HT02 and HT03. **(5 marks)**

(b) The material used by HT plc is also used in a wide variety of other applications and is in relatively limited supply. As business conditions improve in general, there will be pressure for the price of this material to rise, but strong competition in HT plc's sector of the market would make it unlikely that increased material costs can be passed on to customers in higher product prices. The position on material supplies is that HT plc can obtain 20,000 kgs at current prices.

In addition, reductions in the skilled labour force made during a recession mean that the number of available direct labour hours is estimated at no more than 257,600 hours for the next year.

Demand for each product over the year is forecast to be as follows.

	Units
HT01	16,000
HT02	10,000
HT03	6,000

Required

Formulate a linear programme from the above data in order to obtain the annual production/sales plan which will maximise HT plc's contribution earnings and profit. (You are not required to solve the problem.) **(12 marks)**

(c) The following is the final tableau, obtained as a result of running the linear programme.

Final tableau

HTO1	HTO2	HTO3	S_1	S_2	S_3	S_4	S_5	Bij
0.0	0.0	1.0	0.0	0.0	0.0	0.0	1.0	6,000.0
1.0	1.2	1.3	0.0	0.0	0.0	0.0	0.0	10,304.0
0.0	−1.2	−1.3	−0.0	0.0	1.0	0.0	0.0	5,696.0
0.0	1.0	0.0	0.0	0.0	0.0	1.0	0.0	10,000.0
0.0	0.8	1.7	−0.0	1.0	0.0	0.0	0.0	9,696.0
0.0	2.0	1.5	0.7	0.0	0.0	0.0	0.0	180,320.0

Where S_1, S_2, S_3, S_4, S_5 are the slack variables for labour, materials, HTO1, HTO2 and HTO3 respectively.

Required

Provide as complete an interpretation of the final tableau as you can and give an estimate of the final net profit figure. **(8 marks)**

(Total = 25 marks)

---

18 DFG (MADM, 11/07)   45 mins

DFG manufactures two products from different combinations of the same resources. Unit selling prices and unit cost details for each product are as follows:

Product	D £/unit	G £/unit
Selling price	115	120
Direct material A (£5 per kg)	20	10
Direct material B (£3 per kg)	12	24
Skilled labour (£7 per hour)	28	21
Variable overhead (£2 per machine hour)	14	18
Fixed overhead*	28	36
Profit	13	11

*Fixed overhead is absorbed using an absorption rate per machine hour. It is an unavoidable central overhead cost that is not affected by the mix or volume of products produced.

The maximum weekly demand for products D and G is 400 units and 450 units respectively and this is the normal weekly production volume achieved by DFG. However, for the next four weeks the achievable production level will be reduced due to a shortage of available resources. The resources that are expected to be available are as follows:

Direct material A	1,800kg
Direct material B	3,500kg
Skilled labour	2,500 hours
Machine time	6,500 machine hours

Required

(a) Using graphical linear programming identify the weekly production schedule for products D and G that maximises the profits of DFG during the next four weeks. **(15 marks)**

(b) The optimal solution to part *(a)* shows that the shadow prices of Skilled labour and Direct material A are as follows:

Skilled labour £NIL
Direct material A £5.82

Explain the relevance of these values to the management of DFG. **(6 marks)**

(c) Using the graph you have drawn in part *(a)* explain how you would calculate by how much the selling price of Product D could rise before the optimal solution would change.

Note: Assume that demand is not affected by the selling price. You are **not** required to perform any calculations. **(4 marks)**

(Total = 25 marks)

19 Five products (9/10)   18 mins

A company manufactures five products in one factory. The company uses a Just-in-Time (JIT) production system. The company's budgeted fixed costs for the next year are $300,000. The table below summarises the budgeted sales and contribution details for the five products for the next year.

Product	A	B	C	D	E
Unit selling price ($)	40	15	40	30	20
Total sales ($000)	400	180	1,400	900	200
Contribution/sales ratio (%)	45	30	25	20	(10)

The following diagram has been prepared to summarise the above budget figures:

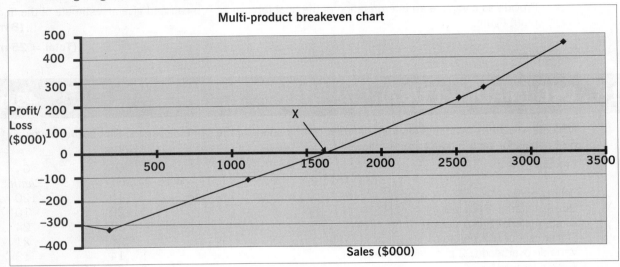

After the diagram had been prepared, the Marketing Director has said that Products A and E are complementary products. The budget assumes that there are no sales of Product A without also selling Product E and no sales of Product E without selling Product A.

Required

(a) (i)   Explain two reasons why the chart does not provide a useful summary of the budget data provided.
            (4 marks)

     (ii) Explain the meaning of point X on the chart.   **(2 marks)**

(b) Calculate the breakeven revenue for the next year using the budgeted sales mix.

     All workings must be shown.
                                                                                    (4 marks)
                                                                          (Total = 10 marks)

20 POD and L   18 mins

(a) POD Ltd makes and sells three products, X, Y and Z. The selling price per unit and costs are as follows.

	X	Y	Z
Selling price per unit	£80	£50	£70
Variable cost per unit	£50	£10	£20
Fixed costs per month	£160,000		

The maximum sales demand per month is 2,000 units of each product and the minimum sales demand is 1,000 of each.

Required

(i) Comment on the potential profitability of the company. **(2 marks)**

(ii) Suppose that there is a fixed demand for X and Y of 1,500 units per month, which will not be exceeded, but for which firm orders have been received. Calculate the number of units of Z that would have to be sold to achieve a profit of at least £25,000 per month. **(3 marks)**

(b) L Ltd achieved the following results in 20X1.

	£'000	£'000
Sales (200,000 units)		2,000
Cost of sales		
Direct materials	800	
Direct labour	400	
Overheads	600	
		1,800
Profit		200

Throughout 20X1, sales were £10 per unit, and variable overheads, which vary with the number of units produced, amount to £1 per unit.

Required

Using CVP analysis, calculate the sales volume necessary to achieve a profit of £330,000 in 20X2 if, at beginning of the year, the sales price is increased by £0.50 per unit, while the increases in costs above 20X1 levels are expected to be as follows. Comment on the result obtained.

	%
Direct material	10
Direct labour	15
Variable overhead	10
Fixed overhead	20

(5 marks)

(Total = 10 marks)

21 RDF Ltd (IMPM, 5/04)　　　　　　45 mins

RDF Ltd offers four services to television companies The number of services provided is measured in service units and details of RDF Ltd's draft budget for its year ending 30 June 20X5 are as follows.

	Service K	Service L	Service M	Service N
Number of service units	1,000	2,300	1,450	1,970
Selling price per unit ($)	18	16	12	20
Variable cost per unit ($)	8	10	13	13
Fixed cost per unit ($)	2	3	2	4

The budgeted level of activity shown in the table above has been based on fully meeting the forecasted market demand for each type of service.

The following chart has been prepared based on the draft budget above.

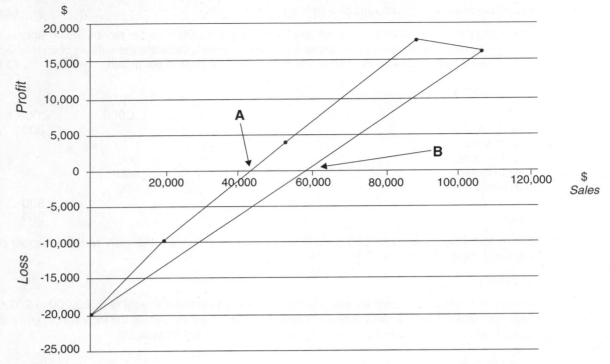

Required

(a) Explain the meaning of the values shown as points A and B on the chart. (*Note*. Calculations are not required.) **(4 marks)**

(b) Further investigation into the nature of the fixed costs has shown that some of those shown in the original budget are incurred as a direct result of providing specific services as follows.

	$
Service K	4,400
Service L	3,700
Service M	NIL
Service N	2,650

The remaining budgeted fixed costs are general fixed costs that will be incurred regardless of the type and number of services provided.

RDF Ltd entered into a three-year contract in June 20X2 which requires it to provide 500 units of service M per year or suffer significant financial penalties. These services are included in the budgeted demand.

Required

(i) Evaluate the financial viability of each of the four services currently provided. **(6 marks)**

(ii) Recommend the operating plan that will maximise profit for the year ended 30 June 20X5 and state the resulting profit. Explain the assumptions that led to your decision and other factors that should be considered. **(5 marks)**

(iii) Calculate the overall breakeven sales value for the operating plan you have recommended in answer to (b)(ii), stating clearly the assumptions made in your calculations. **(5 marks)**

(iv) Comment on any limitations of using breakeven analysis for decision making purposes. **(5 marks)**

(Total = 25 marks)

22 GHK plc (MADM, 5/06)   45 mins

GHK manufactures four products from different combinations of the same direct materials and direct labour. An extract from the flexible budgets for next quarter for each of these products is as follows.

Product	G		H		J		K	
Units	3,000	5,000	3,000	5,000	3,000	5,000	3,000	5,000
	$'000	$'000	$'000	$'000	$'000	$'000	$'000	$'000
Revenue	30	50	60	100	45 0	75.0	90	150
Direct Material A (note 1)	9	15	12	20	4.5	7.5	18	30
Direct Material B (note 2)	6	10	6	10	13.5	22.5	36	60
Direct labour (note 3)	6	10	24	40	22.5	37.5	9	15
Overhead (note 4)	6	8	13	19	11.0	17.0	11	17

Notes

1   Material A was purchased some time ago at a cost of $5 per kg. There are 5,000 kgs in inventory. The costs shown in the flexible budget are based on this historical cost. The material is in regular use and currently has a replacement cost of $7 per kg.

2   Material B is purchased as required; its expected cost is $10 per kg. The costs shown in the flexible budget are based on this expected cost.

3   Direct labour costs are based on an hourly rate of $10 per hour. Employees work the number of hours necessary to meet production requirements.

4   Overhead costs of each product include a specific fixed cost of $1,000 per quarter which would be avoided if the product was to be discontinued. Other fixed overhead costs are apportioned between the products but are not affected by the mix of products manufactured.

GHK has been advised by the only supplier of material B that the quantity of material B that will be available during the next quarter will be limited to 5,000 kgs. Accordingly the company is being forced to reconsider its production plan for the next quarter. GHK has already entered into contracts to supply one of its major customers with the following:

> 500 units of product G
> 1,600 units of product H
> 800 units of product J
> 400 units of product K

Apart from this, the demand expected from other customers is expected to be

> 3,600 units of product G
> 3,000 units of product H
> 3,000 units of product J
> 4,000 units of product K

The major customer will not accept partial delivery of the contract and if the contract with this major customer is not completed in full, then GHK will have to pay a financial penalty of $5,000.

Required

(a)   For each of the four products, calculate the relevant contribution per $ of material B for the next quarter.
(6 marks)

(b)   It has been determined that the optimum production plan based on the data above is to produce 4,100 units of product G, 4600 units of product H, 800 units of product J, and 2,417 units of product K. Determine the amount of financial penalty at which GHK would be indifferent between meeting the contract or paying the penalty.
(5 marks)

(c)   Calculate the relevant contribution to sales ratios for each of the four products.
(2 marks)

(d)   Assuming that the limiting factor restrictions no longer apply, prepare a sketch of a multi product profit volume chart by ranking the products according to your contribution to sales ratio calculations based on total market demand. Your sketch should plot the products using the highest contribution to sales ratio first.
(6 marks)

(e) Explain briefly, stating any relevant assumptions and limitations, how the multiproduct profit volume chart that you prepared in *(d)* above may be used by the manager of GHK to understand the relationships between costs, volume and profit within the business. **(6 marks)**

(Total = 25 marks)

23 Preparation questions: Pricing   40 mins

The following questions are provided to give you practice on calculating optimal prices. Some of them are past exam questions from old syllabus P2 *Management Accounting – Decision Management*.

(a) RJD Ltd makes and sells a single product, Z. The selling price and marginal revenue equations for product Z are as follows:

Selling price = £50 – £0.001x
Marginal revenue = £50 – £0.002x

The variable costs are £20 per unit and the fixed costs are £100,000.

  (i) Calculate what the selling price should be in order to maximise profit. **(3 marks)**
  (ii) If the selling price was set to maximise **revenue**, calculate the resulting profit. **(3 marks)**

(b) A company is considering the pricing of one of its products. It has already carried out some market research with the following results:

The quantity demanded at a price of $100 will be 1,000 units.

The quantity demanded will increase/decrease by 100 units for every $50 decrease/increase in the selling price.

The marginal cost of each unit is $35.

Note that if selling price (P) = a – bx then marginal revenue = a – 2bx

Calculate the selling price that maximises company profit. **(4 marks)**

(c) A company is launching a new product. Market research shows that if the selling price of the product is $100 then demand will be 1,200 units, but for every $10 increase in selling price there will be a corresponding decrease in demand of 200 units and for every $10 decrease in selling price there will be a corresponding increase in demand of 200 units. The estimated variable costs of the product are $30 per unit. There are no specific fixed costs but general fixed costs are absorbed using an absorption rate of $8 per unit.

Calculate the selling price at which profit is maximised.

Note: When Price = a – bx then Marginal Revenue = a – 2bx **(4 marks)**

(d) A company is considering the price of a new product. It has determined that the variable cost of making the item will be $24 per unit. Market research has indicated that if the selling price were to be $60 per unit then the demand would be 1,000 units per week.

However, for every $10 per unit increase in selling price, there would be a reduction in demand of 50 units; and for every $10 reduction in selling price there would be an increase in demand of 50 units.

Calculate the optimal selling price.

Note. If Price P = a – bx then Marginal Revenue = a – 2bx **(4 marks)**

(e) A company is considering the price of one of its products for next year. It expects that the variable cost of making the item will be $15 per unit. It has also determined that if the selling price were to be $35 per unit then the demand would be 500 units per week.

However, for every $5 increase in selling price, there would be a reduction in demand of 50 units per week; and for every $5 reduction in selling price, there would be an increase in demand of 50 units per week.

Calculate the optimal selling price.

Note. If Price P = a – bx then Marginal Revenue = a – 2bx **(4 marks)**

(Total = 22 marks)

24 ML (MADM, 11/05)
18 mins

ML is an engineering company that specialises in providing engineering facilities to businesses that cannot justify operating their own facilities in-house. ML employs a number of engineers who are skilled in different engineering techniques that enable ML to provide a full range of engineering facilities to its customers. Most of the work undertaken by ML is unique to each of its customers, often requiring the manufacture of spare parts for its customers' equipment, or the building of new equipment from customer drawings. As a result most of ML's work is short-term, with some jobs being completed within hours while others may take a few days.

To date ML has adopted a cost plus approach to setting its prices. This is based upon an absorption costing system that uses machine hours as the basis of absorbing overhead costs into individual job costs. The Managing Director is concerned that over recent months ML has been unsuccessful when quoting for work with the consequence that there has been an increase in the level of unused capacity. It has been suggested that ML should adopt an alternative approach to its pricing based on marginal costing since 'any price that exceeds variable costs is better than no work'.

Required

With reference to the above scenario:

(a)   briefly explain absorption and marginal cost approaches to pricing;
(b)   discuss the validity of the comment 'any price that exceeds variable costs is better than no work'.

(10 marks)

25 PT (5/11)
18 mins

PT manufactures and sells a number of products. All of its products have a life cycle of six months or less. PT uses a four stage life cycle model (Introduction; Growth; Maturity; and Decline) and measures the profits from its products at each stage of their life cycle.

PT has recently developed an innovative product. Since the product is unique it was decided that it would be launched with a market skimming pricing policy. However PT expects that other companies will try to enter the market very soon.

This product is generating significant unit profits during the Introduction stage of its life cycle. However there are concerns that the unit profits will reduce during the other stages of the product's life cycle.

Required

For each of the

(i)   Growth; and
(ii)   Maturity stages of the new product's life cycle

explain the likely changes that will occur in the unit selling prices AND in the unit production costs, compared to the preceding stage.   **(10 marks)**

26 PQ (5/10)
18 mins

PQ manufactures and sells consumer electronics. It is constantly working to design the latest gadgets and "must-haves" which are unique in the market place at the time they are launched. The management of PQ are aware of the short product life cycles in this competitive market and consequently use a market skimming pricing strategy at the introduction stage.

Required

Explain the changes that are likely to occur in the following items at the three later stages in the product life cycle of a typical PQ product.

(i)   Selling price
(ii)   Production costs
(iii)   Selling and marketing costs

(10 marks)

27 WX (5/11)   18 mins

WX is reviewing the selling price of one of its products. The current selling price of the product is $25 per unit and annual demand is forecast to be 150,000 units at this price. Market research indicates that the level of demand would be affected by any change in the selling price. Detailed analysis from this research shows that for every $1 increase in selling price, annual demand would reduce by 25,000 units and that for every $1 decrease in selling price, annual demand would increase by 25,000 units.

A forecast of the annual costs that would be incurred by WX in respect of this product at differing activity levels is as follows:

Annual production (units)	100,000	160,000	200,000
	$000	$000	$000
Direct materials	200	320	400
Direct labour	600	960	1,200
Overhead	880	1,228	1,460

The cost behaviour patterns represented in the above forecast will apply for the whole range of output up to 300,000 units per annum of this product.

Required

(a) (i) Calculate the total variable cost per unit.   **(2 marks)**

     (ii) Calculate the selling price of the product that will maximise the company's profits. **(4 marks)**

     Note: If Price (P) = a – bx then Marginal Revenue = a – 2bx

(b) Explain TWO reasons why the company might decide NOT to use this optimum selling price. **(4 marks)**

                                                              (Total = 10 marks)

28 W (MADM, 11/06)   18 mins

W has recently completed the development and testing of a new product which has cost $400,000. It has also bought a machine to produce the new product costing $150,000. The production machine is capable of producing 1,000 units of the product per month and is not expected to have a residual value due to its specialised nature.

The company has decided that the unit selling prices it will charge will change with the cumulative numbers of units sold as follows.

Cumulative sales units	Selling price $ per unit in this band
0 to 2,000	100
2,001 to 7,000	80
7,001 to 14,500	70
14,501 to 54,500	60
54,501 and above	40

Based on these selling prices, it is expected that sales demand will be as shown below.

Months	Sales demand per month (units)
1 – 10	200
11 – 20	500
21 – 30	750
31 – 70	1,000
71 – 80	800
81 – 90	600
91 – 100	400
101 – 110	200
Thereafter	NIL

Unit variable costs are expected to be as follows.

	$ per unit
First 2,000 units	50
Next 12,500 units	40
Next 20,000 units	30
Next 20,000 units	25
Thereafter	30

W operates a Just in Time (JIT) purchasing and production system and operates its business on a cash basis.

A columnar cash flow statement showing the cumulative cash flow of the product after its Introduction and Growth stages has already been completed and this is set out below.

	Introduction	Growth	
Months	1–10	11–30	
Number of units produced and sold	2,000	5,000	7,500
Selling price per unit	$100	$80	$70
Unit variable cost	$50	$40	$40
Unit contribution	$50	$40	$30
Total contribution	$100,000	$425,000	
Cumulative cash flow	($450,000)	($25,000)	

Required

(a)   Complete the cash flow statement for each of the remaining two stages of the product's life cycle. **Do not copy the Introduction and Growth stages in your answer.** Ignore the time value of money.   **(5 marks)**

(b)   Explain, using your answer to (a) above and the data provided, the possible reasons for the changes in costs and selling prices during the life cycle of the product.   **(5 marks)**

(Total = 10 marks)

29   HJ (Specimen paper)   18 mins

HJ is a printing company that specialises in producing high quality cards and calendars for sale as promotional gifts. Much of the work produced by HJ uses similar techniques and for a number of years HJ has successfully used a standard costing system to control its costs.

HJ is now planning to diversify into other promotional gifts such as plastic moulded items including key fobs, card holders and similar items. There is already a well established market place for these items but HJ is confident that with its existing business contacts it can be successful if it controls its costs. Initially HJ will need to invest in machinery to mould the plastic, and it is likely that this machinery will have a life of five years. An initial appraisal of the proposed diversification based on low initial sales volumes and marginal cost based product pricing for year 1, followed by increases in both volumes and selling prices in subsequent years, shows that the investment has a payback period of four years.

Required

(a)   Explain the relationship between target costs and standard costs and how HJ can derive target costs from target prices.

(5 marks)

(b)   Discuss the conflict that will be faced by HJ when making pricing decisions based on marginal cost in the short term and the need for full recovery of all costs in the long term.

(5 marks)

(Total = 10 marks)

30   HS (MADM, 11/07)   18 mins

HS manufactures components for use in computers. The business operates in a highly competitive market where there are a large number of manufacturers of similar components. HS is considering its pricing strategy for the next twelve weeks for one of its components. The Managing Director seeks your advice to determine the selling price that will maximise the profit to be made during this period.

You have been given the following data:

Market Demand

The current selling price of the component is $1,350 and at this price the average weekly demand over the last four weeks has been 8,000 components. An analysis of the market shows that for every $50 increase in selling price the demand reduces by 1,000 components per week. Equally, for every $50 reduction in selling price the demand increases by 1,000 components per week.

Costs

The direct material cost of each component is $270. This price is part of a fixed price contract with the material suppliers and the contract does not expire for another year.

Production labour and conversion costs, together with other overhead costs and the corresponding output volumes, have been collected for the last four weeks and they are as follows:

| Week | Output volume | |
	Units	$'000
1	9,400	7,000
2	7,600	5,688
3	8,500	6,334
4	7,300	5,446

No significant changes in cost behaviour are expected over the next twelve weeks.

Required

(a)   Calculate the optimum (profit maximising) selling price of the component for the period.

Note. If Price = a – bx then Marginal Revenue = a – 2bx

(6 marks)

(b)   Identify and explain two reasons why it may be inappropriate for HS to use this theoretical pricing model in practice.

(4 marks)

(Total = 10 marks)

31   Electrical appliances (9/10)   45 mins

A manufacturer of electrical appliances is continually reviewing its product range and enhancing its existing products by developing new models to satisfy the demands of its customers. The company intends to always have products at each stage of the product life cycle to ensure the company's continued presence in the market.

Currently the company is reviewing three products:

Product K was introduced to the market some time ago and is now about to enter the maturity stage of its life cycle. The maturity stage is expected to last for ten weeks. Each unit has a variable cost of $38 and takes 1 standard hour to produce.

The Managing Director is unsure which of four possible prices the company should charge during the next ten weeks. The following table shows the results of some market research into the level of weekly demand at alternative prices:

Selling price per unit	$100	$85	$80	$75
Weekly demand (units)	600	800	1,200	1,400

Product L was introduced to the market two months ago using a penetration pricing policy and is now about to enter its growth stage. This stage is expected to last for 20 weeks. Each unit has a variable cost of $45 and takes 1.25 standard hours to produce. Market research has indicated that there is a linear relationship between its selling price and the number of units demanded, of the form P = a - bx. At a selling price of $100 per unit demand is expected to be 1,000 units per week. For every $10 increase in selling price the weekly demand will reduce by 200 units and for every $10 decrease in selling price the weekly demand will increase by 200 units.

Product M is currently being tested and is to be launched in ten weeks' time. This is an innovative product which the company believes will change the entire market. The company has decided to use a market skimming approach to pricing this product during its introduction stage.

The company currently has a production facility which has a capacity of 2,000 standard hours per week. This facility is being expanded but the extra capacity will not be available for ten weeks.

Required

(a) (i) Calculate which of the four selling prices should be charged for product K, in order to maximise its contribution during its maturity stage. **(3 marks)**

and as a result, in order to utilise all of the spare capacity from your answer to (i) above,

(ii) Calculate the selling price of product L during its growth stage. **(6 marks)**

(b) Compare and contrast penetration and skimming pricing strategies during the introduction stage, using product M to illustrate your answer. **(6 marks)**

(c) Explain with reasons, for each of the remaining stages of M's product life cycle, the changes that would be expected in the

(i) average unit production cost
(ii) unit selling price **(10 marks)**

(Total = 25 marks)

32 TQ (MADM, Pilot paper)   45 mins

(a) TQ manufactures and retails second generation mobile (cell) phones. The following details relate to one model of phone:

	$/unit
Budgeted selling price	60
Budgeted variable cost	25
Budgeted fixed cost	10

Period	Period 1	Period 2	Period 3
Budgeted production and sales (units)	520	590	660
Fixed overhead volume variance	$1,200 (A)	$1,900 (A)	$2,600 (A)

There was no change in the level of stock during any of periods 1 to 3.

The Board of Directors had expected sales to keep on growing but, instead, they appeared to have stabilised. This has led to the adverse fixed overhead volume variances. It is now the start of period 4 and the Board of Directors is concerned at the large variances that have occurred during the first three periods of the year. The Sales and Marketing Director has confirmed that the past trend of sales is likely to continue unless changes are made to the selling price of the product. Further analysis of the market for the mobile phone suggests that demand would be zero if the selling price was raised to $100 or more.

Required

(i)   Calculate the price that TQ should have charged for the phone assuming that it wished to maximise the contribution from this product.

Note. If price = a – bx then marginal revenue = a – 2bx   **(7 marks)**

(ii)   Calculate the difference between the contribution that would have been earned at the optimal price and the actual contribution earned during period 3, assuming the variable costs per unit were as budgeted.   **(3 marks)**

(b)   TQ is currently developing a third generation mobile phone. It is a 'state of the art' new handheld device that acts as a mobile phone, personal assistant, digital camera (pictures and video), and music player. The Board of Directors seeks your advice as to the pricing strategy that it should adopt for such a product.

The company has incurred a significant level of development costs and recognises that the technology for these products is advancing rapidly and that the life cycle for the product is relatively short.

Prepare a report, addressed to the Board of Directors that discusses the alternative pricing strategies available to TQ.   **(15 marks)**

(Total = 25 marks)

SECTION B – COST PLANNING AND ANALYSIS FOR COMPETITIVE ADVANTAGE

Questions 33 to 73 cover cost analysis for competitive advantage, the subject of Part B of the BPP Study Text for Paper P2.

33 Wye hotel group (IMPM, 5/01, amended)   18 mins

The Wye hotel group operates a chain of 50 hotels. The size of each hotel varies, as do the services that each hotel provides. However, all of the hotels operated by the group provide a restaurant, swimming pool, lounge bar, guest laundry service and accommodation. Some of the hotels also provide guest entertainment, travel bureaux and shopping facilities. The managing director of the group is concerned about the high level of running costs being incurred by the hotels.

Required

Explain how cost reduction and value analysis could be used by the WYE hotel group to improve the profitability of its hotels.   **(10 marks)**

34 JYT (5/11)   18 mins

JYT manufactures and sells a range of products. It is not dominant in the market in which it operates and, as a result, it has to accept the market price for each of its products. The company is keen to ensure that it continues to compete and earn satisfactory profit at each stage throughout a product's life cycle.

Required

Explain how JYT could use Target Costing AND Kaizen Costing to improve its future performance.

Your answer should include an explanation of the differences between Target Costing and Kaizen Costing.

(10 marks)

35 Financial advisors (MADM, 5/06)   18 mins

A firm of financial advisors has established itself by providing high quality, personalised, financial strategy advice. The firm promotes itself by sponsoring local events, advertising, client newsletters, having a flexible attitude towards the times and locations of meetings with clients and seeking new and innovative ideas to discuss with its clients.

The senior manager of the firm has recently noticed that the firm's profitability has declined, with fewer clients being interested in the firm's new investment ideas. Indeed, many clients have admitted to not reading the firm's newsletters.

The senior manager seeks your help in restoring the firm's profitability to its former level and believes that the techniques of *Value Analysis* and *Functional Analysis* may be appropriate.

Required

(a) Explain the meanings of, and the differences between, Value Analysis and Functional Analysis.

(4 marks)

(b) Briefly explain the series of steps that you would take to implement Value Analysis for this organisation.

(6 marks)

(Total = 10 marks)

36 Batch production (3/11)   18 mins

The standard direct labour cost of one batch of 100 units of a product is $50.40. This assumes a standard time of 4.2 hours, costing $12 per hour. The standard time of 4.2 direct labour hours is the average time expected per batch based on a product life of 12,800 units or 128 batches. The expected time for the first batch was 20 hours and an 80% learning curve is expected to apply throughout the product's life.

The company has now completed the production of 32 batches of the product and the total actual direct labour cost was $3,493. The following direct labour variances have also been calculated:

Direct labour rate $85 Adverse
Direct labour efficiency $891 Adverse

Further analysis has shown that the direct labour efficiency variance was caused solely by the actual rate of learning being different from that expected. However, the time taken for the first batch was 20 hours as expected.

Required:

(a)   Calculate the actual rate of learning that occurred.   **(6 marks)**

(b)   Assuming that the actual rate of learning and the actual labour rate continue throughout the life of the product, calculate the total direct labour cost that the company will incur during the life of the product.
                                                                                   (4 marks)

                                                                         (Total = 10 marks)

37 The learning curve effect (11/10)   18 mins

The following variances have been calculated in respect of a new product:

        Direct labour efficiency variance $14,700 Favourable
        Direct labour rate variance $ 5,250 Adverse

The variances were calculated using standard cost data which showed that each unit of the product was expected to take 8 hours to produce at a cost of $15 per hour. Actual output of the product was 560 units and actual time worked in the manufacture of the product totalled 3,500 hours at a cost of $57,750.

However, the production manager now realises that the standard time of 8 hours per unit was the time taken to produce the first unit and that a learning rate of 90% should have been anticipated for the first 600 units.

Required

(a)   Calculate planning and operating variances following the recognition of the learning curve effect.
                                                                                   (6 marks)

(b)   Explain the importance of learning curves in the context of Target Costing. **(4 marks)**

      Note: The learning index for a 90% learning curve is -0.1520

                                                                         (Total = 10 marks)

38 New Product (5/10)   18 mins

The budget for the production cost of a new product was based on the following assumptions:

(i)   Time for the 1st batch of output = 10 hours

(ii)   Learning rate = 80%

(iii)   Learning will cease after 40 batches, and thereafter the time per batch will be the same as the time of the final batch during the learning period, i.e. the 40th batch

(iv)   Standard direct labour rate per hour = $12·00

An extract from the out-turn performance report based on the above budget is as follows.

	Budget	Actual	Variance
Output (batches)	60	50	10 adverse
Direct labour hours	163·53	93·65	69·88 favourable
Direct labour cost	$1,962	$1,146	$816 favourable

Further analysis has shown that, due to similarities between this product and another that was developed last year, the rate of learning that should have been expected was 70% and that the learning should have ceased after 30 batches. Other budget assumptions for the new product remain valid.

Required

(a)   Prepare a revised out-turn performance report for the new product that

    (i)   shows the flexed budgeted direct labour hours and direct labour cost based on the revised learning curve data, and

    (ii)   shows the variances that reconcile the actual results to your flexed budget in as much detail as possible. **(7 marks)**

(b)   Explain why your report is more useful to the production manager than the report shown above. **(3 marks)**

    Note. The learning index values for an 80% and a 70% learning curve are -0·3219 and -0·5146 respectively.

(Total = 10 marks)

39   S (Specimen paper)   18 mins

S uses a standard absorption costing system to control its production costs and monitors its performance using monthly variance reports.

S has recently launched a new product which is being manufactured in batches of 100 units. An extract from the standard cost details per unit for this new product is as follows:

5·3 hours of direct labour @ $10 per hour = $53·00

It is now realised that the standard cost details were based on an average learning period target of 5·3 hours per unit, and that a batch related period of learning was expected. The time expected for the initial batch was 1,000 hours and 90% learning rate was anticipated.

During August production commenced on the product, and 400 units were produced in four batches of 100 units using 2500 hours of direct labour at a cost of $26,000. The direct labour variances that were reported in respect of this product were:

Direct labour rate variance	$1,000 Adverse
Direct labour efficiency variance	$3,800 Adverse

Required

(a)   Calculate the expected length of the learning period in batches (to the nearest whole batch). **(4 marks)**

(b)   Calculate planning and operating variances for August. **(4 marks)**

(c)   Explain why the variances you have calculated in (b) above provide more meaningful information to the managers of S. **(2 marks)**

(Total = 10 marks)

40 Learning curve (MADM, 5/07) 18 mins

A company is planning to launch a new product. It has already carried out market research at a cost of $50,000 and as a result has discovered that the market price for the product should be $50 per unit. The company estimates that 80,000 units of the product could be sold at this price before one of the company's competitors enters the market with a superior product. At this time any unsold units of the company's product would be of no value.

The company has estimated the costs of the initial batch of the product as follows:

	$'000
Direct materials	200
Direct labour ($10 per hour) *2 Show*	250
Other direct costs	100

Production was planned to occur in batches of 10,000 units and it was expected that an 80% learning curve would apply to the direct labour until the fourth batch was complete. Thereafter the direct labour cost per batch was expected to be constant. No changes to the direct labour rate per hour were expected.

The company introduced the product at the price stated above, with production occurring in batches of 10,000 units. Direct labour was paid using the expected hourly rate of $10 and the company is now reviewing the profitability of the product. The following schedule shows the actual direct labour cost recorded:

Cumulative number of batches	Actual cumulative direct labour costs
	$'000
1	280
2	476
4	809
8	1,376

MaMa **Required**

3 (a) Calculate the revised expected cumulative direct labour costs for the four levels of output given the actual cost of $280,000 for the first batch.

3 (b) Calculate the actual learning rate exhibited at each level of output.

4 (c) Discuss the implications of your answers to (a) and (b) for the managers of the company.   **(10 marks)**

41 Small company – learning curves (MADM, 11/07) 18 mins

You are the management accountant of a new small company that has developed a new product using a labour intensive production process. You have recently completed the budgets for the company for next year and, before they are approved by the Board of Directors, you have been asked to explain your calculation of the labour time required for the budgeted output. In your calculations, you anticipated that the time taken for the first unit would be 40 minutes and that a 75% learning curve would apply for the first 30 units.

Required

(a) Explain the concept of the learning curve and why it may be relevant to the above company.   **(3 marks)**

(b) Calculate the expected time for the 6th unit of output.   **(3 marks)**

(c) Discuss the implications of the learning curve for a company adopting a penetration pricing policy.

(4 marks)

(Total = 10 marks)

42 Q Organisation (MADM, 5/05) — 45 mins

(a) The Q organisation is a large, worldwide respected manufacturer of consumer electrical and electronic goods. Q constantly develops new products that are in high demand as they represent the latest technology and are 'must haves' for those consumers that want to own the latest consumer gadgets. Recently Q has developed a new handheld digital DVD recorder and seeks your advice as to the price it should charge for such a technologically advanced product.

Required

Explain the relevance of the product life cycle to the consideration of alternative pricing policies that might be adopted by Q. **(10 marks)**

(b) Market research has discovered that the price demand relationship for the item during the initial launch phase will be as follows:

Price £	Demand Units
100	10,000
80	20,000
69	30,000
62	40,000

Production of the DVD recorder would occur in batches of 10,000 units, and the production director believes that 50% of the variable manufacturing cost would be affected by a learning and experience curve. This would apply to each batch produced and continue at a constant rate of learning up to a production volume of 40,000 units when the learning would be complete.

Thereafter, the unit variable manufacturing cost of the product would be equal to the unit cost of the fourth batch. The production director estimates that the unit variable manufacturing cost of the first batch would be £60 (£30 of which is subject to the effect of the learning and experience curve, and £30 of which is unaffected), whereas the average unit variable manufacturing cost of all four batches would be £52.71.

There are no non-manufacturing variable costs associated with the DVD recorder.

Required

(i) Calculate the rate of learning that is expected by the production director. **(4 marks)**

(ii) Calculate the optimum price at which Q should sell the DVD recorder in order to maximise its profits during the initial launch phase of the product. **(8 marks)**

(iii) Q expects that after the initial launch phase the market price will be £57 per unit. Estimated product specific fixed costs during this phase of the product's life are expected to be £15,000 per month. During this phase of the product life cycle Q wishes to achieve a target monthly profit from the product of £30,000.

Calculate the number of units that need to be sold each month during this phase in order that Q achieves this target monthly profit. **(3 marks)**

(Total = 25 marks)

43 AVX plc (MADM, 5/06) — 45 mins

AVX plc assembles circuit boards for use by high technology audio video companies. Due to the rapidly advancing technology in this field, AVX Plc is constantly being challenged to learn new techniques.

AVX plc uses standard costing to control its costs against targets set by senior managers. The standard labour cost per batch of one particular type of circuit board (CB45) is set out below:

	£
Direct labour – 50 hours @ £10 /hour	500

The following labour efficiency variances arose during the first six months of the assembly of CB45:

Month	Number of batches assembled and sold	Labour efficiency variance £
November	1	NIL
December	1	170.00 (F)
January	2	452.20 (F)
February	4	1,089.30 (F)
March	8	1,711.50 (F)
April	16	3,423.00 (F)

An investigation has confirmed that all of the costs were as expected except that there was a learning effect in respect of the direct labour that had not been anticipated when the standard cost was set.

Required

(a) (i) Calculate the monthly rates of learning that applied during the six months

(ii) Identify when the learning period ended and briefly discuss the implications of your findings for AVX plc. **(10 marks)**

(b) AVX plc initially priced each batch of CB45 circuit boards on the basis of its standard cost of £960 plus a mark up of 25%. Recently the company has noticed that, due to increasing competition, it is having difficulty maintaining its sales volume at this price.

The finance director has agreed that the long run unit variable cost of the CB45 circuit board is £672·72 per batch. She has suggested that the price charged should be based on an analysis of market demand. She has discovered that at a price of £1,200 the demand is 16 batches per month, for every £20 reduction in selling price there is an increase in demand of 1 batch of CB45 circuit boards, and for every £20 increase in selling price there is a reduction in demand of 1 batch.

Required

Calculate the profit maximising selling price per batch using the data supplied by the Finance Director

Note. If Price (P) = a – bx then marginal revenue (MR) = a – 2bx **(8 marks)**

(c) The technical director cannot understand why there is a need to change the selling price. He argues that this is a highly advanced technological product and that AVX Plc should not reduce its price as this reflects badly on the company. If anything is at fault, he argues, it is the use of standard costing and he has asked whether target costing should be used instead.

Required

(i) Explain the difference between standard costs and target costs.

(ii) Explain the possible reasons why AVX plc needs to re-consider its pricing policy now that the CB45 circuit board has been available in the market for six months. **(7 marks)**

(Total = 25 marks)

44 Cost management techniques again (IDEC, 11/02, amended)
18 mins

Traditional cost control systems focused on cost containment rather than cost reduction. Today, cost management focuses on process improvement and the identification of how processes can be more effectively and efficiently performed to result in cost reductions.

Required

Discuss how activity based management differs from the traditional cost containment approach and how it seeks to achieve cost reduction. **(10 marks)**

45 Software development company (MADM, 5/09)   18 mins

A software development company sells three software products: AXPL1, FDR2 and VBG3. The company's marketing department adds a 25% mark-up to product costs to calculate the selling prices of the company's products. The current selling prices are based on the product costs that were calculated using a traditional absorption costing system. The company has just installed an activity based costing system and consequently changed its working practices with the result that all costs are now treated as effectively variable. The marketing department has not yet been informed about the revised product costs.

The company has carried out some market research and there is a linear relationship between the price it charges for its software products and the resulting market share. The research shows that a change in price causes there to be a proportionate change in market share. A summary of the research shows that for every $2 increase in selling price there would be a 3% reduction in market share and for every $2 decrease in selling price there would be a 3% increase in market share. For example, if the selling price of AXPL1 were to be increased to $52 per unit its market share would reduce to 42%.

The following data relate to the three software products:

	AXPL1	FDR2	VBG3
Current unit selling price ($)	50·00	75·00	65·00
Current market share %	45%	15%	80%
Market size for the remaining life of the product (units)	2,500	3,000	4,000
Activity based cost per unit ($)	48.00	42.00	75.00

Required

(a)   Explain, using the above information, why VBG3 currently has a high market share.   **(3 marks)**

(b)   The marketing department is now considering using the new product costings to set the selling price by adding 25% mark-up to the unit Activity Based Cost.

Calculate the impact on the remaining lifetime profits of each software product and the company as a result of the marketing department using this approach.   **(7 marks)**

(Total = 10 marks)

46 Pharmacy   18 mins

QR Ltd operates two pharmacies, X and Z.

A Pareto analysis has been carried out on the retail sales and closing stock for the last trading year for the two pharmacies. The results of the analysis are shown below.

Sales in X and Z

		X					Z		
				Cumulative					Cumulative
Rank	Category	Sales		Sales	Rank	Category	Sales		sales
		£'000	£'000	%			£'000	£'000	%
1	OTC	35	35	21.9	1	OTC	24	24	24
2	Toiletries	30	65	40.6	2	Toiletries	20	44	44
3	Photo	25	90	56.3	3	Food/drink	15	59	59
4	Food/drink	20	110	68.8	4	Photo	12	71	71
5	Baby	10	120	75.0	5	Cosmetic	6	77	77
5	Sanpro	10	130	81.3	6	Baby	5	82	82
5	Other	10	140	87.5	6	Sanpro	5	87	87
8	Foot	6	146	91.3	6	Other	5	92	92
9	Cosmetics	5	151	94.4	9	Foot	4	96	96
9	Hair	5	156	97.5	10	Hair	2	98	98
11	Perfume	4	160	100.0	11	Perfume	2	100	100

Stock in X and Z

Rank	Category	X Stock £'000	X Cumulative stock £'000	X %	Rank	Category	Z Stock £'000	Z Cumulative stock £'000	Z %
1	Toiletries	12.0	12.0	26.1	1	Toiletries	13.0	13.0	30.2
2	Cosmetics	8.0	20.0	43.5	2	Cosmetics	9.0	22.0	51.2
3	OTC	7.0	27.0	58.7	3	OTC	8.0	30.0	69.8
4	Photo	4.0	31.0	67.4	4	Food/drink	4.0	34.0	79.1
4	Food/drink	4.0	35.0	76.1	5	Photo	2.5	36.5	84.9
6	Other	2.6	37.6	81.7	6	Perfume	1.5	38.0	88.4
7	Baby	2.0	39.6	86.1	7	Baby	1.0	39.0	90.7
7	Sanpro	2.0	41.6	90.4	7	Sanpro	1.0	40.0	93.0
7	Hair	2.0	43.6	94.8	7	Foot	1.0	41.0	95.3
7	Perfume	2.0	45.6	99.1	7	Hair	1.0	42.0	97.7
11	Foot	0.4	46.0	100.0	7	Other	1.0	43.0	100.0

Required

On the basis of the Pareto analysis, write a concise report to QR Ltd's management on your findings, highlighting points of importance. **(10 marks)**

47 W manufacturing (Specimen paper)   18 mins

W is a manufacturing company that produces three products: X, Y and Z. Each uses the same resources, but in different quantities as shown in the table of budgeted data for 20X0 below:

Product	X	Y	Z
Budgeted production	1500	2500	4000
Direct labour hours per unit	2	4	3
Machine hours per unit	3	2	3
Batch size	50	100	500
Machine setups per batch	2	3	1
Purchase orders per batch	4	4	6
Material movements per batch	10	5	4

W's budgeted production overhead costs for 20X0 are $400,000 and current practice is to absorb these costs into product costs using an absorption rate based on direct labour hours. As a result the production overhead cost attributed to each product unit is:

Product X $32   Product Y $64   Product Z $48

The management of S are considering changing to an activity based method of attributing overhead costs to products and as a result have identified the following cost drivers and related cost pools:

Cost pool	$	Cost driver
Machine maintenance	100,000	machine hours
Machine setups	70,000	machine setups
Purchasing	90,000	purchase orders
Material handling	60,000	material movements

The remaining $80,000 of overhead costs are caused by a number of different factors and activities that are mainly labour related and are to be attributed to products on the basis of labour hours.

Required

(a)   Calculate the production overhead cost attributed to each product unit using an activity based approach. **(7 marks)**

(b)   Explain how W has applied Pareto Analysis when determining its cost drivers and how it may continue to use Pareto Analysis to control its production costs. **(3 marks)**

(Total = 10 marks)

48 XY Accountancy Services (11/10) — 18 mins

XY provides accountancy services and has three different categories of client: limited companies, self employed individuals, and employed individuals requiring taxation advice. XY currently charges its clients a fee by adding a 20% mark-up to total costs. Currently the costs are attributed to each client based on the hours spent on preparing accounts and providing advice.

XY is considering changing to an activity based costing system. The annual costs and the causes of these costs have been analysed as follows:

	$
Accounts preparation and advice	580,000
Requesting missing information	30,000
Issuing fee payment reminders	15,000
Holding client meetings	60,000
Travelling to clients	40,000

The following details relate to three of XY's clients and to XY as a whole:

	Client			XY
	A	B	C	
Hours spent on preparing accounts and providing advice	1,000	250	340	18,000
Requests for missing information	4	10	6	250
Payment reminders sent	2	8	10	400
Client meetings held	4	1	2	250
Miles travelled to meet clients	150	600	0	10,000

Required

Prepare calculations to show the effect on fees charged to each of these three clients of changing to the new costing system.

(10 marks)

49 ST (9/10) — 18 mins

ST is a distribution company which buys a product in bulk from manufacturers, repackages the product into smaller packs and then sells the packs to retail customers. ST's customers vary in size and consequently the size and frequency of their orders also varies. Some customers order large quantities from ST each time they place an order. Other customers order only a few packs each time.

The current accounting system of ST produces very basic management information that reports only the overall company profit. ST is therefore unaware of the costs of servicing individual customers. However, the company has now decided to investigate the use of Direct Customer Profitability Analysis (DCPA).

ST would like to see the results from a small sample of customers before it decides whether to fully introduce DCPA.

The information for two customers, and for the whole company, for the previous period was as follows:

	Customer		
	B	D	Company
Factory contribution ($000)	75	40.5	450
Number of:			
Packs sold (000)	50	27	300
Sales visits to customers	24	12	200
Orders placed by customers	75	20	700
Normal deliveries to customers	45	15	240
Urgent deliveries to customers	5	0	30

Activity costs:	$000s
Sales visits to customers	50
Processing orders placed by customers	70
Normal deliveries to customers	120
Urgent deliveries to customers	60

Required

(a) Prepare a Direct Customer Profitability Analysis for each of the two customers **(6 marks)**

(b) Explain how ST could use DCPA to increase its profits. **(4 marks)**

(Total = 10 marks)

50 ZP plc (MADM, 11/05)   45 mins

ZP plc is a marketing consultancy that provides marketing advice and support to small and medium sized enterprises. ZP plc employs four full time marketing consultants who each expect to deliver 1,500 chargeable hours per year and each receive a salary of £60,000 per year. In addition the company employs six marketing support/administration staff whose combined total salary cost is £120,000 per year.

ZP plc has estimated its other costs for the coming year as follows:

	£'000
Office premises: rent, rates, heating	50
Advertising	5
Travel to clients	15
Accommodation whilst visiting clients	11
Telephone, fax, communications	10

ZP plc has been attributing costs to each client (and to the projects undertaken for them) by recording the chargeable hours spent on each client and using a single cost rate of £75 per chargeable hour. The same basis has been used to estimate the costs of a project when preparing a quotation for new work.

ZP plc has reviewed its existing client database and determined the following three average profiles of typical clients:

	Client profile		
	D	E	F
Chargeable hours per client	100	700	300
Distance (miles) to client	50	70	100
Number of visits per client	3	8	3
Number of clients in each profile	10	5	5

The senior consultant has been reviewing the company's costing and pricing procedures. He suggests that the use of a single cost rate should be abandoned and where possible, activities should be costed individually. With this is mind he has obtained the following further information:

- It is ZP plc's policy that where a visit is made to a client and the distance to the client is more than 50 miles, the consultant will travel the day before the visit and stay in local accommodation so that the maximum time is available for meeting the client the following day.

- The cost of travel to the client is dependent on the number of miles travelled to visit the client.

- Other costs are facility costs – at present the senior consultant cannot identify an alternative basis to that currently being used to attribute costs to each client.

Required

(a) Prepare calculations to show the cost attributed to each client group using an activity based system of attributing costs. **(7 marks)**

(b) Discuss the differences between the costs attributed using activity based costing and those attributed by the current system and advise whether the senior consultant's suggestion should be adopted. **(9 marks)**

(c) In a manufacturing environment activity based costing often classifies activities into those that are: unit; batch; product sustaining; and facility sustaining. Discuss, giving examples, how similar classifications may be applied to the use of the technique in consultancy organisations such as ZP plc. **(9 marks)**

(Total = 25 marks)

51 KL (MADM, 11/06)   45 mins

(a) KL manufactures three products, W, X and Y. Each product uses the same materials and the same type of direct labour but in different quantities. The company currently uses a cost plus basis to determine the selling price of its products. This is based on full cost using an overhead absorption rate per direct labour hour. However, the managing director is concerned that the company may be losing sales because of its approach to setting prices. He thinks that a marginal costing approach may be more appropriate, particularly since the workforce is guaranteed a minimum weekly wage and has a three month notice period.

Required

Given the managing director's concern about KL's approach to setting selling prices, discuss the advantages and disadvantages of marginal cost plus pricing **AND** total cost plus pricing.   **(6 marks)**

(b) The direct costs of the three products are shown below:

Product	W	X	Y
Budgeted annual production (units)	15,000	24,000	20,000
	$ per unit	$ per unit	$ per unit
Direct materials	35	45	30
Direct labour ($10 per hour)	40	30	50

In addition to the above direct costs, KL incurs annual indirect production costs of $1,044,000.

Required

Calculate the full cost per unit of each product using KL's current method of absorption costing.

(4 marks)

(c) An analysis of the company's indirect production costs shows the following:

	Cost driver	$
Material ordering costs	Number of supplier orders	220,000
Machine setup costs	Number of batches	100,000
Machine running costs	Number of machine hours	400,000
General facility costs	Number of machine hours	324,000

The following additional data relate to each product:

Product	W	X	Y
Machine hours per unit	5	8	7
Batch size (units)	500	400	1,000
Supplier orders per batch	4	3	5

Required

(i)   Calculate the full cost per unit of each product using activity based costing.   **(8 marks)**

(ii) Explain how activity based costing could provide information that would be relevant to the management team when it is making decisions about how to improve KL's profitability. **(7 marks)**

(Total = 25 marks)

52 Retail outlet (MADM, 11/07)   45 mins

A small retail outlet sells four main groups of products: Basic Foods (milk, bread, etc); Newspapers & Magazines; Frozen Foods; and Canned Foods. A budgeted weekly profit statement is shown below:

	Basic foods $	Newspapers and Magazines $	Frozen foods $	Canned foods $
Sales revenue	800	1,000	1,500	2,400
Cost of sales	600	700	550	1,200
Gross margin	200	300	950	1,200
Power for freezers*			100	
Overheads**	100	100	200	400
Net margin	100	200	650	800

*The freezers would be emptied and switched off as necessary during redecoration.

**Overhead costs comprise general costs of heating and lighting, rent and rates, and other general overhead costs. These costs are attributed to products in proportion to the floor area occupied by each product group which is as follows:

	Basic foods	Newspapers and Magazines	Frozen foods	Canned foods
Floor area (m^3)	50	50	100	200

For each product group, analysis has shown that the sales revenue achieved changes in direct proportion to the floor space allocated to the product.

The owner of the retail outlet has decided that the premises need to be redecorated but is undecided as to which of the following two options would be the most profitable.

Option 1

Close the retail outlet completely for four weeks while the redecoration takes place. The company that is to complete the redecoration would charge $2,500 under this option. It is expected that following the re-opening of the retail outlet there would be a loss of sales for the next 12 weeks because customers would have had to find alternative suppliers for their goods. The reduction in sales due to lost customers has been estimated to be 30% of the budgeted sales during the first four weeks of reopening; 20% during the next four weeks; and 10% during the third four weeks. In addition, in order to encourage customers to return to the retail outlet, there would be a 10% price reduction on all Basic Foods and Canned Foods for the entire 12 week period.

Option 2

Continue to open the retail outlet while the redecoration takes place but with a reduced amount of floor area. The useable floor area would be reduced to 40% of that originally available. After three weeks, the retail outlet would be closed for 0·5 weeks while the goods are moved to the newly redecorated area. The retail outlet would then continue to operate using 40% of its original floor area for a further three weeks before the work was fully completed. The company that is to complete the redecoration would charge $3,500 under this option, and in addition there would be product movement costs of $1,000. The owner has determined that in order to avoid losing customers there should be no reduction in the amount of floor area given to Basic Foods and Newspapers and Magazines throughout this period. The floor area to be used by Frozen Foods and Canned Foods should be determined on the basis of their profitability per unit of area. However, the Frozen Foods are presently kept in four freezers, and therefore any reductions in floor area must be determined by complete freezer units. It may be assumed that each freezer unit incurs equal amounts of power costs.

Required

(a) Advise the owner of the retail outlet which option to choose in order to minimise the losses that will occur as a result of the decision. All workings must be shown.   **(15 marks)**

(b) Explain how Activity Based Costing may be used in a retail environment to improve the decision making and profitability of the business.   **(10 marks)**

(Total = 25 marks)

53 RS plc (IDEC, Pilot paper) — 45 mins

RS plc is a retail organisation. It has fifteen supermarkets, all of which are the same size. Goods are transported to RS plc's central warehouse by suppliers' vehicles, and are stored at the warehouse until needed at the supermarkets – at which point they are transported by RS plc's lorries.

RS plc's costs are:

Warehouse costs, per week

	£'000
Labour costs	220
Refrigeration costs	160
Other direct product costs	340
	720

Head office costs, per week

	£'000
Labour costs	80
Other costs	76
	156

Supermarket costs per shop, per week

	£'000
Labour costs	16
Refrigeration costs	24
Other direct product costs	28
	68

Transport costs per trip

	£
Standard vehicles	3,750
Refrigerated vehicles	4,950

The company has always used retail sales revenue less bought-in price to calculate the relative profitability of the different products. However, the chief executive is not happy with this method and has asked for three products – baked beans, ice cream and South African white wine – to be costed on a direct product profit basis. The accountant has determined the following information for the supermarket chain.

	Baked beans	Ice cream	White wine
No of cases per cubic metre (m³)	28	24	42
No of items per case	80	18	12
Sales per week – items	15,000	2,000	500
Time in warehouse – weeks	1	2	4
Time in supermarket – weeks	1	2	2
Retail selling price per item	£0.32	£1.60	£3.45
Bought-in price per item	£0.24	£0.95	£2.85

Additional information:

Total volume of all goods sold per week	20,000 m³
Total volume of refrigerated goods sold per week	5,000 m³
Carrying volume of each vehicle	90 m³
Total sales revenue per week	£5m
Total sales revenue of refrigerated goods per week	£650,000

Required

(a) Calculate the profit per item using the direct product profitability method. **(13 marks)**

(b) Discuss the differences in profitability between the company's current method and the results of your calculations in (a), and suggest ways in which profitability could be improved. **(7 marks)**

(c) Explain how the direct product profit method differs from traditional overhead absorption. **(5 marks)**

(Total = 25 marks)

54 BPR   18 mins

Explain the contribution the management accountant should make to the planning and implementation of a business process re-engineering programme.   **(10 marks)**

55 PR (3/11)   18 mins

PR currently uses a constant flow production system to manufacture components for the motor industry. The demand from the motor industry is higher in certain months of the year and lower in others. PR holds inventory so that it can supply the components as they are demanded. Increasingly, the costs to PR of holding inventory are having a significant effect on its profits and the management of PR are considering changing the production system to one that operates on a just-in-time (JIT) basis.

Required

(a)   Explain the concepts of a JIT production system.   **(4 marks)**

(b)   Explain TWO reasons why the profit of PR may NOT increase as a result of changing to a JIT production system.   **(6 marks)**

(Total = 10 marks)

56 CAL (11/10)   18 mins

CAL manufactures and sells solar panels for garden lights. Components are bought in and assembled into metal frames that are machine manufactured by CAL. There are a number of alternative suppliers of these solar panels. Some of CAL's competitors charge a lower price, but supply lower quality panels; whereas others supply higher quality panels than CAL but for a much higher price.

CAL is preparing its budgets for the coming year and has estimated that the market demand for its type of solar panels will be 100,000 units and that its share will be 20,000 units (i.e. 20% of the available market). The standard cost details of each solar panel are as follows:

		$ per unit
Selling price		60
Bought - in components (1 set)	15	
Assembly & machining cost	25	
Delivery cost	5	45
Contribution		15

An analysis of CAL's recent performance revealed that 2% of the solar panels supplied to customers were returned for free replacement, because the customer found that they were faulty. Investigation of these returned items shows that the components had been damaged when they had been assembled into the metal frame. These returned panels cannot be repaired and have no scrap value. If the supply of faulty solar panels to customers could be eliminated then, due to improved customer perception, CAL's market share would increase to 25%.

Required

(a)   Explain, with reference to CAL, quality conformance costs and quality non-conformance costs and the relationship between them.   **(4 marks)**

(b)   Assuming that CAL continues with its present systems and that the percentage of quality failings is as stated above:

(i)   Calculate, based on the budgeted figures and sales returns rate, the total relevant costs of quality for the coming year.   **(4 marks)**

(ii) Calculate the maximum saving that could be made by implementing an inspection process for the solar panels, immediately before the goods are delivered.   **(2 marks)**

(Total = 10 marks)

57 QW (11/10)   18 mins

QW is a company that manufactures machine parts from sheet metal to specific customer order for industrial customers. QW is considering diversification into the production of metal ornaments. The ornaments would be produced at a constant rate throughout the year. It then plans to sell these ornaments from inventory through wholesalers and via direct mail to consumers.

Presently, each of the machine parts is specific to a customer's order. Consequently, the company does not hold an inventory of finished items but it does hold the equivalent of one day's production of sheet metal so as to reduce the risk of being unable to produce goods demanded by customers at short notice. There is a one day lead time for delivery of sheet metal to QW from its main supplier though additional supplies could be obtained at less competitive prices.

Demand for these industrial goods is such that delivery is required almost immediately after the receipt of the customer order. QW is aware that if it is unable to meet an order immediately the industrial customer would seek an alternative supplier, despite QW having a reputation for high quality machine parts.

The management of QW is not aware of the implications of the diversification for its production and inventory policies.

Required

(a)   Compare and contrast QW's present production and inventory policy and practices with a traditional production system that uses constant production levels and holds inventory to meet peaks of demand.

(5 marks)

(b)   Discuss the importance of a Total Quality Management (TQM) system in a just-in-time (JIT) environment. Use QW to illustrate your discussion.   **(5 marks)**

(Total = 10 marks)

58 Consumer goods (9/10)   18 mins

HT manufactures and sells consumer goods. The market in which it operates is highly competitive and HT is constantly designing new products in order to maintain its market share. The life cycle of products in the market is extremely short with all of the manufacturers constantly introducing new products or variations on existing products.

Consumers consider two main factors when buying these products: price and quality. HT uses a penetration pricing policy when launching its products and is always striving to improve its quality from product design stage through to customer care. As a result it has a 15% market share, and its largest competitor has a 6% market share with around 30 other companies sharing the remainder of the market.

Required

(a)   Compare and contrast

- Costs of quality conformance; and
- Costs of quality non-conformance.   **(3 marks)**

(b)   Discuss the relationship between quality conformance costs and product selling prices in HT.   **(4 marks)**

(c)   Explain how Kaizen principles could be used by HT to extend the life of its products.   **(3 marks)**

(Total = 10 marks)

59 XY Timber (5/10) — 18 mins

XY, a company that manufactures a range of timber products, is considering changing to a just-in-time (JIT) production system.

Currently XY employs staff who are contracted to work and be paid for a total of 3,937·75 hours per month. Their labour efficiency ratio is 96% and, as a result, they are able to produce 3,780 standard hours of output each month in normal working hours.

Overtime working is used to meet additional demand, though the management of XY try to avoid the need for this because it is paid at a 50% premium to the normal hourly rate of $10 per hour. Instead, XY plan production so that in months of lower demand inventory levels increase to enable sales demand to be met in other months. XY has determined that the cost of holding inventory is $6 per month for each standard hour of output that is held in inventory.

XY has forecast the demand for its products for the next six months as follows.

Month	Demand (Standard hours)
1	3,100
2	3,700
3	4,000
4	3,300
5	3,600
6	4,980

Required

(a)   With the current production system,

    (i)   Calculate for each of the six months and the period in total, the total inventory holding costs.

    (ii)   Calculate the total production cost savings made by changing to a JIT production system.

(6 marks)

(b)   Explain TWO other factors that should be considered by XY before changing to a JIT production system.

(4 marks)

(Total = 10 marks)

60 X Group (MADM, 5/05) — 18 mins

The X Group is a well-established manufacturing group that operates a number of companies using similar production and inventory holding policies. All of the companies are in the same country though there are considerable distances between them.

The group has traditionally operated a constant production system whereby the same volume of output is produced each week, even though the demand for the group's products is subject to seasonal fluctuations. As a result there is always finished goods inventory in the group's warehouses waiting for customer orders. This inventory will include a safety inventory equal to two weeks' production.

Raw material inventories are ordered from suppliers using the Economic Order Quantity (EOQ) model in conjunction with a computerised inventory control system which identifies the need to place an order when the re-order level is reached. The purchasing department is centralised for the group. On receiving a notification from the computerised inventory control system that an order is to be placed, a series of quotation enquiries are issued to prospective suppliers so that the best price and delivery terms are obtained for each order. This practice has resulted in there being a large number of suppliers to the X Group. Each supplier delivers directly to the company that requires the material.

The managing director of the X Group has recently returned from a conference on World Class Manufacturing and was particularly interested in the possible use of Just in Time (JIT) within the X Group.

Required

Write a report, addressed to the managing director of the X Group, that explains how the adoption of JIT might affect its profitability.   **(10 marks)**

61 Quality costs (MADM, 5/06) 18 mins

The Managing Director of a manufacturing company based in Eastern Europe has recently returned from a conference on modern manufacturing. One of the speakers at the conference presented a paper entitled 'Compliance versus Conformance – the quality control issue'. The Managing Director would like you to explain to her some of the concepts that she heard about at the conference.

Required

Prepare a report, addressed to the Managing Director, that discusses quality costs and their significance for the company. Your report should include examples of the different quality costs and their classification within a manufacturing environment. **(10 marks)**

Note: 2 marks are available for report format

62 JIT and TQM (MADM, 5/08) 18 mins

A company experiences changing levels of demand but produces a constant number of units during each quarter. The company allows inventory levels to rise and fall to satisfy the differing quarterly demand levels for its product.

Required

(a) Identify and explain the reasons for **three** cost changes that would result if the company changed to a Just-In-Time production method for 20X9.

Assume there will be no inventory at the start and end of the year. **(6 marks)**

(b) Briefly discuss the importance of Total Quality Management to a company that operates a Just-In-Time production method. **(4 marks)**

(Total = 10 marks)

63 PK plc (MADM, 11/05) 18 mins

You are the assistant management accountant within PK plc. PK plc manufactures high quality self-assembly furniture from raw materials utilising highly skilled labour within a computer-controlled manufacturing facility. The company produces a range of furniture, and because of the lead time to receive delivery of its raw materials, has a finished goods inventory policy of holding an average of two weeks estimated sales in inventory. Customer demand is seasonal and as a consequence, this finished goods inventory level fluctuates throughout the year. The company also holds inventories of raw materials based upon estimates of its production requirements. An absorption costing system is used to attribute all manufacturing costs to win customer orders.

Required

Prepare a report addressed to the Management Team of PK plc that explains the changing nature of cost structures in the modern manufacturing environment and the implications for PK plc's:

(a) Inventory valuation
(b) Short-term decision-making

Note. There are two marks available for format and presentational style. **(10 marks)**

64 AVN (MADM, 11/06) 18 mins

AVN designs and assembles electronic devices to allow transmission of audio / visual communications between the original source and various other locations within the same building. Many of these devices require a wired solution but the company is currently developing a wireless alternative. The company produces a number of different devices depending on the number of input sources and the number of output locations, but the technology used within each device is identical. AVN is constantly developing new devices which improve the quality of the audio / visual communications that are received at the output locations.

The managing director recently attended a conference on world class manufacturing entitled 'The extension of the value chain to include suppliers and customers' and seeks your help.

Required

Explain

(a)   The components of the extended value chain   **(3 marks)**
(b)   How each of the components may be applied by AVN   **(7 marks)**

(Total = 10 marks)

65 Chains   18 mins

Your managing director remarks to you that he is aware of a number of business initiatives about which he knows embarrassingly little. He mentions in particular that a management consultant keeps talking to him about the supply chain and the value chain, and how they should be managed to add value. He is vaguely aware that initiatives such as e-procurement and outsourcing are examples of improvements the consultant has in mind.

Required

Explain what is meant by the terms 'supply chain' and 'value chain', and the purpose of supply chain management and value chain management. As part of your explanation, suggest how e-procurement and outsourcing are initiatives that might feature in supply chain management as a means of improving performance.

(10 marks)

66 Partnering   18 mins

'In contrast with traditional "arms-length" procurement and contract management approaches, partnering is characterised by a greater degree of openness, communication, mutual trust and sharing information. The aims of partnering arrangements are often expressed in terms of business outcomes rather than specific outputs or improvements; their success is particularly dependent on the people and relationship aspects.'

(from the Office of Government Commerce website)

Required

(a)   Briefly describe the circumstances in which partnering is appropriate, and those when it is unsuitable.
(b)   Briefly describe some of the common pitfalls associated with partnering.   **(10 marks)**

67 DT Group (Specimen paper)   18 mins

You are engaged as a consultant to the DT group. At present the group source their raw materials locally, manufacture their products in a single factory, and distribute them worldwide via an international distribution company. However, their manufacturing facilities are restricting them from expanding so they are considering outsourcing some of their manufacturing operations to developing economies.

Required

(a)   Discuss the concept of the value chain and how the changes being considered by the DT group may impact on the management of contribution/profit generated throughout the chain.   **(6 marks)**

(b)   Discuss how gain sharing arrangements might be used by the DT group in the context of the changes being considered. Suggest one non-financial target that may be used as part of these gain sharing arrangements.   **(4 marks)**

(Total = 10 marks)

68 XY engineering company (MADM, 5/08) — 18 mins

You are the management accountant of XY, an engineering company that assembles components into engines for sale to the automotive industry. The company is constantly under pressure from its customers to provide more efficient engines, which are also less damaging to the environment. The company uses value chain analysis as a tool in the management of its activities.

The Managing Director of XY has recently been invited to a conference to give a presentation entitled 'The concept of the value chain and the management of profits generated throughout the chain in XY'.

Required

Prepare a report for the Managing Director explaining the points that should be covered in the presentation.

(10 marks)

69 ZX (3/11) — 18 mins

ZX is a new banking organisation which is about to open its first branches. ZX believes that it needs to offer potential customers a new banking experience if it is to win customers from other banks.

Whereas other banks have focused on interest rates and levels of bank charges, ZX believes that quality and availability of service is an important factor in the choice made by customers.

Required

Explain how Total Quality Management (TQM) would enable ZX to gain competitive advantage in the banking sector. **(10 marks)**

70 TQM (MADM, 5/09) — 18 mins

You have recently been appointed as a company's Assistant Management Accountant. The company has recently begun operating a just-in-time production system but is having problems in meeting the demands of its customers because of quality failures within its production function. Previously, the company used to hold sufficient levels of finished goods inventory so that quality problems did not lead to lost sales. However, it was costly to hold high inventories and, as a result, the company decided to adopt the just-in-time approach. The Production Director believes that higher expenditure on Compliance costs is necessary to avoid the costs of Non-compliance, but he is having difficulty convincing the Managing Director and seeks your help.

Required

Prepare a report addressed to the Managing Director that explains:

- Briefly the principles of Total Quality Management
- The four categories of quality costs
- The relationship between Compliance and Non-compliance costs in the context of Total Quality Management **(10 marks)**

71 C1, C2, C3 (IDEC, 11/02, amended) 45 mins

X Ltd manufactures and distributes three types of car (the C1, C2 and C3). Each type of car has its own production line. The company is worried by the extremely difficult market conditions and forecasts losses for the forthcoming year.

Current operations

The budgeted details for the next year are as follows.

	C1 £	C2 £	C3 £
Direct materials	2,520	2,924	3,960
Direct labour	1,120	1,292	1,980
Total direct cost per car	3,640	4,216	5,940
Budgeted production (cars)	75,000	75,000	75,000
Number of production runs	1,000	1,000	1,500
Number of orders executed	4,000	5,000	5,600
Machine hours	1,080,000	1,800,000	1,680,000

Annual overheads

	Fixed £'000	Variable £
Set ups	42,660	13,000 per production run
Materials handling	52,890	4,000 per order executed
Inspection	59,880	18,000 per production run
Machining	144,540	40 per machine hour
Distribution and warehousing	42,900	3,000 per order executed

Proposed JIT system

Management has hired a consultant to advise them on how to reduce costs. The consultant has suggested that the company adopts a just-in-time (JIT) manufacturing system. The introduction of the JIT system would have the following impact on costs (fixed and variable):

Direct labour	Increase by 20%
Set ups	Decrease by 30%
Materials handling	Decrease by 30%
Inspection	Decrease by 30%
Machining	Decrease by 15%
Distribution and warehousing	Eliminated

Required

(a) Based on the budgeted production levels, calculate the total annual savings that would be achieved by introducing the JIT system. **(6 marks)**

(b) The following table shows the price/demand relationship for each type of car per annum.

C1		C2		C3	
Price £	Demand	Price £	Demand	Price £	Demand
5,000	75,000	5,750	75,000	6,500	75,000
5,750	65,000	6,250	60,000	6,750	60,000
6,000	50,000	6,500	45,000	7,750	45,000
6,500	35,000	7,500	35,000	8,000	30,000

Required

Assuming that X Ltd adopts the JIT system and that the revised variable overhead cost per car remains constant (as per the proposed JIT system budget), calculate the profit-maximising price and output level for each type of car. **(12 marks)**

(c) Write a report to the management of X Ltd which explains the conditions that are necessary for the successful implementation of a JIT manufacturing system. **(7 marks)**

(Total = 25 marks)

72 MN Ltd

45 mins

MN Ltd manufactures automated industrial trolleys, known as TRLs. Each TRL sells for £2,000 and the material cost per unit is £600. Labour and variable overhead are £5,500 and £8,000 per week respectively. Fixed production costs are £450,000 per annum and marketing and administrative costs are £265,000 per annum.

The trolleys are made on three different machines. Machine X makes the four frame panels required for each TRL. Its maximum output is 180 frame panels per week. Machine X is old and unreliable and it breaks down from time to time – it is estimated that, on average, between 15 and 20 hours of production are lost per month. Machine Y can manufacture parts for 52 TRLs per week and machine Z, which is old but reasonably reliable, can process and assemble 30 TRLs per week.

The company has recently introduced a just-in-time (JIT) system and it is company policy to hold little work-in-progress and no finished goods stock from week to week. The company operates a 40-hour week, 48 weeks a year (12 months × 4 weeks) but cannot meet demand. The demand for the next year is predicted to be as follows and this is expected to be typical of the demand for the next four years.

	Units per week		Units per week
January	30	July	48
February	30	August	45
March	33	September	42
April	36	October	40
May	39	November	33
June	44	December	30

The production manager has suggested that the company replaces machine Z with machine G which can process 45 TRLs per week. The maintenance manager is keen to spend £100,000 on a major overhaul of machine X as he says this will make it 100% reliable.

Required

(a) Calculate the throughput accounting ratio (defined below) for the key resource for an average hour next year.

$$\text{Throughput accounting ratio} = \frac{\text{return per factory hour}}{\text{cost per factory hour}}$$

where $\text{return per factory hour} = \dfrac{\text{sales price} - \text{material cost}}{\text{time on key resource}}$

(5 marks)

(b) Briefly describe the uses to which advocates of throughput accounting suggest that the ratio be put. **(4 marks)**

(c) Suggest two other ratios which may be used by a company operating throughput accounting and explain the use to which they may be put. **(5 marks)**

(d) Explain how the concept of contribution in throughput accounting differs from that in marginal costing. **(6 marks)**

(e) Machine G is purchased and Machine X is overhauled. Describe the impact that this should have on monitoring and reporting production activities. **(5 marks)**

(Total = 25 marks)

73 Various cost management techniques   18 mins

(a)   ABC Inc makes product A using three types of labour, unskilled, semi-skilled and highly skilled. All three types of labour are interchangeable. The company budgeted to make 480 units last month but actually produced less.

The standard cost card is shown below.

Standard (1 unit)

	Hours	£	£
Unskilled	6	6.00	36
Semi-skilled	18	8.00	144
Highly skilled	6	12.00	72
	30		252

The actual cost information is shown below.

Actual (380 units produced)

	Hours	£
Unskilled	2,160	12,096
Semi-skilled	6,600	54,120
Highly skilled	2,200	26,840
		93,056

Required

Calculate the labour rate, mix and productivity (yield) variances.   **(5 marks)**

(b)   A company operates two divisions, A and B. Division A manufactures two products X and Y. Product X is sold to the external market for £84 per unit. Product Y which is partly completed is sold to division B only.

Division B can obtain the partly completed product Y from the external market as well as from division A. The price of the partly completed product Y on the external market is £75 per unit. Division A is able to manufacture products X and Y in any combination.

The production costs in division A are as follows:

	X	Y
	£	£
Variable costs per unit	64	70
Fixed overheads per unit	10	10
Total unit costs	74	80

Required

Based on the above information, provide advice on an appropriate transfer price for product Y from division A to division B under each of the following circumstances.

(i)   Assume that division A has spare capacity and demand for product X is limited.

(ii)   How would your advice differ if division A was operating at full capacity and there was unsatisfied external demand for product X?   **(5 marks)**

(Total = 10 marks)

SECTION C – BUDGETING AND MANAGEMENT CONTROL

Questions 74 to 91 cover budgeting and management control, the subject of Part C of the BPP Study Text for Paper P2.

74 Preparation question: MPL Ltd   29 mins

MPL Ltd is a company specialising in providing consultancy services to the catering industry. MPL Ltd prepared its operating statement for period 5 of the year ending 31 August 20X0. This was as follows.

	Budget	Actual	Variance
Chargeable consultancy hours	2,400	2,500	100
	£	£	£
Administration staff salaries – fixed	15,000	15,750	750
Consultants' salaries – fixed	80,000	84,000	4,000
Casual wages – variable	960	600	360
Motor and travel costs – fixed	4,400	4,400	–
Telephone – fixed	600	800	200
Telephone – variable	2,000	2,150	150
Printing, postage & stationery – variable	2,640	2,590	50
Premises and equipment costs – fixed	3,200	3,580	380
Total costs	110,400	116,480	6,080
Fees charged	180,000	200,000	20,000
Profit	69,600	83,520	13,920

While the directors are pleased that the actual profit exceeded their budget expectations they are interested to now how this has been achieved. After the budgets had been issued to them, the consultants expressed concern at the apparent simplicity of assuming that costs could be classified as being either fixed or varying in direct proportion to chargeable consultancy hours.

Required

As the newly appointed management accountant, prepare a report addressed to the board of directors of MPL Ltd which:

(a)   Explains the present approach to budgeting adopted in MPL Ltd and discusses the advantages and disadvantages of involving consultants in the preparation of future budgets   **(10 marks)**

(b)   Critically discusses the format of the operating statement for period 5   **(6 marks)**

(Total = 16 marks)

75 Budgeting and budgetary control   45 mins

(a)   Briefly outline the main features of 'feedback control' and the 'feedback loop' and explain how, in practice, the procedures of feedback control can be transformed into 'feed-forward control'.   **(5 marks)**

(b)   Briefly outline the advantages and disadvantages of allowing profit centre managers to participate actively in the setting of the budget for their units.   **(5 marks)**

(c)   Define the 'controllability principle' and give arguments for and against its implementation in determining performance measures.   **(5 marks)**

(d)   A general insurance company is about to implement a balanced scorecard. You are required to:

   (i)   State the four perspectives of a balanced scorecard.

   (ii)   Recommend one performance measure that would be appropriate for a general insurance company, for each of the four perspectives, and give a reason to support each measure. (You must recommend one measure only for each perspective.)   **(5 marks)**

(e)   Briefly discuss three different circumstances where participation in setting budgets is likely to contribute to poor performance from managers.   **(5 marks)**

(Total = 25 marks)

76 SFG (5/11)   18 mins

SFG is a national hotel group that operates more than 100 hotels. The performance of the manager of each hotel is evaluated using financial measures.

Many of the hotel's managers are not happy. They believe that there can be conflict between good performance and achieving short-term profits. They are also unhappy that their profit reports include a share of head office costs and other costs that they cannot control.

Required

(a) Explain why non-financial performance measures are important in the service sector.   **(2 marks)**

(b) Recommend, with reasons, TWO non-financial performance measures that SFG could use to evaluate the performance of the hotel managers.   **(4 marks)**

(c) Explain why, and how, non-controllable costs should be shown on the profit reports.   **(4 marks)**

(Total = 10 marks)

77 College (3/11)   18 mins

A college is preparing its budget for 20X2. In previous years the director of the college has prepared the college budget without the participation of senior staff and presented it to the college board for approval.

Last year the college board criticised the director over the lack of participation of his senior staff in the preparation of the budget for 20X1 and requested that for the 20X2 budget the senior staff were to be involved.

Required

Discuss the potential advantages and disadvantages to the college of involving the senior staff in the budget preparation process.   **(10 marks)**

78 DW (11/10)   18 mins

DW, a transport company, operates three depots. Each depot has a manager who reports directly to the Operations Director.

For many years the depot managers have been asked by the Operations Director to prepare a budget for their depot as part of the company's annual budgeting process. A new depot manager has been appointed to the Southern region and he has concerns about the validity of these annual budgets. He argues that they soon become out of date as operational circumstances change. At a recent manager's meeting he said, "They are restrictive. They do not permit the depot managers to make decisions in response to operational changes, or change working practices for next year until that year's budget has been approved."

Required

(a) Explain the differences between the above annual budgeting system and a rolling budget system.

(4 marks)

(b) Discuss how the Southern region depot manager could use a rolling budget system to address his concerns.   **(6 marks)**

(Total = 10 marks)

79 CW (9/10)   18 mins

CW is a retail company that operates five stores. Each store has a manager and there is also a General Manager who reports directly to the Board of directors of the company.

For many years the General Manager has set the budgets for each store and the store managers' performances have been measured against their respective budgets even though they did not actively participate in their preparation. If a store manager meets his budgeted target then he is financially rewarded for his performance.

The company has recently appointed a new Finance Director who has questioned this previous practice and suggested that each store manager should be involved in the preparation of their own budget. The General Manager is very concerned about this. She thinks that the store managers will overstate their costs and resource requirements in order to make it easier for them to achieve their budget targets.

Required

(a)   Explain the problems that could arise, for planning and decision making purposes within CW, if the store managers did overstate their budgeted costs and resource requirements.   **(4 marks)**

(b)   Discuss the behavioural issues that could arise if excess costs and resources are removed from the store managers' budget.   **(6 marks)**

(Total = 10 marks)

80 Solicitors (5/10)   18 mins

A firm of solicitors is using budgetary control during 20X0. The senior partner estimated the demand for the year for each of the firm's four divisions: Civil, Criminal, Corporate, and Property. A separate partner is responsible for each division.

Each divisional partner then prepared a cost budget based on the senior partner's demand estimate for the division. These budgets were then submitted to the senior partner for his approval. He then amended them as he thought appropriate before issuing each divisional partner with the final budget for the division. He did not discuss these amendments with the respective divisional partners. Actual performance is then measured against the final budgets for each month and each divisional partner's performance is appraised by asking the divisional partner to explain the reasons for any variances that occur.

The Corporate partner has been asked to explain why her staff costs exceeded the budgeted costs for last month while the chargeable time was less than budgeted. Her reply is below.

"My own original estimate of staff costs was higher than the final budgeted costs shown on my divisional performance report. In my own cost budget I allowed for time to be spent developing new services for the firm's corporate clients and improving the clients' access to their own case files. This would improve the quality of our services to clients and therefore increase client satisfaction. The trouble with our present system is that it focuses on financial performance and ignores the other performance indicators found in modern performance management systems."

Required

(a)   Discuss the present budgeting system and its likely effect on divisional partner motivation.   **(6 marks)**

(b)   Explain two non-financial performance indicators (other than client satisfaction and service quality) that could be used by the firm.   **(4 marks)**

(Total = 10 marks)

81 Budgets for solicitors (Specimen paper)   18 mins

A firm of solicitors is preparing its budgets for 20X0. The structure of the firm is that it has a managing partner who is responsible for client and staff management, the firm's accounts and compliance matters and three other partners who each take responsibility for case matters depending on the branch of law that is involved in each case.

For a number of years the managing partner has prepared the budgets for the firm. These include budgets for fee income and costs analysed by each partner, and a cash budget for the firm as a whole. The firm has overdraft facilities which are renewable in June each year and sets cash balance targets for each month that reflect the seasonality of some of its work.

At the end of each month there is a partners' meeting at which the managing partner presents a statement that compares the actual results of the month and the year to date with the corresponding budget. At this meeting all partners are asked to explain the reasons for the variances that have arisen.

The managing partner recently attended a course on "Budget Planning & Cost Control" at which the presenter argued that each of the partners in the firm should be involved in the budget setting process. However, the managing partner is not convinced by this argument as she believes that this could lead to budget manipulation.

Required

(a) Explain feedback and feed-forward control systems and give an example of each in the context of the firm of solicitors. **(5 marks)**

(b) Discuss ONE potentially beneficial consequence and ONE potentially adverse consequence of involving the firm's other partners in the budget setting process of the firm. **(5 marks)**

(Total = 10 marks)

82 Budget planning   18 mins

(a) Explain, giving examples, how budgets can be used for feedback control and feed-forward control. **(5 marks)**

(b) Briefly explain **three** reasons why budgetary planning and control might be inappropriate in a rapidly changing business environment **(5 marks)**

(Total = 10 marks)

83 X plc (MAPE, 11/06, amended)   18 mins

X plc manufactures specialist insulating products that are used in both residential and commercial buildings. One of the products, Product W, is made using two different raw materials and two types of labour. The company operates a standard absorption costing system and is now preparing its budgets for the next four quarters. The following information has been identified for Product W:

Sales

Selling price: £220 per unit

Sales demand

	Units		Units
Quarter 1	2,250	Quarter 4	2,050
Quarter 2	2,050	Quarter 5	1,250
Quarter 3	1,650	Quarter 6	2,050

Costs

Materials

A	5 kgs per unit @ £4 per kg
B	3 kgs per unit @ £7 per kg

Labour

Skilled	4 hours per unit @ £15 per hour
Semi-skilled	6 hours per unit @ £9 per hour

Annual overheads £280,000

40% of these overheads are fixed and the remainder varies with total labour hours. Fixed overheads are absorbed on a unit basis.

Inventory holding policy

Closing inventory of finished goods	30% of the following quarter's sales demand
Closing inventory of materials	45% of the following quarter's materials usage

The management team are concerned that X plc has recently faced increasing competition in the market place for Product W. As a consequence there have been issues concerning the availability and costs of the specialised materials and employees needed to manufacture Product W, and there is concern that these might cause problems in the current budget setting process.

Required

(a) X Plc has just been informed that Material A may be in short supply during the year for which it is preparing budgets. Discuss the impact this will have on budget preparation and other areas of X plc.

(5 marks)

(b) Assuming that the budgeted production of Product W was 7,700 units and that the following actual results were incurred for labour and overheads in the year:

Actual production: 7,250 units

		£
Actual overheads:	Variable	185,000
	Fixed	105,000
Actual labour costs	Skilled – £16.25 per hour	568,750
	Semi-skilled – £8 per hour	332,400

Prepare a flexible budget statement for X plc showing the total variances that have occurred for the above four costs only.

(5 marks)

(Total = 10 marks)

84 W Limited   18 mins

W Limited designs and sells computer games. There are many other firms in this industry. For the last five years the senior management has required detailed budgets to be produced for each year with slightly less detailed plans for the following two years.

The managing director of W Limited has recently attended a seminar on budgeting and standard costing and heard the 'Beyond Budgeting' arguments that have been advanced by Hope and Fraser, among others.

Required

(i) Briefly describe the 'beyond budgeting' approach; and

(2 marks)

(ii) Advise the management of W Limited whether or not it should change its current budgeting system to a 'beyond budgeting' approach.

(3 marks)

(Iii) Briefly discuss three reasons why standard costing may not be appropriate in a modern business environment.

(5 marks)

(Total = 10 marks)

85 M plc (MAPE, 5/06, amended)   45 mins

M plc designs, manufactures and assembles furniture. The furniture is for home use and therefore varies considerably in size, complexity and value. One of the departments in the company is the assembly department. This department is labour intensive; the workers travel to various locations to assemble and fit the furniture using the packs of finished timbers that have been sent to them.

Budgets are set centrally and they are then given to the managers of the various departments who then have the responsibility of achieving their respective targets. Actual costs are compared against the budgets and the managers are then asked to comment on the budgetary control statement. The statement for April for the assembly Department is shown below.

	Budget	Actual	Variance
Assembly labour hours	6,400	7,140	
	$	$	$
Assembly labour	51,970	58,227	6,257 (A)
Furniture packs	224,000	205,000	19,000 (F)
Other materials	23,040	24,100	1,060 (A)
Overheads	62,060	112,340	50,280 (A)
Total	361,070	399,667	38,597 (A)

Note. The costs shown are for assembling and fitting the furniture (they do not include time spent travelling to jobs and the related costs). The hours worked by the manager are not included in the figure given for the assembly labour hours.

The manager of the assembly department is new to the job and has very little previous experience of working with budgets but he does have many years' experience as a supervisor in assembly departments. Based on that experience he was sure that the department had performed well. He has asked for your help in replying to a memo he has just received asking him to 'explain the serious overspending in his department'. He has sent you some additional information about the budget:

(1)   The budgeted and actual assembly labour costs include the fixed salary of $2,050 for the manager of the assembly department. All of the other labour is paid for the hours they work.

(2)   The cost of furniture packs and other materials is assumed by the central finance office of M plc to vary in proportion to the number of assembly labour hours worked.

(3)   The budgeted overhead costs are made up of three elements: a fixed cost of $9,000 for services from central headquarters, a stepped fixed cost which changes when the assembly hours exceed 7,000 hours, and some variable overheads. The variable overheads are assumed to vary in proportion to the number of assembly labour hours. Working papers for the budget showed the impact on the overhead costs of differing amounts of assembly labour hours:

Assembly labour hours	5,000	7,500	10,000
Overhead costs	$54,500	$76,500	$90,000

The actual fixed costs for April were as budgeted.

Required

(a)   Prepare, using the additional information that the manager of the assembly department has given you, a budgetary control statement that would be more helpful to him.   **(9 marks)**

(b)   Discuss the differences between the format of the statement that you have produced and that supplied by M plc.   **(3 marks)**

(c)   Discuss whether M plc should change to a system of participative budgeting.   **(8 marks)**

(d)   Outline the difference between budgets for **planning** and budgets for **control**, citing an example of each.
                                                                                                       (5 marks)

                                                                                           (Total = 25 marks)

86   AHW plc

45 mins

AHW plc is a food processing company that produces high-quality, part-cooked meals for the retail market. The five different types of meal that the company produces (products A to E) are made by subjecting ingredients to a series of processing activities. The meals are different, and therefore need differing amounts of processing activities.

Budget and actual information for October 20X2 is shown below:

Budgeted data

	Product A	Product B	Product C	Product D	Product E
Number of batches	20	30	15	40	25

Processing activities per batch

	Product A	Product B	Product C	Product D	Product E
Processing activity W	4	5	2	3	1
Processing activity X	3	2	5	1	4
Processing activity Y	3	3	2	4	2
Processing activity Z	4	6	8	2	3

Budgeted costs of processing activities

	£'000
Processing activity W	160
Processing activity X	130
Processing activity Y	80
Processing activity Z	200

All costs are expected to be variable in relation to the number of processing activities.

Actual data

Actual output during October 20X2 was as follows:

	Product A	Product B	Product C	Product D	Product E
Number of batches	18	33	16	35	28

Actual processing costs incurred during October 20X2 were:

	£'000
Processing activity W	158
Processing activity X	139
Processing activity Y	73
Processing activity Z	206

Required

(a)   Prepare a budgetary control statement (to the nearest £'000) that shows the original budget costs, flexible budget costs, the actual costs, and the total variances of each processing activity for October 20X2.

(11 marks)

(b)   Your control statement has been issued to the managers responsible for each processing activity and the finance director has asked each of them to explain the reasons for the variances shown in your statement. The managers are not happy about this as they were not involved in setting the budgets and think that they should not be held responsible for achieving targets that were imposed upon them.

Required

Explain briefly the reasons why it might be preferable for managers *not* to be involved in setting their own budgets. **(6 marks)**

(c)   (i)   Explain the difference between fixed and flexible budgets and how each may be used to control production costs and non-production costs (such as marketing costs) within AHW plc.

(ii)   Give two examples of costs that are more appropriately controlled using a fixed budget, and explain why a flexible budget is less appropriate for the control of these costs. **(8 marks)**

(Total = 25 marks)

87 DVD and Blu-ray (5/11)   18 mins

A company produces and sells DVD players and Blu-ray players.

Extracts from **the budget** for April are shown in the following table:

	Sales (players)	Selling price (per player)	Standard cost (per player)
DVD	3,000	$75	$50
Blu-ray	1,000	$200	$105

The Managing Director has sent you a copy of an e-mail she received from the Sales Manager. The content of the e-mail was as follows:

> *We have had an excellent month. There was an adverse sales price variance on the DVDs of $18,000 but I compensated for that by raising the price of Blu-ray players. Unit sales of DVD players were as expected but sales of the Blu-rays were exceptional and gave a total sales volume profit variance of $19,000. I think I deserve a bonus!*

The Managing Director has asked for your opinion on these figures. You obtained the following information:

Actual results for April were:

	Sales (players)	Selling price (per player)
DVD	3,000	$69
Blu-ray	1,200	$215

The total market demand for DVD players was as budgeted but as a result of distributors reducing the price of Blu-ray discs the total market for Blu-ray players grew by 50% in April. The company had sufficient capacity to meet the revised market demand for 1,500 units of its Blu-ray players and therefore maintained its market share.

Required

(a)   Calculate the following operational variances based on the revised market details:

    (i)   The total sales mix profit margin variance   **(2 marks)**
    (ii) The total sales volume profit variance   **(2 marks)**

(b)   Explain, using the above scenario, the importance of calculating planning and operational variances for responsibility centres.   **(6 marks)**

(Total = 10 marks)

88 KHL (3/11)   18 mins

KHL manufactures a single product and operates a budgetary control system that reports performance using variances on a monthly basis. The company has an agreement with a local supplier and calls off raw materials as and when required. Consequently there is no inventory of raw materials.

The following details have been extracted from the budget working papers for 2011:

	Annual Activity (units)		
	50,000	70,000	90,000
	$000	$000	$000
Sales revenue	3,200	4,480	5,760
Direct materials (3 kgs per unit)	600	840	1,080
Direct labour (2 hours per unit)	1,000	1,400	1,800
Variable overhead (2 hours per unit)	400	560	720
Fixed overhead (2 hours per unit)*	600	600	600

*The fixed overhead absorption rate of $5 per hour was based on an annual budget of 60,000 units of the product being produced at a constant monthly rate throughout the year, with the fixed overhead cost being incurred in equal monthly amounts.

The following actual performance relates to February 20X1:

	$	$
Sales revenue (5,700 units)		330,600
Direct materials (18,600 kgs)	70,680	
Direct labour (11,500 hours)	128,800	
Variable overhead (11,500 hours)	47,150	
Fixed overhead absorbed	60,000	
	306,630	
Finished goods inventory adjustment	15,000	291,630
Gross profit		38,970
Fixed overhead over-absorption		3,000
Profit		41,970

For February 20X1 budgeted sales were 6,000 units, the selling price variance was $34,200 Adverse and the sales volume profit variance was $4,200 Adverse. The actual fixed overhead incurred was $57,000.

Budgeted profit for February 20X1 was $84,000.

Required

Prepare a statement for February 20X1 that reconciles the budgeted profit of $84,000 with the actual profit of $41,970.

You should show the variances in as much detail as possible given the data provided. **(10 marks)**

89 Direct labour requirements (9/10)   18 mins

The following details show the direct labour requirements for the first six batches of a new product that were manufactured last month:

	Budget	Actual
Output (batches)	6	6
Labour hours	2,400	1,950
Total labour cost	$16,800	$13,650

The Management Accountant reported the following variances:

Total labour cost variance	$3,150 favourable
Labour rate variance	Nil
Labour efficiency variance	$3,150 favourable

The Production Manager has now said that he forgot to inform the Management Accountant that he expected a 90% learning curve to apply for at least the first 10 batches.

Required

(a) Calculate planning and operational variances that analyse the actual performance taking account of the anticipated learning effect. **(6 marks)**

   Note: The learning index for a 90% learning curve is -0.1520.

(b) Explain the differences between standard costing and target costing. **(4 marks)**

(Total = 10 marks)

90 WC

45 mins

WC is a company that installs kitchens and bathrooms for customers who are renovating their houses. The installations are either pre-designed 'off the shelf' packages or highly customised designs for specific jobs.

The company operates with three divisions: Kitchens, Bathrooms and Central Services. The Kitchens and Bathrooms divisions are profit centres but the Central Services division is a cost centre. The costs of the Central Services division, which are thought to be predominantly fixed, include those incurred by the design, administration and finance departments. The Central Services costs are charged to the other divisions based on the budgeted Central Services costs and the budgeted number of jobs to be undertaken by the other two divisions.

The budgeting and reporting system of WC is not very sophisticated and does not provide much detail for the Directors of the company.

Budget details

The budgeted details for last year were:

	Kitchens	Bathrooms
Number of jobs	4,000	2,000
	$	$
Average price per job	10,000	7,000
Average direct costs per job	5,500	3,000
Central Services recharge per job	2,500	2,500
Average profit per job	2,000	1,500

Actual details

The actual results were as follows:

	Kitchens	Bathrooms
Number of jobs	2,600	2,500
	$	$
Average price per job	13,000	6,100
Average direct costs per job	8,000	2,700
Central Services recharge per job	2,500	2,500
Average profit per job	2,500	900

The actual costs for the Central Services division were $17·5 million.

Required

(a)   Calculate the sales price variances and the sales mix profit and sales quantity profit variances.

(6 marks)

(b)   Prepare a statement that reconciles the budgeted and actual profits and shows appropriate variances in as much detail as possible. **(10 marks)**

(c)   Using the statement that you prepared in part *(b)* above, discuss

(i)   the performance of the company for the year; and

(ii)   potential changes to the budgeting and reporting system that would improve performance evaluation within the company. **(9 marks)**

(Total = 25 marks)

91 Planning & control variances (MAPE, 11/08, amended) 45 mins

A company manufactures two types of fertilizer (FA and FB). The company uses a standard costing system for planning and control purposes. Standards are set annually but budgets and variance reports are prepared each period.

Chemicals

Three chemicals (C1, C2 and C3) are used to make the fertilizers. C2 and C3 can be input directly to the manufacturing process but C1 has to be treated before it can be used. The treatment results in a loss of 30% of the chemicals treated. There are no further losses in the manufacturing process.

Details of the standards for the chemicals are as follows:

	C1	C2	C3
Price per kg	$8	$15	$12
Treatment loss	30%		
Content of finished product:			
per unit of FA	0.20 kg	0.15 kg	NIL
per unit of FB	0.20 kg	NIL	0.25 kg

Inventory policies

Chemicals: end of period holdings must be equal to 50% of the following period's requirements.

Treated C1 is used immediately. There are never any inventories of treated C1 at the start or end of any period.

Fertilizers: no finished products are to be held.

Period 1: output and sales

	Budget Units	Actual Units
FA	40,000	38,000
FB	24,000	25,000

Periods 2 and 3: sales budgets

	Period 2 Units	Period 3 Units
FA	40,000	44,000
FB	24,000	33,000

Required

(a) During Period 1, the quantity of C1 used was 17,740 kg. Calculate for Period 1 for C1:

    (i) The materials usage variance for the whole process

    (ii) The treatment loss percentage **(6 marks)**

(b) In Period 1, the company purchased and used 6,450 kg of C3. The cost of this purchase was $94,000. It has now been realised that the standard price of C3 should have been $14·50 per kg for Period 1.

    (i) Calculate the planning variance, and the operational price and usage variances for C3 for Period 1. **(7 marks)**

    (ii) Explain two problems associated with the reporting of planning variances. **(3 marks)**

(c) 'Variance analysis presents results after the actual events have taken place and therefore it is of little use to management for planning and control purposes, particularly in a modern manufacturing environment'.

    Discuss the above statement. **(9 marks)**

(Total = 25 marks)

92 LMN (5/10)   18 mins

LMN comprises three trading divisions plus a Head Office. There is a director for each trading division and, in addition, there is a Managing Director who is based in Head Office. Divisional directors are empowered to make decisions concerning the day to day operations of their division and investment decisions requiring an initial investment up to $100,000. Investment decisions involving greater initial expenditure must be authorised by the Managing Director. Inter-divisional trading occurs between all of the trading divisions. The transfer prices are determined by Head Office. Head Office provides services and facilities to each of the trading divisions.

At the end of each month, the actual costs of Head Office are apportioned to the trading divisions. Each Head Office cost is apportioned to the trading divisions using an appropriate basis. The bases used are: number of employees; value of sales; capital invested; and standard hours of service delivered.

The Head Office costs, together with the costs and revenues generated at divisional level, are summarised in a divisional performance statement each month. The divisional directors are not happy with the present performance statement and how it is used to appraise their performance.

Required

(a) Explain, using examples from the scenario, three issues that LMN should consider when designing a new divisional performance statement. **(6 marks)**

LMN is thinking of introducing Activity Based Costing at its Head Office to help with the apportionment of all its costs to the divisions.

(b) Discuss the advantages of applying Activity Based Costing to apportion all of the Head Office costs.

(4 marks)

(Total = 10 marks)

93 C plc   18 mins

C plc is a large company that manufactures and sells wooden garden furniture. It has three divisions:

The Wood Division (WD) purchases logs and produces finished timber as planks or beams. Approximately two-thirds of its output is sold to the Products Division, with the remainder sold on the open market.

The Products Division (PD) manufactures wooden garden furniture. The policy of C plc is that the PD must buy all its timber from the WD and sell all its output to the Trading Division.

The Trading Division (TD) sells wooden garden furniture to garden centres, large supermarkets, and similar outlets. It only sells items purchased from PD.

The current position is that all three divisions are profit centres and C plc uses return on investment (ROI) measures as the primary means to assess divisional performance. Each division adopts a cost-plus pricing policy for external sales and for internal transfers between divisions. The senior management of C plc has stated that the divisions should consider themselves to be independent businesses as far as possible.

Required

(a) For each division suggest, with reasons, the behavioural consequences that might arise as a result of the current policy for the structure and performance evaluation of the divisions. **(5 marks)**

(b) The senior management of C plc has requested a review of the cost-plus transfer pricing policy that is currently used.

Suggest with reasons, an appropriate transfer pricing policy that could be used for transfers from PD to TD, indicating any problems that may arise as a consequence of the policy you suggest. **(5 marks)**

(Total = 10 marks)

94 SK plc (1)   18 mins

(a) SK plc is divided into five divisions that provide consultancy services to each other and to outside customers. Discuss the implications for SK plc, and the consequences for the managers of the supplying and receiving divisions, of two of the following possible cost-based approaches to setting a transfer price.

    (i)   Marginal cost   (iii) Cost plus

    (ii)   Total cost   (iv) Opportunity cost   **(5 marks)**

(b) Discuss whether standard costs or actual costs should be used as the basis for cost-based transfer prices.

(5 marks)

(Total = 10 marks)

95 SK plc (2)   18 mins

(a) Discuss the problems that arise specifically when determining transfer prices where divisions are located in different countries.

(5 marks)

(b) State one context in which a transfer price based on marginal cost would be appropriate and briefly describe any issues that may arise from such a transfer pricing policy.

(5 marks)

(Total = 10 marks)

96 SWZ (11/10)   45 mins

SWZ is a manufacturing company that has many trading divisions. Return on Investment (ROI) is the main measure of each division's performance. Each divisional manager's salary is linked only to their division's ROI.

The following information summarises the financial performance of the S division of SWZ over the last three years:

Year ending 31 October:

	20X8	20X9	20Y0
	$'000	$'000	$'000
Turnover	400	400	400
Cost of sales	240	240	240
Gross profit	160	160	160
Other operating costs	120	104	98
Pre-tax operating profit	40	56	62
Capital invested as at the end of the year	400	320	256

Other operating costs include asset depreciation calculated at the rate of 20% per annum on a reducing balance basis.

The figures shown in the above table for the capital invested as at the end of the year is the net book value of the division's fixed assets.

All of the above values have been adjusted to remove the effects of inflation. There have been no additions or disposals of fixed assets within the S division during this period.

Required

(a) Discuss the performance of the S division over the three year period.   **(9 marks)**

The manager of the S division is now considering investing in a replacement machine. The machine that would be replaced would be sold for its net book value which was $40,000 at 31 October 20Y0 and the new machine would cost $100,000. The new machine would have an expected life of five years and would be depreciated using the same depreciation rates as the existing machinery. The new machine would reduce the division's cost of sales by 10%. At the end of five years it would be sold for its net book value.

The divisional cost of capital is 8% per annum. The company has evaluated the investment and correctly determined that it has a positive Net Present Value (NPV) of $24,536.

Required

(b) Prepare calculations to show why the manager of the S division is unlikely to go ahead with the investment.

Ignore taxation.   **(11 marks)**

(c) Prepare calculations to show how the use of Residual Income (RI) as the performance measure would have led to a goal congruent decision by the manager of the S division in relation to the purchase of the replacement machine.

Ignore taxation.   **(5 marks)**

(Total = 25 marks)

97 H (5/10)   45 mins

H manufactures perfumes and cosmetics by mixing various ingredients in different processes, before the items are packaged and sold to wholesalers. H uses a divisional structure with each process being regarded as a separate division with its own manager who is set performance targets at the start of each financial year which begins on 1 January. Performance is measured using Return on Investment (ROI) based on net book value of capital equipment at the start of the year. The company depreciates its capital equipment at the rate of 20% per annum on a reducing balance basis. The annual depreciation is calculated at the start of the financial year and one-twelfth of this annual amount is included as monthly depreciation in the fixed overhead costs of each process. Output transferred from one process to another is valued using transfer prices based on the total budgeted costs of the process plus a mark-up of 15%.

Process B

This is the first process. Raw materials are blended to produce three different outputs, two of which are transferred to Processes C and D respectively. The third output is accounted for as a by-product and sold in the external market without further processing. The equipment used to operate this process originally cost $800,000 on 1 January 20X5. The Process B account for April 20Y0 was as follows.

	Litres	$		Litres	$
Opening WIP	Nil	Nil	Normal loss	3,000	3,000
Material W	10,000	25,000	By-product	5,000	5,000
Material X	5,000	10,000	Output to C	9,000	82,800
Material Y	12,000	24,000	Output to D	10,000	92,000
Direct labour		30,000	Closing WIP	Nil	Nil
Overhead		75,000			
Profit & Loss		18,800			
Totals	27,000	182,800		27,000	182,800

The material costs are variable per unit of input and direct labour costs are fixed in the short term because employees' contracts provide them with a six month notice period. Overhead costs include a share of Head Office costs, and of the remaining overhead costs some vary with the input volume of the process. The level of activity in April 20Y0 was typical of the monthly volumes processed by the company.

Process C

This process receives input from Process B to which is added further materials to produce a finished product that is sold in the external market at the budgeted selling price of $20 per litre. The equipment used to operate this process originally cost $500,000 on 1 January 20X8.

The Process C account for April 20Y0 was as follows.

	Litres	$		Litres	$
Opening WIP	1,000	11,200	Normal Loss	3,000	1,500
Input from B	9,000	82,800	Abnormal Loss	1,500	750
Material Z	3,000	15,000	Output	7,500	150,000
Direct Labour		20,000	Closing WIP	1,000	11,200
Overhead		50,000			
			Profit & Loss		15,550
Totals	13,000	179,000	Totals	13,000	179,000

The material costs are variable per unit of input and direct labour costs are fixed in the short term because employees' contracts provide them with a six month notice period. Overhead costs include a share of Head Office costs, and of the remaining overhead costs some vary with the input volume of the process. The level of activity that occurred in April 20Y0 was typical of the monthly volumes processed by the company, and the opening and closing work in process are identical in every respect.

The process is regarded as an investment centre and completed output and losses are valued at their selling prices. The manager of Process C is concerned at the level of output achieved from the input volume and is considering investing in new equipment that should eliminate the abnormal loss. This would involve investing $1,000,000 in new processing equipment on 1 January 20Y1; the existing equipment would be sold on the same date at a price equal to its net book value.

Process D

This process receives input from Process B which is further processed to produce a finished product that is sold in the external market at the budgeted selling price of $16 per litre. The equipment used to operate this process originally cost $300,000 on 1 January 20X0.

The Process D account for April 20Y0 was as follows.

	Litres	$		Litres	$
Opening WIP	1,000	5,500	Normal Loss	1,000	3,000
Input from B	10,000	92,000	Output	9,000	144,000
Direct Labour		30,000	Closing WIP	1,000	5,500
Overhead		30,000	Profit & Loss		5,000
Totals	11,000	157,500	Totals	11,000	157,500

Direct labour costs are fixed in the short term because employees' contracts provide them with a six month notice period. Overhead costs include a share of Head Office costs, and of the remaining overhead costs some vary with the input volume of the process. The level of activity in April 20Y0 was typical of the monthly volumes processed by the company, and the opening and closing work in process are identical in every respect. The process is regarded as an investment centre and completed output and losses are valued at their selling prices. The manager of Process D believes that the transfer price from Process B is unfair because the equivalent material could be purchased in the open market at a cost of $7·50 per litre.

Required

(a) (i) Calculate the annualised Return on Investment (ROI) achieved by each of the process divisions during April 20Y0. **(4 marks)**

(ii) Discuss the suitability of this performance measure in the context of the data provided for each process division. **(4 marks)**

(b) (i) Calculate the effect on the annualised Return on Investment in 20Y1 of Process Division C investing in new capital equipment. **(4 marks)**

(ii) Discuss the conflict that may arise between the use of NPV and ROI in this investment decision. **(4 marks)**

(c) Discuss the transfer pricing policy being used by H from the viewpoints of the managers of Process Division B and Process Division D. **(9 marks)**

(Total = 25 marks)

98 Responsibility centres and performance appraisal (1) 18 mins

(a) Explain the value and use of non-financial performance measures. **(5 marks)**

(b) Discuss the relative merits of ROI and RI as performance indicators. **(5 marks)**

(Total = 10 marks)

99   Responsibility centres and performance appraisal (2)   18 mins

(a)   Explain and discuss the similarities and differences between Residual Income and Economic Value Added (EVA®) as methods for assessing the performance of divisions.   **(5 marks)**

(b)   (i)   Briefly explain the main features of Economic Value Added (EVA®) as it would be used to assess the performance of divisions.   **(2 marks)**

(ii)   Briefly explain how the use of EVA® to assess divisional performance might affect the behaviour of divisional senior executives.   **(3 marks)**

(Total = 10 marks)

100   Y and Z plc (MAPE, 11/05, amended)   45 mins

(a)   A large organisation, with a well developed cost centre system, is considering the introduction of profit centres and/or investment centres throughout the organisation, where appropriate. As management accountant, you will be providing technical advice and assistance for the proposed scheme.

Required

Explain what conditions are necessary for the successful introduction of profit centres and investment centres.   **(5 marks)**

(b)   Y and Z are two divisions of a large company that operate in similar markets. The divisions are treated as investment centres and every month they each prepare an operating statement to be submitted to the parent company. Operating statements for these two divisions for October are shown below:

Operating statements for October

	Y £'000	Z £'000
Sales revenue	900	555
Less variable costs	345	312
Contribution	555	243
Less controllable fixed costs (includes depreciation on divisional assets)	95	42
Controllable income	460	201
Less apportioned central costs	338	180
Net income before tax	122	21
Total divisional net assets	£9.76m	£1.26m

The company currently has a target return on capital of 12% per annum. However, the company believes its cost of capital is likely to rise and is considering increasing the target return on capital. At present the performance of each division and the divisional management are assessed primarily on the basis of return on investment (ROI).

Required

(i)   Calculate the annualised return on investment (ROI) for divisions Y and Z, and discuss the relative performance of the two divisions using the ROI data and other information given above. **(9 marks)**

(ii)   Calculate the annualised residual income (RI) for divisions Y and Z, and explain the implications of this information for the evaluation of the divisions' performance.   **(6 marks)**

(iii)   Briefly discuss the strengths and weaknesses of ROI and RI as methods of assessing the performance of divisions. Explain two further methods of assessment of divisional performance that could be used in addition to ROI or RI.   **(5 marks)**

(Total = 25 marks)

101 The DE Company (5/11)

45 mins

The DE Company has two divisions. The following statement shows the performance of each division for the year ended 30 April 20X1:

	D $'000	E $'000
Sales	500,200	201,600
Variable cost	380,400	140,000
Contribution	119,800	61,600
Fixed costs	30,000	20,000
Operating profit	89,800	41,600

Division E manufactures just one type of component. It sells the components to external customers and also to Division D. During the year to 30 April 20X1, Division E operated at its full capacity of 140,000 units. The transfer of 70,000 units to Division D satisfied that division's total demand for that type of component. However the external demand was not satisfied. A further 42,000 components could have been sold to external customers by Division E at the current price of $1,550.

The current policy of the DE Company is that internal sales should be transferred at their opportunity cost. Consequently during the year, some components were transferred to Division D at the market price and some were transferred at variable cost.

Required

(a)   Prepare an analysis of the sales made by Division E that shows clearly, in units and in $, the internal and external sales made during the year.
(3 marks)

(b)   Discuss the effect of possible changes in external demand on the profits of Division E, assuming the current transfer pricing policy continues.
(6 marks)

Division E is considering investing in new equipment which would reduce its unit variable costs by 20% and increase its capacity by 10% for each of the next five years. The capital cost of the investment is $120m and the equipment would have no value after five years. The DE company and its divisional managers evaluate investments using net present value (NPV) with an 8% cost of capital.

External annual demand for the next five years will continue to be 112,000 components at $1,550 each but the DE Company will insist that the internal annual demand for 70,000 components must be satisfied.

Required

(c)   Assuming that the current transfer pricing policy continues:

(i)   Evaluate the investment from the perspective of the manager of Division E.
(6 marks)

(ii)   Evaluate the investment from the perspective of the DE Company.
(4 marks)

Note: Ignore inflation and taxation.

(d)   Explain TWO factors that should be considered when designing divisional performance measures.
(6 marks)

(Total = 25 marks)

102   PZ Group (3/11)   45 mins

The PZ Group comprises two companies: P Limited and Z Limited. Both companies manufacture similar items and are located in different regions of the same country. Return on Capital Employed (ROCE) is used as the group's performance measure and is also used to determine divisional managers' bonuses. The results of the two companies and of the group for the year ended 31st December 20X0 and the balance sheets at that date are as follows:

	P Limited $'000	Z Limited $'000	PZ Group $'000
Revenue	200,000	220,000	400,000
Cost of sales	170,000	160,000	310,000
Gross profit	30,000	60,000	90,000
Administration costs	10,000	30,000	40,000
Interest payable	10,000		10,000
Pre-tax profit	10,000	30,000	40,000
Non-current assets:			
Original cost	1,000,000	1,500,000	2,500,000
Accumulated depreciation	590,400	1,106,784	1,697,184
Net book value	409,600	393,216	802,816
Net current assets	50,000	60,000	110,000
	459,600	453,216	912,816
Non-current borrowings	150,000		150,000
Shareholders' funds	309,600	453,216	762,816
Capital employed	459,600	453,216	912,816

Notes

1   During the year Z Limited sold goods to P Limited that had cost Z Limited $10,000. The transactions relating to this sale have been eliminated from the PZ Group results stated above.

2   Both companies use the group depreciation policy of 20% per annum on a reducing balance basis for their non-current assets. Neither company made any additions or disposals of non-current assets during the year.

Required

(a)   Calculate the Return on Capital Employed (ROCE) ratios for each of the two companies for the year and analyse these into their secondary ratio components of:

(i)   Pre-tax profit %
(ii)   Asset Turnover   **(3 marks)**

(b)

(i)   Calculate Z's gross profit margin on its internal sales and compare this to the gross profit margin on its external sales.   **(4 marks)**

(ii)   Discuss the performance of the two companies EXCLUDING the effects of the intra group transactions.   **(11 marks)**

Due to operational difficulties, the directors of the PZ Group are to impose a transfer pricing policy.

(c)   Explain THREE factors that they should consider when setting the transfer pricing policy.   **(7 marks)**

      (Total = 25 marks)

103 The Alpha group (9/10)   45 mins

The Alpha group comprises two companies, X Limited and Y Limited both of which are resident in a country where company profits are subject to taxation at 30%.

X Limited

X Limited has two trading divisions:

Consultancy division - provides consultancy services to the engineering sector.

Production division - assembles machinery which it sells to a number of industry sectors. Many of the components used in these machines are purchased from Y Limited.

Y Limited

Y Limited manufactures components from raw materials many of which are imported. The components are sold globally. Some of the components are sold to X Limited.

Financial results

The financial results of the two companies for the year ended 30 September 20X0 are as follows

| | X Limited | | Y Limited |
| | Consultancy division | Production division | |
	$'000	$'000	$'000
External sales	710	1,260	400
Sales to X Limited			350
			750
Cost of sales	240	900*	250
Administration costs	260	220	130
Operating profit	210	140	370
Capital employed	800	2,000	4,000

* includes the cost of components purchased from Y Limited.

Required

(a)   DiscuSs the performance of each division of X Limited and of Y Limited using the following three ratios:

    (i)   Return on Capital Employed (ROCE)
    (ii)   Operating Profit Margin
    (iii)   Asset Turnover   **(9 marks)**

Transfer Prices

The current policy of the group is to allow the managers of each company or division to negotiate with each other concerning the transfer prices.

The manager of Y Limited charges the same price internally for its components that it charges to its external customers. The manager of Y argues that this is fair because if the internal sales were not made he could increase his external sales. An analysis of the market demand shows that currently Y Limited satisfies only 80% of the external demand for its components.

The manager of the Production division of X Limited believes that the price being charged by Y Limited for the components is too high and is restricting X Limited's ability to win orders. Recently X Limited failed to win a potentially profitable order which it priced using its normal gross profit mark-up. The competitor who won the order set a price that was less than 10% lower than X Limited's price.

An analysis of the cost structure of Y Limited indicates that 40% of the cost of sales is fixed costs and the remaining costs vary with the value of sales.

Required

(b) (i) Discuss how the present transfer pricing policy is affecting the overall performance of the group.

(5 marks)

(ii) Explain, including appropriate calculations, the transfer price or prices at which the components should be supplied by Y Limited to X Limited.

(8 marks)

(c) The group Managing Director is considering relocating Y Limited to a country that has a much lower rate of company taxation than that in its current location.

Required

Explain the potential tax consequences of the internal transfer pricing policy if Y Limited were to relocate.

(3 marks)

(Total = 25 marks)

104 DEF (Specimen paper)   45 mins

DEF is a trading company that is divided into three divisions: D, E and F. Each division maintains its own accounting records and prepares an annual summary of its results. These performance summaries are shown below for the year ended 30 September 20X9.

Division	D	E	F
	$000	$000	$000
Sales (net of returns)	150	200	400
Variable production costs	50	70	230
Fixed production costs	60	50	80
Administration costs	30	25	40
Profit	10	55	50
Capital Employed	400	550	415

1   Divisions are free to trade with each other without any interference from Head Office. The managers of the respective divisions negotiate transfer prices between themselves. During the year and included in the above costs and revenues are the following transactions:

• Division D sold goods for $20,000 to Division E. The price negotiated was agreed on a unit basis between the managers of the two divisions. The variable production cost of these items in Division D was $18,000. Division D was operating under capacity and agreed to a transfer price that was little more than its own variable cost.

• Division F sold goods for $15,000 to Division E. The price negotiated was agreed on a unit basis between the managers of the two divisions. The variable production cost of these items in Division F was $9,000. Division F was operating under capacity and negotiated a transfer price based on its total production cost.

2   Included in the Administration costs for each division are the following management charges from Head Office:

D $10,000
E $8,000
F $15,000

3   At the start of each year Head Office sets each division a target Return on Capital Employed. The target depends on their nature of the work and their industry sector. For the year ended 30 September 20X9 these targets were:

D   6%
E   3%
F   15%

Required

(a)   Discuss the shortcomings of the above performance summaries when measuring the performance of each division.   **(5 marks)**

(b)   Discuss the potential problems of negotiated transfer pricing, and how these have impacted on the performance of each of Divisions D, E, and F for the year ended 30 September 20X9.   **(6 marks)**

(c)   Prepare an alternative statement that is more useful for measuring and reporting the performance of Divisions D, E, and F.   **(8 marks)**

(d)   Discuss how the use of "Dual" transfer prices could affect the measurement of divisional performance within DEF. Illustrate your answer with suggested dual prices.   **(6 marks)**

(Total = 25 marks)

105   ACF Group   45 mins

Division A, which is part of the ACF Group, manufactures only one type of product, a Bit, which it sells to external customers and also to division C, another member of the group. ACF Group's policy is that divisions have the freedom to set transfer prices and choose their suppliers.

The ACF Group uses residual income (RI) to assess divisional performance and each year it sets each division a target RI. The group's cost of capital is 12% a year.

Division A

Budgeted information for the coming year is as follows.

Maximum capacity	150,000 Bits
External sales	110,000 Bits
External selling price	£35 per Bit
Variable cost	£22 per Bit
Fixed costs	£1,080,000
Capital employed	£3,200,000
Target residual income	£180,000

Division C

Division C has found two other companies willing to supply Bits.

X could supply at £28 per Bit, but only for annual orders in excess of 50,000 Bits.

Z could supply at £33 per Bit for any quantity ordered.

Required (Note. Ignore taxation)

(a)   Division C provisionally requests a quotation for 60,000 Bits from division A for the coming year.

(i)   Calculate the transfer price per Bit that division A should quote in order to meet its annual profit target of £564,000.   **(5 marks)**

(ii)   Calculate the two prices division A would have to quote to division C, if it became group policy to quote transfer prices based on opportunity costs.   **(4 marks)**

(b)   Evaluate and discuss the impact of the group's current and proposed polices on the profits of divisions A and C, and on group profit. Illustrate your answer with calculations.   **(16 marks)**

(Total = 25 marks)

106 FD and TM   45 mins

CTD Ltd has two divisions: FD and TM. FD is an iron foundry division which produces mouldings that have a limited external market and are also transferred to TM division. TM division uses the mouldings to produce a piece of agricultural equipment called the 'TX' which is sold externally. Each TX requires one moulding. Both divisions produce only one type of product.

The performance of each divisional manager is evaluated individually on the basis of the residual income (RI) of his or her division. The company's average annual 12% cost of capital is used to calculate the finance charges. If their own target residual income is achieved, each divisional manager is awarded a bonus equal to 5% of his or her residual income. All bonuses are paid out of head office profits.

The following budgeted information is available for the forthcoming year.

	TM division TX per unit	FD division Moulding per unit
	£	£
External selling price	500	80
Variable production costs	366*	40
Fixed production overheads	60	20
Gross profit	74	20
Variable selling and distribution cost	25	4**
Fixed administration overhead	25	4
Net profit	24	12

	TM division TX per unit	FD division Moulding per unit
Normal capacity (units)	15,000	20,000
Maximum production capacity (units)	15,000	25,000
Sales to external customers (units)	15,000	5,000
Capital employed	£1,500,000	£750,000
Target RI	£105,000	£85,000

* The variable production cost of TX includes the cost of an FD moulding.
** External sales only of the mouldings incur a variable selling and distribution cost of £4 per unit.

FD division currently transfers 15,000 mouldings to TM division at a transfer price equal to the total production cost plus 10%.

Fixed costs are absorbed on the basis of normal capacity.

Required

(a)   Calculate the bonus each divisional manager would receive under the current transfer pricing policy and discuss any implications that the current performance evaluation system may have for each division and for the company as a whole.   **(7 marks)**

(b)   Both divisional managers want to achieve their respective residual income targets. Based on the budgeted figures, calculate:

(i)   The **maximum** transfer price per unit that the divisional manager of TM division would pay.
(ii)   The **minimum** transfer price per unit that the divisional manager of FD division would accept.
                                                                                                        (7 marks)

(c)   Write a report to the management of CTD Ltd that explains, and recommends, the transfer prices which FD division should set in order to maximise group profits. Your report should also:

(i)   Consider the implications of actual external customer demand exceeding 5,000 units

(ii)   Explain how alternative transfer pricing systems could overcome any possible conflict that may arise as a result of your recommended transfer prices

Note. Your answer must be related to CTD Ltd. You will not earn marks by just describing various methods for setting transfer prices.   **(11 marks)**

                                                                                        (Total = 25 marks)

107 Sports equipment manufacturer (MAPE, 5/09) — 45 mins

A multi-national sports equipment manufacturer has a number of autonomous divisions throughout the world. Two of the divisions are in America, one on the west coast and one on the east coast. The west coast division manufactures cycle frames and assembles them into complete cycles using bought-in components. The east coast division produces wheels that are very similar to the wheel sets that are used by the Frames Division but it currently only sells them to external customers. Details of the two divisions are given below.

Frames Division (west coast)

The Frames Division buys the wheels that it needs from a local supplier. It has negotiated a price of $870 per set (there are two wheels in a set). This price includes a bulk purchase discount which is awarded if the division purchases 15,000 sets per year. The production budget shows that 15,000 sets will be needed next year.

Wheels Division (east coast)

The Wheels Division has a capacity of 35,000 sets per year. Details of the budget for the forthcoming year are as follows:

Sales	30,000 sets

Per set	$
Selling price	950
Variable costs	650

The fixed costs of the division at the budgeted output of 30,000 sets are $8m per year but they would rise to $9m if output exceeds 31,000 sets.

Note: The maximum external demand is 30,000 sets per year and there are no other uses for the current spare capacity.

Group Directive

The Managing Director of the group has reviewed the budgets of the divisions and has decided that in order to improve the profitability of the group the Wheels Division should supply wheel sets to the Frames Division. She is also thinking of linking the salaries of the divisional managers to the performance of their divisions but is unsure which performance measure to use. Two measures that she is considering are 'profit' and the 'return on assets consumed' (where the annual fixed costs would be used as 'assets consumed').

The manager of the Wheels Division has offered to supply wheel sets to the Frames Division at a price of $900 per set. He has offered this price because it would earn the same contribution per set that is earned on external sales (this is after adjusting for distribution and packaging costs).

Required

(a) Assume that the 15,000 wheel sets are supplied by the Wheels Division at a transfer price of $900 per set. Calculate the impact on the profits of each of the divisions and the group. **(4 marks)**

(b) Calculate the minimum price at which the Manager of the Wheels Division would be willing to transfer the 15,000 sets to the Frames Division if his performance is to be measured against maintaining:

(i) The profit of the division (currently $1m)

(ii) The return on assets consumed by the division (currently 12·5%). **(7 marks)**

(c) Produce a report to the Managing Director of the group that:

(i) Explains the problems that may arise from the directive and the introduction of performance measures. **(9 marks)**

(ii) Explains how the problems could be resolved. **(5 marks)**

Note. You should use your answers to parts (a) and (b) and other relevant calculations, where appropriate, to illustrate points in your report.

(Total = 25 marks)

ANSWERS

SECTION A – PRICING AND PRODUCT DECISIONS

Answers 1 to 32 cover pricing and product decisions, the subject of Part A of the BPP Study Text for Paper P2.

1 Z Ltd

Top tips. Think about the possible methods for apportioning joint costs and see if there is any relationship between the cost per litre for the three products. This should tell you that litres is the basis of apportionment.

In part (b) remember to only look at the incremental revenues and costs after the common process.

Easy marks. This question requires very simple calculations. Therefore, work out the basis of the common apportionment first.

Examiner's comments. This question was poorly answered, particularly part (a). Only one to two percent of candidates attempted to explain why it was necessary to apportion the common costs.

Many students did not appreciate the simplicity of part (b).

Common errors noted by the examiner include:

- Misreading part (a) and answering that the method used to apportion meant absorption costing or ABC.

- In part (b) calculating full profitability statements rather than simply comparing incremental costs and revenue.

- Ignoring or misunderstanding the viability of the common process and whether it generated an overall profit.

(a)

Product	Value at end of process (i) $	Litres (ii)	Value per litre from process ((i)/(ii)) $
M	141,875	25,000	5.675
N	85,125	15,000	5.675
P	255,375	45,000	5.675
	482,375	85,000	

As $482,375/85,000 = $5.675 the method used to apportion common costs between the joint products is litres produced.

This method is only suitable when products remain in the same state that is don't separate into liquid and gas products. It also doesn't take into account the relative income earning potential of each product.

However, it does allow values to be put on the products for stock and financial reporting purposes.

It is necessary to apportion the common costs between each product to put a value on stock for financial reporting and so sales can be matched with the cost the of sales.

(b) (i) <u>Viability of the common process</u>

Product	Selling price after common process $/litre	Litres	Total revenue $
M	6.25	25,000	156,250
N	5.20	15,000	78,000
P	6.80	45,000	306,000
			540,250

Less costs at end of common process (per (a) above)	(482,375)
Net revenue at the end of the common process	57,875

Therefore the common process is viable as net revenue is positive.

(ii) Optimal processing plan for each product

Product	Selling price now $	Selling price after $	Extra variable costs $	Contribution $
M	6.25	8.40	1.75	6.65
N	5.20	6.45	0.95	5.50
P	6.80	7.45	0.85	6.60

Products M and N should be processed further as the contribution per unit of each of these products is greater than the selling price before extra processing takes place (net revenue is positive). Product P should not be processed further as Z Ltd would be worse off by ($6.80 − $6.60) = $0.20 per unit.

2 Exe

Text references. Refer to Chapter 1A for the basis for making decisions based on relevant cash flows.

Top tips. Don't forget to provide your reasons for using each of the values in your estimate.

Easy marks. You should be able to identify that most overheads will not be relevant costs as they are incurred anyway irrespective of an individual job. Costs that are specifically incurred for this job, for instance the brass fittings would be relevant costs. Costs that have already been incurred such as estimating time are sunk costs.

	Notes	$
Direct materials		
Steel	1	55.00
Brass fittings		20.00
Direct labour		
Skilled	2	300.00
Semi-skilled	3	–
Overhead	4	7.50
Estimating time	5	–
		382.50
Administration overhead	6	–
Profit	7	–
Selling price		382.50

Lowest cost estimate = £382.50

Notes

1   $10m^2 \times \$5.50$ (the replacement cost)

2   **Overtime option** – 25 hrs × $8 × 1.5 = £300

Reduction in production of another product option = 25 × $(8 + 13) = £525

∴ It is cheaper to work overtime and hence this will be the relevant cost.

3   There is no incremental cost involved since the employees are currently being paid to be idle.

4   **General fixed costs will be incurred regardless of whether or not the order is accepted** and so are not relevant. The relevant cost therefore relates to the machine usage and is 10 hrs × $0.75.

5   This is a **sunk cost** and is therefore not relevant.

6   Administration costs will be incurred regardless of whether or not the order is accepted and so are not relevant.

7   We are asked to produce a **lowest cost estimate** which is one which just covers incremental costs and makes no profit. The **profit mark up** is therefore **not relevant**.

3 Z

Text reference. Read Chapter 1A if you get stuck with this question.

Top tips. You are being tested on how you make decisions. You are being asked to **state recommendations** and **state assumptions** in parts(a) and (b). **So don't just tackle this as a calculation exercise.** You will need to produce calculations but also be able to explain these.

Easy marks. The calculations in part(a) are quite simple. You need to compare the **incremental revenue** from the later products with the **incremental cost** to make these products. You can take much of this data straight from the question.

(a) Further processing decision

	Selling price now $	Selling price after $	Extra variable costs $	Contribution $
R	3.00	6.00	1.40	4.60
S	5.00	5.75	0.90	4.85
T	3.50	6.75	1.00	5.75

Recommendations

The table shows that the further processing of products R and T into RZ and TZ will be profitable as these result in additional net revenue (that is, the contribution per unit with further processing is greater than the selling price with no further processing.) Let's assume that the monthly output of product TZ remains at 1,200kg (no loss in further processing for instance). It is clear that even by accounting for these fixed costs it is profitable to convert T into TZ. So:

1,200 kg × $2.25 − $600 = $2,100

However, it is not profitable to process S further into product SZ. Nonetheless, other factors must also be considered. We do also need to consider whether the sales of these products are related so that, say, the sale of product T depends on that of S. So it may be necessary to continue selling a loss-making product to maintain a market presence.

(b) Validity of the common process

(i) Assuming an external market for products R, S and T

We are considering the **validity of the common process.** So we need to compare the combined cost of producing the three products with the combined market prices for each as given in the question.

		Product		
	R $	S $	T $	Total $
Revenue				
R/S/T (W1)	2,400	10,000	4,200	16,600
Cost (W2)				17,500
Net revenue/loss				(900)

Working

(1) Take the output from the common process for each product and multiply by the unit market prices given. So for product R, this would be 800kg × $3.00/kg.

(2) Total cost taken from process account in question.

Recommendation

The calculations in the table tell us that the common process is not viable given the costs and/or current market prices for the products.

(ii) Assuming no external market for products R, S and T

We need to work out a **notional sales value** for each product if there isn't a market price. This can be achieved by working backwards from the further products which do have a sales value.

	RZ	*Product* *SZ*	*TZ*	*Total*
	$	*$*	*$*	*$*
Revenue				
RZ/SZ/TZ (W1)	4,800	11,500	8,100	24,400
Common costs				17,500
Further costs (W2)	1,120	1,800	1,800	4,720
Net revenue/loss				2,180

Workings

(1) Take the unit market prices in the question and multiply by the outputs from the common process. So taking product R/RZ, 800kg × $6/kg = $4,800.

(2) Take the output from the common process and multiply by the specific costs in the question. Remember to include the fixed costs relating to product TZ.

Recommendation

The calculations in the table tell us that the common process is viable given the costs and/or notional market prices for the products. However this does of course depend on how reliable the notional prices are in reflecting market prices for the products.

4 Hotel

Text references. Relevant costing is covered in Chapter 1A.

Top tips. Carefully read through the scenario, noting the relevant costs and their causes as you do so. There is a lot of information to prepare for part (a) so presentation is key. Remember to show all of your workings!

(a) Hotel plan

	Peak *($)*	*Mid* *($)*	*Low* *($)*	*Total* *($)*
Room revenue	855,000	720,000	412,500	1,987,500
Guest related cost (guests (W1) × $12)	(184,680)	(162,000)	(108,000)	(454,680)
Room costs (Days × rooms (W1) × $8, $9, $11)	(68,400)	(81,000)	(82,500)	(231,900)
Avoidable general costs (W4)	(225,000)	(300,000)	(375,000)	(900,000)
Room / Guest contribution	376,920	177,000	(153,000)	400,920
Snack contribution (W3)	4,617	12,150	8,100	24,867
Cook costs (W5)	(5,000)	(6,667)	(8,333)	(20,000)
Restaurant contribution (W2)	17,313.75	33,750	47,250	98,313.75
Staff costs (W6)	(13,500)	(18,000)	(22,500)	(54,000)
Total contribution	380,350.75	198,233	(128,483)	450,100.75
Non-avoidable costs (W7)	(75,000)	(100,000)	(125,000)	(300,000)
Net contribution	305,350.75	98,233	(253,483)	150,100.75
Annual fixed costs				(200,000)
Annual profit / (loss)				(49,899.25)

Workings

1   Number of hotel guests

Season	Days	Rooms	Occupants	Guests
Peak	90	× 95	× 1.8	15,390
Mid	120	× 75	× 1.5	13,500
Low	150	× 50	× 1.2	9,000

2   Restaurant contribution

Season	Guests	Daily demand	Contribution	Gross contribution ($)
Peak	15,390	× 0.3 × $15	× 0.25	17,313.75
Mid	13,500	× 0.5 × $20	× 0.25	33,750.00
Low	9,000	× 0.7 × $30	× 0.25	47,250.00

3   Snacks contribution

Season	Guests	Daily demand	Contribution	Gross contribution ($)
Peak	15,390	× 0.1 × $10	× 0.30	4,617
Mid	13,500	× 0.3 × $10	× 0.30	12,150
Low	9,000	× 0.3 × $10	× 0.30	8,100

4   Avoidable general costs

Forecast general costs for the next year are as follows. Costs could be reduced by 75% if the hotel were to close temporarily for one or more seasons of the year.

Peak	$300,000 × 0.75	= $225,000
Mid	$400,000 × 0.75	= $300,000
Low	$500,000 × 0.75	= $375,000

5   Cook costs

The hotel employs a cook on a salary of $20,000 per year.

Peak (90 days)	$20,000 × (90/360)	= $5,000
Mid (120 days)	$20,000 × (120/360)	= $6,667
Low (150 days)	$20,000 × (150/360)	= $8,333

6   Staff costs

The hotel employs two chefs on a combined salary of $54,000 per year.

Peak (90 days)	$54,000 × (90/360)	= $13,500
Mid (120 days)	$54,000 × (120/360)	= $18,000
Low (150 days)	$54,000 × (150/360)	= $22,500

7   Non-avoidable costs

Forecast general costs for next year are as follows. Costs could be reduced by 75% (W4). Therefore, 25% are non-avoidable.

Peak	$300,000 × 0.25	= $75,000
Mid	$400,000 × 0.25	= $100,000
Low	$500,000 × 0.25	= $125,000

(b) (i) Part-closure

The above statement shows that the hotel makes an overall **annual loss**. Further analysis shows that the hotel could be profitable if the hotel was **closed during the low season** when it makes a significant loss.

Snack service

Also, since the snack service is only **profitable during the mid season** it could be closed down during the other seasons to further increase the profitability of the hotel.

(ii) Regular guests

One factor that should be considered are the regular guests who stay at the hotel throughout the year. If the hotel closes for the low season these guests may find an alternative hotel for the whole year which may **reduce profitability** in the other seasons. There may also be a **loss of reputation** as guests feel the hotel isn't customer focused.

Snack service

In addition, closing the snack service for parts of the year may raise issues over the possibility of only opening it for 120 days a year and whether current staff will accept this arrangement. Alternatively would more guests use the restaurant if there was no snack service at all?

5   M Group

> **Text references.** Relevant costing is covered in Chapter 1A.
>
> **Top tips.** Ensure that you answer all three elements of part (a) for each item on the cost estimate.
>
> **Easy marks.** There are easy marks in part (a) for discussing the basis of valuation for each item in the cost estimate and in part (c) for discussing non-financial matters that are relevant to the project decision.

(a) **Engineering specification (1)**

The cost of $1,500 has been calculated as the 3 days taken for the engineer to meet the manufacturing company and prepare the specification for the machine at a cost of $500 per day. However the meeting with the manufacturing company has already taken place, therefore the fee of $1,500 is a sunk cost and should not be included within the cost estimate of the machine. The relevant value for the cost estimate is $NIL.

Direct material A (2)

The cost of $61,000 has been calculated using the weighted average basis:

10,000 square metres	× $6.00	=	$60,000
5,000 square metres	× $6.10	=	$30,500

15,000 square metres in total = $91,500 = $6.10 per square metre.

This is not the correct valuation for direct material A. The 10,000 square metres required by the machine should be valued at the replacement cost (current market price of $7.00/metre) as the material is currently in use by PQR. The relevant value for the cost estimate is $70,000.

Direct Material B (3)

The cost of $2,500 has been calculated as the 250 metre lengths of material required by the machine at a cost of $10 per metre length. Material B is not currently used by PQR and would need to be purchased specifically for this work. The supplier of the material has a minimum order size of 300 metre lengths and PQR does not foresee any future use of the 50 unused lengths of material B. The relevant value for the cost estimate should be calculated based on the minimum order size multiplied by the market price:

300 metre lengths (minimum order size) × $10 = $3,000

Components (4)

The cost of $6,000 has been calculated as the 500 components at a price of $8 per component plus the 50% mark-up charged by HK in line with the transfer pricing policy within M group. This valuation is not correct and the relevant cost to M group should be calculated as the variable costs of manufacturing the components plus any contribution foregone as a result of reducing the volume of other components that are currently manufactured by HK and sold to the external market.

PQR could buy the components from the external market at a cost of $14 each. This is an irrelevant cost as it is cheaper for PQR to manufacture the components internally.

The relevant cost of components is calculated as:

350 components	×	$8 variable cost/component	= $2,800
150 components	×	($8 variable cost + $3 lost contribution)	= $1,650
Total relevant cost	=	$4,450	

Direct Labour (5)

The cost of $12,500 has been calculated as the 1,000 hours of skilled labour required to operate the machine at a labour rate of $12.50 per hour. However, the engineers employed by PQR do not currently have spare capacity and the cost estimate should be revised to take account of transferring the engineers from their existing duties and replacing them with temporary engineers at a labour rate of $14.00 per hour. The current market rate for engineers with the appropriate skills ($15.00 per hour) is not a relevant cost as it is cheaper for PQR to transfer skilled engineers from their existing duties.

The relevant cost of direct labour is calculated as:

1,000 hours of skilled labour × $14.00 per hour = $14,000

Supervision (6)

The cost of $350 has been calculated as one month salary of the senior engineer ($42,000 / 12 months = $3,500) multiplied by the time the engineer is expected to spend on the project (10%) = $350. However, the salary of the senior engineer is not a relevant cost. The senior engineer is already employed by PQR and will continue to be regardless whether the project goes ahead or not. If the supplier can not complete the work required within normal working hours, they will work overtime which is unpaid. The relevant cost is $NIL.

Machine hire (7)

The cost of $2,500 has been calculated as the hire of the specialist machine for 5 days during the project at a rate of $500 per day. However the relevant cost should be calculated as the lower of:

5 days hire × $500 per day = $2,500
$5,000 (monthly hire) − $3,000 (sub-let income $150 x 20 days) = $2,000

The total relevant cost is $2,000.

Overhead costs (8)

The cost of $5,500 has been calculated based on latest annual forecast of total overheads and the normal operating capacity of 80% as follows:

$220,000 forecast overheads	/	(50,000 labour hours × 80%)	= $5.50 per hour
1,000 skilled labour hours	×	$5.50 per hour	= $5,500

However, this is not a relevant cost. There is no evidence to suggest that the fixed costs are project-specific. The costs will be incurred regardless of whether the project is undertaken or not. The relevant cost is $NIL.

Revised schedule of relevant costs:

	Note	$
Engineering specification	1	Nil
Direct material A	2	70,000
Direct material B	3	3,000
Components	4	4,450
Direct Labour	5	14,000
Supervision	6	Nil
Machine hire	7	2,000
Overhead costs	8	Nil
Total		$93,450

(b)   Under PQR routine accounting practices, the profit from the project which is reported to the Board of M would be $8,150 ($100,000 - $91,850 per original cost estimate). The profit reported to the Board under a relevant cost basis would be $6,550 ($100,000 - $93,450 per relevant cost schedule). The difference of $1,600 is caused by the **different accounting methods** used for decision making compared to those used for inventory valuation and profit reporting.

The usage of material A on the project will be valued at the replacement cost of $7 per square metre under the relevant cost schedule as opposed to $6.10 per square metre using the weighted average method under PQR routine accounting practices:

	Cost per sq metre ($)	Total cost ($)
10,000 sq metres (cost estimate)	$6.10	$61,000
10,000 sq metres (relevant cost)	$7.00	$70,000
	Difference	$9,000

PQR routine accounting practices aim to allocate overhead costs to the project using an overhead absorption rate based on budgeted overheads and activity levels. Whilst this is relevant for profit reporting, it is **not appropriate for short-term decision making** as these costs will not be affected by the decision, resulting in a cost difference of $5,500.

(c)   One non-financial matter that should be considered is **the morale of the existing workforce**. Workers may become **de-motivated if they are transferred from their existing duties** to work on the new project. Paying temporary workers a rate of $14 per hour to perform the same duties as permanent employees who are currently paid $12.50 per hour **could cause conflict** within the workforce and adversely affect productivity levels or even lead to existing workers leaving the company.

The Board of M and PQR should also consider the existing consumer base of HK. If HK focuses on manufacturing components for PQR there is a risk that it could **lose touch with external customers who may find an alternative supplier**. This could result in HK losing market share.

6 H

Text reference. You will find most of the information to answer this question in Chapters 1A and 2.

Top tips. To tackle part (a), we suggest you list the costs and profit mark-up in a table with a space for the reasons why you consider each to be relevant or non-relevant costs. Keep any workings that you need to do separate and cross reference these to your main table. Remember that relevant costs are **future, incremental cash flows** and frame your reasons with this definition in mind. Other terms you could use to describe relevant costs are **differential, avoidable** or **opportunity** costs.

In part(b), you are being tested on how well you understand the differences between **relevant costing** and **absorption costing**. Make sure you use the data you have already calculated to make your points illustrating the differences.

Easy marks. You should be able to get a couple of easy marks in part (a). At least some of the costs are clearly relevant or non-relevant.

(a) Relevant costs

	Cost $	Reason
Technical report	0	This is a sunk cost.
Material A	15,000	3,400 sheets in existing inventory that have an existing use so they will need to be replaced if they are used in this contract. Also 6,600 new sheets are needed. The current market price is $1.50/sheet.
Material B	2,000	250 litres of ink need to be bought in at $8/litre to provide 200 litres for this contract. There is no foreseen alternative use for the excess 50 litres which were brought in to fulfil this contract.
Direct labour	500	50 hours at the overtime rate only are **differential costs**. The other hours are paid under a guaranteed minimum wage.
Supervision	0	Existing supervisor and no suggestion that this work will require overtime or taking her off other duties.
Machine A	240	There are 30 unused hours of capacity that have an alternative market so an **opportunity cost** arises at 20 hours × $12/hour.
Machine B	100	This machine will need to be run at overtime rates so this is an **incremental cost** of 25 machine hours at $4/hr
Despatch	400	This is a specific cost relating to this contract.
Fixed overheads	0	Fixed overheads which aren't specifically attributable to this contract as they are general fixed overheads.
Profit mark-up	0	Profit is not a relevant cost.
	18,240	

(b) Relevant costing, absorption costing, selling prices and profitability

Short-term pricing

In the short-term, a product or service can be priced using **relevant cost** to enable a contract to be won on a one-off basis. However in the longer term, organisations will need to cover costs that don't fall under the 'relevant' category but are nonetheless still incurred. In the example in (a) above, the organisation needs to set prices in the longer term to cover the sunk costs and overheads that arise but aren't deemed relevant to this contract.

Profitability and absorption costing

Absorption costing attributes **full costs** to inventory using an agreed basis of allocation such as labour hours. Therefore non-relevant costs will be attributed to the catalogues as part of the absorption of overheads based on a measure such as labour hours taken or machine hours used. The cost of the materials included in the catalogues will also be based on a standard LIFO, FIFO or AVCO valuation.

If we take the cost of **material A,** this will be calculated at the original cost of $1.40/sheet for the existing inventory plus the cost of buying in the extra sheets at $1.50 each.

So total cost will be $1.40 × 3,400 + $1.50 × 6,600 = $14,660 instead of $15,000 under the relevant cost basis.

Material B will be costed based on the **materials used**. Therefore the cost will be $1,600 instead of $2,000.

The **direct labour** will be charged at the full cost of employee time and wages spent on the catalogues so at $8 × 150 hours or $1,200 compared to $500.

Overheads will be charged to the catalogues at $20 per direct labour hour. At 150 hours this results in an absorption of $3,000 of overheads.

In summary the differences are:

Materials	$ (740) less
Labour	$ 700 more
Overheads	$3,000 more

If management have based their pricing of the catalogues on a relevant cost of $18,240 it is likely that then using an absorption costing system to attribute costs will see a loss on the contract as costs are nearly $3,000 higher.

7 Engineering company with limiting factors

Text references. Relevant cash flows for decisions are covered in Chapter 1A. Short term decisions are dealt with in Chapter 1B.

Top tips. Layout is important in part (a) so that it is clear how you arrive at your conclusions. Don't forget to answer the narrative part of part (a), as it is easy to get too engrossed in calculations.

Part (b) links the contribution per m^2 of the limiting factor to prices. The maximum price should not only include the contribution the company would earn from the production of the extra units, but also the current price of the material.

In part (c), you have to consider the size of the penalty that would make the company indifferent to the contract (almost like a breakeven point). You should compare the contribution the company would lose by fulfilling the contract with the contribution it would gain from the contract itself.

Easy marks. The calculations in part (a) are quite straightforward if you have studied relevant costing.

(a)　The most profitable course of action can be determined by ranking the products and components according to **contribution per unit of the limiting factor**. Direct material M1 is the limiting factor in this case, therefore the highest rank will be given to the product/component with the greatest contribution per m^2 of this material.

	Product P4 $	Product P6 $	Component C3 $	Component C5 $
Selling price	125	175	–	–
Opportunity cost			75	95
Direct materials:				
M1	15	10	5	10
M2	10	20	15	20
Direct labour	20	30	16	10
Variable overhead	10	15	8	5
Total direct costs	55	75	44	45
Contribution/unit	70	100	31	50
m^2 of M1/unit	0.75	0.5	0.25	0.5
Contribution/m^2	$93.33	$200	$124	$100
Ranking	4	1	2	3

Optimal production schedule

	m_2
Material available	1,000
Produce: 1,500 units of P6	750
	250
500 units of C3	125
	125
$\dfrac{125m^2}{0.5}$ = 250 units of C5	125
	NIL

Optimal production plan is therefore:

P4	No units
P6	1,500 units
C3	500 units
C5	250 units

Other factors to be considered (only three are required).

(i) Will the non-production of P4 have an effect on the sales of other products?

(ii) What is the likelihood of the price of Material M1 remaining at $20 per m²?

(iii) Is there a possibility of replacing Material M1 with another material that is in more plentiful supply?

(iv) What are the future prospects for product P4? Should production be terminated completely? Would this affect the company's overall market position?

(b) The company would purchase further material in order to satisfy demand for component C5 and product P4.

As component C5 has a **greater contribution per m²**, outstanding demand for this would be **satisfied first**.

Total units to be produced = (1,000 units − 250) = 750
Total m² of M1 required = 750 × 0.5 = 375m²
Saving per m² = $100 per m² (see part (a))

Therefore maximum price would be $100 + 20 = $120.

Product P4

Total units = 2,000
Total m² = 2,000 × 0.75 = 1,500

Contribution per m² = $93.33 (see part (a))

Therefore maximum price would be $93.33 + 20 = $113.33.

(c) Material required to fulfil the contract = 500 × 0.75m² = 375m²

This would be taken from current production, starting with the item with the lowest contribution per m².

		$
C5	125m² at a contribution of $100 per m²	12,500 lost
C3	125m² at a contribution of $124 per m²	15,500 lost
P6	125m² at a contribution of $200 per m²	25,000 lost
	Total contribution lost	53,000

Minimum financial penalty = Lost contribution − contribution from contract
= $53,000 − ($93.33 × 375)
= $18,001.25

8 Engineering project

Text references. Relevant costing is covered in Chapter 1A.

Top tips. The question does not only ask for a list of relevant costs – it also asks for an explanation of the reason for using each cost value. The question tests you on most aspects of relevant costs, such as opportunity costs, replacement costs and internal costs. Some of the costs require more than one calculation in order to determine the relevant cost – you should assume that the firm will choose the lower cost option when faced with more than one alternative. Don't forget that depreciation is never a relevant cost as it is not a cash cost! Absorbed overheads and sunk costs are also irrelevant so when you see these in the question make sure you immediately mark them as such!

Part (b) might have thrown you slightly but all it is really asking for is the differences between using absorption costing for pricing purposes and using relevant costing.

Easy marks. If you can remember that depreciation is never a relevant cost as it is not a cash cost, you should be able to gain a couple of easy marks.

(a) Statement of relevant costs

		$	$	$
(1)	Hire cost (4,000 × $10)		40,000	
	Purchase option:			
	Cost	250,000		
	Less scrap value	150,000		
			100,000	
	Income from hiring out machine			
	(30 x $2,500)		7,000	
	Net cost			25,000

The relevant cost is the lower cost option – that is, to buy the machine and hire it out when not in use   25,000

(2) **Running costs**: 10 weeks × $720   7,200

The relevant cost is the running cost that will be incurred in the future if the project was to go ahead

(3) **Depreciation**

Depreciation is not relevant as it is not a cash cost   NIL

(4) **Labour**

External option: pay 9,000 hours at $12 per hour   108,000
Internal option: replacements for internal workers paid at $11 per hour for 9,000 hours   99,000

The relevant cost is the lower cost option of using internal workers and paying for replacements at $11 per hour. The existing rate per hour is irrelevant as the company is paying this regardless of whether the project is undertaken.   99,000

(5) **Unskilled labour**: 12,000 hours x $8   96,000

The relevant cost is the recruitment cost of the unskilled labour, as this will only be incurred if the project goes ahead.

(6) **Supervision costs**

The relevant cost is the bonus paid to the supervisor, which would not Be paid if the project does not go ahead. The supervisor's salary is irrelevant as it is being paid anyway. The overtime hours are also irrelevant as the supervisor is not paid overtime.   500

		$	$	$
(7)	**Material A**			

(7) **Material A**

The relevant cost is the purchase cost as the materials have to be purchased especially for the project. ... 15,000

Material B

Current material in inventory can be used (5,000 sq metres) Relevant cost is the resale value foregone ($2 per sq metre) ... 10,000

Purchase price of remaining material ($5 x 5,000 sq metres) ... 25,000

... 35,000

The original purchase cost of the inventory is not relevant as this is a sunk cost.

(8) **Analysis cost**

This is not relevant as it is a past (sunk) cost. ... NIL

(9) **Absorbed overheads**

These are not relevant as they are incurred anyway – they are not specific to the project. Overheads would only be relevant if they are specific to the project. ... NIL

(10) **Profit**

This is not relevant as it is not a cost. ... NIL

TOTAL RELEVANT COST ... 277,700

(b) **Absorption costing** is used in financial reporting in order to calculate **total costs**, rather than relevant costing. In some cases both methods will give the same results, in others the totals will be different.

For example, **depreciation** is included as part of the total cost with absorption costing, as are overheads and a proportion of supervision costs. Relevant costing excludes those items as this method only includes **future incremental cash flows**.

However, with **unskilled labour**, the relevant cost is the same as the cost under absorption costing as it is an incremental cost. With Material B, the resale value (opportunity cost) will not be considered – the historical inventory value of $20,000 would be included as part of the total cost.

9 QP plc

Text references. Chapter 9A should give you enough information to answer part (a). Then use Chapter 2 to answer the limiting factor calculation. Finally, refer to Chapter 4 for the simplex method.

Top tips. This question covered throughput accounting and decision making with both one and two limiting factors. Remember that throughput accounting takes contribution to be sales revenue less directly attributable variable costs. In the modern manufacturing environment the only truly variable cost in the short term is materials. Part (c) could be answered in isolation. Part (b) needed you to read the question carefully as two limiting factors then become one.

In part (a) two thirds of the six marks available are for explaining the effect of throughput accounting on constraints and scarce resources and the remainder for its impact on contribution.

In part (b) the marks were evenly spread (ie five marks each) for calculating the contribution per kg of material L, and for the product mix that maximises the value of contribution.

In part (c) one mark per value was awarded with a maximum of nine marks.

> **Easy marks.** Part (c) should be easy enough if you remember what all the simplex values represent.
>
> **Examiner's comments.** In general, the question was well answered although there were two common errors:
>
> - Including labour costs in the calculation of the contribution
>
> - Describing production processes and bottle-necks in detail. This relates to the theory of constraints rather than throughput accounting.

(a)   Throughput accounting

Throughput accounting (TA) is a **cost and management system** used in a **JIT environment**. It emphasises **throughput**, **minimisation of inventory** and **cost control**.

It aims to identify and eliminate **bottleneck resources**, which inhibit throughput and therefore hinder conversion of WIP to finished goods and hence to sales.

TA uses a series of measures to **rank products** in order to allocate scarce resources for short-term decision making purposes. One of these is the TA ratio which is (sales price- material cost)/(labour + overhead).

Because TA differentiates between fixed and variable costs it is often compared with marginal costing and **some people argue that there is no difference between marginal costing and throughput accounting**. Two techniques are identical in some respects, but **marginal costing is generally thought of as being purely a short-term decision-making technique** while **TA, or at least TOC, was conceived with the aim of changing manufacturing strategy to achieve evenness of flow. It is therefore much more than a short-term decision technique.**

Because **TA combines all conversion costs** together and does not attempt to examine them in detail it is particularly **suited to use with ABC**, which examines the behaviour of these costs and assumes them to be variable in the long-run.

In throughput accounting, the limiting factor is the bottleneck. The return per time period measure can be adapted and used for **ranking products to optimise production** in the **short term**.

$$\text{Product return per minute} = \frac{\text{sales price} - \text{material costs}}{\text{minutes on key/bottleneck resource}}$$

Ranking products on the basis of throughput contribution per minute (or hour) on the bottleneck resource is **similar in concept to maximising contribution per unit of limiting factor**. Such product rankings are for **short-term production scheduling only**. In throughput accounting, bottlenecks should be eliminated and so rankings may change quickly. Customer demand can, of course, cause the bottleneck to change at short notice too.

(b)   Calculations for the production mix that will maximise QP's profit

This is an example of production with a scarce resource (ingredient L) and so limiting factor analysis should be used. Note that ingredient M is not scarce by virtue of the existence of a non-scarce substitute ingredient.

If resources are limiting factors, then contribution is maximised by earning the biggest possible contribution per unit of limiting factor.

 STEP ①   Ascertain whether material L is the limiting factor

Product	TR	PN	BE	Total
Kgs of L per batch (kg)	7	9	4	
Kgs of L needed to meet sales demand	3,500	3,600	1,400	8,500
Kgs available				7,000
Shortfall				1,500

STEP 2   <u>Calculate contribution per unit of scarce resource and rank ingredients</u>

Product	TR	PN	BE
Contribution per batch (£)	90	165	95
Kgs per batch	7	9	4
Contribution per kg (£)	12.86	18.33	23.75
Ranking	3	2	1

STEP 3   <u>Determine the optimum product mix</u>

Product	Demand Batches	Ingredient L required kgs	Ingredient L available kgs*	Batches produced
BE	350 (× 4)	1,400	7,000 (1,400) 5,600	350
PN	400 (×9)	3,600	(3,600)	400
TR	500 (×7)	3,500	2,000 (1,995) 5	285

* Demand includes a requirement to produce 50 batches as a minimum.

(c)   This is a linear programming solution using the simplex method because there are more than two decision variables.

    (i)   **Objective function value**. This is the optimal contribution of £110,714 (on the assumption the value is not in £'000).

    (ii)   **TR value**. This is the optimal number of batches of TR that should be produced, being 500.

    (iii)   **PN value**. Likewise, the optimum batch quantity is 357.

    (iv)   **BE value**. Likewise, 71 batches of BE should be produced.

    (v)   **TR slack value** of 0 represents the unsatisfied demand in batches.

    (vi)   **PN slack value** of 43 represents the unsatisfied demand in batches.

    (vii)   **BE slack value** of 279 represents the unsatisfied demand in batches.

    (viii)   **L value** is the shadow price of material L which indicates the amount by which the optimal contribution would increase if an extra kg of material L was available at its normal variable cost.

    (ix)   **M value** is the shadow price for material M and indicates that contribution would increase by this amount if an extra kg of M were available.

10 Fertiliser 1

> **Top tips**. Provided you work carefully through the steps required to formulate a linear programming model you should be able to pick up the majority of the ten marks on offer for this question.
>
> **Easy marks.** There are three products so a simplex method is needed.

Calculate contribution per tonne

	X1 £ per tonne	X2 £ per tonne	X3 £ per tonne
Nitrate, at £150 per tonne	15	15	30
Phosphate, at £60 per tonne	6	12	6
Potash, at £120 per tonne	24	12	12
Filler, at £10 per tonne	6	6	6
Other manufacturing costs	11	11	11
	62	56	65
Sales price	83	81	81
Contribution	21	25	16

The **linear programming model** is formulated as follows.

Define variables: The three products are X1, X2 and X3

Establish objective function: Maximise contribution (C) = 21X1 + 25X2 + 16X3

Establish constraints

Nitrate	$0.1X1 + 0.1X2 + 0.2X3 \leq 1,200$
Phosphate	$0.1X1 + 0.2X2 + 0.1X3 \leq 2,000$
Potash	$0.2X1 + 0.1X2 + 0.1X3 \leq 2,200$
Non-negativity	$X1, X2, X3 \geq 0$

Introduce slack variables X4, X5 and X6 and redefine constraints

(a)　Slack variable X4 represents the amount of unused nitrate, in tonnes, so that
$$0.1X1 + 0.1X2 + 0.2X3 + X4 = 1,200$$

(b)　Slack variable X5 represents the amount of unused phosphate, in tonnes, so that
$$0.1X1 + 0.2X2 + 0.1X3 + X5 = 2,000$$

(c)　Slack variable X6 represents the amount of unused potash, in tonnes, so that
$$0.2X1 + 0.1X2 + 0.1X3 + X6 = 2,200$$

Redefine objective function

$$C - 21X1 - 25X2 - 16X3 + 0X4 + 0X5 + 0X6 = 0$$

11 Fertiliser 2

> **Top tips**. The interpretation required is relatively straightforward, especially if you have worked through a number of examples.
>
> Attempted in conjunction with Fertiliser I, these questions provide an excellent example of simplex. Work through them again and again until you are 100% confident.

The **optimal solution** is to make and sell:

(a)   4,000 tonnes of X1
(b)   8,000 tonnes of X2
(c)   nothing of X3

There will be 600 tonnes of unused potash (X6). Total contribution will be £284,000.

X4 and X5 (nitrate and phosphate) will be fully used up, with means that they have a **shadow price**, as follows.

(a)   For each **extra tonne of nitrate (X4)** that could be made available, the production plan could be rearranged so as to **increase total contribution by £170**.

(b)   Similarly, for each **extra tonne of phosphate** (X5) that could be made available, the production schedule could be re-arranged so as to **increase total contribution** by £40.

(c)   The **shadow price of X3** is £22. If a decision were taken to increase production of X3 from zero tonnes, total contribution would fall by £22 per tonne of X3 made and sold, given existing constraints on materials supply. The contribution per tonne of X3 would have to rise by £22 or more to make production of X3 worthwhile.

12 Company C

> **Text references.** Limiting factor analysis is covered in Chapter 2. Linear programming – the graphical method is covered in Chapter 3.
>
> **Top tips.** Use a full side of your answer booklet for the graph in part (b)(i).

(a)   The optimum production plan is determined by reference to the product contributions earned per unit of scarce resource.

STEP 1 – CONFIRM THE LIMITING FACTOR IS SOMETHING OTHER THAN SALES DEMAND

The question states that the total number of direct labour hours for November 20X9 is limited to 4,000 hours. All other production resources are readily available.

By comparing the number of direct labour hours required to meet maximum demand, with the number of direct labour hours available, it is evident that there is a shortfall of 650 direct labour hours.

	Direct labour hours required to meet demand	Direct labour hours available	Shortfall
Demand from Company D:			
Product X (500 units)	1,000		
Product Y (300 units)	450		
Additional demand in Nov:			
Product X (1,000 units)	2,000		
Product Y (800 units)	1,200		
Total	4,650	4,000	650

STEP 2 – IDENTIFY THE CONTRIBUTION EARNED BY EACH PRODUCT PER UNIT OF SCARCE RESOURCE (LABOUR HOURS WORKED)

Product	X	Y
	$/unit	$/unit
Selling price	86	74
Direct labour	16	12
Direct material A	12	15
Direct material B	12	8
Other variable costs	20	15
Contribution	26	24
Direct labour hours per unit	2 hours	1.5 hours
Contribution per labour hour	13	16
Rank	2	1

STEP 3 – DETERMINE THE BUDGETED PRODUCTION

Sufficient X's and Y's will be made to meet the demand from Company D, thus avoiding the financial penalty. Sufficient Y's will be made to meet full market demand, and the remaining labour hours available will then be used to make X's:

Product	Units	Hours per unit	Hours available
			4,000
Y (contract)	300	1.5	(450)
			3,550
X (contract)	500	2	(1,000)
			2,550
Y (market)	800	1.5	(1,200)
			1,350
X (market)	675	2	(1,350)
			Nil

Total production:

Product X	1,175 units
Product Y	1,100 units

(b) (i)

STEP 1 – DEFINE VARIABLES AND CALCULATE RESOURCES AVAILABLE

Let X = number of units of X produced

Let Y = number of units of Y produced

Resource	Available (per question)	Contract requires (Product X)	Contract requires (Product Y)	Resources remaining
Direct labour (hours)	5,450	1,000	450	4,000
Material A (kgs)	11,000	2,000	1,500	7,500
Material B (kgs)	6,100	1,500	600	4,000

STEP 2 – ESTABLISH OBJECTIVE FUNCTION

Maximise contribution 26X + 24Y, subject to constraints.

STEP 3 – ESTABLISH CONSTRAINTS

Direct labour	$2X + 1.5Y \le 4,000$
Material A	$4X + 5Y \le 7,500$
Material B	$3X + 2Y \le 4,000$
Product X maximum market demand in December	$X \le 1,300$
Product Y maximum market demand in December	$Y \le 1,400$
Iso-contribution function	$26X + 24Y$

STEPS 4 & 5 – GRAPH THE PROBLEM AND ESTABLISH FEASIBLE REGION

Constraint		*Point 1*	*Point 2*
Direct labour	$2X + 1.5Y \leq 4,000$	Let X = 0 $1.5Y = 4,000$ Y = 2,667	Let Y = 0 $2X = 4,000$ X = 2,000
Material A	$4X + 5Y \leq 7,500$	Let X = 0 $5Y = 7,500$ Y = 1,500	Let Y = 0 $4X = 7,500$ X = 1,875
Material B	$3X + 2Y \leq 4,000$	Let X = 0 $2Y = 4,000$ Y = 2,000	Let Y = 0 $3X = 4,000$ X = 1,333
Product X maximum market demand in December	$X \leq 1,300$		X = 1,300
Product Y maximum market demand in December	$Y \leq 1,400$	Y = 1,400	
Iso-contribution function	$26X + 24Y = 20,000$ (using $20,000 as a target contribution)	Let X = 0 $24Y = 20,000$ Y = 833	Let Y =0 $26X = 20,000$ X = 769

Graph to Show Optimal Production Plan For December

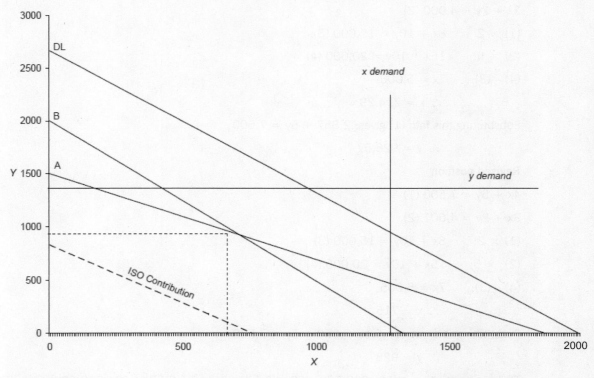

The optimum production plan is to produce 725 units of X and 925 units of Y, in addition to fulfilling the contract with Company D.

(ii)   If the contract was not fulfilled, the resources allocated to the contract would be used to make additional units of X and Y for sale to the external market.

The graph shows that the two material resources are more binding than the direct labour constraint so the optimal use of the resources released can be calculated using simultaneous equations:

$4x + 5y = 3,500$ (1)

$3x + 2y = 2,100$ (2)

(1) × 2: $\quad 8x + 10y = 7,000$ (3)

(2) × 5: $\quad 15x + 10y = 10,500$ (4)

(4) − (3): $\quad 7x = 3,500$

$\therefore x = 500$

Substituting this into (1) gives: $2,000 + 5y = 3,500$

$\therefore y = 300$

This is the same as the resource utilisation for the contract, so revenues can be compared.

All of the production capacity can be sold in the open market at the full selling prices, so if the penalty value were equal to the loss of sales revenue, the company would be indifferent between the contract and market sales. This amounts to:

500 Units of X at $13 per unit plus 300 units of Y at $12 per unit = $10,100

(iii)   Both material constraints are binding. If material B were less scarce then the output would change:

Existing position

$4x + 5y = 7,500$ (1)

$3x + 2y = 4,000$ (2)

(1) × 2: $\quad 8x + 10y = 15,000$ (3)

(2) × 5: $\quad 15x + 10y = 20,000$ (4)

(4) − (3): $\quad 7x = 5,000$

$\therefore x = 714.29$

Substituting this into (1) gives: $2,857 + 5y = 7,500$

$\therefore y = 928.57$

Revised position

$4x + 5y = 7,500$ (1)

$3x + 2y = 4,001$ (2)

(1) × 2: $\quad 8x + 10y = 15,000$ (3)

(2) × 5: $\quad 15x + 10y = 20,005$ (4)

(4) − (3): $\quad 7x = 5,005$

$\therefore x = 715$

Substituting this into (1) gives: $2,860 + 5y = 7,500$

$\therefore y = 928$

There is a reduction in Y by 928.57 − 928 = 0·57 units losing 0.57 × $24 $13·68 contribution.

There is an increase in X by 715 − 714.29 = 0·71 units gaining 0.71 × $26 = $18·46 contribution.

This is a net increase in contribution of $4·78. The maximum price that should be paid per kg is $8·78 which is the original cost per kg of material B ($4) plus the contribution value.

13 WZ manufacturing

> **Text references.** Short-term decisions are covered in Chapter 1B and limiting factor analysis is covered in Chapter 2. Linear programming is covered in Chapter 3.
>
> **Top tips.** Show all of your supporting workings to maximise your score. Use the rankings determined in part (a) to prepare a statement showing the optimum usage of scarce material in part (b).
>
> **Easy marks.** There are easy marks in part (c) for explaining two non-financial factors that should be considered as part of the decision process.

(a)   STEP 1 – CALCULATE THE INTERNAL MANUFACTURING COST OF COMPONENT P

	$/unit
Direct labour (1 hour × $8 per hour)	8.00
Direct material B (2kg × $5 per kg)	10.00
Variable overhead (W1)	
Direct labour (1 hour × $0.50 per hour)	0.50
Machine hours (0.5 hours × $0.25 per hour)	0.125
	18.625

STEP 2 – COMPARE THE INTERNAL MANUFACTURING COST WITH THE BUYING PRICE

The buying price of component P is $35 per unit, so the company should manufacture the component if resources are readily available. As resources are scarce in the next 10 weeks the contribution from the component needs to be compared with the contribution that can be earned from the other products (see Step 4).

STEP 3 – ESTABLISH WHICH MATERIAL, IF ANY, IS SCARCE

Resource	J	K	L	M	P	Total (litres/kg)	Available (litres/kg)	Shortfall (kg)
Material A (W2)	2,200	3,700	0	14,250	0	20,150	21,000	–
Material B (W2)	2,200	0	8,850	19,000	1,000	31,050	24,000	7,050

It can be seen above that material B is a binding constraint and so the contributions from each product and the component, per kg of material B must be compared. As product K does not use the scarce material it can be omitted.

STEP 4 – RANK PRODUCTS IN ORDER OF CONTRIBUTION EARNED PER KG OF MATERIAL B

	J	L	M	P
	$/unit	$/unit	$/unit	$/unit
Selling price / buying cost	56.00	78.00	96.00	35.00
Direct labour	20.00	24.00	20.00	8.00
Material A	6.00	0.00	9.00	0.00
Material B	10.00	15.00	20.00	10.00
Overhead:				
Labour	1.25	1.50	1.25	0.50
Machinery	1.25	0.75	1.00	0.125
Contribution	17.50	36.75	44.75	16.375
Kg of material B per unit	2kg	3kg	4kg	2kg
Contribution per kg of material B	8.75	12.25	11.19	8.19
Rank	3	1	2	4

Since component P has the lowest ranking, WZ should continue to purchase the component from the external supplier so that the available resources can be used to manufacture products L, M and J.

Workings

1 Variable overhead rates per hour

Variable overhead rates per hour can be calculated by referring to any product. Using product J the rates are as follows.

Labour related variable overhead per unit $1.25
Direct labour hours per unit = $20/8 = 2.5 hours
Labour related variable overhead per hour = $1.25 / 2.5 hours = $0.50 per hour

Machine related variable overhead per unit $1.25
Labour related variable overhead per hour = $1.25 / 5 hours = $0.25 per hour

2 Material requirements

Product J

Weekly units = 1,000 + 100 = 1,100

Material A weekly usage = 2 litres × 1,100 = 2,200 litres

Material B weekly usage = 2 kg × 1,100 = 2,200 kg

Product K

Weekly units = 3,500 + 200 = 3,700

Material A weekly usage = 1 litre × 3,700 = 3,700 litres

Material B weekly usage = 0 kg × 3,700 = 0 kg

Product L

Weekly units = 2,800 + 150 = 2,950

Material A weekly usage = 0 litres × 2,950 = 0 litres

Material B weekly usage = 3 kg × 2,950 = 8,850 kg

Product M

Weekly units = 4,500 + 250 = 4,750

Material A weekly usage = 3 litres × 4,750 = 14,250 litres

Material B weekly usage = 4 kg × 4,750 = 19,000 kg

Component P

Weekly units = 500

Material A weekly usage = 0 litres × 500 = 0 litres

Material B weekly usage = 2 kg × 500 = 1,000 kg

(b) The optimum weekly usage of material B is based on the ranking calculated above.

	Kg of material B per unit	Kg used	Total kg remaining
Contract units:			24,000
Product L (150 units)	3	450	
Product M (250 units)	4	1,000	
Product J (100 units)	2	200	(1,650)
			22,350
Normal weekly demand:			
Product L (2,800 units)	3	8,400	(8,400)
			13,950
Product M (3,487.5 units *)	4	13,950	(13,950)
			–

* 13,950kg remaining / 4kg per unit = 3,487.5 units.

Weekly production plan

Product J = 100 units

Product L = 2,950 units

Product M = 3,737.5 units

(c)   (i)   The decision to purchase component P would change if the contribution from manufacturing the component is equal to the lowest contribution from the products produced that use material B. From the weekly production plan, product J is only manufactured to satisfy the contractual demand. The lowest contribution (per kg) for products manufactured to cater for 'normal' weekly demand is from product M.

          Product M has a contribution per kg of $11.19 which is $3 per kg higher than from component P. As each unit of P uses 2 kgs of material B then the buying price would have to be 2 × $3 = $6 per component higher to have the same rank as product M. Therefore the buying price at which the decision would change is $35 + $6 = $41.

   (ii)   There are a number of non-financial factors that should be considered.

<u>Employee skill level</u>

          WZ should consider whether the employees have the necessary skill level to produce component P. If not, WZ should purchase the component from external suppliers to ensure the components are of appropriate quality.

<u>Control</u>

          WZ may prefer to control / oversee the production of component P and may not wish to be dependent on a third party for delivering component P on time and with adequate quality. In this case, WZ should take steps to enable component P to be manufactured internally.

(d)   <u>Objective function</u>

Maximise contribution (C) = 17.5J + 18.0K + 36.75L + 44.75M, subject to the following constraints:

2J + 1K + 0L + 3M ≤ 21,000   Material A supply

2J + 0K + 3L + 4M ≤ 24,000   Material B supply

14   LM

Text references. Limiting factor analysis is covered in Chapter 2 and linear programming: the simplex method is covered in Chapter 4.

Top tips. Set out your workings in stages for the single limiting factor scenario in part (a). In part (b), remember the contract has to be fulfilled first. The constraints can then be drawn for the remaining demand.

(a)   The optimum production plan is determined by reference to the product contributions earned per unit of scarce resource.

STEP 1 – CONFIRM THE LIMITING FACTOR IS SOMETHING OTHER THAN SALES DEMAND

The question states that the resource availability for December 20X0 is as follows:

Direct labour	3,500 hours
Direct materials	6,000 kg
Machine hours	2,000 hours

By comparing the resources required to meet maximum demand with the resources available, we are able to identify the limiting factor.

	Direct labour (hours)	Direct materials (kg)	Machine hours
Resource available	3,500	6,000	2,000
Demand in December 20X0:			
Product L (400 units)	1,600	800	400
Product M (700 units)	1,400	6,300	1,400
	3,000	7,100	1,800
Surplus / (shortfall)	500	(1,100)	200

Direct material is the limiting factor.

STEP 2 – IDENTIFY THE CONTRIBUTION EARNED BY EACH PRODUCT PER UNIT OF SCARCE RESOURCE (DIRECT MATERIAL USED)

Product	L	M
	$/unit	$/unit
Selling price	70	90
Direct labour	28	14
Direct material	10	45
Machine hours	10	20
Contribution per unit	22	11
Direct material per unit	2 kg	9 kg
Contribution per labour kg	11	1.22
Rank	1	2

STEP 3 – DETERMINE THE BUDGETED PRODUCTION

Sufficient L's will be made to meet full market demand, and the remaining material available will then be used to make M's:

Product	Units	Kg per unit	Kg available
			6,000
L	400	2	(800)
			5,200
M	577*	9	(5,193)
			7

* 5,200kg / 9kg per unit of M

Total production:

		Contribution ($)
Product L	400 units	8,800
Product M	577 units	6,347
		15,147

(b) The revised resource available is as follows:

	Direct labour (hours)	Direct material (kg)	Machine hours
Original resource	3,500	6,000	2,000
20% reduction	(700)	(1,200)	(400)
	2,800	4,800	1,600
Less: 250 units of product M	(500)	(2,250)	(500)
Revised resource	2,300	2,550	1,100

<u>Revised resource constraints and objective function</u>

Direct labour	4L + 2M ≤ 2,300
Direct material	2L + 9M ≤ 2,550
Machine hours	1L + 2M ≤ 1,100

C = 22L + 11M

(c) Product L (value 1: 400, value 2: 0)

Value 1 (400) represents the optimum production of product L (400 units). This has been calculated as part of the **optimum production plan** in part (a). Value 2 (0) represents the **unsatisfied demand**. This is zero because the output from the optimum production plan is equal to the maximum demand for product L in December (400 units).

Product M (value 1: 194, value 2: 506)

Value 1 (194) represents the **optimum number of units of product M** to be produced under the revised production plan calculated in part (b). Value 2 (506) is the **unsatisfied demand for product M**. Demand for product M in December is 700 units and only 194 units are to be produced.

Direct Labour (312)

The value of 312 is the number of **unused direct labour hours** under the revised production plan calculated in part (b).

Direct material ($1.22)

The value of $1.22 is the **shadow price of the direct materials**. This is the **maximum additional price that should be paid for an extra kg of material above the standard cost** of $5 per kg. The fact that there is a shadow price confirms that **direct material is a binding constraint**.

An extra 1kg of direct material would be used to increase production of product M. Each unit of product M requires 9kg so 0.11 additional units of M could be produced from 1kg extra of direct material. Each unit of M yields a contribution of $11. So 0.11 units yields $1.22 contribution.

Machine hours (312)

The value of 312 is the number **of unused machine hours** under the revised production plan. This has been calculated in part (b).

Contribution ($10,934)

The value of $10,934 is the **contribution earned from the revised production plan** calculated in part (b). This is calculated below.

	$
400 units of L earn $22 each	8,800
194 units of M earn $11 each	2,134
	10,934

15 Staff uniforms

Text references. Look at Chapter 2, which should give you steps for working out the limiting factor. Chapter 3 will give you a plan for working out the optimal solution to part (b) and graphing this.

Top tips. The question was slightly ambiguous as it was not completely clear whether the previously accepted contract was included in the demand figures. It was!

In Step 2 of part (a) you could have worked out the contribution per $1 of machine cost instead of per hour of machine time.

In (b), you had to calculate revised contribution figures as the selling prices had changed. If you are not sure about the accuracy of your graph, verify your answer by solving simultaneous equations.

Easy marks. Part (a) is a straightforward limiting factor analysis with limited freedom of action. You needed to begin by checking which of the resources, if any, were scarce. Label graph and draw neatly for presentation. State whether selling prices should be revised in (b)(ii) for a mark.

(a) **STEP 1** <u>Establish which of the resources, if any, are scarce</u>

Cleaning materials

	Litres
Required Laundry ($^2/_{10}$ × 8,000)	1,600
Dry cleaning ($^3/_{10}$ × 10,500)	3,150
	4,750
Available	5,000
Spare	250

Therefore, **not scarce**

Direct labour hours

	Hours
Required Laundry ($^{1.2}/_6$ × 8,000)	1,600
Dry cleaning ($^2/_6$ × 10,500)	3,500
	5,100
Available	6,000
Spare	900

Therefore, **not scarce**

Machine hours

	Hours
Required Laundry ($^{0.5}/_3$ × 8,000)	1,333.3
Dry cleaning ($^{1.5}/_3$ × 10,500)	5,250.0
	6,583.3
Available	5,000.0
Shortfall	1,583.3

Therefore, **scarce**

 STEP 2 <u>Rank the services in terms of contribution per hour of machine time</u>

	Laundry	Dry cleaning
Unit contribution		
$(2.15 + 1.15)	$3.30	
$(3.25 + 2.25)		$5.50
Machine hours per service		
($0.5/$3)	$^1/_6$	
($1.5/$3)		$^1/_2$
Contribution per hour of machine time	$19.80	$11
Ranking	1	2

STEP 3 <u>Determine a production plan</u>

	Demand	Machine hours required	Machine hours available
			5,000
Contracted services			
Laundry	1,200 (× $^1/_6$)	200	4,800
Dry cleaning	2,000 (× $^1/_2$)	1,000	3,800
Non-contracted services			
Laundry	6,800* (× $^1/_6$)	1,133 $^1/_3$	2,666 $^2/_3$
Dry cleaning	5,333** (× $^1/_2$)	2,666 $^2/_3$	

*   8,000 – 1,200
**   2,666 $^2/_3$ ÷ $^1/_2$

<u>Profit-maximising mix of services</u>

Laundry: 8,000 services
Dry cleaning: 7,333 services

(b) (i) <u>Define variables</u>

Let l = number of laundry services provided

Let d = number of dry cleaning services provided

<u>Establish objective function</u>

Fixed costs will be the same irrespective of the optimal mix and so the objective is to maximise contribution (c).

Laundry: revised contribution = $5.60 − $(2 + 1.2 + 0.5) = $1.90

Dry cleaning: revised contribution = $13.20 − $(3 + 2 + 1.5) = $6.70

Maximise c = 1.9l + 6.7d, subject to the constraints below.

<u>Establish constraints</u>

Cleaning materials: $^2/_{10}l + {}^3/_{10}d \leq 5,000$

$$^1/_5l + {}^3/_{10}d \leq 5,000$$

Direct labour: $^{1.2}/_6l + {}^2/_6d \leq 6,000$

$$^1/_5l + {}^1/_3d \leq 6,000$$

Variable machine cost: $^{0.5}/_3l + {}^{1.5}/_3d \leq 5,000$

$$^1/_6l + {}^1/_2d \leq 5,000$$

Maximum and minimum services (for contract): $14,000 \geq l \geq 1,200$
$$9,975 \geq d \geq 2,000$$

(ii) <u>Establish coordinates to plot lines representing the inequalities.</u>

Cleaning materials: If l = 0, d = 16,667
                     If d = 0, l = 25,000

Direct labour: If l = 0, d = 18,000
                If d = 0, l = 30,000

Variable machine cost: If l = 0, d = 10,000
                        If d = 0, l = 30,000

Also plot the lines l = 1,200 and d = 2,000, and l = 14,000 and d = 9,975

<u>Construct an iso-contribution line</u>

c = 1.9l + 6.7d

If c = (1.9 × 6.7 × 1,000) = 12,730

then: if l = 6,700, d = 0
       if d = 1,900, l = 0

Draw the graph

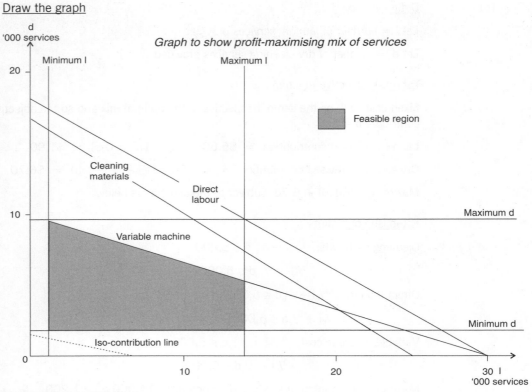

Graph to show profit-maximising mix of services

Find the optimal solution

By moving the iso-contribution line out across the graph, it is clear that the optimal solution lies at the intersection of lines representing the constraints for minimum number of laundry services and machine hours.

Therefore, optimal solution occurs when:

$l = 1{,}200$ and $\frac{1}{6}l + \frac{1}{2}d = 5{,}000$

If $l = 1{,}200$, then $d = (5{,}000 - 200) \times 2 = 9{,}600$

The **optimal solution** is to carry out 1,200 laundry services and 9,600 dry cleaning services.

Check the validity of revising selling prices

Maximum profit per mix in (a)

		$
Contribution		
Laundry:	8,000 × unit contribution of $3.30	26,400.0
Dry cleaning:	7,333 × unit contribution of $5.50	40,331.5
		66,731.5
Less: fixed costs ((8,000 × $1.15) + (10,500 × $2.25))		(32,825.0)
		33,906.5

Maximum profit based on revised selling prices

		$
Contribution		
Laundry:	1,200 × unit contribution of $1.90	2,280
Dry cleaning:	9,600 × unit contribution of $6.70	64,320
		66,600
Less: fixed costs		32,825
		33,775

By revising the selling prices, maximum profit achievable falls by $(33,906.5 - 33,775) = $131.50

Therefore, In theory, **prices should not be revised** but the difference is so small that management should check carefully the reasonableness of the estimates used.

16 RT

> **Test references.** Limiting factor analysis is covered in Chapter 2. Linear programming – the graphical method is covered in Chapter 3.
>
> **Top tips.** Use a full side of your answer booklet for the graph in part (c).
>
> **Easy marks.** There are easy marks available in part (d) for discussing how the graph in part (c) can be used to help determine the optimum production plan.
>
> **Examiner's comments.** Parts (a) and (b) were generally well answered. Many candidates only earned half marks on part (c) due to a number of issues including poorly constructed graphs, presenting an inaccurate sketched graph and not providing a final answer.

Marking scheme

			Marks
(a)	Identifying the limiting factor	2	
	Ranking of products based on direct labour hours	1	
	Optimal production plan	2	
	Contribution from optimal plan	1	
			6
(b)	Recognising market demand is unsatisfied	1	
	Calculation	1	
	Comparison	1	
			3
(c)	Constructing equations for each resource constraint identified	4	
	Constructing equations for demand constraints	1	
	Plotting constraints on graph	3	
	Identifying the feasible region	1	
	Providing a solution	2	
			11
(d)	1 mark per point		
	Points include		
	– Most binding constraints		
	– Shifts to the right		
	– If no changes to direct labour, other constraints have no effect		
	– Parallel to existing constraint		
	– Material A becomes binding		
		Max 5	5
			25

(a) The optimum production plan is determined by reference to the product contributions earned per unit of scarce resource.

 STEP 1 <u>Confirm the limiting factor is something other than sales demand</u>

The resource requirements to meet the maximum product demand levels for June (including the order with the commercial customer) are as follows:

	R	T	Total
Total demand	750 units	1,150 units	
Direct labour (hours)	2,250	5,750	8,000
Material A (kgs)	3,750	4,600	8,350
Material B (kgs)	1,500	1,150	2,650
Machine hours	2,250	4,600	6,850

By comparing the resources required to meet maximum demand with the resource available, it is evident that the limiting factor is direct labour hours:

	Resource required to meet maximum demand	Resource available	Shortfall
Direct labour (hours)	8,000	7,500	500
Material A (kgs)	8,350	8,500	-
Material B (kgs)	2,650	3,000	-
Machine hours	6,850	7,500	-

 STEP 2

Identify the contribution earned by each product per unit of scarce resource (labour hours worked)

Product	R	T
	$/unit	$/unit
Selling price	130	160
Direct labour	24	40
Material A	15	12
Material B	14	7
Machine time	30	40
	83	99
Contribution	47	61
Direct labour hours per unit	3 hours	5 hours
Contribution per labour hour	15.67	12.20
Rank	1	2

 STEP 3

Determine the budgeted production

Sufficient R's will be made to meet the full sales demand, and the remaining labour hours available will then be used to make T's:

Product	Units	Hours per unit	Hours available
			7,500
R (contract)	250	3	(750)
			6,750
R (market)	500	3	(1,500)
			5,250
T (contract)	350	5	(1,750)
			3,500
T (market)	700	5	(3,500)
			Nil

The yield a contribution of:

Product R	Contract	250 × $17	$4,250	
	Market	500 × $47	$23,500	$27,750
Product T	Contract	350 × $36	$12,600	
	Market	700 × $61	$42,700	$55,300
				$83,050

(b) The mix calculated in part (a) leaves market demand of 100 units of product T unsatisfied.

The lost contribution is $6,100 (100 units x $61). This is less than the financial penalty for non-delivery of any part of the commercial contract ($10,000) and so the commercial order should be completed in full as shown in part (a).

(c)

 STEP 1 Calculate resources available.

Resource	Per question	Less 10%	Contract requires	Resources available
Direct labour (hours)	7,500	6,750	2,500	4,250
Material A (kgs)	8,500	7,650	2,650	5,000
Material B (kgs)	3,000	2,700	850	1,850
Machine hours	7,500	6,750	2,150	4,600

 STEP 2 Establish constraints

Constraint	
Direct labour	$3R + 5T \leq 4,250$
Material A	$5R + 4T \leq 5,000$
Material B	$2R + 1T \leq 1,850$
Machine hours	$3R + 4T \leq 4,600$
Product R maximum market demand in June	$R \leq 500$
Product T maximum market demand in June	$T \leq 800$
Iso-contribution function	$47R + 61T$

 STEP 3 Graph the problem and establish feasible region

Constraint		Point 1	Point 2
Direct labour	$3R + 5T \leq 4,250$	Let R = 0 5T = 4,250 T = 850	Let T = 0 3R = 4,250 R = 1,417
Material A	$5R + 4T \leq 5,000$	Let R = 0 4T = 5,000 T = 1,250	Let T = 0 5R = 5,000 R = 1,000
Material B	$2R + 1T \leq 1,850$	Let R = 0 T = 1,850	Let T = 0 2R = 1,850 R = 925
Machine hours	$3R + 4T \leq 4,600$	Let R = 0 4T = 4,600 T = 1,150	Let T = 0 3R = 4,600 R = 1,533
Product R maximum market demand in June	$R \leq 500$		R = 500
Product T maximum market demand in June	$T \leq 800$	T = 800	
Iso-contribution function	$47R + 61T = 2,867$	Let R = 0 61T = 2,867 T = 47	Let T = 0 47R = 2,867 R = 61
	Multiply T and R by 10 to plot on graph	T = 470	R = 610

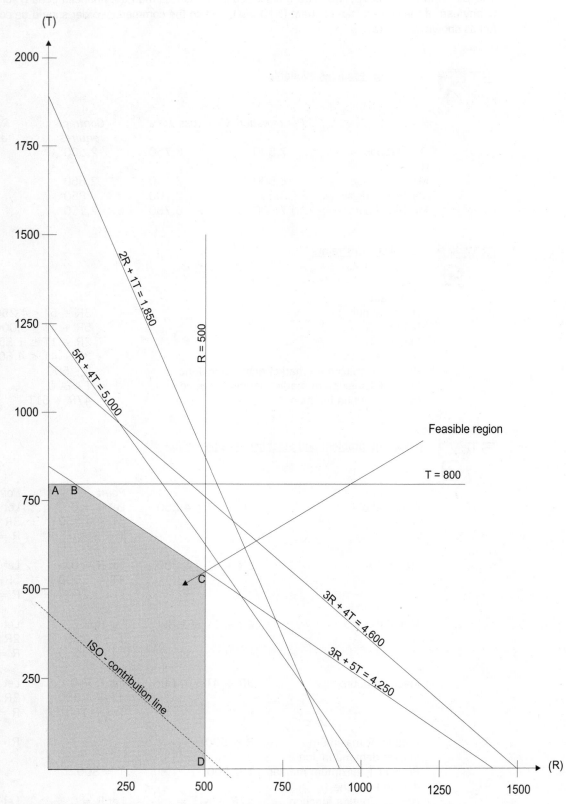

The feasible region on the graph is shown as the shaded area ABCDO.

In addition to fulfilling the contact, the optimal plan is to produce 500 units of Product R and 550 units of product T.

(d)   The graph shows that the most prominent constraints are the availability of direct labour hours and the level of demand for product R.

If the direct labour constraint remains unchanged, movement of any of the other resource constraints would have no effect on the production plan.

If the direct labour constraint were to move to the right, the optimal production values would change until the material A constraint became binding.

17 HT plc

> **Text references.** If you get stuck or want some help, look at Chapter 4 which will give you material for answering the question.
>
> **Top tips.** Notice the checking we have performed in part (c). It may boost your confidence to know that your interpretation is correct!
>
> **Easy marks.** If you are confident with manipulating functions and following the steps involved, these are standard and so practice is key to gain confidence here.

(a)   The regression equation indicates that HT plc's overheads consist of:

£4,000 per week fixed overhead
£0.50 per hour spent on production of HT01
£0.70 per hour spent on production of HT02
£0.80 per hour spent on production of HT03

The **total variable product costs** are therefore as follows.

	HT01 £	HT02 £	HT03 £
Direct labour	100.0	120	132.0
Direct materials	20.0	40	40.0
Variable overhead:			
HT01 (£100/£4 × £0.50)	12.5		
HT02 (£120/£4 × £0.70)		21	
HT03 (£132/£4 × £0.80)			26.4
	132.5	181	198.4

(b)   Contribution earned by each product

	HT01 £	HT02 £	HT03 £
Price	150.0	200	220.0
Variable production costs (see part (a))	132.5	181	198.4
	17.5	19	21.6

Define variables

Let a, b, c be the number of HT01, HT02 and HT03 produced respectively.

Establish objective function

The objective function is to maximise contribution C, given by:

$C = 17.5a + 19b + 21.6c$

Establish constraints

The constraints are as follows.

$25a + 30b + 33c \leq 257{,}600$ (labour hours)
$a + 2b + 2c \leq 20{,}000$ (materials)
$a \leq 16{,}000$ (demand for HT01)
$b \leq 10{,}000$ (demand for HT02)
$c \leq 6{,}000$ (demand for HT03)
$a, b, c \geq 0$

Introduce slack variables

Let S_1 be the number of unused labour hours.

Let S_2 be the number of unused kilograms of material.

Let S_3, S_4, S_5 respectively be the number of units produced of HT01, HT02 and HT03 less than the maximum demand.

Reformulate constraints

$25a + 30b + 33c + S_1 = 257,600$
$a + 2b + 2c + S_2 = 20,000$
$a + S_3 = 16,000$
$b + S_4 = 10,000$
$c + S_5 = 6,000$
$a, b, c \geq 0$

Reformulate objective function

The objective function is to maximise C, given by:

$C - 17.5a - 19b - 21.6c + 0S_1 + 0S_2 + 0S_3 + 0S_4 + 0S_5 = 0$

(c)　In the final tableau the **variables** represented in the **solution column** are respectively S_5, HT01, S_3, S_4, S_2. The **optimal solution** is therefore to produce 10,304 units of HT01, with no production of HT02 or HT03. The contribution arising from this policy is given in the solution row as £180,320 (check: 10,304 × £17.50 = £180,320).

The **remaining figures in the solution column** indicate the following.

$S_5 = 6,000$　(production of HT03 should be 6,000 less than demand, ie nil)

$S_3 = 5,696$　(production of HT01 should be 5,696 less than demand ie 10,304 (16,000 − 5,696) as indicated above)

$S_4 = 10,000$　(production of HT02 should be 10,000 less than demand, ie nil)

$S_2 = 9,696$　(there will be 9,696 kilograms of unused material (check: 20,000 − (10,304 × 1) = 9,696)

Since there is **no value for S_1,** it follows that **labour hours will be fully utilised** (check: 10,304 × 25 = 257,600).

The **shadow prices of HT02 and HT03** are £2.00 and £1.50 respectively. This means that for every unit of HT02 or HT03 made, contribution would fall by £2 and £1.50 respectively. In other words, the contribution from HT02 and HT03 would need to rise by at least those respective amounts before it became profitable to manufacture them at the expense of HT01.

Adoption of the **optimum production plan** will lead to the following **results**.

	£
Contribution earned	180,320
Less: fixed overheads (46 × £4,000)	184,000
Net loss for year	3,680

The **shadow price of one hour of labour (S_1)** is £0.70. This means that for every extra hour of labour made available at its normal cost of £4 per hour, contribution could be increased by 70p. (Check: one hour of labour would produce 1/25th of a unit of HT01 at a contribution of £17.50/25 = £0.70.) This interpretation is only valid while labour hours are a constraint on production.

18 DFG

> **Text reference**: Linear Programming is covered in Chapter 3.
>
> **Top tips**: This was quite a straightforward linear programming question. Make sure you follow the instructions in part (c) – you are **not** required to perform any calculations! You can use the shadow prices in part (b) to check whether your graph is correct – if skilled labour is one of your binding constraints, you have done something wrong!
>
> **Easy marks**: If you have read the Study Text, most of this question should be quite straightforward. There are a number of easy marks to be obtained in part (a), such as defining the objective function and constraints.

(a) **Define variables**

Let D be the number of product D produced
Let G be the number of product G produced

 Resources required by each product

	D	G
Direct Material A	$^{20}/_5 = 4$kg	$^{10}/_5 = 2$kg
Direct Material B	$^{12}/_3 = 4$kg	$^{24}/_3 = 8$kg
Skilled Labour	$^{28}/_7 = 4$ hours	$^{21}/_7 = 3$ hours
Machine time	$^{14}/_2 = 7$ hours	$^{18}/_2 = 9$ hours

 Establish objective function

The objective function should be to maximise **contribution** rather than profit, as fixed overheads are not affected by the mix or volume of products produced.

	D	G
	$	$
Selling price	115	120
Total variable costs	74	73
Contribution per unit	41	47

The objective function to be maximised is:

Contribution = 41D + 47G.

 Establish constraints

Use the per unit resources required that were calculated in Step 2.

Direct Material A:	$4D + 2G \leq 1,800$
Direct Material B:	$4D + 8G \leq 3,500$
Skilled Labour:	$4D + 3G \leq 2,500$
Machine Time:	$7D + 9G \leq 6,500$
Product D demand:	$D \leq 400$
Product G demand:	$G \leq 450$
Non-negativity:	$D \geq 0; G \geq 0$

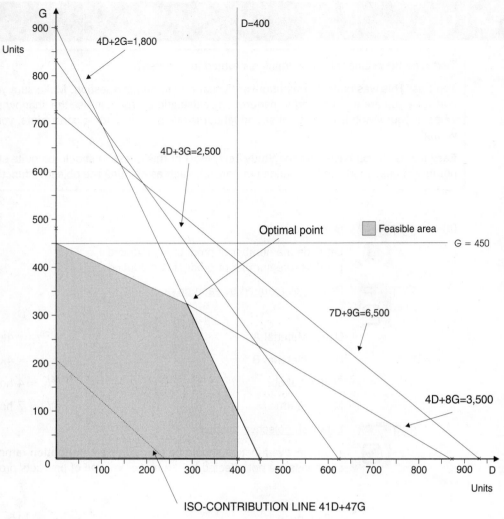

ISO-CONTRIBUTION LINE 41D+47G

The optimal point is reached at the intersection between:

4D+2G=1,800 (1)
4D+8G=3,500 (2)

Deduct equation (1) from equation (2)

6G = 1,700
G = 283

Substitute G=283 into equation (1)

4D+(2×283) = 1,800

4D+566 = 1,800

4D = 1,234

$D = \dfrac{1,234}{4}$

D = 309

Therefore, profit is maximised when 309 units of D and 283 units of G are produced. Contribution would be $25,970.

(b)   Shadow prices

The shadow price of a resource which is a limiting factor on production is the amount by which total contribution would fall if the organisation was deprived of one unit of that resource. Alternatively, it is the amount by which total contribution would rise if an extra unit of that resource became available.

Skilled labour: Shadow price = £0

This indicates that skilled labour, although a limiting factor, is not a **binding constraint** on production, given the current status of the other resources. Contribution would not be affected if skilled labour was increased or reduced by one hour.

Direct Material A: Shadow price = £5.82

If direct material A was increased by one kg, contribution would increase by £5.82. Similarly if supply of this material was reduced by one kg, contribution would fall by £5.82. Direct Material A is a **binding constraint** on production as the shadow price is greater than zero.

(c) Selling price sensitivity analysis

The sensitivity of the optimal solution to changes in the selling price of Product D can be determined by changing the slope of the iso-contribution line. As the selling price of Product D increased, the slope of the iso-contribution line would become steeper. The optimal solution will change when the slope of the iso-contribution line is such that its last point in the feasible region is no longer 309 units of Product D and 283 units of Product G.

19 Five products

Text references. Multi-product breakeven analysis is covered in Chapter 5.

Top tips. Ensure that you clearly show all workings to part (b) to maximise your mark.

Easy marks. Explaining the meaning of point 'X' on the chart should be relatively straightforward.

Examiner's comments. This question was answered poorly. It was clear that most candidates did not fully understand a multi-product breakeven chart. In particular, candidates did not understand that the charts can be constructed with the products with the highest or lowest C/S ratio first.

Marking scheme

		Marks
(a)	Need to establish an order of product sales	1
	Sales will consist of a mix of products	1
	Products A and E should be combined	1
	Product B has the highest C/S ratio	1
	Point X is the highest value of sales at which breakeven will occur	2
		6
(b)	Total annual budgeted sales and contribution	1
	Budgeted C/S ratio	2
	Budgeted breakeven sales revenue	1
		4

(a) (i) <u>Complementary products</u>

The Marketing Director said that Products A and E are complementary products **after** the chart had been prepared. As a result the chart does not recognise the effect of A and E being complementary products and the fact that sales of one do not occur without sales of the other. For this reason, sales data for Products A and E should be combined and viewed as a single product.

<u>Order of sale</u>

Multi-product breakeven charts are constructed based on the **assumption that products will be sold in order of their contribution to sales (C/S) ratio**. The order can be highest to lowest or lowest to highest. This assumption is not representative of real-life trading conditions where it is likely that a mix of all products will be sold each month assuming each product is readily available for sale.

(ii) Assuming that the budgeted sales values are the maximum achievable for each product, point 'X' on the chart shows the highest value of sales at which breakeven will occur.

(b) <u>Breakeven revenue for next year using the budgeted sales mix</u>

The overall budgeted contribution to sales ratio is $744,000 / $3,080,000 = 24.156% (W)

Therefore, the budgeted breakeven revenue using the budgeted sales mix is:

$300,000 fixed costs / 0.24156 = $1,241,927

Workings

<u>Budgeted sales and related contribution</u>

	Sales $'000	C/S ratio	Contribution $'000
A	400	45%	180
B	180	30%	54
C	1,400	25%	350
D	900	20%	180
E	200	(10%)	(20)
Total	3,080		744

20 POD and L

Top tips. When there is no indication about whether marginal costing or absorption costing is in use, it is simpler (and more informative too) to assess profitability with contribution analysis and marginal costing. This is the requirement in part (a)(i) of the problem. The obvious analysis to make is a calculation of the worst possible and best possible results.

The second part of the problem (a)(ii) is a variation of a 'target profit' calculation.

(a) (i)

	Best possible			*Worst possible*		
	Sales units	Cont'n per unit £	Total cont'n £	Sales units	Cont'n per unit £	Total cont'n £
X	2,000	30	60,000	1,000	30	30,000
Y	2,000	40	80,000	1,000	40	40,000
Z	2,000	50	100,000	1,000	50	50,000
Total contribution			240,000			120,000
Fixed costs			160,000			160,000
Profit/(loss)			80,000			(40,000)

The company's potential profitability ranges from a profit of £80,000 to a loss of £40,000 per month.

(ii)

	£	£
Required (minimum) profit per month		25,000
Fixed costs per month		160,000
Required contribution per month		185,000
Contribution to be earned from:		
product X 1,500 × £30	45,000	
product Y 1,500 × £40	60,000	
		105,000
Contribution required from product Z		80,000

Contribution per unit of Z: £50

Minimum required sales of Z per month: 1,600 units

(b) In 20X1 sales were 200,000 units. **The variable cost per unit** is therefore as follows.

	20X1	20X2 prediction
	£	£
Direct materials	4	4.40
Direct labour	2	2.30
Variable overhead	1	1.10
Per unit	7	7.80

Fixed costs

	£
20X1 total overhead (fixed plus variable)	600,000
Variable overhead in 20X1 (200,000 × £1)	200,000
Fixed overhead in 20X1	400,000
Add 20%	80,000
Estimated fixed overhead in 20X2	480,000

In 20X2, a **profit of £330,000 is required.**

	£
Required profit	330,000
Fixed costs	480,000
Required contribution	810,000

Contribution per unit in 20X2 (£10.50 – £7.80) = £2.70

Required sales $\dfrac{£810,000}{£2.70}$ = 300,000 units

This is an increase of 50% on 20X1 volumes. It is first of all **questionable** whether such a **large increase** could be **achieved** in one year. Secondly, given such an increase, it is likely that **output** will be **outside** the **relevant range** of output. Thirdly, **estimates** of fixed costs and variable costs are **unlikely to be reliable**.

21 RDF Ltd

Text references. Refer to Chapter 5 for information to answer part (a). Part (b) draws on prior knowledge as in the introductory chapter, and Chapter 5 for the C/S ratio.

Top tips. You should have been able to interpret the graph in (a) as details are provided in the BPP Study Text. Remember that on a multi-product P/V chart, products (or services) are plotted from left to right, starting with the product/service with the highest C/S ratio. These ratios were not provided but you should have been able to compute and compare them in your head.

Part (b)(i) was very straightforward – so straightforward, in fact, that you might have thought you had misunderstood the requirements. For both this part of the question and part (b)(iii) you had to apply marginal costing principles so that you arrived at figures for contribution which can be used for decision making.

In part (b)(ii) it was vital to take account of the financial penalty that would be incurred if RDF Ltd did not honour the contract to supply 500 units of service M per annum, as this had a significant impact on the profit-maximising operating plan.

In the text we use the C/S ratio of one standard mix of products to determine the breakeven point. In part (b)(iv) we assume that just one mix is sold, that being the total sales mix.

Part (b)(iv) requires knowledge of the assumptions underlying breakeven analysis and the limitations of these assumptions.

(a) **Point A** is the company's **breakeven point** on the **assumption that the services are sold in order of their C/S ratio**, all of the service with the highest C/S ratio (service K) being sold first, all of the service with the second highest C/S ratio (service L) second, and so on until the breakeven sales value is reached. We base the ratio on gross contribution (ie before any fixed costs).

Point B is the **average breakeven point** for RDF Ltd on the **assumption that the services are sold in the ratio 1,000: 2,300: 1,450, 1,970** until the breakeven sales value is reached.

(b) (i)

	K Per service $	K Total $	L Per service $	L Total $	M Per service $	M Total $	N Per service $	N Total $	Overall total $
Selling price	18		16		12		20		
Variable cost	8		10		13	*	13		
Gross contribution	10	10,000	6	13,800	(1)	(1,450)	7	13,790	36,140
Attributable fixed costs		4,400		3,700		–		2,650	10,750
Net contribution		5,600		10,100		(1,450)		11,140	25,390
General fixed costs (W)									8,930
Profit									16,460

* Includes ($500) relating to contract for 500 units of M per year.

Working

Total fixed costs = $(1,000 \times \$2) + (2,300 \times \$3) + (1,450 \times \$2) + (1,970 \times \$4) = \$19,680$

General fixed costs = $\$(19,680 - 4,400 - 3,700 - 2,650) = \$8,930$

The above table shows that **services K, L and N are financially viable** as they make a **positive contribution** towards the organisation's general fixed costs. Each unit of **service M** provided results in a **negative contribution** of $1, however, and hence the service **should not be offered unless there are other business reasons** for continuing to provide it, such as the three-year **contract** already in force.

(ii) The **contract** for the 500 units of product M should be **fulfilled** to avoid the significant financial penalties that RDF Ltd would incur if it were to break the terms.

This level of provision is below the budgeted number of 1,450 service units and so leaves spare resources that can be employed in the provision of additional units of the other three services if there is demand for them.

Insufficient data has been provided to determine how these spare resources should be used, however, and so they have not been taken into account in the budget profit statement below.

(iii) We can calculate the breakeven point using the average C/S ratio. We assume that one 'mix' of products is sold (which represents the budgeted volumes as per the budget profit statement in (iii) above).

Total sales revenue $= (1,000 \times \$18) + (2,300 \times \$16) + (500 \times \$12) + (1,970 \times 20)$
$= \$100,200$

Total gross contribution =	Total gross contribution (from profit statement in (i))	$36,140
	Add back (1,450 units – 500 units)* × $1	950
		$37,090

* RDF is only required to produce 500 units of M in order to meet the requirements of the contract and avoid the financial penalty.

Average C/S ratio $= \dfrac{37,090}{100,200} \times 100\% = 37\%$

Breakeven point in sales revenue $= \dfrac{\text{Fixed costs}}{\text{C/S ratio}} = \dfrac{\$10,750 + \$8,930}{0.37} = \$53,189$

(iv) Although breakeven analysis can give firms an indication of the minimum sales revenue or sales units that are required to cover total costs, it is based on a number of assumptions that really form the basis for its limitations.

- It is assumed that units are sold in a **constant mix** which is unlikely to be the case in reality. The proportions in which products are sold vary according to such factors as changing consumer tastes, availability of substitute products, changes in prices and so on.

- **Selling price is assumed to remain constant** regardless of the number of units sold. This is unrealistic for most 'normal' products as consumers are often only persuaded to purchase more if prices are reduced. As soon as selling prices change, the breakeven point will change, which makes it necessary to conduct the analysis again.

- **Inventory levels are ignored** as it is assumed that production and sales are the same. Although firms are increasingly striving to carry less inventory, it is unlikely that production and sales will exactly match.

- The analysis suggests that any **activity level above the breakeven point** will result in profits being made. This is not necessarily the case in reality, as changes in costs and revenues as more units are sold may result in a second breakeven point after which losses may be made. This is particularly true of electronic products such as computer games that have a very short shelf life.

- Costs are expected to behave in a linear fashion. Unit variable costs are expected to remain constant regardless of activity levels and fixed costs are not expected to change. This assumption ignores the possibility of economies of scale that could result in lower unit variable costs, or the fact that fixed costs may have to increase after a certain level of activity due to, for example, the need to rent additional premises.

22 GHK plc

Text references. Chapter 1A for relevant costs, Chapter 5 for C/S ratios and P/V charts, and Chapter 2 for limiting factors.

Top tips. Do not be put off by the length of the solution to this question. We have carefully led you through each step in detail but you would not be expected to reproduce this length of answer in the exam.

Part (a) requires you to calculate the relevant contribution per $ for six marks (five marks for calculating the relevant contributions for each product and one for the relevant contribution per $ for material B).

Just be a bit careful and don't calculate contribution per kg instead. This was a common mistake according to the examiner, who also remarked that this part of the question was poorly answered.

Set out your workings in a table like the one we have prepared. You need to use the high-low method for the overhead costs. Deduct the specific fixed costs first and then work out the variable cost per unit. Use the replacement cost of materials for Material A.

Part (b) basically requires you to do the following.

Step 1. Calculate the contribution from the contract to supply the major customer. This uses the relevant contributions calculated in part (a) for each product. There were two marks for this.

Step 2. Calculate the contribution from the alternative use of resources (ie fulfilling other demand expected as stated in the question). You need to compare demand and the optimum production plan capacity. There are two products where demand is more than capacity (J and K) and so you would look at switching capacity to produce these. Note however that one product (J) has a negative contribution so you wouldn't want to produce any more of this product. So look at switching resources from the minimum contract to satisfy the demand for product J. There were two marks for this part.

Step 3. Lastly, compare the contribution from the contract with the contribution from the alternative use of resources and state the financial penalty at which the company would be indifferent between meeting the contract or paying the penalty. There was one mark for this part.

Part (c) was well answered according to the examiner, which is not surprising given how easy it is!

The examiner reported that part (d) was not well answered as many candidates could not sketch the graph. We take you through how to do this in our answer below but we also have a nice example in Chapter 5 of the Study Text which you can work through and practise sketching a graph yourself. Make sure that you don't lose marks for not labelling axes. There were two marks for plotting the fixed costs and four marks for plotting the products by their contribution/sales ratios from lowest to highest.

Part (e) was also not well answered and many answers failed to relate to the scenario in the question.

The marks are spread evenly across the five parts to the question so there are plenty of possibilities for at least a couple of marks in each part.

Easy marks. You should have found part (a) easy and should have been able to pick up at least a couple of marks. Part (c) can be answered very, very easily straight from your answer to part (a) and just applying the C/S ratios. Part (d) also uses some of the calculations done in part (a) for overhead costs.

(a)

Product	G $	H $	J $	K $
Selling price (W1)	10.00	20.00	15.00	30.00
Material A (W2)	4.20	5.60	2.10	8.40
Material B (W3)	2.00	2.00	4.50	12.00
Direct labour (W4)	2.00	8.00	7.50	3.00
Overhead (W5)	1.00	3.00	3.00	3.00
Total costs	9.20	18.60	17.10	26.40
Relevant contribution per unit	0.80	1.40	(2.10)	3.60
Relevant contribution per $ of Material B (W6)	0.40	0.70	(0.47)	0.30

Workings

1 Take the revenue in $ as stated in the question and divide by the number of units. So for product G, take $30,000 and divide by 3,000 units to get $10 per unit selling price.

2 Costs shown in the budget are based on $5 per kg but the relevant cost will be the $7 replacement cost of material A. So taking Product G as an example:

Cost of material A per unit of G was $\frac{\$9,000}{3,000\,units} = \$3$

Kgs of material A per unit of G = $^{\$3}/_{\$5}$

Revised cost of material A per unit of G = $(^{\$3}/_{\$5}) \times \$7 = \$4.20$

3 The relevant cost here is based on the $10 per kg replacement cost so there is no need to substitute a replacement cost as in working 2 above and you can use the figures straight from the budget.

4 Likewise, the relevant cost here is the $10 hourly rate and you can take the cost from the budget.

5 You need to use the high-low method to calculate the variable element of the overheads, after deducting the specific fixed cost of $1,000.

Product	G $	G Units	H $	H Units	J $	J Units	K $	K Units
High volume	5,000	3,000	12,000	3,000	10,000	3,000	10,000	3,000
Low volume	7,000	5,000	18,000	5,000	16,000	5,000	16,000	5,000
Difference	2,000 (1)	2,000 (2)	6,000	2,000	6,000	2,000	6,000	2,000

Variable cost per unit ((1)/(2))	$\frac{2,000}{2,000} = \$1$	$3	$3	$3

6 Let's consider product G again. The cost of material B per the table above is $2 per unit. Apply this to the relevant contribution per unit you have already worked out and you will get the relevant contribution per $ of material B.

(b) Optimum production plan and financial penalty

In our Top tips above, we suggest the steps that you should take to work through this part of the question. So here goes......

 Calculate the contribution from the contract to supply the major customer

The data for units comes straight from the question and you should then use the relevant contributions calculated in part (a) for each product.

	G	H	J	K	Total
Units in the contract	500	1,600	800	400	
Relevant contribution per unit ($)	0.80	1.40	(2.10)	3.60	
Total contribution ($)	400	2,240	(1,680)	1,440	2,400

STEP 2 — <u>Calculate the contribution from the alternative use of resources</u>

First, you need to compare demand and the optimum production plan for each product. These are stated in the question in the body of the question and in part (b). Clearly you will only want to produce more where demand is greater than capacity, and you can look at switching resources to meet this demand.

Product	G	H	J	K
Demand for Units	3,600	3,000	3,000	4,000
Optimum production plan	4,100	4,600	800	2,417
Therefore spare capacity	0 (W1)	0 (W1)	2,200 (W2)	1,583 (W3)
Plus additional spare capacity if no contract				400
Total useful spare capacity				1,983

Workings

1   There are two products where demand is more than capacity, so there is no spare capacity.

2   You would not want to produce more of product J as this has a negative contribution, so look at producing more of product K.

3   The demand from other customers for product K is 4,000 units but the optimum production plan recommends a production level of 2,417 units. Without the contract, the production level would be 2,417 – 400 = 2,017 units, so there are 1,983 units of unsatisfied demand.

Then look at switching resources from the minimum contract to satisfy the demand for product K.

Product	G	H	J	K	Total
Units in the contract	500	1,600	800	400	
Material B (kg) per unit (W)	0.20	0.20	0.45	1.20	
Total kg released	100	320	360	480	1,260

Working

Refer to the budget in the question. For product K , for example, at 3,000 units the cost of material B is $36,000 so the cost per unit is $12.00. Divide by the expected cost per unit for material B of $10 to give 1.20 kg of material B per unit of K.

<u>Contribution from alternative use of resources</u>

This all relates to product K

Capacity in units (see above)	1,983
Material B (kg) per unit(see above)	1.20
Total kg required (1,983 × 1.2 kgs)	2,380
Available kg from switching (See above)	1,260
Additional units from available kgs (1,260 kgs /1.2 kgs per unit) (W)	1,050
Contribution from alternative use of resources (1,050 × $3.60)	$3,780

Working

The 1,983 units would require (x 1.2 kgs) 2,379.6 kgs of material B, which is more than the 1,260 made available if the contract does not go ahead. Therefore the additional units are limited by the 1,260 kgs made available.

With the extra 1,260 kgs, an extra 1,050 units of K can be produced (divide by 1.2).

Lastly, compare the contribution from the contract with the contribution from the alternative use of resources and state the financial penalty at which the company would be indifferent between meeting the contract or paying the penalty.

Minimum contract

	$
Total contribution (Step 1 above)	2,400
Less fixed cost not incurred (W)	(1,000)
Net contribution from the minimum contract	1,400
Contribution from alternative use of resources	3,780

Difference between two options ($(3,780 – 1,400)) = $2,380

Working

If the contract did not go ahead product J would not be produced (because it has a negative contribution) and specific fixed costs of $1,000 would be saved, so the contribution from the contract is a net figure of $1,400.

Conclusion. The penalty at which it is worthwhile to switch from the contract to other production is therefore $2,380.

Alternatively:

If GHK is indifferent between meeting the contract and paying the penalty:

Penalty + lost contribution from contract = extra contribution from production of additional product K

Therefore penalty = $3,780 – $1,400 = $2,380

(c)   Relevant contribution to sales ratios for all four products

Take the information calculated in part (a) above and use to calculate C/S ratios for each product.

Product	G	H	J	K
	$	$	$	$
Selling price	10.00	20.00	15.00	30.00
Relevant contribution	0.80	1.40	(2.10)	3.60
Contribution to sales ratios (%)	8%	7%	(14%)	12%

(d)   Sketch a graph showing multi product profit volume (PV) chart

A P/V chart has revenue on the x axis and profit on the y axis, and so for each product you need to know the revenue that can be earned from total market demand (contract + other customers) and the profit from this level of revenue. Remember that the limiting factor restriction on material B no longer applies as demand will be the sum of that for the minimum contract plus the demand expected from other customers.

Product	G	H	J	K	Total
Total demand (units) (W1)	4,100	4,600	3,800	4,400	
	$	$	$	$	$
Sales revenue (W2)	41,000	92,000	57,000	132,000	322,000
Contribution to sales ratios (%) (W3)	8%	7%	(14%)	12%	
Contribution	3,280	6,440	(7,980)	15,840	17,580

Workings

1   You need to add the demand from the minimum contract to the other demand stated, for each product. All information is in the question.

2   Use the selling price you calculated in part (a) × total demand for units

3   From part (c)

STEP 2

You need a 'starting point' for the graph (ie at the point of nil revenue on the x axis) and so you need to determine the profit when revenue is nil (the point on the y axis). Profit – or loss – when revenue is nil = fixed costs.

Product	G $	H $	J $	K $	Total $
Overhead costs per the question	6,000	13,000	11,000	11,000	
Units	3,000	3,000	3,000	3,000	
Variable overhead cost per unit (from (a))	$1	$3	$3	$3	
Total variable costs (units x variable cost per unit)	3,000	9,000	9,000	9,000	
Fixed cost (total overhead costs – total variable costs)	3,000	4,000	2,000	2,000	11,000
Less avoidable fixed cost (from note 4 of question)					(4,000)
Fixed cost at which sales are nil					7,000

STEP 3

The question states that the products are to be plotted in order of their C/S ratios so (from (c) they need to be plotted in the order KGHJ

You now need to work out cumulative revenues and profits

As each product is produced, a directly attrib fixed cost is incurred - we'll assume – immediately ie at zero revenue

Products	Revenue $	Cumulative revenue (x axis coordinate) $	Profit $	Cumulative profit (y axis coordinate) $
None	None	None	(7,000)	(7,000)
Start selling K	None	None	(1,000)	(8,000)
Finish selling K	132,000	132,000	15,840	7,840
Start selling G	None	132,000	(1,000)	6,840
Finish G	41,000	173,000	3,280	10,120
Start selling H	None	173,000	(1,000)	9,120
Finish selling H	92,000	265,000	6,440	15,560
Start selling J	None	265,000	(1,000)	14,560
Finish selling J	57,000	322,000	(7,980)	6,580

Multi product profit volume chart

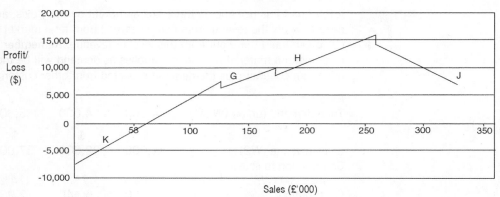

(e) The chart would **show further information about the contribution earned by each product individually**, so that their performance and profitability can be compared.

By convention, the **products are shown individually** on a P/V chart from **left to right**, in **order of the size of their C/S ratio**. In the question, product K will be plotted first, then products G and H and finally product J. The **jagged line** is used to show the **cumulative profit/loss and the cumulative sales** as each product's sales and contribution in turn are added to the sales mix.

It is also possible to plot a single line from the two end points on the **line** to indicate **the average profit, which** will be earned from sales of the products in this mix.

The diagram **highlights** the following points.

(i) Since K is the most profitable in terms of C/S ratio, it might be worth considering an increase in the sales of K, at the expense of less profitable products such as J.

(ii) Alternatively, the pricing structure of the products should be reviewed and a decision made as to whether the price of product J should be raised so as to increase its C/S ratio (although an increase is likely to result in some fall in sales volume).

The **multi-product P/V chart** therefore helps to **identify** the following.

(i) The overall company breakeven point.

(ii) Which products should be expanded in output and which, if any, should be discontinued.

(ii) What effect changes in selling price and sales volume will have on the company's breakeven point and profit.

Assumptions

1 The technique assumes that all variable costs are the same per unit at all levels of output and that fixed costs are the same in total.

2 It also assumes that sales price will be the same across all levels of activity.

3 There are no changes in levels of inventory so the consequences of increases and decreases in inventory levels are ignored.

23 Preparation questions: Pricing

(a) Marginal cost = £20
Profits are maximised when marginal cost = marginal revenue
ie when $20 = 50 - 0.002x$
ie when $x = 15,000$

When $x = 15,000$, selling price $= £50 - £(0.001 \times 15,000) = £35$

Maximum revenue occurs when marginal revenue = £0

ie when $0 = £50 - £0.002x$
ie when $x = 25,000$

When $x = 25,000$, selling price $= £50 - (£0.001 \times 25,000) = £25$

Profit = contribution – fixed costs
= $(25,000 \times £(25 - 20)) - £100,000 = £25,000$

(b) Marginal cost = $35

Profits are maximised when marginal revenue = marginal cost, ie when $35 = a - 2bx$

$a = \$100 + (1,000/100 \times \$50) = \$600$

$b = \$50/100$

Therefore, $35 = \$600 - x$

Therefore, $x = \$565$

$P = a - bx$

$= \$600 - \$50/100 \times \$565$

$= \$317.50$

(c) The question states the formulae for the demand curve and for marginal revenue. What you need to do is work out the values of 'a' and 'b' to substitute into the two formulae. You can then work out the profit-maximising price using MR = MC. Remember that 'a' is the price at which demand would be nil and 'b' is the amount by which price falls for each stepped change in demand.

STEP 1 Find the price at which demand would be NIL

Assuming demand is linear, each increase of $10 in the price would result in a fall in demand of 200 units. So if the price goes up by $60, the demand will fall by:

200 units × 6 = 1,200. Therefore a = $160.

 STEP 2 Extract figures from the question

We know that P = a –bx and a = $160. We have also defined b above. So taking data from the question, and ignoring currency

b = $^{10}/_{200}$ = 0.05

So the demand equation will be:

P = 160 – 0.05x

And the MR equation will be:

MR = 160 – 0.10x

STEP 3 Calculate the selling price at which profit is maximised

MR = MC so

160 – 0.10x = 30

x = 1,300

Substitute this value of x into the demand equation to obtain the **profit-maximising selling price**

P = 160 – 0.05 × 1,300 = $95

(d) $a = 60 + \dfrac{10 \times 1,000}{50} = \$260$

b = $10/50 = 0.2
P = 260 – 0.2x
MR = 260 – (2 × 0.2)x = 260 – 0.4x

Profit is maximised (optimal selling price and output) when MR = MC

Marginal cost = variable cost per unit = $24

Optimal output:

260 – 0.4x = 24
0.4x = 260 – 24
x = 590 units

Optimal selling price:

P = 260 – 0.2 × 590 = $142

(e) a = the price at which demand is zero

b = the amount by which price falls for each stepped change in demand

STEP 1 Find the price at which demand would be NIL

Assuming demand is linear, for every $5 increase in selling price demand falls by 50 units per week and vice versa.

For demand to be zero, demand must fall by 500 units (which means that price must go up by $(500 ÷ 50) × 5 = 50). Therefore a = $35 + $50 = $85.

Alternative approach

You could simply use the formula approach to replace step 1 above.

$P = a - bx$
$35 = a - 0.1 \times 500$
$35 = a - 50$
$a = 85$

 STEP 2 Extract figures from the question

$P = a - bx$ $a = 85$ (from step 1 above)

$b = 5 ÷ 50 = 0.1$

The **demand equation** is:

$P = 85 - 0.1x$

Marginal revenue $= 85 - 0.2x$

 STEP 3 Calculate the selling price at which profit is maximised

This occurs when MR = MC (where marginal cost is assumed to be the variable cost per unit)

$85 - 0.2x = 15$

$0.2x = 85 - 15$

$x = 350$

Substitute this value of x into the demand equation to obtain the **optimal selling price**

$P = 85 - (0.1 \times 350)$
P = $50

---

24 ML

Top tips. This was a reasonable written question on pricing methods. You need to read through the scenario and refer to the pertinent characteristics of ML that would add to your discussion. The examiner gave up to three marks for explaining the differences between the two costing methods and another two marks for how the system would affect pricing decisions. The remainder of the marks could be earned for your comments in part (b).

Easy marks. You could earn useful marks by just repeating from memory what you know of the approaches to pricing. Better marks would accrue from applying these to the scenario but put down your general points first and then expand on these in the 18 minutes.

(a)   (i)   Absorption costing

Traditionally the costing of production has included a **'fair share'** of overheads. This is justified by the argument that all production overheads arise **as a result of production** and so **each unit produced should incur some overhead costs**. This includes both variable and fixed overheads.

By adding a margin for profit to the full cost of production, the sale price can be calculated. This is known as **'full cost plus'** pricing. This method is particularly **appropriate** for companies who do jobbing or contract work **where no standard sales prices can be fixed**.

ML has used a **cost plus approach** to pricing based on absorption costing. **This approach** is appropriate to a company, which like ML, undertakes **ad hoc work** that may need to be **individually priced**.

An **absorption costing basis** may be **inappropriate** when overheads apportioned to a job **do not reflect the overheads** a job has caused. Thus ML uses a machine hours basis but a **labour hours basis may be more appropriate** given the skilled engineers appear to drive the work carried out. Alternatively, **activity based costing** may be more appropriate. ML may be losing work because they have set the profit margin too high and hence quoted prices too high.

It is not clear if they are using the same margin on all products, but ML could **consider varying the margin** depending on the type of work and/or customers. Because there is unused capacity, the use of absorption costing does not necessarily imply fixed costs are covered.

(ii) <u>Marginal costing</u>

Marginal costing values inventory at its **variable cost** thereby excluding fixed overheads, which are treated as a **cost of the accounting period** rather than being apportioned to production. There is a direct relationship between output and profitability as contribution varies directly with sales. Fixed overheads are charged as they are incurred.

Marginal costing is simple and easy to use. It is most appropriate when there is a **readily identifiable unit cost**, for instance in retail industries which is not the case with ML. However, it ignores fixed costs and so the **mark-up must be sufficiently high** to ensure they are covered.

Nonetheless the mark-up % can be varied so management can use their discretion when quoting for individual jobs. This may help ML win more quotes.

(b) <u>Comment on the Managing Director's remark</u>

A price based on variable costs reflects the **marginal costing approach** to pricing.

Any price that exceeds variable cost will at least offer some **contribution** toward fixed costs, but in the long term, this approach is **not sustainable**. The price must at least cover fixed costs for a profit to be made.

In the short term, ML could consider this approach in an effort to win business, but it may prove **difficult to raise prices** in the future without again losing business. In addition, low prices might give the impression that work is of an **inferior quality** to that of competitors.

25 PT

> **Text references**. The product life cycle is covered in Chapter 6.
>
> **Top tips**. Do not waste valuable time describing the introduction and decline stages of the product life cycle. Use headings and short paragraphs to make your answer easy to mark.

(i) <u>Growth stage</u>

In comparison to the introduction stage the following changes are likely to occur.

<u>Unit selling prices</u>

Selling **prices** are likely to be **decreasing** for a number of reasons.

The product will **no longer be unique** as competitors will be introducing their own versions of the product.

In an attempt to make the market less attractive to other companies PT may wish to lower their selling price and reduce the level of profitability on each unit.

The selling **price** may need to be **lowered** to attract **different market segments** to the product which will then lead to an increase in sales volume.

Unit production costs

Production costs are also likely to **decrease**.

Increasing production volume will give the opportunity to **buy in greater bulk** and take advantage of discounts which will reduce unit material costs.

Learning and experience curve effects may mean that direct labour will be more efficient which may **reduce direct labour costs**.

Variable overhead costs per unit may reduce if there are larger batches in production, especially if the variable element is not totally related to volume.

Fixed production costs will **fall** as they are being shared amongst a **greater number of units**.

(ii)   Maturity stage

In comparison to the growth stage the following changes are likely to occur.

Unit selling prices

Selling prices are likely to reduce from the growth stage as the product has become **established in the market**.

The selling price is likely to remain fairly constant throughout this stage as the company looks to **consolidate** its position.

Unit production costs

Direct labour costs are unlikely to reduce any further as the effect of the **learning and curve** has ended. Labour costs could even increase if workers choose to focus on the next product.

Direct material costs are likely to remain fairly constant at this stage. Lower quantities of material may be required in comparison to the growth stage. This could reduce **negotiating power** with suppliers, leading to an increase in prices.

Overhead costs are likely to be similar to those at the end of the growth stage as optimum batch sizes have been established.

26 PQ

Test references. The product life cycle is covered in Chapter 6.

Top tips. Ensure you spend appropriate time on each part of the question.

Easy marks. Explaining the likely sales price at different stages in the product life cycle in part (i) should be straightforward.

Examiner's comments. This question was generally well answered. A number of students presented answers in bullet points which reduced the number of marks that could be awarded. The question asked candidates to 'explain the changes' and so a fuller answer was required.

Marking scheme

		Marks
(i)	Selling price changes (2 marks for growth stage, 1 mark per other stage)	4
(ii)	Production cost changes (1 mark per stage)	3
(iii)	Selling & marketing costs changes (1 mark per stage)	3
	Max	10

PQ operates a market skimming pricing strategy. This involves charging high prices when a product is first launched and spending heavily on advertising and sales promotion to obtain sales.

(i) Selling price changes

As the product moves into the later stages of its life cycle, **progressively lower prices will be charged**.

PQ may first reduce sales prices at the **growth** stage in a bid to prevent competitors from entering the market. Reducing the price at this stage is likely to increase demand.

Sales prices are likely to decrease significantly at the **maturity** stage. Competitors will have flooded the market with alternative products and PQ is likely to lower sales prices as a means of sustaining demand for its products.

At the **saturation and decline** stage, the market will have bought enough of PQ's products and demand will start to fall. Due to the competitive market in which the company operates, products may become obsolete. For a while, PQ products will still be profitable in spite of declining sales but eventually products will become loss-making and the company may decide to stop selling the product.

PQ may attempt to prolong the life of its products buy reducing selling prices significantly at this stage.

(ii) Production cost changes

To an extent, production costs will change in line with unit sales over the course of the product life cycle.

Production costs per unit are likely to be highest at the **growth stage** as demand for PQ products increases and sales increase. PQ products should begin to make a profit at this stage as the initial costs of investment in new products are gradually recovered. Production costs per unit could be reduced through economies of scale.

At the **maturity** stage, the growth in demand for products will slow down. PQ may choose to modify or improve products as a means of preserving demand. Such a strategy is likely to lead to an increase in production costs.

As outlined above, demand for PQ products will decrease at the **saturation and decline** stage. In line with the reduced demand, fewer products are likely to be produced which will lead to a reduction in production costs. This could be offset by an increase in costs due to machine breakdowns and inefficiencies.

(iii) Selling and marketing cost changes

Sales and marketing costs likely to remain high at the **growth** stage as PQ aims to justify high selling prices by distinguishing itself from the competition and attempting to make it difficult for other companies to enter the consumer electronics market.

Sales and marketing costs are likely to decrease at the **maturity** stage as the product is established in the market and therefore does not require extensive advertising and marketing campaigns.

As with production costs, sales and marketing costs can be expected to decrease significantly at the **saturation and decline** stage as the product is nearing the end of its life.

27 WX

Text references. The profit-maximising price / output level is covered in Chapter 6.

Top tips. Present all of your workings clearly to maximise your score.

Easy marks. Calculating the total variable cost per unit using the high-low method in part (a) should be straight forward.

(a) (i) From the data in the question it can be seen that direct materials and direct labour are fully variable.

These variable costs total $8 per unit [($200,000 + $600,000)/100,000]

The overhead costs appear to be semi-variable and will be analysed using the **high-low method**.

	Units	$'000
High	200,000	1,460
Low	100,000	880
Difference	100,000	580

The variable element of the overhead is 580,000/100,000 = $5.80 per unit

Total variable cost = $8 + $5.80 = $13.80 per unit.

(ii)   Profit maximisation occurs when marginal revenue = marginal cost (assumed to be variable cost).

P = a – bx   where:

P = the selling price

x = the quantity demanded at that price

a = the price at which demand would be nil

b = the change in price required to change demand by one unit
    (change in price / change in quantity)

Demand falls by 25,000 for every $1 selling price increase above $25. Therefore there will be zero demand at a price of $31. [$25 + (150,000/25,000)] = $31.

The equation of the selling price is therefore

$31 – (1/25,000)x

= $31 – 0.00004x

Then from the formula given in the question (MR = a–2bx) marginal revenue is

$31 – 2 × 0.00004x

= $31 – 0.00008x

Profit maximisation occurs when marginal revenue = marginal cost

$31 – 0.00008x = $13.80

$17.20 = 0.00008x

x = 215,000

If the number of units is 215,000, the price is

$31 – (0.00004 × 215,000) = $22.40

(b)   There are a number of reasons why this price may not be used.

Demand

The model assumes that **price** is the **only determinant of demand**. In reality **other factors** such as advertising, changes in trends or fashion, competitor activity and economic factors can influence demand.

The model assumes a **static relationship** between **price** and **demand**, but in practice this **changes** on a regular basis.

Marginal (variable) cost

The **assumption** that marginal cost equals variable cost **may also be false**, but even if this assumption is true then the assumption that variable costs all vary in line with volume is **unlikely to be realistic** as some of these costs will be driven by factors other than volume.

The assumption that variable cost is unchanged once it has been determined may also not hold in the long run.

28 W

> **Top tips**. You will find the data you need scattered throughout the question. This makes it a bit difficult for you to remember to use it all but keep a clear head and cross off data as you use it. In part(a) you are required to complete the cash flow statement for the two remaining stages in the product life cycle. Remember that you need to produce a **cumulative statement** as well as stating cash flows for a period. You will need to remember the **four stages of the product life cycle** and their features so that you can select the **correct sales and cost characteristics** of the two remaining stages.
>
> Part (b) you need to make some clear points about the reasons why costs and sales change during the life cycle of a product. You must remember to **apply study text knowledge** to the scenario in the question. There are four stages in the lifecycle so you should score at least one mark for a comment on each stage.
>
> **Easy marks**. Part (a) is easy in principle. You are calculating a cash flow using data from the question and using the format suggested in the question. So you could earn a few useful marks by just setting out the format for the two remaining periods and slotting in some of the easier calculations such as sales demand for the maturity stage. In part (b) set out your answer with headings so the marker can pick out the four stages clearly and award marks more easily.

(a)   (i)

	Maturity (1)	Maturity (2)	Decline
Months	*31–70*	*51-70*	*71–110*
Number of units produced and sold (W1)	20,000	20,000	20,000
Selling price per unit ($)	60	60	40
Unit variable cost ($)	30	25	30
Unit contribution ($)	30	35	10
Total contribution($)	600,000	700,000	200,000
Cumulative cash flow(W2)	575,000	1,275,000	1,475,000

Workings

1   *Months 31–70*. 1,000 units per month × 40 months = 40,000 units.

   Months 71–110 are calculated as follows:

   (10 × 800) + (10 × 600) + (10 × 400) + (10 × 200) = 20,000 units.

   The clue to knowing which sales demand applies to which life cycle stage is to look at the sales demand over the life cycle. Monthly sales levels continue to increase up to months 31-70. Thereafter they decline. The growth stage typically shows a **rapid increase** in sales and the maturity stage shows a slow down in sales **growth**. However, it is only at the decline stage that sales actually **decline.**

2   Cumulative cash flow brought forward = $(25,000).

(b)   **The possible reasons for the changes in cost and selling prices during the life cycle of the product**. There are **four stages** in a product life cycle. Each stage has different features in relation to costs and sales. These are:

<u>Introductory stage</u>

The principal aim during this stage is to **introduce a product and build demand**. The organisation is likely to **spend significant amounts on advertising and distribution** to get the product or service known. Production costs ie **unit variable costs** are also likely to be high as the product has not yet achieved **economies of scale.** This is also the time in the product lifecycle where **research and development costs** are incurred. Prices are generally high if a **market skimming** policy is adopted to take advantage of being an early entrant to the market and so recoup costs. However an organisation may choose a **market penetration** strategy so prices are low to gain market share. For W, costs are high at $50/unit and the selling price is also (compared with those over the entire lifecycle) high at $100/unit. An unit contribution of $50/unit sold is the highest contribution over the product life cycle. W therefore appears to be seeking to recoup as much R&D expenditure and fixed asset expenditure as possible at this stage.

Growth stage

The aim during this stage is to **build market share**. **Costs will still be high** as more promotion is needed to advertise the product more widely. Distribution channels may be expanded to take up more market share. **The price will be high** but may need to fall if demand is seen as falling. W charges between $70 and $80/unit sold and the price drops over the period in response to market conditions. However, the unit variable cost is also falling. Margins are falling but volume has risen so the product is contributing more at this stage than the last one.

Maturity stage

This is the **most profitable stage** of the product's life cycle. **Costs will begin to fall** as economies of production are achieved. Advertising costs should fall as product awareness is stronger. Marketing is concentrated in reaching new customers. **The price will fall** in response to competition and to retain market share. Profitability is shown by the contribution of $1.3m that is the highest over the life cycle of the product despite a fall in selling price/unit. This is achieved by volume sales as well as the unit cost continuing to fall.

Decline stage

This is the stage at which the product is **losing popularity and market share is falling**. W can adopt a **choice of strategies** including running the product down or discontinuing it. Costs fall as marketing support is withdrawn but economies of scale begin to decline so the **unit variable cost actually rises** again to $30/unit. **Prices are reduced** to mop up market share.

29 HJ

> **Text references**. Target costs are covered in Chapter 7.
>
> **Top tips**. Remember to explain the stages HJ will go through to derive target costs from target prices.
>
> **Easy marks**. Being able to define target costs and standard costs in part (a) and marginal cost in part (b) should earn you a few marks.

(a)   Standard costs

The standard cost approach is to **develop a product**, determine the **expected standard production cost** of that product and then set a selling price (probably based on cost). Costs must be kept within the standard cost limit and variances are calculated to check that this has happened.

Target costs

The target cost approach is to develop a product concept and then determine the **price that customers would be willing to pay** for the product. The desired profit margin is deducted from the price, leaving a figure that represents total cost. This is the target cost and the product **must be capable of being produced for this amount** otherwise the product will not be manufactured. Because target costing places emphasis on continual cost reduction and focuses on profit margins, it is a useful tool that can help to strengthen an organisation's competitive position.

How HJ can derive target costs from target prices

HJ should start by examining prices charged by competitors for the new range of promotional gifts or carry out **market research to establish the price that customers are willing to pay** for key fobs, card holders and similar items. HJ should then decide on the profit that it requires from the new product range in order to deliver sufficient return on its investment in new machinery. HJ should **subtract the profit from the selling price** to derive the **target cost** for the plastic moulded products. HJ will then need to review its production methods to ensure that the new range of products can be produced for the calculated target cost.

(b)   Marginal cost pricing is the method of determining the sales price for a product by **adding a profit margin** on to either the marginal cost of production or the marginal cost of sales. The marginal-cost model is often used to **break into new markets** that are well established but is unlikely to be financially viable in the long term as businesses need to recover fixed costs and deliver a return on investment.

If HJ make price decisions based on the need for full recovery of all costs sales prices are likely to be higher than if a marginal cost approach was used, assuming a similar mark-up is applied. It is therefore important that HJ is seen to **add value to the product range in order to justify the higher selling price**.

HJ could add value by designing products from the new gift range in the same style as the cards and calendars that are part of the original product range that the company specialises in. For example, key fobs and card holders could be designed in the same colours as the calendars, thus encouraging customers to purchase the full range of matching products.

30 HS

Text references: Deriving profit – maximising selling prices is covered in Chapter 6. Target costing is in Chapter 7.

Top tips: Part (a) requires a methodical approach to ensure you have calculated all the required elements, so make sure you label all your workings. There is a temptation to use the material cost of $270 as the marginal cost, but the true marginal (variable) cost has to be calculated using the high-low method.

Easy marks: If you remember the formula for a, and the steps in calculating profit – maximising prices, you should be able to pick up the majority of the marks in part (a).

(a)   STEP 1   <u>Determine a and b for use in the Marginal Revenue equation</u>

$$b = \frac{\$50}{1,000} = 0.05$$

$$a = \$1,350 + (8,000 \times 0.05) = \$1,750$$

 STEP 2   <u>Calculate Marginal Revenue using the equation given in the question</u>

MR= 1,750 – (2×0.05)q
MR= 1,750 – 0.1q

STEP 3   <u>Calculate Marginal Cost using the high-low method</u>

	Units		$'000
Highest output	9,400	Total cost	7,000
Lowest output	7,300	Total cost	5,446
Change in units	2,100	Change in cost	1,554

$$\text{Variable (marginal) cost per unit} = \frac{\text{Change in cost}}{\text{Change in units}}$$

$$= \frac{1,554,000}{2,100}$$

$$= \$740 \text{ per unit}$$

 STEP 4   <u>Calculate optimum selling price</u>

Profit is maximised where MR = MC

ie where 1,750 – 0.1q = 740 + 270

0.1q = 1,750 – 1,010

q = 7,400 (profit-maximising demand)

Price = a – bq
= 1,750 – (0.05 x 7,400)
= $1,380

Profit maximising price is $1,380.

(b)   <u>Why this theoretical pricing model may be inappropriate:</u>

It is extremely difficult to determine a demand factor with any degree of accuracy, therefore HS may end up making the wrong pricing decision. In a highly competitive environment, this could prove to be disastrous, as customers will simply switch to a different supplier.

Rather than aiming for maximum profit, most organisations will try to achieve a target profit. As HS operates in a highly competitive environment, profit maximisation is unrealistic –it would be more appropriate (and motivational) to have a target profit in mind and price accordingly.

31   Electrical appliances

Text references. Pricing strategies and the product life cycle are covered in Chapter 6.

Top tips. The discussion elements of this questions were straightforward. Note that 16 marks were available for comparing pricing strategies and explaining likely production costs and selling prices at different stages in the product life cycle. Present your answer using sub-headings to ensure you answer all elements of the question and maximise your score.

Examiner's comments. The marks attained by most candidates were extremely high. The most common fault was the length of answers, sometimes covering several pages. This practice deprives candidates of valuable time for other questions.

Marking scheme

			Marks
(a)	Contribution for each price and identifying the price that maximises contribution		3
	The remaining capacity		1
	The number of units of L to utilise the available capacity		1
	The selling price at which demand is matched to available capacity		<u>4</u>
			<u>9</u>
(b)	Explanation of penetration pricing		2
	Explanation of skimming pricing		3
	Relating the answer to the scenario		<u>1</u>
			<u>6</u>
(c)	Unit production costs and unit selling prices at		
	- Growth stage		
	- Maturity stage		
	- Decline stage		
	Up to 4 marks for explanation of costs and selling prices at each stage		Max 10

(a)   (i)   <u>Selling price for product K to maximise contribution during the maturity stage</u>

Selling price / unit ($)	100	85	80	75
Contribution / unit ($)	62	47	42	37
Demand (units)	600	800	1,200	1,400
	<u>37,200</u>	<u>37,600</u>	<u>50,400</u>	<u>51,800</u>

From the above table it is clear that a selling price of $75 / unit maximises contribution for Product K.

The company production facility has a capacity of 2,000 hours per week. 1,400 units of Product K will take 1,400 hours to produce (standard production time of 1 hour per unit). This leaves 600 hours remaining to produce Product L.

Production of Product L takes 1.25 hours per unit. Therefore the maximum number of units of Product L that can be produced in a week is 480 units.

(ii)   <u>The selling price of product L during the growth stage</u>

When demand is linear the equation for the demand curve is P = a – bx

Where P   =   the selling price

x   =   the quantity demanded at that price

a   =   theoretical maximum price. If price is set at "a" or above, demand will be zero

b   =   the change in price required to change demand by one unit.

a and b are constants and are calculated as follows:

$$a = \$ \text{ (current price)} + \left(\frac{\text{Current quantity at current price}}{\text{Current quantity when price changed by \$b}} \times \$b \right)$$

$$b = \frac{\text{Change in price}}{\text{Change in quantity}}$$

 Find the price at which demand would be nil

The question states that there is a linear relationship between the selling price of the product and the number of units demanded. Therefore, each increase of $10 in the price would result in a fall in demand of 200 units. For demand to be nil, the price needs to rise from its current level by as many times as there are 200 units in 1,000 units (expected demand per week for the product).

(1,000/200 = 5) ie to $100 + (5 × $10) = $150.

Using the formula above, this can be shown as a = $100 + ((1,000/200) × $10)= $150

 Calculate b

$$b = \frac{\text{change in price}}{\text{change in quantity}} = \frac{\$10}{200} = 0.05$$

The demand equation is therefore P = 24 – 0.05x

Where x represents the quantity demanded. We know from part (a)(i) that the maximum level of production for Product L is 480 units a week.

 Complete the equation
P = 150 – (0.05x)
P = 150 – (0.05 x 480units)
P = 150 - 24
P = 126

Product L should be sold for $126 per unit at the growth stage.

(b)   <u>Penetration pricing</u>

Penetration pricing is a policy of **low prices** when the product is **first launched** in order to obtain sufficient penetration into the market.

Product M is an innovative product that the manufacturer believes will change the whole market once it is launched. A strategy of penetration pricing could be effective in **discouraging potential new entrants** to the market.

However, the product is believed to be unique and as such **demand** is likely to be fairly **inelastic**. In this instance a policy of penetration pricing could **significantly reduce revenue** without a corresponding increase in sales.

Market skimming

Market skimming pricing involves charging **high prices** when a product is **first launched** and spending heavily on **advertising and sales promotions** to obtain sales.

The aim of market skimming is to **gain high unit profits early in the product's life**, allowing the costs of developing the product to be recovered.

Product M is new and different. A policy of market skimming appears most appropriate as customers are prepared to pay high prices for innovative products that are expected to change the market.

(c)   Unit production costs

Unit production costs of Product M are likely to change throughout the product's life cycle.

Production costs at the growth stage

The impact of **learning and experience curves** is likely to result in a reduction in production costs per unit at the growth stage. Costs may also decrease due to **economies of scale**.

The extent to which costs fall will depend upon the **skill level** and **experience** of the workforce and the complexity of the manufacturing process.

Production costs at the maturity stage

The workforce is likely to have become used to the manufacturing process by the maturity stage. The **learning period** will have ended and production costs per unit are likely to remain fairly constant.

Production costs at the decline stage

Sales volumes at the decline stage are likely to be low as the product is **surpassed by new exciting products** that have been introduced to the market. Furthermore, the workforce may be less interested in manufacturing a declining product and may be looking to learn new skills. For both of these reasons, **unit production costs are likely to increase** at the decline stage.

Unit selling price

The selling price will initially be high if a policy of **market skimming** is employed. The uniqueness of the product should **justify the high selling price** and will enable the company to quickly **recoup product development costs**.

Selling price at the growth stage

The high selling price will encourage competitors to attempt to produce the same product at a lower cost. Competitors may attempt to do this through **reverse engineering**.

The company should **reduce the selling price** at the growth stage to maximise unit sales as the product is more affordable to lower social economic groups.

Selling price at the maturity stage

It is likely that the price of the product will be lowered further at the maturity stage in a bid to **preserve sales volumes**. The company may attempt to preserve sales volumes by employing an **extension strategy** rather than reducing the selling price. For example, they may introduce product add-ons to the market that are compatible with Product M.

Selling price at the decline stage

At the decline stage, Product M is likely to have been **surpassed by more advanced products** in the market and consequently will **become obsolete**. The company will not want to incur **inventory holding costs** for an obsolete product and is likely to sell Product M at **marginal cost or perhaps lower.**

32 TQ

> **Text references.** Chapter 6 covers profit-maximising price calculations and the material to put in the report on different pricing strategies.
>
> **Top tips.** You may have floundered around for a few minutes at the beginning of this question, not knowing quite how to start. Unless the examiner is being very mean and the information about the volume variance and the budgeted production and sales volumes are red herrings, you could always use it to find out actual volumes (given that the volume variance is the difference between budgeted and actual volumes). As the link between the demand curve and marginal revenue is provided, hopefully you realised that you had to derive the demand curve, which you couldn't do without the actual volumes. Part (i) certainly needed a fair amount of mathematical ability, but once you grasp the key steps in these questions you should find they become easier with practice.
>
> **Easy marks.** Start part (b) first. Part (b) was far more straightforward although, as is the case with all written answers, there is no point simply regurgitating book knowledge. You must apply it to the details and circumstances described in the question scenario.

(a) (i) $P = a - bx$

When $P = 100$, $x = 0$

Therefore, using above equation, $a = 100$

Using fixed overhead volume variance to find actual sales units:

Fixed overhead volume variance = (Budgeted units – actual units) × standard fixed overhead rate

Rearranging:

Actual units = budgeted units – $\dfrac{\text{Fixed overhead volume variance}}{\text{Standard fixed overhead rate}}$

Period	Budgeted units	–	$\dfrac{\text{Fixed overhead volume variance}}{\text{Standard fixed overhead rate}}$	–	Actual units
1	520	–	$\dfrac{1,200}{10}$	–	400
2	590	–	$\dfrac{1,900}{10}$	–	400
3	660	–	$\dfrac{2,600}{10}$	–	400

Using high-low method to calculate b:

$b = \dfrac{\text{Change in P}}{\text{Change in x}}$

When

$P = 60, \ x = 400$

$ = 100, \ x = 0$

$b = \dfrac{(100 - 60)}{400}$

$ = 0.10$

So, we can now write equations as:

$P = 100 - 0.1x$

$MR = 100 - 0.2x$

To maximise contribution: MR = MC

We assume that MC = variable cost per unit of $25

$100 - 0.2x = 25$

$x = 375$

To sell 375 units:

$$P = 100 - (0.1 \times 375)$$
$$= \$62.50 \text{ (this is the price at which contribution will be maximised).}$$

(ii)

	Optimal price $	Actual price $
Selling price	62.50	60.00
Variable costs	25.00	25.00
Contribution per unit	37.50	35.00
Units sold	375 units	400 units
Total contribution	$14,062.50	$14,000

Difference in contribution = $62.50.

(b) <u>REPORT</u>

To:	Board of directors
From:	Management accountant
Date:	13 March 20X3
Subject:	<u>Alternative pricing strategies</u>

Following our recent meeting to discuss pricing of our new mobile phone, I set out below a number of alternative strategies that we should consider.

<u>Market skimming</u>

This pricing strategy involves charging **high prices when a product is first launched** and spending heavily on advertising and promotion to obtain sales so as to exploit any price insensitivity in the market. As the product moves into **later stages of its life cycle**, **prices can be reduced** in order to remain competitive. The aim is therefore to gain high unit profits early in the product's life.

A **high price** makes it more likely that **competitors** will **enter** the market, however, and so there must be significant **barriers to entry** or the product must be **differentiated** in some way. The fact that our product is 'state of the art' should provide some level of differentiation.

Such a strategy could be **appropriate** for a number of reasons.

(i)   Our product will be new and different and so high prices can be charged to take advantage of its **novelty appeal**.

(ii)   Charging high prices in the early stages of the product's (expected) very short life cycle would generate the **high initial cash flows** needed to cover the significant level of development costs we have incurred.

(iii)   Once the market has become **saturated**, the product's price could be **reduced** to attract that part of the market that has not been exploited.

<u>Market penetration pricing</u>

This is a policy of **low prices when a product is first launched** in order to **achieve high sales** volumes and hence **gain a significant market share**. If we adopt this strategy it might **discourage competitors** from entering the market. You should note that demand for our **product** is likely to be **inelastic**, however, whereas **penetration pricing** is most suited to products for which demand is **elastic** and so responds well to low prices.

<u>Demand-based approach</u>

This approach is based on the **assumption that there is a profit-maximising combination of price and demand** because demand is elastic. We would need to commission some market research if we were to adopt such a strategy, however, to obtain information about levels of demand at various prices.

There are some significant **drawbacks** to this approach to pricing, however.

(i)   It can be difficult to predict the demand curve, even with market research.

(ii)   It ignores the market research costs of acquiring the necessary information.

(iii) It assumes that price is the only influence on the quantity demanded. Other factors such as quality of the product, levels of after sales service and so on could also impact.

(iv)   It assumes that we have no production constraints that prevent the equilibrium point between supply and demand being met.

The **advantages** of the approach are that if would force management to think about price/demand relationships and to consider the market in which we operate.

Premium pricing

This strategy would involve highlighting the product's 'state of the art' features as a **differentiating factor** to justify a **premium price**.

Price discrimination

A **different price** for the product would be charged to **different groups of buyers** if this strategy were adopted. For example, we could charge a different price if the product were bought on-line to the price charged in retail outlets.

I hope this information proves useful. If you would like to discuss any of the issues further, please get in touch.

SECTION B – COST ANALYSIS FOR COMPETITIVE ADVANTAGE

Answers 33 to 73 cover analysis for competitive advantage, the subject of Part B of the BPP Study Text for Paper P2.

33 Wye hotel group

> **Top tips.** This question has been included so that you can see how to apply your knowledge to different scenarios.

Cost reduction

Cost reduction is a planned and positive approach to **reducing the unit cost** of goods/services below current budgeted or standard levels **without impairing their suitability for the use intended**. It should not be confused with cost control, which is all about keeping costs within acceptable (standard or budgeted) limits.

A cost reduction programme in the WYE hotel group would therefore look at how to reduce the cost of a guest staying a night in the hotel, a meal being served in the restaurant and so on, without the customer perceiving any fall in the value of the service provided.

How to reduce costs

The **improvement of efficiency levels** might be considered.

(a)   Improving materials usage (eg the use of food in restaurants or guest supplies in bedrooms)

(b)   Improving labour productivity (eg changing work methods to eliminate unnecessary procedures, perhaps in the work required to prepare rooms for new guests)

(c)   Improving efficiency of equipment usage (eg allowing members of the public to use the swimming pool at certain times of the day/year for payment of a fee)

A programme could also consider ways to **reduce the costs of resources**.

(a)   It might be possible to find cheaper suppliers for, say, wines and beers.

(b)   Increased automation of certain guest services, say the travel bureaux, would reduce labour costs.

Other aspects of a cost reduction programme might include **increased control over spending decisions**.

Value analysis

Conventional cost reduction techniques try to achieve the lowest unit costs for a specific product design or specific way of providing a service. Value analysis tries to find the **least-cost method of making a product or providing a service that achieves the desired function/outcome**.

Value analysis of a particular service within the hotel group would involve the systematic investigation of both the costs connected with the service and the way in which it is provided, with the **aim of getting rid of all unnecessary costs**. An unnecessary cost is an **additional cost incurred without adding** to the following aspects of value.

- **Use value** – the purpose fulfilled by the service
- **Exchange value** – the market value of the service
- **Esteem value** – the prestige the guest attaches to the service

Applying value analysis

A value analysis of the guest entertainment provided might therefore pose the following questions.

(a)   **Are all parts of the entertainment programme necessary?** Could the cabaret show be removed from the programme without affecting guests' perception of the quality of the overall programme?

(b)   **Could the programme be provided at a lower cost without affecting its value?** For example, could children's films be shown instead of using a live entertainer?

From the analysis **a variety of options** can be **devised** and **the least cost alternative which maintains or improves the value of the service to the guests can be selected**.

34 JYT

> **Text references**. Target costing is covered in Chapter 7. Kaizen costing is covered in Chapter 9A.
>
> **Top tips**. Ensure you refer back to the scenario throughout your answer.
>
> **Easy marks**. Explaining the key differences between target costing and Kaizen costing will earn you quick and easy marks.

Target costing

Target costing is a costing system that can be used when a company (such as JYT) is **unable to dictate a selling price** and is forced to accept the prevailing market selling price for a product.

After the specification of the product is completed, JYT will determine the price that the market is **prepared to pay** for the product (this may be by considering similar products already available or by carrying out market research). JYT then would subtract a target profit from the selling price to determine its **cost target**. If the expected cost of the product already meets the target cost over its lifecycle, including any expected cost reductions, then production can commence. If the expected cost exceeds the target cost then major changes are introduced to reduce costs so that the target cost is achieved. If JYT cannot achieve the target cost then the product will be abandoned.

Kaizen costing

Kaizen costing has been used by some Japanese firms for over twenty years and is now widely used in the electronics and automobile industries. 'Kaizen' translates as **continuous improvement**.

Functional analysis is applied at the design stage of a new product, and a **target cost for each function** is set. The functional target costs are added together and the total becomes the **product target cost**. Once the product has been in production for a year, the actual cost of the first year becomes the starting point **for further cost reduction**. It is this **process of continuous improvement, encouraging constant reductions by tightening the 'standards'**, that is known as kaizen costing.

JYT could apply Kaizen costing as follows. The previous year's actual production cost serves as the cost base for the current year's production cost. A reduction rate and reduction amount are set. **Actual performance** is **compared** to the **Kaizen goals** throughout the year and **variances are monitored**. At the end of the current year, the current actual cost becomes the cost base for the next year. New (lower) Kaizen goals are set and the whole process starts again.

Differences

One of the main differences between the two methods is that target costing is applied **before** production commences, but Kaizen costing is applied **after** production has started.

Another difference is that target costing requires significant changes to be made, but Kaizen costing involves making a number of small improvements to the whole process as part of continuous improvement.

35 Financial advisers

> **Top tips**. In part (a) you must ensure that you describe value analysis and not the value chain. This was a mistake made by many candidates according to the examiner. Also ensure that you are clear about the different focus of each technique. Value analysis has a focus on reducing cost without sacrificing the function to the customer, whereas functional analysis looks at the value to the customer of each function of a product or service.
>
> You need to read through the scenario and refer to the pertinent steps to implement the technique to answer Part (b). There were six marks for this part. Keep your answer brief, however, as you only have 18 minutes to complete the question.
>
> **Easy marks**. You could earn a few useful marks by just repeating from memory what you know of the two techniques.
>
> The question then guides you to earn easy marks from applying the steps of value analysis to the scenario. Put down the steps first (you'll get some marks for this) and then apply these to the scenario in the time allowed.

(a) Value analysis is a planned, scientific approach to cost reduction which reviews the material composition of a product and production design so that modifications and improvements can be made which do not reduce the value of the product to the customer or to the user.

Functional analysis is concerned with improving profits by attempting to reduce costs and/or by improving products by adding new features in a cost-effective way that are so attractive to customers that profits actually increase.

Value analysis focuses on cost reduction through **a review of the processes** required to produce a product or service. **Functional analysis** focuses on the **value to the customer of each function** of the product or service and then makes decisions about whether cost reduction is needed.

(b) There are seven steps in value analysis, which need to be followed through before implementation. These are:

Select a product or service for study. The service provided by the firm is high quality, personalised financial strategy advice.

Obtain and record information. The questions to be asked include: What do the clients want from the service? Does it succeed? Are there alternative ways of providing it? What do these alternatives cost?

Analyse the information and evaluate the service. Each aspect of the service should be analysed. Any cost reductions must be achieved without the loss of use or esteem value. (Or at least, cost savings must exceed any loss in value suffered, and customers would then have to be compensated for the loss in use or esteem value in the form of a lower selling price.) The type of questions to be asked and answered in the analysis stage is as follows.

(i) Are all the activities undertaken necessary? So does the firm need to undertake all of sponsorship, newsletters and seek new and innovative ideas, for instance. It is clear that many clients don't read the newsletter so does this still need to be produced?

(ii) Can the service be provided at a lower cost?

(iii) Can any part of the service be standardised?

(iv) Does the value provided by each aspect of the service justify its cost?

Consider alternatives. From the analysis, a variety of options can be devised. This is the 'new ideas' stage of the study, and alternative options would mix ideas for eliminating unnecessary services or standardising certain features of the service.

Select the least cost alternative. The costs (and other aspects of value) of each alternative should be compared.

Recommend. The preferred alternative should then be recommended to the decision makers for approval.

Implement and follow-up. Once a value analysis proposal is approved and accepted, its implementation must be properly planned and co-ordinated. Management should review the implementation and, where appropriate, improve the new service in the light of practical experience.

To be successful, value analysis programmes must have the full backing of senior management.

36 Batch production

> **Text references.** The learning curve is covered in Chapter 7.
>
> **Top tips.** You can solve part (a) using the learning curve formula in reverse.

(a) $Y_x = aX^b$

  Where Y_x = Cumulative average time per unit to produce X units

  a = The time required to produce the first unit of output

  X = The cumulative number of units

  b = The learning coefficient (log of the learning rate / log of 2)

The standard cost of the actual labour hours worked is the actual cost less the adverse direct labour rate variance.

$3,493 – $85 = $3,408.

At a standard rate of $12 per hour this equates to $3,408 / $12 = 284 labour hours (actual hours worked).

With a total of 32 batches the average time per batch is as follows.

284 / 32 = 8.875 hours per batch

32 batches represents 5 doublings of output.

The learning rate is calculated as follows

$^5\sqrt{(8.875/20)} = 0.85 = 85\%$

(b)   The actual labour rate paid is $3,493 / 284 = $12.30 per hour.

  b = log of the learning rate / log of 2

  b = log 0.85 / log 2 = - 0.2345

  Using the formula $Y_x = aX^b$ will give the average batch time

  $Y_{128} = 20 \times 128^{-0.2345}$

  $Y_{128} = 6.41$ hours

  Total cost   = average time $\times$ no of batches $\times$ actual labour rate

  = 6.41 $\times$ 128 $\times$ $12.30

  = $10,092

37 The learning curve effect

> **Text references.** The learning curve is covered in Chapter 7. Planning and operating variances are covered in the Introduction Chapter.
>
> **Top tips.** Ensure that you clearly show all workings to part (a) to maximise your mark.
>
> **Easy marks.** Explaining the concept of target costing in part (b) will earn you some easy marks.

(a)   Total time allowed for actual production   1,712 hours
  Actual hours   3,500 hours
  Original standard hours (560 units $\times$ 8 hours/unit)   4,480 hours

Planning variance

	Hrs
Original standard	4,480
Revised standard	1,712
	2,768 (F)

Difference valued at standard labour rate (2,768 hours × $15) — $41,520 (F)

Operating variance

	Hrs
560 units should have taken	1,712
But did take	3,500
	1,788 (A)

Difference valued at standard labour rate (1,788 hours × $15) — $26,820 (A)

Workings

Average time per unit for the first 560 units assuming a 90% learning curve

$Y = aX^b$

Where
Y = Cumulative average time per unit to produce X units

a = The time required to produce the first unit of output

X = The cumulative number of units

b = The learning coefficient

$Y = 8 \times 560^{-0.1520}$

$Y = 3.057$ hours

Total time for 560 units

Total time for 560 units = 560 × 3.057 hours = 1,712 hours

(b) The importance of learning curves in the context of target costing

The **target costing approach** is to develop a **product concept** and then to **determine the price customers would be willing to pay** for that concept. The **desired profit margin** is deducted from the price leaving a figure that represents **total cost**.

This is the **target cost** and the product must be capable of being produced for this amount otherwise the product will not be manufactured.

The importance of learning curves in the context of target costing **depends on the nature of the manufacturing process**.

Target costs may only be achieved once a certain level of activity (the **learning period**) has been reached in **labour intensive environments**.

In contrast, **learning curves may not exist** in machine-intensive environments consisting of a number of **automated processes**. In such environments, learning curves could be said to be irrelevant to target costing.

38 New Product

Test references. Variances are covered within the Introduction chapter. Flexed budgets are covered in Chapter 10.

Top tips. Remember to show all your workings for part (a) to maximise your mark.

Easy marks. Explaining why your report is more useful to the production manager will earn you 3 easy marks.

Examiner's comments. Answers to this question were disappointing, especially given that the calculations required to flex the budget and the calculation of two basic variances relate to the C01 syllabus.

Candidates were unable to make simple calculations relating to the learning curve and many failed to put forward acceptable benefits of the reconstructed report.

Marking scheme

		Marks
(a)	Time for the 30th batch	2
	Time for 50 batches	1
	Direct labour cost for flexed budget	1
	Efficiency and rate variances (1 mark each)	2
	Format	$\frac{1}{7}$
(b)	1 mark per reason	$\frac{3}{10}$

(a) **Revised turn-out performance report**

	Flexed Budget	Actual	Variance
Output (batches)	50	50	
Direct labour hours	68.91 (W2)	93.65	24.74 (Adverse)
Direct labour cost ($) (W3)	826.92	1,146.00	319.08 (Adverse)
Direct labour efficiency ($) (W4)			296.88 (Adverse)
Direct labour rate ($)			22.20 (Adverse)

WORKINGS

The question states that the learning should have ceased after 30 batches.

W1 – Average time for 30 batches (using learning curve data)

$Y = ax^b$

$Y = 10 \times 30^{-0.5146} = 1.737$ hours

Total time for 30 batches = 30 x 1.737 hours = 52.11 hours

W2 – Average time for 29 batches (using learning curve data)

$Y = ax^b$

$Y = 10 \times 29^{-0.5146} = 1.768$ hours

Total time for 29 batches = 29 x 1.768 hours = 51.27 hours

Therefore, time for the 30th batch = 52.11 hours -51.27 hours = 0.84 hours

Total time for 50 batches = 52.11 hours + (20 batches x 0.84 hours) = 68.91 hours

W3 – Total labour cost variance

	$
Actual hours paid should cost (68.91 hours x $12 standard rate)	826.92
Actual hours paid did cost	1,146.00
Total variance	319.08 (A)

W4 – Flexed budget direct labour efficiency variance

	Hours
Actual production should use	68.91
Actual production did use	93.65
Difference	24.74 (A)
Valued at $12 standard cost per hour	296.88 (A)

(b) The above performance report is more useful to the production manager than the original report for a number of reasons.

The **assumptions concerning the learning curve** in the original budget are inaccurate.

The comparison in the original report is inaccurate as actual output is less than budget and no adjustment has been made to account for this (to expected direct labour hours or direct labour cost).

The revised report compares actual performance for 50 batches with expected costs based on the same level of output.

The **revised performance report analyses the direct labour cost variance** by slitting it into the labour efficiency variance and the labour rate variance. This will enable the production manager to see the proportion of the adverse variance that is due to resource utilisation and labour rates.

39 S

> **Text references**. The learning curve is covered in Chapter 7.
>
> **Top tips**. Remember to apply the standard direct labour rate when calculating the planning and operating variances in part (b).
>
> **Easy marks**. Explaining the variances that you have calculated in part (b) should be straightforward.

(a)

Number of batches completed	Average time per batch
1	1,000 hours
2	900 hours
4	810 hours
8	729 hours
16	656 hours
32	590 hours
64	531 hours

Note: With a 90% learning rate, the cumulative average time per unit of output will fall to 90% of what it was before, every time output is doubled.

Expected length of learning period = 64 batches

(Average time of 5.3 hours per unit; 530 hours per batch of 100 after 64 batches have been completed).

(b) S produced 4 batches of the new product in August. The average time per batch should have been 810 hours (as shown in the answer to (a) above).

4 batches should have taken	(4 × 810 hrs)	3,240 hours
4 batches did take		2,500 hours
		740 hours (F)
Standard rate		$10/hr
Operating efficiency variance		$7,400 (F)

The planning variance is calculated by comparing the standard target time with the revised target time:

Original standard	(5.3hrs × 400 units)	2,120 hours
Revised standard	(4 x 810 hrs)	3,240 hours
		1,120 hours (A)
Standard rate		$10/hr
Planning efficiency variance		$11,200 (A)

(c) The split of the efficiency variance into planning and operational variances will provide the management of S with **more meaningful information** by showing the true efficiency of operations.

Only 4 batches of the new product were produced in August and as the learning period continues to around 64 batches (see part (a) above), it would appear **unfair to measure current performance against a post-learning standard**.

The operating efficiency variance shows that the 4 batches produced in August took less time than expected. Management of S **should congratulate the workforce on their efficiency**.

40 Learning curve

> **Text reference.** Chapter 7 will help you with learning curves.
>
> **Top tips.** You should spot straight away that this question is testing your knowledge of learning curves. Part (a) asks you to apply the **expected rate of learning** to an initial **actual cost** for the first batch. Remember that the learning curve measures the **cumulative average labour cost per unit.** You will need to multiply the average time by the cumulative number of units to arrive at the costs asked for. Part (b) then gets you to calculate an **actual rate of learning** based on **actual cost** data. Part (c) is testing your understanding of how your findings in parts (a) and (b) affect management.
>
> **Easy marks. Draw up tables as we have done to answer parts (a) and (b).** Otherwise, you can use the formula for the learning curve which is given in the exam. However as the batches double, i.e. 1,2,4 and 8 you do not need to use the formula.

(a) <u>Revised expected cumulative direct labour costs</u>

Cumulative batches	Rate of learning	Average direct labour cost per batch	Cumulative direct labour cost
	%	$'000	$'000
1	–	280.00	280.00
2	80	224.00	448.00
4	80	179.20	716.80
8 (W)	–	153.10	1,224.80

Working

You will need to use the learning curve formula to work out the labour cost for batch 4 as this is when the rate of learning ends. **Remember that this is not the same as the average direct labour cost for batch 4.** Then use this to calculate the labour costs of the later batches. We know the cumulative labour cost for four batches, which is $716.80. So to work out the labour cost for the fourth batch we need to work out the cumulative direct labour cost for the first **three** batches. So here goes.

 STEP 1

$Y_x = aX^b$

Where $a = 280$

$X^b = 3^b$

$b = \dfrac{\text{Log } 0.80}{\text{Log } 2} = \dfrac{-0.0969}{0.301} = -0.3219$

Therefore $3^b = 3^{-0.3219} = 0.702$ and substituting this into the main formula for the learning curve gives

$Y_x = 280 \times 0.702$
$= \$196.60 \text{ (rounded)}$

 STEP 2

Multiply this by three batches to get $196.60 \times 3 = \$589.8$.

 STEP 3

Deduct this from the cumulative labour cost for four batches to give the labour cost for the fourth batch.

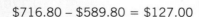

$716.80 - \$589.80 = \$127.00$

 STEP 4

Multiply this by four to give the total costs of batches 5–8 and then add this to the cumulative direct labour cost for batch 4 to give the cumulative direct labour cost for the eight batches. In numbers:

$127 \times 4 = \$508$

$716.80 + \$508 = \$1,224.80$

 STEP 5

You can then **divide** this by eight to get the average direct labour cost for eight batches.

(b) <u>Actual learning rate</u>

Cumulative batches	Actual cumulative direct labour cost $'000	Average direct labour cost per batch $'000	Rate of learning %
1	280	280.00	0
2	476	238.00	85
4	809	202.25	85
8	1,376	172.00	85

(c) <u>Implications of the findings in parts (a) and (b)</u>

The actual rate of learning based on **the actual costs** recorded shows that the rate of learning is lower than expected. Costs are decreasing at a slower rate than anticipated given the budgeted direct labour cost. The learning period is longer than anticipated.

Moreover, the **actual direct labour cost** of the first batch is $30 higher than originally planned. This is due to a longer or slower production than expected paid at a standard labour rate so slower than expected.

Management need to consider how these changes will affect the profitability of the new product as these will increase the cost above that estimated. If price is based on cost then management may have to re-consider how price is calculated. They could also look at methods of reducing costs such as target costing, and value analysis.

We have drawn up a table here that shows how these changes affect contribution.

	Original estimate Batch 1 $'000	Revised estimate Batch 1 $'000	Revised estimate Batch 8 $'000	Actual Batch 8 $'000
Market price	500	500	4,000	4,000
Direct costs other than labour 300,000/batch	300	300	2,400	2,400
Direct labour (W)	250	280	1,224.80	1,376
Contribution	50.00	(80.00)	375.20	224.00

Working

Estimate. The direct labour figure for batch 8 of $1,224.80 is calculated in Step 3 and Step 4 in the solution to part (a) above.

41 Small company – learning curves

Text references: Chapter 7 for learning curve theory and formula; Chapter 6 for penetration pricing.

Top tips: Remember to relate your answer to part (a) to the company mentioned in the scenario – it is tempting to write all you know about learning curve theory, but this would only be answering part of the question. In part (c), avoid just defining penetration pricing – relate what you know about the circumstances in which learning curve theory may be applied to those in which penetration pricing may be used.

Easy marks: If you know the learning curve formula, part (b) provides 3 easy marks.

(a) The **learning curve's concept** is that, as complex and labour-intensive tasks are repeated, the **average time taken** to complete each task will **decrease**. In addition, learning curve theory states that the **cumulative average time** taken per unit or task **will fall** by a constant percentage every time total output doubles.

The learning curve concept is **relevant** to this company as its product is produced using a **labour intensive** production process. The company is also **developing a new product** , for which a learning curve effect could be expected. As the company is a small one, it may be that the product will be made in **relatively small quantities**, a characteristic of production for which labour time should be expected to declare as output increases.

(b)   Expected time for the 6th unit of output:

Learning curve formula:

$Y_x = aX^b$

$Y_6 = 40 \times 6^{-0.415}$

$Y_6 = 19$ minutes (to the nearest minute)

$Y_5 = 40 \times 5^{-0.415}$

$= 20.511$ or 20 minutes (to the nearest minute)

Cumulative units	Cumulative average time per unit (mins)	Total time (mins)
6	19	114
5	20	100
		14

The expected time for the 6th unit of output is therefore 14 minutes.

(c)   Implications of the learning curve where a penetration pricing policy is adopted:

One of the circumstances in which **penetration pricing** may be appropriate is where significant **economies of scale** can be made from producing high levels of output, and companies therefore initially charge very low prices to gain a foothold in the market. **Learning curve theory** is more appropriate for **products that are produced in small quantities**, therefore a company adopting penetration pricing are less likely to be using a highly labour intensive process, given the desire to produce large volumes. **Learning curve theory does not apply itself to highly mechanised processes** that are generally employed to achieve high levels of output.

However, learning curve theory can be useful when quoting selling prices that are calculated on a **'cost plus'** basis. Penetration pricing tends to involve setting the **lowest possible price** whilst still covering costs (a "cost plus zero" approach). Learning curve theory may be useful for **identifying the cost** of producing a product and thus identifying the lowest possible price that could be charged.

42   Q Organisation

Text references. Chapter 6 explains the product life cycle and pricing. Chapter 7 explains the learning curve, Chapter 6 again should give you material to help you calculate an optimum price.

Top tips. Part (a) of the question requires you to identify the four stages of the product life cycle and the appropriate pricing policies for each stage. Think about the product and apply your knowledge to this specific product.

Part (b)(i) requires you to remember how to calculate a rate of learning and a learning curve.

Part (b)(ii) should just follow on: once you have total variable costs for each level of demand you can calculate the optimal contribution.

Part (b)(iii) requires a careful reading of the question – you need to calculate the average variable cost for each learning stage after the initial phase identified in part (ii).

Examiner's comments. Most students made a good attempt at this question but many did not actually answer the question. In part (b), too many candidates had only a basic understanding of the learning curve!

Common errors included:

- Describing life cycle costing rather than the product life cycle
- Not relating appropriate pricing policies to the stage of the product life cycle
- Suggesting inappropriate pricing policies
- Not using initiative by introducing the figure calculated in part (b)(i) into part (b)(ii)
- Applying the learning curve formula incorrectly especially when the quantity being produced falls outside the 'doubling' process (part (b)(ii))
- Applying the learning curve effect to the full £60
- Not understanding what was required in part (iii)

(a)   The product life cycle comprises four stages:

> **Easy marks**. The examiner gave two marks for identifying the four stages correctly.

Introduction

In the **introduction stage** the company needs to price the product to achieve its market strategy using either **penetration or skimming pricing policies**.

A penetration policy is used with the objective of achieving a high level of demand very quickly by using a low price that is affordable to a large number of potential customers. This has the effect of discouraging new suppliers to the market because the unit profitability is relatively low, but the high volume of sales enables the initial supplier to recover their development costs.

A skimming policy is particularly appropriate to a product that has a novelty value or that is technologically advanced. Such a policy uses a price that is high and this restricts the volume of sales since only high worth customers can afford the product, but the high unit profitability enables the initial supplier to recover their development costs. However, the high unit profitability attracts competitors to the market so that it is important for the initial supplier to be able to reduce the price and can prevent new entrants to the market from being able to reverse engineer the product and make significant profits from little or no development investment.

The Q organisation is launching a technologically advanced product which will be demanded by high worth customers who are proud to be amongst the first to own such a state of the art product. This is exactly the type of product for which a price skimming policy is appropriate.

The initial price will be high as this will quickly recover the development costs of the product. The high worth customers will not be deterred from buying the product as it will be sold on the basis of its technological value rather than its price.

Growth

Competitors will be attracted to the product by its high price and will seek to compete with it by introducing their own version of the product at much lower development costs (by reverse engineering Q's product) so it is important for Q to **reduce the price** during the **growth stage** of the product's life cycle There may be many price reductions during this phase so that the product gradually becomes more affordable to lower social economic groups.

Maturity

As the product enters the **maturity stage** the price will need to be **lowered further**, though a profitable contribution ratio would continue to be earned. Oligopolistic competition is often found in this stage, but provided Q has gained market share and survived until this stage the opportunity to make profit and cash surpluses should exist. **However, in this type of market the price will tend to be set by the market and Q will have to accept that price**. Thus Q will need to focus on the control of its costs to ensure that the product will remain profitable.

Decline

When the product enters the **decline phase** a **loyal group of customers** may continue to be prepared to pay **a reasonable price** and at this price the product will continue to be profitable, especially as costs continue to reduce. **Eventually the price will be lowered to marginal cost or even lower in** order to sell off inventories of what is now an obsolete product as it has been replaced by a more technologically advanced item.

> **Top tips**. Eight marks were available for discussing the pricing policies appropriate to each stage of the product life cycle.
>
> See the comments in bold – these are key phases that will get you marks.
>
> Remember to look at Q's specific product to determine which pricing policy applies.

(b) (i)

Cumulative number of units	Total variable cost/unit £	Affected by learning £	Not affected by learning £
10,000	60.00	30.00	30.00
20,000	56.10 (W2)	26.10	30.00
30,000	54.06 (W3)	24.06	30.00
40,000	52.71	22.71	30.00

Workings

1 Calculation of rate of learning

At 10,000 units, variable cost affected by learning = £30

At 40,000 units, variable cost affected by learning = £22.71

Let the rate of learning be r.

$30r^2 = 22.71$

$r^2 = 0.757$

$r = 0.87$

2 We can now derive the variable cost affected by learning for 20,000 units, $= 30r = 30 \times 0.87 = 26.10$

The variable cost affected by learning for 30,000 units will require the use of a formula for the learning curve.

a = £30

X = 3 (cumulative number of batches)

$b = \dfrac{\text{Log } 0.87}{\text{Log } 2}$

  = –0.201

Thus $Y = aX^b$

  $= 30 \times 3^{-0.201}$

  $= \underline{24.06}$

(ii) Optimum price at which the DVD recorder should be sold.

Demand in Units	Price/unit £	Variable cost /unit £	Contribution/ unit £	Total contribution £
10,000	100	60.00	40.00	400,000
20,000	80	56.10	23.90	478,000
30,000	69	54.06	14.94	448,200
40,000	62	52.71	9.29	371,600

The price which gives the optimum contribution is £80/unit.

> **Top tips.** Doing this calculation and identifying the best price would get you three marks.

(iii) The initial launch phase identified in (b)(ii) is up to a level of at 20,000 units.

The target contribution is £45,000 per month.

To determine unit costs if after the initial phase, total volume is between 20,000 and 30,000 units, the average cost would be

$$\frac{30,000 \times 54.06 - 20,000 \times 56.10}{10,000} = £49.98$$

Likewise between 30,000 and 40,000 units, the average cost would be:

$$\frac{40,000 \times 52.71 - 30,000 \times 54.06}{10,000} = £48.66$$

Therefore, at between 20,000 and 30,000 units, the required sales level is calculated as:

$$\frac{£45,000}{£(57 - 49.98)} = \underline{6,410 \text{ units}}$$

Likewise between 30,000 and 40,000 units, required sales are:

$$\frac{£45,000}{£(57 - 48.66)} = \underline{5,396 \text{ units}}$$

43 AVX plc

Text references. Look at Chapter 7 to answer part (a), Chapter 6 for part (b) and Chapters 6 and 7 for part (c).

Top tips. We have given you a lot of information to help you answer this question. What you need to do can be broken down into easily managed parts.

The answer may look very long but this is mainly because we have shown both methods. You will only use one method during the exam so don't be put off!

You may have struggled to know where to start with part (a)(i), and may not have known how to work out the rates of learning. So one approach is to look at the information in the question and see if you can work out what you need to do once you have established the information available. You have a table with batches that double in each subsequent month. What does this remind you of from reading your text? You have standard labour hours and you have labour efficiency variances from which you can work out actual hours.

First, what you need to do is work out the actual hours per month by deducting the favourable efficiency variance (translated into hours by dividing by £10/h) for each month from the standard labour hours for each month. Even if your knowledge of variances is a bit vague it should be possible to work out that a labour efficiency variance is measuring a **speeding up** in activity by labour and so it is measuring how much **quicker** workers become over the six months.

Then work out the cumulative actual hours.

Use this to calculate the cumulative average actual hours.

Finally divide each month's cumulative average actual hours by that of the following month and this should give the rate of learning. The examiner gave three marks for this. Remember that learning curve theory states that the cumulative average time per unit falls by a constant percentage [the rate of learning] every time total output of the product doubles.

Part (b) was well answered so we don't need to dwell on this. Four marks could be earned for deriving the price equation and then the rest of the marks were for applying this equation to get a profit-maximising selling price.

Part (c) saw many candidates describing market skimming and penetration rather than identifying that the company needed to move from a cost plus price to a target price method. Up to four marks were possible for the differences between standard and target costs and three marks for explaining the reasons to reconsider pricing policy.

Easy marks. The second part of the question requires you to calculate a profit-maximising selling price using data from the question. The formula is given. If you know that MR = MC (and you should), you just need to slot the data into the formula to calculate the answer.

Then the final part of the question asked in part (i) for an explanation of the difference between standard and target costs. This is book knowledge and should have presented you with few problems.

Examiner's comments. Many candidates couldn't relate the efficiency variant to the learning aim. Part (c) revealed basic flaws in understanding such as not being able to explain 'standard cost' and not picking up from c(i) that AVX needed to move from cost plus pricing to target selling.

(a) (i) Rates of learning

We have drawn up the table below based on the method sketched out in our top tips above. The data has been worked out and set out sequentially as follows:

 Take the number of batches in each month and work out the cumulative batches to date.

 Work out the standard hours per month (standard hours per batch multiplied by the number of batches produced in the month).

 Work out the actual hours per month by deducting the appropriate labour efficiency variance **in hours** (divide the monetary variance by £10 to get the number of hours) from the standard hours per month. We deduct the variance because the actual hours are less than the standard hours, as indicated by the fact that the variance is favourable.

 Work out the cumulative actual hours by adding each month's actual hours to the total of preceding months.

 Work out the cumulative average actual hours by dividing the cumulative actual hours by the cumulative batches produced.

 Finally, work out the rate of learning, which is each month's cumulative average actual hours divided by that of the preceding month.

Month	Batches	Cumulative batches	Standard hours per month	Actual hours per month	Cumulative actual hours	Cumulative Average actual hours	Rate of learning
November	1	1	50.0	50.00	50.00	50.00	
December	1	2	50.0	33.00	83.00	41.50	0.83
January	2	4	100.0	54.78	137.78	34.45	0.83
February	4	8	200.0	91.07	228.85	28.61	0.83
March	8	16	400.0	228.85	457.70	28.61	0.00
April	16	32	800.0	457.70	915.40	28.61	0.00

(ii) From the table it is clear that the **learning period ended** after February when the rate of learning was at 83%. This means that after February the production time taken is no longer decreasing and so labour efficiency savings are not being made. The company could look at training and review processes to see if the **learning process could be continued** or consider switching to a more mechanised process. This also means that the company should make **decisions** involving costs, for instance profit maximisation and pricing policy decisions, **based on this now constant labour time per batch**.

(b) Profit-maximising selling price per batch

The formula as given in the question is $P = a - bx$ and $MR = a - 2bx$, where a= price at which demand is NIL.

Demand is 16 batches at a price of £1,200 (£960 + 25% mark up) and demand varies by 1 batch for every £20 change in price so b = 20.

Marginal cost is £672.72 from the question.

The price at which demand would be nil = £1,200 + £20 × 16 = £1,520.

So, putting these into the equation:

$P = 1,520 - 20x$

Price is maximised when MR = MC

MR = 1,520 – 40x = £672.72
Therefore x = 21.18
And P = 1,520 – 20 × 21.18 = £1,096.40

This is the profit maximising selling price per batch for product CB45.

(c) (i) <u>The difference between standard costs and target costs</u>

A **standard cost** is an expected cost for a unit of product or service based on the resources required (materials, labour etc) and the expected prices for the resources. Standard costs are used in standard costing systems, which aim to control an organisation's costs.

A **target cost** is calculated by deducting a target profit from a predetermined selling price based on customers' views. Functional analysis, value engineering and value analysis are used to change production methods and/or reduce expected costs so that the target cost is met. This is all part of a target costing system.

Target costs are therefore based on the price set by the external market, a factor over which an organisation has no control. Standard costs, on the other hand, are internally-derived costs to be used as part of an internal control system.

(ii) <u>Review of pricing policy</u>

When the product was **new** and the price was first set, this was possibly the **only product of its kind in the market**. So the price charged was **high**. The price was based on earning a 25% margin on the cost, to ensure a profit was made. This strategy of setting high prices when a product is first launched is known as **market skimming**.

The product has now been on the market for six months. **Competitors** have entered the market with their own versions. They have able to work out how the product is made and hence **copy** it. AVX plc is therefore probably facing competition and is unable to sell at £1,200 per batch. The price therefore needs to be **successively lowered** in order to **maintain some market share** and continue to earn profits. By adopting **target costing** and applying continual pressure to ensure target costs are met, the organisation can charge prices that the market will pay and maintain profits.

44 Cost management techniques again

> **Top tips.** To score well on this question you must cover the traditional approaches too.

<u>Activity based management</u>

<u>Traditional approach</u>

Traditional costing systems, notably **absorption costing, assume** that all products **consume resources in proportion to their production volumes**. While this may be true for overheads such as power costs, it does not necessarily hold for all overheads, or an increasing proportion of them, especially those connected with support services. The amount of **overhead allocated** to individual products by absorption costing therefore bears **very little resemblance** to the **amount of overhead actually incurred** by the products and hence gives management **minimal understanding of the behaviour of overhead costs and**, consequently, they have a lack of **ability to control/reduce them**.

<u>ABC/ABM approach</u>

Activity based costing (**ABC**) attempts to overcome this problem by identifying the activities or transactions (**cost drivers**) which underlie an organisation's activities and which cause the incidence of the activity, and hence the cost of the activity (overheads) to increase. Costs can then be attributed to products according to the number of cost drivers they cause/consume using cost driver rates.

Activity based management (ABM) is the term given to those **management processes that use the information provided by an activity-based cost analysis to improve organisational profitability.**

ABM and cost reduction

Because ABM analyses costs on the basis of what causes them, rather than on the basis of type of expense/cost centre, it provides management with vital information on why costs are being incurred. If management can **reduce the incidence of the cost driver, they can reduce the associated cost.**

ABM involves a variety of **cost reduction techniques**.

(a)   Ensuring activities are performed as efficiently as possible
(b)   Controlling, reducing or eliminating the need to perform activities that do not add value for customers
(c)   Minimising cost drivers
(d)   Improving the design of products

In short, it aims to **ensure that customer needs are met while fewer demands are made on organisational resources**.

45   Software development company

Text references. Activity based costing is covered in Chapter 8 of the Study Text.

Top tips. In part (a), you are really being asked for differences between costs using absorption costing and costs using ABC. As ABC tends to give a truer picture of costs (and probably a higher total cost as a result), selling prices based on mark-up on costs will be higher and this will have an effect on market share.

Part (b) is asking for a comparison of profits between the current use of absorption costing to find selling prices and the new regime of ABC. Remember to answer the question – that is, assess the impact on remaining profits – rather than just calculate the profits under each technique and leave it at that. The calculations themselves are not difficult – the main issue in this question was determining what the question is asking for. In the absence of any other figures for absorption costing, we have to assume that the profit using this technique is the difference between the given selling prices and the activity based cost per unit.

Easy marks. The calculation of revised selling prices using a 25% mark up on ABC is quite straightforward, as is the calculation of revised profit.

(a)   The company has been using traditional absorption costing to calculate product costs and thus selling price. However, activity based costing (ABC) gives a truer reflection of total costs and will probably give a higher total cost of the products. This means that when the same mark-up is added to the ABC total cost figure, the selling price will be higher. An increase in selling price will result in a lower market share

Market share for VBG3 in particular seems to be very high which suggests that the mark-up percentage is being applied to an artificially low total cost. In fact, the total cost under ABC is higher than the current selling price, suggesting that the product is being sold at a loss.

(b)

	AXPL1	FDR2	VBG3
	$	$	$
Total cost using ABC	48.00	42.00	75.00
25% mark-up	12.00	10.50	18.75
Selling price	60.00	52.50	93.75
Current selling price	50.00	75.00	65.00
Increase/(decrease)	10.00	(22.50)	28.75

For every $2 increase in price there will be a 3% reduction in market share. For every $2 decrease in selling price there will be a 3% increase in market share.

	AXPL1	FDR2	VBG3
Increase/(decrease) in market share (W1)	(15%)	33.75%	(43.125%)
Revised market share	30%	48.75%	36.875%
Market share (units)	750	1,462.5	1,475
Profit per unit (W2)	$12.00	$10.50	$18.75
Lifetime profit (units x profit)	$9,000	$15,351	$27,656.25

Total lifetime profit = $52,007.25

Workings

1   For AXPL1: price has increased by $10 therefore market share will decrease by:

$(^{10}/_2) \times 3 = 15\%$

For FDR2: price has decreased by $22.50 therefore market share will increase by:

$(^{22.50}/_2) \times 3 = 33.75\%$

For VBG3: price has increased by $28.75 therefore market share will decrease by:

$(^{28.75}/_2) \times 3 = 43.125\%$

2   Profit per unit = Selling price using ABC – ABC per unit

<u>Current lifetime profitability based on traditional absorption cost pricing</u>

	AXPL1	FDR2	VBG3
Profit/(loss) per unit (W3)	$2.00	$33.00	$(10.00)
Market share (units)	1,125	450	3,200
Lifetime profit/(loss)	$2,250	$14,850	$(32,000)

Total lifetime loss = $(14,900)

Overall increase in profitability = $52,007.25 + 14,900 = $66,907.25

3   Profit/(loss) per unit = Original selling price using absorption costing – ABC per unit

46   Pharmacy

Text references. Chapter 8 covers Pareto analysis in detail.

Top tips. The report in (b), the types of comment which usually result from a Pareto analysis (on the lines that 'these categories account for X% of sales but only Y% of stock') are not really appropriate in this case and you are advised to concentrate on the rankings of the different categories. Focus on the range of discussion points raised when reviewing the answer. Interpretation of results will be where marks are awarded in exam questions.

REPORT

To: Management
From: Management accountant
Date: XX November 20X7
Subject: <u>Sales and stock in pharmacies X and Z</u>

1   <u>Introduction</u>

1.1   A **Pareto analysis** has been carried out using last year's sales and stock figures for pharmacies X and Z. The findings and some comments on points of importance are given below.

2   <u>Findings</u>

2.1   There is a **marked difference** between the two pharmacies in terms of the **amount of stock held relative to sales**.

Pharmacy	Sales	Stock	
	£'000	£'000	%
X	160	46	29
Z	100	43	43

2.2 The table below shows the **sales rank minus the stock rank** for each category.

Category	Difference in ranks of sales and stock	
	X	Z
OTC	–2	–2
Toiletries	1	1
Photo	–1	–1
Food/drink	0	–1
Baby	–2	–1
Sanpro	–2	–1
Other	–1	–1
Foot	–3	2
Cosmetics	7	3
Hair	2	3
Perfume	4	5

As can be seen from the table, the rankings for sales are **broadly similar** to **those for stock** in both pharmacies, with three **exceptions**.

2.3 **Exception 1. Cosmetics** stands out as the category which has particularly **high stock levels** compared to sales. This is the case in both pharmacies but is specially marked in X where the category is second in stock and only ninth in sales.

2.4 **Exception 2. Perfumery** is another category which has quite markedly **high stock levels** compared to sales, being eleventh in sales and sixth in stock in Z and, to a lesser extent, hair-care products also seem to involve high stock levels.

2.5 **Exception 3.** The categories which require lower stock levels than might be expected from their sales are shown by the negatives in the table and are not specially marked. In both pharmacies, OTC has a sales level ranked two points better than its stock level.

2.6 Comparing the two pharmacies, aside from the points made above, the **rankings of sales and stock are broadly similar.**

3 Recommendations

3.1 Management should give further consideration to a number of issues.

3.2 **Issue 1. The proportionately high level of stock being held in Z.** Can it be reduced to something closer to the 29% of pharmacy X?

3.3 Issue 2. Cosmetics, perfumery and hair-care all seem to require, to different extents, high stock levels. Is this necessary or can stock levels be reduced?

3.4 **Issue 3.** It might be a useful exercise, prior to taking action over the 'problem' categories, to **investigate the categories**, such as OTC, **which have low stock levels**.

Signed: Management accountant

47 W manufacturing

Text references. Activity based costing is covered in Chapter 7.

Top tips. You may find it easier to calculate the cost driver rates per batch. Divide the balance by the number of units per batch to derive the unit cost.

Easy marks. If you are familiar with Pareto analysis you will pick up a few marks for explaining the concept.

(a) Calculation of cost driver rates:

Machine maintenance
$100,000 / ((1,500 x 3) + (2,500 x 2) + (4,000 x 3)) = \$4·65 per machine hour

Machine setups
$70,000 / [{(1,500/50) x 2} + {(2,500/100) x 3} + {(4,000/500) x 1}] = \$489·51 per setup

Purchasing

$90,000 / [{(1,500/50) x 4} + {(2,500/100) x 4} + {(4,000/500) x 6}] = $335·82 per order

Material Handling

$60,000 / [{(1,500/50) x 10} + {(2,500/100) x 5} + {(4,000/500) x 4}] = $131·29 per movement

Other Costs

$80,000 / ((1,500 x 2) + (2,500 x 4) + (4,000 x 3)) = $3·20 per labour hour

Product	X ($)	Y ($)	Z ($)
Batch costs:			
Machine setup	979.02	1,468.53	489.51
Purchasing	1,343.28	1,343.28	2,014.92
Material handling	1,312.90	656.45	525.16
	3,635.20	3,468.26	3,029.59
Batch size	50	100	500
Unitised batch costs	72.70	34.68	6.06
Machine maintenance	13.95	9.30	13.95
Other costs	6.40	12.80	9.60
Product overhead costs	93.05	56.78	29.61

(b) Pareto analysis is based on the general principle that 80% of wealth is owned by 20% of the population (**the 80:20 rule**). W believes that 80% ($320,000) of its overhead costs relate to 4 activities (cost drivers). The remaining $80,000 (20%) is considered to be attributable to a number of other factors.

By monitoring the 4 cost drivers identified and measuring actual results against budget on a regular basis, **W will be controlling 80% of production overhead costs**.

48 XY Accountancy Services

> **Text references.** Activity-based costing is covered in Chapter 8.
>
> **Top tips.** Clearly show your workings for each cost driver to maximise your score.
>
> **Easy marks.** You should score well in this question providing you show all workings and calculate the difference between the old and new costing systems.

Fees charged to clients under new ABC costing system

	Client A $	Client B $	Client C $
Accounts preparation and advice	32,222	8,055	10,955
Requesting missing information	480	1,200	720
Issuing fee payment reminders	75	300	375
Holding client meetings	960	240	480
Travelling to clients	600	2,400	0
Total costs	34,337	12,195	12,530
Total cost on original basis *	40,280	10,070	13,695
Client fees – new basis (20% mark-up on total cost)	41,204	14,634	15,036
Client fees – original basis (20% mark-up on total cost)	48,336	12,084	16,434
Increase / (Decrease)	(7,132)	2,550	(1,398)

*$725,000 (total costs) / 18,000 hours = $40.28 per hour

Workings

Cost driver rates

Activity	Working	Rate	Client A	Client B	Client C
Accounts preparation and advice	$580,000 / 18,000 hours	$32.22 per hour	1,000 hours	250 hours	340 hours
Requesting missing information	$30,000 / 250 times	$120.00 per request	4 requests	10 requests	6 requests
Issuing fee payment reminders	$15,000 / 400 times	$37.50 per reminder	2 reminders	8 reminders	10 reminders
Holding client meetings	$60,000 / 250 meetings	$240.00 per meeting	4 reminders	1 reminder	2 reminders
Travelling to clients	$40,000 / 10,000 miles	$4.00 per mile	150 miles	600 miles	0 miles

49 ST

Marking scheme

		Marks
(a)	Cost driver rates	2
	Customer costs	2
	Measurement of customer profits	2
		6
(b)	Explanation of two examples relevant to scenario (2 marks each)	4

(a)   <u>Direct Customer Profitability Analysis for each customer</u>

	B	D
	$'000	$'000
Factory contribution	75	40.5
Sales visits	6	3
Order processing	7.5	2
Normal deliveries	22.5	7.5
Urgent deliveries	<u>10</u>	<u>0</u>
	<u>46</u>	<u>12.5</u>
Profit	<u>29</u>	<u>28</u>

Workings

Cost driver rates

Activity	Working	Rate	B	D
Sales visits	$50,000 cost / 200 sales visits	$250 per visit	24 sales visits × $250= $6,000	12 sales visits × $250= $3,000
Order processing	$70,000 cost / 700 orders placed	$100 per order	75 orders placed × $100 = $7,500	20 orders placed × $100= $2,000
Normal delivery	$120,000 cost / 240 normal deliveries	$500 per normal delivery	45 normal deliveries × $500 = $22,500	15 normal deliveries × $500= $7,500
Urgent deliveries	$60,000 cost / 30 urgent deliveries	$2,000 per urgent delivery	5 urgent deliveries × $2,000 = $10,000	0 urgent deliveries

(b) How ST could use DCPA to increase its profits

Customer profitability analysis (CPA) provides important information which allows an organisation to determine both which **classes of customers it should concentrate** on and the **prices it should charge**. CPA applies the principles of activity-based costing to split customer costs into key activities.

ST could improve profitability by considering how it could **alter its internal processes** to reduce the costs of the key activities. For example, ST could no longer offer an urgent delivery service to customers.

The company could also **reflect** the **costs caused by customer behaviour** by increasing the sales price of the product to yield greater margins.

50 ZP plc

Text references. Chapter 8 covers the material needed to answer this question.

Top tips. You might have come unstuck in part (a). However what the examiner appears to want is for you to pick out only those costs that can be identified to customers and attribute costs to them using appropriate cost drivers. Part (b) then asks for you to compare and contrast your calculations in (a) with the current costing system and make recommendations. Part (c) asks for a written answer on ABC cost classifications and how these would apply to ZP plc.

In part (a) roughly equal marks could be earned for calculating travel costs, accommodation costs, and other costs, for each client profile. In part (b) once again marks were evenly spread between comparing costs recognising the similarity of costs using each system, pros and cons of using ABC, and other benefits of ABC. Part (c) awarded four marks each to ABC classifications as that could be used by ZP and examples in ZP of each.

Easy marks. Even if you think the values you calculate in (a) are incorrect, base your comments in (b) on your results. Make sensible suggestions.

(a) Attribute costs to client group using an ABC system

	Working	D £'000	E £'000	F £'000	Total £'000
Consultants' salaries	1	40	140	60	240
Travel	2	4	7	4	15
Accommodation	3	0	8	3	11
Other costs					
Facility costs	4	31	108	46	185
		75	263	113	451

This table gives the activity-based costs of supporting each customer group based on the factors that cause the costs to be incurred as noted in the Working notes.

Workings

1   These can be attributed as at present on the basis of chargeable hours. Effectively they are direct costs for each client group.

Total cost = £240,000

Budgeted chargeable hours = 6,000

Rate per hour = £40

Cost attributable to each group = chargeable hours per client × number of clients in group × £40

2   The travel cost is driven by the distance in miles to clients

Number of cost driver units = 50 × 3 × 10 + 70 × 8 × 5 + 100 × 3 × 5 = 5,800

Cost per cost driver (ie per mile) = $\dfrac{£15,000}{5,800}$ = £2.59

Cost attributable to each group = number of miles x number of visits × number of clients × £2.59

3   The accommodation cost is driven by the number of visits to clients where the distance to the client is over 50 miles.

The cost of accommodation is therefore not attributable to client group d as the distance is not more than 50 miles.

Number of cost driver units = 8 × 5 + 3 × 5 = 55

Cost per cost driver = £11,000/55 = £200

4   These costs have been attributed to each client group using chargeable hours as a cost driver. It could also be argued however that they would not be attributed to each client group using an activity based system, as they are facility level activities and so would not be driven by an activity which can be related to clients.

(b)   Compare and contrast the current costing system and that using ABC

The current costing system uses chargeable hours as a basis for apportioning costs. Thus, comparing the costs attributed under activity based costing with those attributed by the current system:

	Cost rate	D £'000	E £'000	F £'000	Total £'000
Chargeable hours needed		1,000	3,500	1,500	6,000
Costs attributed using cost rate	£75/hr	75	263	113	451
Costs using ABC		75	263	113	451
Difference		0	0	0	0

Using an activity basis for allocating shows the cost of supporting individual customer groups by relating the costs incurred to the factors or 'cost drivers' that cause them to be incurred in the first place. This shows that the particular cost allocation using cost drivers results in the same allocation as using a blanket chargeable hours basis. However this is perhaps not surprising as the bulk of the costs allocated are the consultants' salaries and these are driven by chargeable hours, as they are direct costs of servicing clients.

However this would not always necessarily be the case especially where a cost driver was say, machine hours for producing tools, yet a chargeable hours basis as used here were adopted.

So in summary, the senior consultant's recommendation on using cost drivers allows a more accurate understanding of the actual costs incurred as a result of the activity for each client group.

(c)   Classifications of activities using ZP plc as an example

The **manufacturing cost hierarchy** categorises costs and activities as unit level, batch level, product/process level and organisational/facility level.

To reflect today's more **complex business environment**, recognition must be given to the fact that **costs are created and incurred because their cost drivers occur at different levels. Cost driver analysis investigates, quantifies and explains the relationships between cost drivers and their related costs**.

Activities and their related costs fall into four different categories, known as the **manufacturing cost hierarchy**. The **categories determine the type of activity cost driver required**.

Traditionally it has been assumed that if costs did not vary with changes in production at the unit level, they were fixed rather than variable. The analysis above shows this assumption to be false, and that costs vary for reasons other than production volume or chargeable hours. To determine an accurate estimate of product or service cost, **costs should be accumulated at each successively higher level of costs**.

Unit level costs are allocated over number of units produced, batch level costs over the number of units in the batch, product level costs over the number of units produced by the product line. These costs are all related to units of product (merely at different levels) and so can be gathered together at the product level to match with revenue. Organisational level costs are not product related, however, and so should simply be deducted from net revenue.

Such an approach gives a far greater insight into product profitability.

Classification level	Cause of cost	Types of cost in ZP plc	Necessity of cost
Unit level activities and costs	Production/acquisition of a single unit of product or delivery of single unit of service	Consultants' salaries	For every hour worked for client
Batch level activities and costs	A group of things being made, handled or processed	Travel to clients, accommodation	Once for each client visit
Product/process level activities and costs	Development, production or acquisition of different items	Support staff, advertising although there is not sufficient information to say what a cost driver for this would be, ordinarily they would be process level costs.	Supports consultants and customers
Organisational/ facility level activities and costs	Some costs cannot be related to a particular product line (or client group); instead they are related to maintaining the buildings and facilities. These costs cannot be related to cost objects with any degree of accuracy and are often excluded from ABC calculations for this reason.	Office premises, telephone, comms and fax.	Supports the overall service process

51 KL

Text references. You will find data to answer this question in the introductory chapter and chapters 6 and 8 of your Study Text.

Top tips. This question is in **four parts** and looks at **three issues**. Firstly, it asks for a discussion of two methods of setting price. Secondly, it asks you to calculate full cost and then activity based cost (ABC) for three products. Finally you are asked to explain how ABC can provide useful management information.

The P2 examiner often sets a question looking at the contrast between traditional costing methods and 'modern' systems such as activity based costing.

Part (a) wants you to **compare and contrast marginal cost plus pricing and total cost plus pricing**. Don't panic – we have made more points in our answer than you would need to in the real exam.

Don't do a mind dump and write all you know, as this will not be rewarded. Make concise points and keep to short paragraphs to make it easier for the marker to read your script.

Part (b) is asking for a **short calculation of full cost** per unit using absorption costing data from the question. There shouldn't be anything tricky for you to consider here.

In (c) you need to calculate the **full cost using activity costing**. The best approach is to break your answer down into manageable workings as we have done and follow these through to the ultimate unit cost calculation asked for.

Part (d) is discursive and wants you to **refer to the company** when making your explanation about ABC.

Easy marks. Parts (a), (b) and (c) are self-contained so you could answer then in any order. Part (b) is very straight forward and should be able to be answered using information you have brought forward into P2 from your earlier studies.

(a)   <u>Problems with and advantages of full cost-plus pricing</u>

There are several **problems** with relying on a full cost approach to pricing.

(i)   It fails to recognise that since demand may be determining price, there will be a profit-maximising combination of price and demand.

(ii)   There may be a need to adjust prices to market and demand conditions.

(iii)   Budgeted output volume needs to be established. Output volume is a key factor in the overhead absorption rate.

(iv)   A suitable basis for overhead absorption must be selected, especially where a business produces more than one product.

However, it is a **quick, simple and cheap** method of pricing which can be delegated to junior managers (which is particularly important with jobbing work where many prices must be decided and quoted each day) and, since the size of the profit margin can be varied, a decision based on a price in excess of full cost should ensure that a company working at normal capacity will **cover all of its fixed costs and make a profit.**

<u>The advantages and disadvantages of a marginal cost-plus approach to pricing</u>

Here are the **advantages**.

(i)   It is a **simple and easy** method to use.

(ii)   The **mark-up percentage can be varied**, and so mark-up pricing can be adjusted to reflect demand conditions.

(iii)   It **draws management attention to contribution**, and the effects of higher or lower sales volumes on profit. In this way, it helps to create a better awareness of the concepts and implications of marginal costing and cost-volume-profit analysis. For example, if a product costs $10 per unit and a mark-up of 150% is added to reach a price of $25 per unit, management should be clearly aware that every additional $1 of sales revenue would add 60 pence to contribution and profit.

There are, of course, **drawbacks** to marginal cost-plus pricing.

(i)   Although the size of the mark-up can be varied in accordance with demand conditions, it does not ensure that sufficient attention is paid to demand conditions, competitors' prices and profit maximisation.

(ii)   It ignores fixed overheads in the pricing decision, but the sales price must be sufficiently high to ensure that a profit is made after covering fixed costs.

(b)   Calculate the full cost per unit of each product using absorption costing

The full cost of each product will include indirect costs allocated to each product using a predetermined overhead absorption rate. In the case of KL, this is based on **direct labour hours**.

	W $	X $	Y $
Variable cost/unit			
Direct materials	35.00	45.00	30.00
Direct labour	40.00	30.00	50.00
Production overhead (W)	18.00	13.50	22.50
Full cost/unit	93.00	88.50	102.50

Working

Total overheads = $1,044,000

	W	X	Y	Total
Total labour hours				
Hrs per unit	4	3	5	
Budgeted annual production	15,000	24,000	20,000	
Total annual direct labour hrs	60,000	72,000	100,000	232,000

$$\text{Overhead absorption rate (OAR)} = \frac{\$1,044}{232,000}$$

OAR per direct labour hour = $4.50/hr per direct labour hour

	W	X	Y
Hrs per unit	4	3	5
Production overhead absorbed per unit	18.00	13.50	22.50

(c)   (i)   Calculate the full cost per unit of each product using ABC

We have listed the steps taken to calculate the unit costs using an ABC system of costing. The references to workings are to the workings below.

STEP 1   Work out the annual activity for each cost driver.

Working

Annual activity

	W	X	Y	Total $
Batches				
Batch size (units)	500	400	1,000	
Annual units	15,000	24,000	20,000	
Annual number of batches	30	60	20	110
Supplier orders				
Per batch	4	3	5	
Annual number of batches	30	60	20	
Annual supplier orders	120	180	100	400
Machine hours				
Per unit	5	8	7	
Annual units	15,000	24,000	20,000	
Annual machine hours	75,000	192,000	140,000	407,000

Use this information to calculate the **activity cost driver rates** in **working below**. You should also be able to use information provided in the table in the question.

Working

Cost driver rates

Material ordering costs $220,000 ÷ 400 supplier orders = $ 550 per supplier order

Machine setup costs $100,000 ÷ 110 batches = $ 909 per batch

Machine running costs $400,000 ÷ 407,000 machine hours = $ 0.98 per machine hour

General facility costs $324,000 ÷ 407,000 machine hours = $ 0.80 per machine hour

Apply these cost driver rates to the supplier orders, batch sizes and machine hours for each product. This will give you the unit cost for each product for each cost pool. See workings 1, 2,3 and 4.

Workings

1		W	X	Y
	Supplier orders per batch	4	3	5
	Batch size	500	400	1,000
	Cost driver (supplier orders) per unit	= 4/500	= 3/400	= 5/1,000
	Activity cost driver rate (per order) $	550	550	550
	Unit cost $	4.40	4.125	2.75

2		W	X	Y
	Batch size in units	500	400	1,000
	Activity cost driver rate (per batch) $	909	909	909
	Unit cost $	1.82	2.27	0.91

3		W	X	Y
	Machine hours per unit	5	8	7
	Activity cost driver rate $ (per machine hour)	0.98	0.98	0.98
	Unit cost $	4.90	7.84	6.86

4		W	X	Y
	Machine hours per unit	5	8	7
	Activity cost driver rate $ (W5)	0.80	0.80	0.80
	Unit cost $	4.00	6.40	5.60

You should now be able to calculate the **full unit cost** using the information you have already calculated slotted into a table as below.

Using **activity based costing**, unit costs for the three products would be as follows.

	W	X	Y
	$/unit	$/unit	$/unit
Direct material	35.00	45.00	30.00
Direct labour	40.00	30.00	50.00
Material ordering costs (W1)	4.40	4.13	2.75
Machine set-up costs (W2)	1.82	2.27	0.91
Machine running costs (W3)	4.90	7.84	6.86
General facility costs (W4)	4.00	6.40	5.60
	90.12	95.64	96.12

<u>Alternative solution</u>

The alternative way to approach this problem, given that we have information on all the products that the costs have to be shared between, is to use **ratios** rather than cost drivers.

 Work out the annual activity for each cost driver (same calculation as in Step 1 above).

 Allocate costs proportionately according to each product's activity in relation to the total.

	W	X	Y
Material ordering costs	$^{120}/_{400} \times 220,000$	$^{180}/_{400} \times 220,000$	$^{100}/_{400} \times 220,000$
	= 66,000	= 99,000	= 55,000
Machine set-up costs	$^{30}/_{110} \times 100,000$	$^{60}/_{110} \times 100,000$	$^{20}/_{110} \times 100,000$
	= 27,273	= 54,545	= 18,182
Machine running costs	$^{75}/_{407} \times 400,000$	$^{192}/_{407} \times 400,000$	$^{140}/_{407} \times 400,000$
	= 73,710	= 188,698	= 137,592
General facility costs	$^{75}/_{407} \times 324,000$	$^{192}/_{407} \times 324,000$	$^{140}/_{407} \times 324,000$
	= 59,705	= 152,845	= 111,450
Total indirect costs	$226,688	$495,088	$322,224

STEP 3 Calculate indirect cost per unit and full cost per unit

	W	X	Y
Total indirect cost	226,688	495,088	322,224
Budgeted annual production (units)	15,000	24,000	20,000
Indirect cost per unit	$15.12	$20.64	$16.12
	$	$	$
Direct costs per unit			
Material	35.00	45.00	30.00
Labour	40.00	30.00	50.00
Full cost per unit	90.12	95.64	96.12

(ii) <u>How ABC could provide information relevant to decisions regarding profitability</u>

The management team of KL will need to look at **price** and **cost** when it considers profitability. ABC can be useful to business in both areas of decision making The unit costs calculated using ABC differ to those calculated under full cost. These are summarised in the table below.

	W	X	Y
	$	$	$
Full cost per unit	93.00	88.50	102.50
ABC cost per unit	90.12	95.64	96.12
Difference	2.88	(7.14)	6.38

<u>Costing</u>

ABC helps with **cost reduction** because it provides an insight into causal activities and allows organisations to consider the possibility of **outsourcing particular activities**, or even of **moving to different areas in the industry value chain**, eg reduce numbers of orders and increase size of batches.

Many **costs are driven by customers** (delivery costs, discounts, after-sales service and so on), but traditional cost accounting does not account for this. Companies may be trading with certain customers at a loss but may not realise it because costs are not analysed in a way that would reveal the true situation. ABC can be **used in conjunction with customer profitability analysis (CPA)** to determine more accurately the profit earned by serving particular customers.

Pricing

ABC establishes a long-run product cost and because it provides data which can be used to evaluate different business possibilities and opportunities it is particularly suited for decisions such as pricing. Pricing has long-term strategic implications and **average cost** is probably **more important** than **marginal cost** in many circumstances. **An ABC cost is an average cost**, but it is **not always a true cost** because some costs such as depreciation are usually arbitrarily allocated to products. An ABC cost is therefore **not a relevant cost for all decisions.**

Profit

The differences in unit costs between full cost, and ABC cost shown in the table show that management need to consider a few actions from the results of ABC costing. Should they increase the price of X which has a higher ABC cost than full cost?

On the other hand should management reduce the price of Y which has a lower ABC cost than full cost?

52 Retail outlet

> **Text references**. Short-term decisions are covered in Chapter 1B; ABC is covered in Chapter 8.
>
> **Top tips**. There is a lot of information in part (a) and it is thus easy to miss something out. Tackle one option at a time and label each working. Make sure you note that the financial information at the start of the question is on a weekly basis and will have to be multiplied by the appropriate number of weeks. An added complication in Option Two was that relating to the freezers which further affected the selling capacity of the frozen foods section. You have to calculate the floor area that will be allocated to this section before you can determine how many freezers can be accommodated. In part (b), make sure you relate your answer to the retail environment, rather than just stating the benefits of ABC.
>
> **Easy marks**. Some of the relevant costs came straight from the question (such as redecoration costs). Calculation of the loss in sales due to the 10% price reduction in Option One is also straightforward.

(a)   Comparison of the two available options

Option One

Relevant costs and savings:

(1)   Redecoration costs $2,500

(2)   Loss of gross profit after reopening

		$
First four weeks = 30% of $2,650 × 4		3,180
Next four weeks = 20% of $2,650 × 4		2,120
Third four weeks = 10% of $2,650 × 4		1,060
		6,360

(3)   Loss of gross profit during shutdown = 4 × $2,650 = $10,600

(4)   Savings in power for freezers = 4 × $100
                                                          = $400

(5)   Price reduction effects

Basic foods: Revised revenue

First 4 weeks = 70% of $800
Next 4 weeks = 80% of $800   } $1,920 × 4 = $7,680
Third 4 weeks = 90% of $800

10% lost due to price reduction = $768

Canned foods:

Revised revenue

First 4 weeks = 70% of $2,400
Next 4 weeks = 80% of $2,400 } $5,760 × 4 = $23,040
Third 4 weeks = 90% of $2,400

10% lost due to price reduction = $2,304

Total price reduction effect = $3,072

Total Relevant Costs

	$
Redecoration costs (W1)	2,500
Loss of profit due to sales reduction (W2)	6,360
Loss in sales revenue (W5)	3,072
Loss of profit during shutdown (W3)	10,600
Savings in freezer power costs (W4)	(400)
Total relevant costs	22,132

It is assumed that general overheads will still be incurred during the shutdown.

Option Two

(1) Revised floor area

Floor area in total is reduced to 40% of 400m² = 160m²

Distribution of reduced floor area:

Basic foods   50 (unchanged)
Newspapers and Magazines   50 (unchanged)
                                     100

Remaining floor area to be divided between other area = 60m²

(2) Distribution of remaining floor area

Profitability per m² of floor area (using gross margin)

Frozen foods $= \dfrac{950}{100} = \$9.50$ per m²

Canned foods $= \dfrac{1,200}{200} = \$6$ per m²

Floor area allocation

As frozen foods give a high profit per m², as much floor space as possible should be allocated to this range.

Floor space per freezer $= \dfrac{100m^2}{4} = 25m^2$

Of the 60m² remaining, 50m² should be allocated to frozen foods, which is enough for two freezers. The remaining 10m² should be allocated to canned foods.

Floor area proportions

	Original %	Revised~ %
Basic foods	$^{50}/_{400} = 12.5$	$^{50}/_{160} = 31.25$
Newspapers and Magazines	$^{50}/_{400} = 2.5$	$^{50}/_{160} = 31.25$
Frozen foods	$^{100}/_{400} = 25$	$^{50}/_{106} = 31.25$
Canned foods	$^{200}/_{400} = 50$	$^{10}/_{160} = 6.25$

Reduction in floor area%

Basic foods; Newspapers and Magazines = 0

$$\text{Frozen foods} = \frac{100 - 50}{100} = 50\%$$

$$\text{Canned foods} = \frac{200 - 10}{200} = 95\%$$

(3) Freezer cost savings

Two freezers will be non-operational for the six weeks of reduced operation

$$\text{Total savings for this period} = 6 \times 2 \times \frac{\$100}{4} = \$300$$

Four freezers will be non-operational for the 0.5 weeks shutdown

Therefore, total savings for this period = $0.5 \times \$100 = \$50$

Total freezer cost savings = $\underline{\$350}$

(4) Reduction in gross profit (for six weeks of reduced operating)

		$
Frozen foods	$950 × 6 × 50%	2,850
Canned foods	$1,200 × 6 × 95%	6,840
Total reduction		9,690

As Basic foods and Newspapers and Magazines are not suffering reduced floor space, sales revenue and gross profit will be unaffected for these areas.

(5) Reduction in gross profit for 0.5 weeks' shutdown

$$\text{Total Gross Profit for all areas} = [\$200 + 300 + 950 + 1,200] \times 0.5$$
$$= \$2,650 \times 0.5$$
$$= \$1,325$$

Total Relevant Costs

	$
Redecoration	3,500
Product Movement Costs	1,000
Freezer cost savings (W3)	(350)
Reduction in gross profit for 6 weeks' reduced operations (W4)	9,690
Lost profit from shutdown (W5)	1,325
	15,165

As Option 2 results in lower losses, the retail outlet should continue to operate at reduced capacity during the redecoration period.

Alternative solution

You could allocate space to frozen foods and canned foods on a proportionate basis of profitability per unit of area, as follows:

$$\text{Frozen foods} = \frac{9.50}{15.50} \times 60m^2 = 37m^2$$

$$\text{Canned foods} = \frac{6}{15.50} \times 60m^2 = 23m^2$$

The floor area assigned to frozen foods is only sufficient for one freezer, so you can

(1)   Either allocate the remaining 12m² (37 – 25) to canned foods or

(2)   Leave the space empty.

	(1)		(2)	
	Frozen	*Canned*	*Frozen*	*Canned*
Floor area proportions (revised)	$\frac{25}{160}$	$\frac{25}{160}$	$\frac{37}{160}$	$\frac{23}{160}$
	= 15.6%	= 15.6%	= 23.1%	= 14.4%
Reduction in floor area	$\frac{100-25}{100}$	$\frac{200-25}{200}$	$\frac{100-37}{100}$	$\frac{200-23}{200}$
	= 75%	= 87.5%	= 63%	= 88.5%

As only one freezer can be accommodated in the 37m² floor space allocated to frozen foods in alternative (2), the reduction in selling space will be the same as for alternative (1) – that is, 75%.

Freezer cost savings (both alternatives)

Three freezers will be non-operational for the six weeks of reduced operation.

$$\text{Total savings} = 6 \times 3 \times \frac{\$100}{4} = \$450$$

Four freezers will be non-operational during the shutdown (as before) – savings of $50.

Total freezer cost savings = $450 + $50 = $500.

Reduction in gross profit (for six weeks of reduced operating)

	(1)	(2)
	$	$
Frozen ($950 × 6 × 75%)	4,275	4,275
Canned ($1,200 × 6 × 87.5%)	6,300	
($1,200 × 6 × 88.5%)		6,372
Total relevant costs	10,575	10,647

	(1)	(2)
	$	$
Redecoration (as before)	3,500	3,500
Product movement costs (as before)	1,000	1,000
Freezer cost savings	500	500
Reduction in gross profit (reduced operations)	10,575	10,647
Lost profit from shutdown (as before)	1,325	1,325
	16,900	16,972

You will notice that each method gives a different answer. You obviously do not have sufficient time to try all three methods to see which one gives the best solution, therefore you should clearly state your assumptions in your answer.

(b)   How activity based costing can be used in a retail environment

More realistic pricing

Activity based costing (ABC) helps to address one of the main problems with traditional costing systems – that is, excessive costs are often charged to high-volume products (product-cost subsidisation). This problem could lead to the low-volume products being underpriced, probably leading to increased customer demand (and vice versa for high volume products). As ABC is based on a fairer system – with costs being allocated using cost drivers that cause the costs to occur in the first place – it helps retail organisations to determine a more realistic price for individual products. This will reduce the likelihood of lower volume products being sold at unprofitable prices, and retailers being accused of predatory pricing.

Allocation of floor space to higher demand products

Linked with the more realistic pricing aspect of ABC, retailers will be able to more accurately predict demand when 'proper' prices are set. When demand can be more accurately predicted, it will be easier to allocate floor space according to this demand, which should help to improve profitability.

Diversity of products, processes and customers

Modern retail organisations deal with numerous products and sell a wide range of products. ABC assists in identifying activities required to support each category of product, for example, and the cost drivers of these activities. By doing so, ABC can help retail organisations to determine the 'real' cost of each category of product which will again help in the pricing process.

Demands on overhead resources

Different customers place different demands on overhead resources. In a service retail environment, such as the hotel industry, a businessman staying in a hotel is more likely to place more demands on available resources (such as the Business Centre) than a leisure guest. By allocating overheads according to cost drivers, the hotel could distinguish room prices between business and leisure stays.

53   RS plc

Text references. Chapter 8 has a section on DPP for answering this question.

Top tips. An alternative approach to calculating the 'other costs' per product is to calculate the costs per m^3 for each product and then a cost per item.

You may have approached the answer in 'total' terms rather than in 'per item' terms. This is perfectly valid.

Easy marks. You can answer part (c) separately and get up to five marks before launching into the numbers.

(a)   Initial costings

		£ per cubic metre
Warehouse costs per week		
Refrigeration	£160,000/5,000	32.00 per week
Other	£560,000/20,000	28.00 per week
Supermarket costs per week		
Refrigeration	15 × £24,000/5,000	72.00 per week
Other	15 × £44,000/20,000	33.00 per week
Transport costs per trip		
Refrigerated	£4,950/90 cubic metres	55.00 per week
Standard	£3,750/90 cubic metres	41.67 per week

Direct product profit (DPP)

	Baked beans		Ice cream		White wine	
	£ per item	£ per item	£ per item	£ per item	£ per item	£ per item
Sales revenue		0.320		1.600		3.450
Direct cost		0.240		0.950		2.850
Gross profit		0.080		0.650		0.600
Warehouse costs						
Refrigeration						
£32÷24÷18 × 2 weeks			0.148			
Other						
£28÷28÷80 × 1 week	0.012					
£28÷24÷18 × 2 weeks			0.130			
£28÷42÷12 × 4 weeks					0.222	
Supermarket costs						
Refrigeration						
£72÷24÷18 × 2 weeks			0.333			
Other						
£33÷28÷80 × 1 week	0.015					
£33÷24÷18 × 2 weeks			0.153			
£33÷42÷12 × 2 weeks					0.131	
Transport						
£41.67÷28÷80	0.019					
£55÷24÷18			0.127			
£41.67÷42÷12					0.083	
		0.046		0.891		0.436
Direct product profit		0.034		(0.241)		0.164
% of sales		10.6%		(15.1%)		4.8%

Traditional method profit

	Baked beans	Ice cream	White wine
£ per item	0.08	0.65	0.60
% of sales	25%	40.6%	17.4%

Using **DPP** the ranking of profits is as follows.

1st   Baked beans
2nd   White wine
3rd   Ice cream – loss-making

Using the **traditional method** the ranking was as follows.

1st   Ice cream
2nd   Baked beans
3rd   White wine

(b)   There are two main causes of the difference in profits between the two methods.

(i)   The **traditional method focused on the gross margin** only and did not apportion overhead costs.

(ii)   With **DPP, ice cream** is charged a **higher proportion of overhead** to **reflect** the fact that it **uses the high cost activities** of refrigerated transport and storage. The beans and the wine absorb only the costs of the (lower cost) resources that they use.

Ways in which profitability could be improved

(i)   **Refrigerated transport**. At £4,950 per trip this is a high cost activity.

(1)   Care must be taken to ensure all journeys using refrigerated transport carry full loads.

(2)   Suppliers of goods requiring refrigeration should be contacted to determine whether they would be able to deliver direct to the store, thus eliminating this cost for RS.

(ii)   **Adjust selling prices**. A full DPP analysis should be carried out and adjustments made to selling prices wherever possible to reflect any costs which are found not to be covered.

   (iii)   **Adjust the product range**. Where prices cannot be increased sufficiently and where the product does not need to be stocked in order to attract customers, consideration might be given to discontinuing that product and replacing it with a line with a higher DPP.

(c)   <u>Ways in which DPP differs from traditional overhead absorption</u>

   (i)   Traditional absorption costing would utilise an overhead rate by department rather than by activity. Products that generate a high level of overhead spending would not be penalised as the spending would be averaged out over all products which use a department's facilities regardless of the level of cost generated by that use.

   (ii)   Traditional overhead absorption may have attempted to include a share of the head office costs whereas DPP would ignore this because the costs are not caused by the individual product units.

   (iii)   DPP is likely to provide better information for planning and control. High cost activities will be recognised and controlled more tightly. The stocking of products which utilise only the low cost activities may be encouraged. Selling prices should more accurately reflect the actual costs generated.

54 BPR

> **Top tips.** Don't fall into the trap of assuming that BPR can be implemented wholly by the management accountant, rather than by a team.

Having overall responsibility for the organisation's information systems, the management accountant will be the **main provider of the information** required by the BPR programme. Because BPR involves the introduction of significant changes to business processes, the organisation's information requirements are likely to change. Users will require alternative types of information in alternative formats.

At the outset there will be no way of knowing for sure the precise information requirements, however, because the chief tool of BPR is a clean sheet of paper. It is only once the programme commences that precise information requirements will become clear.

At the planning stage of a BPR programme the management accountant will therefore need to **liaise with all others on the team** and consider the changes that will be necessary to the **organisation's information systems** as a result of different ways of organising work.

Benchmarking exercises, comparing processes with those used in other organisations may need to be set up, and the management accountant is likely to be heavily involved in devising ways of collecting and analysing data from such exercises.

A **modelling approach** will help to assess the validity and consequences of alternative ways of re-engineering processes.

Costing systems may need to be reappraised: for example it might be useful to set up activity based costing systems, and the consequent changes to information collection and analysis and to accounting software need to be considered.

For reporting purposes, **alternative performance measures will need to be devised**, since information will no longer be required on a departmental/ functional basis but on a process basis.

Contribution of the management accountant to the implementation of a BPR programme

When the BPR programme is being implemented, the management accountant will need to **ensure that managers within the organisation are provided with the information they require**. It is likely that the management accounting function will need to provide a broader range of information than previously, but the emphasis must be on user friendliness and sharing. This is likely to mean the introduction of **new software and telecommunications links**, capable of handling different flows of information.

As one example, sales processes may be re-engineered so that they are geared to types of customer rather than to types of product: information will need to cut across a variety of product categories or brands. Or, re-engineered work may be devolved to lower levels in the organisation hierarchy, and the managers at these levels may have quite different information requirements to those that were catered for previously.

An important aspect of implementation will be **monitoring of progress**: are the expected benefits of BPR being realised, and if not what action is required? Indicators of success might include reduced costs, faster delivery, more satisfied customers and so on, but systems need to be in operation to measure such things.

The **management accounting function itself is likely to need to change**, as part of the BPR programme, so that it can provide the information required.

55 PR

Text references. Just-in-time production is covered in Chapter 9A.

Top tips. You can score easy marks by explaining the main elements of a JIT production system in part (a).

(a) Just-in-time production is a production system which is **driven by demand** for finished products whereby each component on a production line is **produced only when needed** for the next stage.

The objective is to produce or to **procure products** or components **as they are required** (by a customer or for use) rather than for inventory.

This will mean that ideally for PR there will be:

No inventories at any stage including no finished goods inventory as items will be completed just as they are to be delivered to customers.

A system in place so that there is **no work in progress** between the different stages of production.

(b) Changing to a JIT production system will not necessarily improve the profitability of PR for several reasons which include the following.

Purchase discounts

As there will be no holdings of inventory PR will **not be purchasing components in bulk** and will lose out on potential **bulk purchase discounts** as it will need to have more frequent and smaller orders.

If the increased ordering and delivery costs are greater than the reduced inventory holding costs then PR will not be more profitable.

Overtime

As production needs to be **timed to match demand** (which fluctuates), at times of higher demand it may be necessary to work **overtime**.

Overtime is likely to be **paid at a premium rate** which may make **labour costs higher** than the constant flow production system.

56 CAL

Text references. Costs of quality are covered in Chapter 9A.

Top tips. Remember to relate your answer to part (a) to the scenario.

Easy marks. Explaining the relationship between quality conformance costs and quality non-conformance costs in part (a) should be straightforward.

(a) Quality conformance costs

Quality conformance costs are discretionary costs which are incurred with the intention of **eliminating the costs of internal failure and external failure**. Costs of conformance may also be incurred as a result of achieving specified quality standards.

Quality non-conformance costs

Quality non-conformance costs are the **costs of failure to deliver the required standard of quality**. Costs may be incurred as a result of supplying an item of insufficient quality to the customer (**external failure cost**) or due to a product needing to be re-worked (**internal failure cost**).

The cost of non-conformance can only **be reduced by increasing the cost of conformance**. Businesses must decide how to manage this **trade-off**.

Some competitors charge lower prices than CAL for lower quality products, whilst others charge higher prices for higher quality products. **CAL has positioned itself in the middle of the market** in an attempt to maximise market share. If CAL customers demand increased quality, it is likely **that CAL will need to increase prices to cover the costs of conformance** incurred as a result of adhering to any revised quality standards.

(b)   (i)   The total relevant costs of quality for the coming year

	$
Cost of free replacements	18,360
Contribution forgone from failure to increase market share to 25%	75,000
Total relevant costs of quality	93,360

Workings

Cost of free replacements

Customer demand is 20,000 units. 2% of units supplied are faulty and will be replaced free of charge.

20,000 units × 100/98 = 20,408 units (including those that are returned for a free replacement).

408 units × $45 (cost per unit) = $18,360

Contribution forgone

Market share would increase to 25% (an additional 5,000 units) if the supply of faulty solar panels to customers had been eliminated.

Contribution forgone = 5,000 units × $15 (contribution per unit) = $75,000

(ii)   Maximum saving from inspection process

	$
Savings on delivery costs *	2,040
Contribution from increase in market share to 25% **	75,000
Total savings	77,040

* The delivery costs of faulty items (408 units) would also be avoided. $5 per unit × 408 units = $2,040

** The inspection process would eliminate the supply of faulty solar panels to customers. Market share would increase to 25% (an extra 5,000 units). The contribution from these sales is therefore deducted from the annual costs of quality.

57 QW

Text references. Just-in-time and TQM are covered in Chapter 9A.

Top tips. Remember to use points from the scenario to illustrate your answers. It is very easy to simply write everything you know about just-in-time and TQM.

Easy marks. You should be able to pick up a few marks in part (b) by explaining the relationship between just-in-time and TQM.

(a) QW's present production and inventory policy

QW manufactures machine parts to specific customer order and **does not hold an inventory of finished items**. This is an example of a **just-in-time (JIT) production system**.

QW **does not use a JIT purchasing system** and holds the equivalent of one day's production of sheet metal, to reduce the risk of being unable to **cater for customer orders at short notice**. However, raw material **inventory levels are kept to a minimum which is in keeping with the JIT philosophy** and helps to control holding costs.

Traditional production systems

The proposed system for the metal ornaments is an example of a **traditional production system** where products are **produced at a constant rate** throughout the year and **stored in inventory until sold**. This system will enable QW to predict the levels of raw materials that it requires and budget for them accordingly.

However, traditional production systems can lead to **inefficiencies if not monitored** on a regular basis. **Holding high levels of inventory will increase costs** whilst inventory may become **damaged or obsolete** if not managed effectively.

(b) The importance of TQM in a just-in-time environment

Total quality management (TQM) is a philosophy of business behaviour **based on the concepts of employee involvement and continuous improvement in order to improve quality**.

TQM is essential in just-in-time production systems such as that used by QW. **If products are not of sufficient quality, they cannot be replaced as there is no inventory** due to the policy of making machine parts to specific customer order. Such a scenario will adversely impact the company's reputation as well as resulting in lost sales.

In a traditional production system where **products are produced at a constant rate**, any failings or **poor quality products can be 'hidden' within inventory**. It is important that management are notified of any failings to ensure that faulty products are not supplied to customers.

As the focus on quality is often less critical for traditional production systems, it is harder to convince employees to follow quality control procedures.

58 Consumer goods

> **Text references**. Costs of quality and Kaizen are covered in Chapter 9A.
>
> **Top tips**. Remember to relate your answer to part (c) to the scenario.
>
> **Easy marks**. Comparing and contrasting costs of quality conformance and non-conformance in part (a) should be straightforward.
>
> **Examiner's comments**. Answers to this question were satisfactory. Most candidates appeared to have a good understanding of quality costs but failed to address the verbs in the question.

Marking scheme

		Marks
(a)	Explain costs of conformance	1
	Define costs of quality non-conformance	2
		3
(b)	Price vs quality and the impact on cost and selling price	2
	Need to understand the customer profile	2
		4
(c)	Definition of Kaizen	1
	Example relating to scenario	2
		3

(a) <u>Costs of quality conformance</u>

The cost of conformance is a discretionary cost which is incurred with the intention of **eliminating the costs of internal failure and external failure**. Costs of conformance may also be incurred as a result of achieving specified quality standards.

<u>Costs of quality non-conformance</u>

The cost of non-conformance, on the other hand, is the **cost of failure to deliver the required standard of quality**. Costs may be incurred as a result of supplying an item of insufficient quality to the customer (**external failure cost**) or due to a product needing to be re-worked (**internal failure cost**). The cost of non-conformance can only **be reduced by increasing the cost of conformance**.

(b) <u>The relationship between quality conformance costs and product selling prices in HT</u>

The market in which HT operates is highly competitive and **consumers focus on price and quality** when buying products. As a result, there is likely to be a trade-off between price and quality.

HT should consider undertaking **market research** to understand the extent to which customers are willing to **pay for quality**.

The more HT invests in developing quality products, the higher its costs will be. As a result, the selling price of products will need to be higher to cover the development costs and ensure that HT is profitable.

HT will need to decide whether to follow a **high price, high quality strategy** or something closer to a **low price, low quality strategy**. As the market leader with 15% market share, the strategy that HT adopts is likely to be followed by some of its competitors.

(c) <u>The definition of Kaizen</u>

Kaizen principles are built around the theory of **gradual, continuous improvement** and focus on obtaining small **incremental cost reductions** during the production phase of the product life cycle.

<u>How HT can use Kaizen to extend the life of its products</u>

The **life cycle** of products in the market in which HT operates is **extremely short**. **Extending** the life of these products would make HT **more profitable**.

Kaizen principles could achieve this by tightening internal quality standards to improve the overall quality of finished products. Tightening internal quality standards is also likely to result in small reductions in production costs which will improve HT profit margins.

59 XY Timber

Test references. Just-in-time is covered in Chapter 9A.

Top tips. Make your calculations in part (a) easy for the examiner to understand.

Easy marks. There are easy marks in part (b) for stating two factors that the company should consider prior to switching to a JIT production system.

Examiner's comments. The presentation of answers to part (a) was poor. Part (b) was generally well answered, but many candidates spent time describing several factors associated with JIT instead of the two required. This did not earn extra marks and wasted valuable time.

Marking scheme

		Marks
(a)	Average inventory (cost)	1
	Average inventory (units)	2
	Overtime (hours)	1
	Adjust standard hours for 96% efficiency	1
	Cost comparison	1
		6
(b)	Explanation of two factors relevant to JIT system (up to 2 marks each))	4
		10

(a)

Month	Demand (Std hours)	Basic Production Std hours	Inc / (Dec) in Inventory Std hours	Closing inventory Std hours	Average Inventory Std hours	Inventory cost $	Overtime cost $
1	3,100	3,780	680	680	340	2,040	–
2	3,700	3,780	80	760	720	4,320	–
3	4,000	3,780	(220)	540	650	3,900	3,437.55 (W1)
4	3,300	3,780	480	1,020	780	4,680	–
5	3,600	3,780	180	1,200	1,110	6,660	–
6	4,980	3,780	(1,200)	0	600	3,600	18,750.00 (W1)
Total						25,200	22,187.55

The total production cost savings made by switching to a JIT production system = $3,012.45

W1 – CALCULATION OF OVERTIME COST

Month 3 = 220 std hours / 0.96 = 229.17 labour hours x $15 (labour rate incl 50% premium) = 3,437.55
Month 6 = 1,200 std hours / 0.96 = 1,250.00 labour hours x $15= 18,750.00
22,187.55

(b) There are a number of factors that should be considered prior to switching to a JIT production system.

XY staff must be versatile so that they can perform any job within reason to keep production flowing as required. Staff must also be committed to quality.

XY must have strong relationships with suppliers. For a JIT production system to be successful, suppliers must take responsibility for the quality of their goods. The onus is on suppliers to inspect the timber materials before delivery to XY and to guarantee their quality.

60 X Group

Top tips. The examiner's marking guide stated that there were two marks for introducing and explaining JIT. The remaining eight marks were awarded for stating how JIT would affect profitability in X Group.

Therefore, it would be wise to concentrate effort on applying JIT specifically to the X group. The examiner is looking at your application of knowledge.

Easy marks. It is possible to gain two marks from just memorising or paraphrasing CIMA's definitions of JIT included as Key Terms in the P2 Study Text. Look at the format requested in the question – using a report format will earn a mark or so.

<u>REPORT</u>

To: Managing Director
From: Management Accountant
Date: 11 November 20X5
Subject: How the adoption of a JIT system would affect profitability

<u>Introduction</u>

This report addresses how the adoption of a JIT system might affect the profitability of the X Group.

<u>JIT definition</u>

JIT is a customer led production system, also known as a 'pull' system. The objective is to produce products as they are required by the customer rather than build up stock to cater for demand.

<u>Just in time production</u>

A JIT production system is driven by demand for finished products whereby each component in a process is only made when needed for the next stage.

<u>Just in time purchasing</u>

A JIT purchasing system requires material to be purchased so that as far as possible it can be used straight away.

<u>The effect on X Group's profitability</u>

The introduction of a JIT production and purchasing system would have the following impact on profitability:

- A reduction in inventory holding costs as inventories of raw materials and finished goods will disappear.
- An increase is possible for raw material costs to encourage suppliers to deliver to a JIT schedule and so additional flexibility is required.
- As demand may fluctuate, additional labour costs to cover production where no buffer stocks exist.
- Additional requirements for quality control by suppliers to ensure materials and by others to ensure finished goods are acceptable for the customer.
- Increased administration costs to plan throughput.

61 Quality costs

Top tips. You will need to make sure that you state the two main types of quality cost and their sub classifications, giving relevant examples, in your report. Four marks could be earned for this. Then make sure that you discuss them for another four marks. This may all sound obvious but the examiner often says that candidates don't answer the question set and this time he said that candidates did not give relevant examples or even use a report format. Crucially you need to bring out in your discussion the relationship between incurring costs of conformance and avoiding those of non-conformance. You also need to discuss explicitly the relationship between price and quality in your report.

Easy marks. Make sure you use the appropriate headers and so on for a report. Lay out the body of your answer in a report format and end the report appropriately, and there's two marks straight away.

Divide up your report with headings so that it is clear you have covered the points you need to discuss.

<u>REPORT</u>

To: Managing Director
From: Management accountant
Date: 23 May 20X6
Subject: <u>Quality costs and their significance for the organisation</u>

1   <u>Introduction</u>

     This report explains quality costs and their significance for the company.

2   Quality costs

There are two main types of quality cost, these being **costs of conformance** and **costs of non-conformance**. Conformance costs are further analysed into prevention costs, and appraisal costs. Costs of non-conformance can be further analysed into internal failure costs and external failure costs.

Prevention costs are the costs incurred prior or during production to prevent substandard or defective products or services being produced. Examples of these include the costs of quality engineering and design or development of quality control or inspection equipment.

Appraisal costs are the costs incurred to ensure that outputs produced meet required quality standards. Examples would include acceptance testing costs and the cost of inspection of goods inwards.

Internal failure costs are the costs arising from inadequate quality, which are identified before the transfer of ownership from supplier to purchaser. Relevant examples include re-inspection costs and losses due to lower selling prices from sub-quality goods.

External failure costs are the costs arising from inadequate quality discovered after the transfer of ownership from supplier to purchaser. Relevant examples would include product liability costs and costs of repairing products returned from customers.

3   Significance of quality costs for the company

To remain **successful** in the modern business environment, organisations must offer customers a **competitively priced, high-quality** product. Consideration must therefore be given to the **optimum balance between the costs of conformance and the costs of non-conformance**. There is a **trade off** between the two: the higher the expenditure on conformance (to ensure that customers receive the high quality products they demand) the lower the cost of non-conformance (as there are fewer quality failures) and vice versa.

The **problem** organisations face is **determining the level of quality customers expect** and hence the **acceptable level of external failure cost**. Some sort of research into customer preferences could be undertaken maybe with focus groups looking at our products and giving feedback on price and quality.

- A **zero defects** policy could be adopted, but this would be extremely costly and time consuming and would drive up the costs of conformance.

- A **sample testing** approach could be taken. This would keep down the costs of conformance but at the risk of increasing the costs of non-conformance.

Some **research** into customer preferences could be undertaken, possibly using focus groups to provide feedback on acceptable mixes of price and quality.

I hope this information has proved useful but if I can be of any further assistance please do not hesitate to contact me.

Signed: Management accountant

62   JIT and TQM

Test references. Chapter 9A covers Just-In-Time. Total Quality Management is also covered in this chapter.

Top tips. Avoid regurgitating all you know about JIT and TQM – the questions asked are quite specific. Make sure you refer to the particular features of the company in the scenario – the constant production levels are quite significant for a company considering a switch to a JIT system.

Easy marks. There are no really easy marks in this question, although if you are comfortable with JIT and TQM you should be able to score quite highly.

(a)   Cost changes resulting from changing to JIT.

(i)   Non-value added activities

A JIT system seeks to **eliminate** any activities that **do not add value** to the final product. Therefore there should be a reduction in inspection costs and costs of moving products from one department to another.

(ii) <u>Inventory costs</u>

The practice of allowing inventory to rise and fall during the year will be eliminated and with it the cost of storing inventory. The idea behind JIT is that it **responds to demand** – production levels will change to suit demand levels rather than continuing to produce units for inventory. The absence of inventory means that space may be freed up for expansion of production facilities.

(iii) <u>Labour costs</u>

One potential problem with the JIT system for this company is the **possibility of having to pay overtime** to the workforce when demand is heavy. At the moment production is constant, with inventories being used to satisfy fluctuations in demand. If inventories were eliminated, increases in demand could only be met by the workforce working extra hours, at a premium.

(b) <u>Importance of Total Quality Management</u>

When a firm operates a JIT system inspection costs (which check for quality) are eliminated. As a result, it is important for each individual to take responsibility for the quality of their own output. In the context of TQM, quality means **'getting it right first time'** – this is particularly important for a JIT system where there are no inventories to act as a buffer in the event of production problems. Any such problems would result in lost sales. The use of TQM encourages **the delivery of good quality products all the time**, thus reducing the possibility of stoppages due to poor quality.

63 PK plc

> **Top tips.** This question required you to discuss three points being the changing nature of cost structures in modern manufacturing, the implications for PK plc's inventory valuation, and for PK plc's short term decision making. It awarded two points for format and presentation, which seemed to suggest there are only two or three marks for each point you need to discuss.
>
> As suggested in the question, there were two marks for the report format. The remaining eight marks were split 50:50 between explaining traditional cost structures and how these have changed, and the importance of these to valuing stock and short-term decision making.
>
> **Easy marks.** Make sure you use the appropriate headers and so on for a report. Lay out the body of your answer in a report format and end the report appropriately, and there's two marks straight away.
>
> Divide up your report with headings so that it is clear you have covered the three points you need to discuss.

<u>REPORT</u>

To: Management Team of PK plc
From: Assistant management accountant
Date: 23 November 20X5
Subject: <u>Cost structures in the modern manufacturing environment</u>

1 <u>Introduction</u>

This report explains the changing nature of cost structures in the modern manufacturing environment and then considers the implications for PK's inventory valuation and short term decision making.

2 <u>Changing nature of cost structures in the modern manufacturing environment</u>

The traditional **absorption costing** approach to dealing with overheads was developed at a time when most organisations produced only a **narrow range of products** and when **overhead costs** were only a very **small fraction of total costs**, direct labour and direct material costs accounting for the largest proportion of the costs. Errors made in attributing overheads to products were therefore not too significant.

Nowadays, however, the situation is very different and it has been argued that traditional absorption costing is unsuitable for the modern business environment.

(i) **Direct labour may account for as little as 5% of a product's cost**. With the advent of advanced manufacturing technology, **support activities** such as setting-up, production scheduling, first item inspection and data processing have increased. These support activities assist the efficient manufacture of a wide range of products and are not, in general, affected by changes in production volume. To allocate them to products on the basis of some measure of production volume (as would be the case if absorption costing were used) would therefore be entirely inappropriate. The level of such activities tends to vary in the long term according to the **range** and **complexity of the products** manufactured. The wider the range and the more complex the product, the more support services will be required.

(ii) The current business environment is characterised by high levels of **competition**. Management's need for an accurate indication of how much it costs to take on competitors cannot be met by traditional costing systems.

(iii) **Support department costs** have a tendency to increase. Management therefore need additional information to enable them to **manage and control** these costs.

(iv) Traditionally, the management accounting cost object has been the product. Information about the **profitability of customers and market segments** is now vital, however, if organisations wish to compete in the modern business environment.

Given the accessibility of and improvement in **information technology**, and the need for more appropriate information, the reason for the development of new costing approaches, such as activity based costing (ABC), is obvious.

3   Inventory valuation

Absorption costing is used to value inventory for financial reporting purposes where the requirement is to include all costs in 'bringing the product to its present location and condition'. So this would include related production overheads.

However, absorption costing may give an inaccurate record of profit if the absorption basis used is inappropriate in the modern manufacturing environment.

In many circumstances, in the modern manufacturing environment, ABC allocates overheads to products using more relevant cost drivers. ABC therefore produces more realistic product costs and so more realistic inventory valuation.

4   Short-term decision-making

Some commentators argue that only marginal costing provides suitable information for decision making. This is untrue. Marginal costing provides a crude method of differentiating between different types of cost behaviour by splitting costs into their variable and fixed elements. **Marginal costing** can only be used for **short-term decisions** and usually even these have longer-term implications which ought to be considered.

ABC spreads costs across products or other cost units according to a number of different bases. The analysis may show that one activity which is carried out for one or two products is expensive. If costs have been apportioned using the traditional method prior to this the cost of this activity is likely to have been spread across all products, thus hiding the fact that the products using this activity may be loss making. If these costs are not completely variable costs but are, for example, batch costs, marginal costing would not have related them to the products at all. Therefore **ABC** can be used to make **decisions about pricing, discontinuing products**, and so on which are short-term. However, ABC is particularly suited in fact to long term and strategic decisions.

I hope this information has proved useful but if I can be of any further assistance please do not hesitate to contact me.

Signed: Assistant accountant

64 AVN

(a) The **value chain** was described and popularised by Michael Porter. Its ultimate goal is to maximise **value** creation while minimising costs.

The **value chain** is the sequence of business **activities** by which, from the **perspective of the end user**, **value is added** to the products and services produced by an entity.

These activities are known as **primary** and **support** activities and are value activities.

The **primary activities** include: inbound logistics, operations (production), outbound logistics, sales and marketing, and service (maintenance). The **support activities** include: administrative infrastructure management, human resources management, R&D, and procurement.

Costs and value drivers are identified for each **value** activity.

The idea of the value chain has been **extended** beyond individual organisations. Where this occurs, the value chain is known as an **extended value chain**, and it can apply to whole supply chains and distribution networks. Individual value chains combine to deliver value to the end user.

Porter terms this larger interconnected system of **value** chains the 'value' system'. A **value** system includes the value chains of an organisation's supplier (and their suppliers all the way back), the organisation itself, and its distribution channels, retailers, customers and so on to the ultimate end user. Value chains may extend to an extent that they become global.

(b) AVN should be looking at how it can **lower costs** and **enhance value** throughout the extended value chain. So AVN is looking at gaining **competitive advantage** by controlling its value chain.

The first step AVN should take is **to map the extended value chain** to determine the various activities in the chain and allocate costs and revenues to each. The elements of AVN's extended value chain would be **its suppliers, distributors and customers**.

Then AVN needs to look at controlling the **cost drivers** for the costs of each activity. These cost drivers are the executional and structural cost drivers mentioned above.

Suppliers

AVN could look at its **relationships with the suppliers of the parts** in its electronic devices. One way of doing this is through **supply chain management**. This involves AVN looking at ways of **improving its supply chain**. For instance AVN could switch to new suppliers by purchasing on-line.

AVN could require its part suppliers to be located nearby its assembly plant to minimise the cost of transportation. The company could also consider tying its suppliers into a JIT agreement so that inventory levels are kept to a minimum saving on stockholding costs. However this does need to be balanced against the risks of stock-outs and damaging relationships with customers.

AVN could try to **negotiate cheaper prices** for the components it buys in. Furthermore, the organisation could agree quality standards and inventory levels with its suppliers, thereby **building in quality without increasing cost**.

Retailers and customers

AVN should look at price and the company could consider **negotiating better margins** on its products, or consider **undertaking some market research** prior to development of new products to establish exactly what the customer sees as a quality product. This would control the research costs it incurs and direct effort to where value is added. It would also **reduce the complexity of products** being offered if some of these aren't selling. AVN should also consider the transport costs and reliability of supplying its product to customers.

Other ideas

- AVN could **share technology** with suppliers and streamline its expertise.

- AVN could consider **outsourcing** activities that aren't **core**.

- AVN could standardise components and products so it **reduces complexity** without compromising on product availability.

65 Chains

> **Top tips.** Notice how the requirements of this question provide a ready-made framework for your answer – you need to cover the supply chain, the value chain, e-procurement and outsourcing.

The supply chain

The supply chain refers to **all the stages and activities involved in getting a finished product or service delivered to the customer**. In the case of a manufactured product, the supply chain starts with the sources of raw materials, and includes not only production activities, but also distribution (logistics) and storage and support activities such as purchasing.

Managing the supply chain involves **ensuring a smooth flow of the product to the customer**, through all the stages of the chain. It therefore involves **management of the relationship with suppliers**, and **ensuring that suppliers deliver their goods to the required specifications on time**.

The value chain

The value chain also refers to all the stages and activities involved in getting a product or service to the customer, but the **focus is on the value added at each stage of the chain**.

Managing the value chain is concerned with **identifying ways in which more value can be added at each stage** of the chain, perhaps by doing things in a different way. Activities that fail to add value should be identified and eliminated.

E-procurement and outsourcing

E-procurement and outsourcing are **ways** in which it might be **possible to add value in the supply chain**.

E-procurement involves **purchasing** items from suppliers **through the Internet** (although other methods of electronic purchasing, such as EDI or electronic data interchange, might be included in the definition). A company that buys regularly from a supplier might make an arrangement whereby the **computer systems of buyer and seller** might **exchange data** and make supply transactions. There will normally have to be pre-agreed terms and conditions of supply, product specifications and fixed prices or a formula for pricing. A company needing to buy goods from a supplier might be able to generate an automatic order within its own computer system, and despatch the order to the supplier's system. The supplier's system will respond by confirming availability and delivery arrangements. The automatic electronic processing of purchase orders, given an established buyer/supplier relationship, can result in **significant cost savings** as well as **greater purchasing efficiency**. Human intervention and paperwork are removed from this stage of the supply chain.

Outsourcing involves the **purchase of products or services externally**, rather than making the product or performing the service with the organisation's own staff. The outsourcing of production work involves having products made by an external supplier rather than making them in-house. Numerous services might also be outsourced, including IT services, facilities management and the accounting function. The term 'outsourcing' in fact usually refers to putting services out to an external provider. The organisation, having outsourced activities at which it is not particularly specialised, is then able to **focus on its core activities**, where it can **add value** more effectively. The **provider of the outsourced service** should have the **relevant expertise** which will enable it to **perform** the service **more efficiently** than the organisation's own staff. If this is the case, outsourcing can **add value** to the supply chain/value chain. The management of the organisation are responsible for managing the relationship with the service provider, but are no longer responsible for the detailed management of the service itself.

66 Partnering

> **Top tips.** Don't be afraid to add real-life examples to your answer. If relevant, they provide additional evidence that you know what you are talking about!

(a)   Partnering is **particularly appropriate in the following circumstances**.

    (i)   If significant input is required from specialist contractors or subcontractors (such as in the construction of a new airport terminal)

    (ii)   If there is a rapid expansion of a programme of construction (say, if a supermarket chain opens lots of new branches)

    (iii)   If time is a critical factor

    (iv)   If projects are repetitive and based upon a set of standard designs (such as the construction of McDonalds restaurants)

    (v)   If there is a particular construction problem which is best solved by a team of experts (such as the construction of oil rigs)

Partnering is less **suitable in the following circumstances**.

    (i)   If it is important that costs can be predicted with certainty.

    (ii)   If the project is a one-off, commissioned by a one-off customer (as the benefits of team building and supply chain management cannot be easily achieved on a single project)

    (iii)   If the customer has little knowledge of the construction process (as partnering requires active involvement of a knowledgeable client)

    (iv)   If the customer requires significant or complete control over the specification and delivery, so that there is little opportunity for the contractor to propose new ways of doing things.

(b)   (i)   **Using the wrong people.** In some situations, interpersonal skills can be more important than technical understanding.

    (ii)   **Lack of cultural readiness.** All members of both the customer and contractor teams must be ready to make partnering work. Although the benefits of partnering may be obvious and achievable, an organisation may not be ready to work in the new ways required, or to be able to change in a short time.

    (iii)   **Unclear objectives.** If the objectives for both customer and contractor are not clear at the outset, no amount of management effort will make the partnering relationship successful.

    (iv)   **Inadequate performance measurement.** The baseline from which improvements are to be measured can be difficult to establish, even though it is crucial to the way in which the contractor's performance is assessed. And finding appropriate benchmarking measures in order to make meaningful comparisons between contractors can be difficult.

67 DT Group

> **Text references**. The value chain and gain sharing arrangements are covered in Chapter 9B.
>
> **Top tips**. Remember to relate your answer to part (a) to the requirement. It is very easy to write all you know about the value chain, however the question asks you to consider elements of the value chain with regard to the changes being considered by the DT group.
>
> **Easy marks**. Being able to discuss the different elements of the value chain will earn you a few marks.

(a)   The value chain is the **sequence of business activities** by which, from the perspective of the end user, **value is added to an organisation's products and services**. Businesses must have a thorough understanding of the importance of the relationship between all elements in the value chain. These include inbound and outbound logistics, marketing and sales and after sales service (**primary activities**) and procurement, human resource management and firm infrastructure (**support activities**).

DT group currently manufactures products in a single factory, which makes the management of production fairly straight-forward. **Outsourcing** some manufacturing operations to developing economies **could result in communication difficulties** thus making it harder for management to ensure a smooth manufacturing process.

Delays in receiving information could **disrupt the flow of goods to the customer**. Aside from the communication difficulties, the skills of employees at the outsourcing company may not be up to the standard of employees at the current factory. This could **adversely affect the quality of goods and services** that reach the customer. Such instances will make it difficult to attribute profits or losses and contribution to individual elements of the value chain.

(b)   In gain sharing arrangements, **all cost savings and profits are shared between the customer and the contractor**. As the benefits from the arrangement are split equally, there is an **incentive for both parties** to look for cost-cutting opportunities. The arrangements place emphasis on greater openness and shared development and improvement.

DT group may enter into a gain sharing arrangement with the suppliers of the components that are used in the company's products. Both parties may agree to **non-financial targets to include delivery times and quality of components**. **Fewer defects** in components supplied and **deliveries ahead of schedule** would result in a gain that can be shared between DT group and the supplier.

68 XY engineering company

> **Test references**. The value chain is covered in Chapter 9B.
>
> **Top tips**. Although this question might appear to be a general one about value chains, it is important to make your answer relevant to the company in the scenario. You should adapt what you know about value chains to the company in question, and refer to the company frequently in the body of your report. Remember to prepare a report and divide the report into sections with clear headings.
>
> **Easy marks**. You should be able to explain the concept of the value chain.

REPORT

To: Managing Director
From: Management Accountant
Date: 21 May 20X8

The concept of the value chain and the management of profits generated throughout the chain in XY.

This report contains information to assist you in the preparation of your presentation for the upcoming conference.

(1) <u>What is a value chain?</u>

In general, a value chain provides a **'bird's eye'** view of the organisation and its activities. The activities in the value chain are the means by which an organisation **creates value** in its products.

As XY is an engineering company, its **key activities** could be defined as:

Research and development $\Rightarrow$ Design $\Rightarrow \dfrac{\text{Product}}{\text{Assembly}} \Rightarrow$ Marketing $\Rightarrow$ Distribution $\Rightarrow$ Customer service

These activities are the 'primary' activities of XY. They are supported by the 'support' activities, such as human resources, technology and procurement.

(2) <u>Creating value</u>

The value created by the activities is **the difference between the price customers are prepared to pay for XY's engines and the cost of carrying out these activities**.

XY can create value either by carrying out its activities **more efficiently** than its competitors or by combining them to produce **unique products**.

XY can also encourage customers to **purchase value** by making their engines superior to those of their competitors. By doing so, customers will compare XY's engines favourably with competitors' products and 'purchase' the engines for their superior attributes.

(3) <u>Competitive advantage</u>

XY can gain competitive advantage over its competitors by adopting either a **low-cost strategy** or a **differentiation strategy**, whereby the engines will be perceived as being unique, perhaps via design or features.

Value chain analysis is essential when trying to gain or maintain competitive advantage as it can be used to determine the points in the value chain where **cost can be lowered or value enhanced**.

As there is pressure on XY to produce more efficient, environmentally friendly engines, the value chain can be used to identify where such progression could be made in the research and development and design activities. By providing what the customer wants, there is a greater chance of **improving profitability**.

(4) <u>Summary</u>

The value chain, by forcing an external focus, can help XY to improve its profitability. XY can use the technique to **identify opportunities** for improving its competitive advantage and thus build on its existing customer base.

Should you require any further information, please do not hesitate to contact me.

69 ZX

Text references. TQM is covered in Chapter 9A.

Top tips. Do not be tempted to simply write all you know about TQM. Try to relate each point you make to the banking sector and divide your answer into short paragraphs to make each point clear.

Easy marks. If you are familiar with TQM you will pick up a few marks for explaining the concept.

Total Quality Management (TQM) is a management philosophy where **quality is the focus** of the organisation. The **quality experience** of the customer (which may be internal or external) **is key** and the customer must always be satisfied. TQM should foster a consistent, systematic approach to **continuous improvement** that involves every aspect of the organisation.

Improvements in quality may require expenditure. In TQM the **expenditure is seen as an investment** which will lead to future benefits rather than a cost to be minimised.

Customer experience and service

One of the basic principles of TQM is that the cost of **preventing mistakes** is **less than the cost of correcting them** once they occur. The aim should therefore be to **get things right first time**. Every mistake, delay and misunderstanding, directly costs an organisation money through wasted time and effort, including time taken in pacifying customers. The **lost potential** for future revenue because of **poor customer service** must also be **taken into account**.

If ZX invests in TQM it will be able to improve the customer experience and their service. This will enable it to have a competitive advantage over the other banks.

ZX could invest in TQM in a number of ways.

Customer satisfaction

Employees could be given **technical training** in addition to **customer service training**. Customers should then receive a better service from a technical and a customer service perspective. This should lead to **greater customer satisfaction** combined with fewer complaints. ZX may then generate business through personal recommendations.

Customer feedback

ZX should **respond to customer feedback** and implement working practices to help the customer. This could include **longer opening hours** to suit customers and also providing **additional staff** at busy times which will reduce queue sizes. This will all **improve** the **customer experience** and lead to more satisfied customers.

The improved long-term quality measures, although they incur additional expenditure will enable ZX to gain a competitive advantage and should lead to increased profitability for the bank.

70 TQM

Text references. Total Quality Management and continuous improvement are covered in Chapter 9A.

Top tips. Remember to use a report format as this is specifically asked for. This is only a ten mark question so don't write pages and pages about TQM. The question divides your report quite nicely into three distinct parts so your task is made easier! It's always a good idea to give an example of each cost just to demonstrate that you understand what each category means.

Easy marks. If you are familiar with the principles of TQM then the first two bullet points of the question should be quite straightforward

Report

To:	Managing Director
From:	Assistant Management Accountant
Date:	May 20X9
Subject:	Total Quality Management

This report gives a brief overview of the principles of Total Quality Management (TQM), the costs involved and the relationship between compliance and non-compliance costs (also known as conformance and non-conformance costs).

Principles of TQM

The key principle of TQM is **'get it right first time'** – the belief that the costs of preventing mistakes in the first place are less than the costs of correcting these mistakes once they occur.

Another basic principle is dissatisfaction with the status quo – the belief that it is always possible to improve (**'get it right next time'**). This is known as **continuous improvement**.

In order for TQM to work properly, everyone within the organisation must be **committed** to its principles and the ultimate objective of producing good quality goods or services. In order to encourage this commitment, everyone should be **encouraged** to make suggestions that might improve quality and given responsibility for achieving quality results.

Quality costs

There are four categories of costs that are related to TQM.

(a)   Prevention costs

Prevention costs are incurred prior to or during production in order to prevent sub-standard or defective goods being produced. Examples include quality engineering and training staff in aspects of quality control.

(b)   Appraisal costs

These costs are incurred once the goods or services have been produced to ensure that outputs meet quality standards. Examples include inspection costs and acceptance testing.

(c)   Internal failure costs

These are the costs arising from inadequate quality of goods or services that are identified before the customer takes ownership. One example is the loss from failure of purchased items – goods may have to be produced again to fulfil an order due to sub-standard production that is discovered prior to delivery.

(d)   External failure costs

These costs arise from inadequate quality of goods or services that is discovered after the customer has taken ownership. Such costs include administration of the customer complaints section and repair costs of goods returned by customers.

Compliance and non-compliance costs

The four cost categories mentioned above can be divided into costs of **compliance** (conformance) with quality standards – prevention and appraisal costs – and costs of **non-compliance** (non-conformance) with these standards (internal and external failure costs).

There is a trade-off between compliance and non-compliance costs. To achieve low levels of defects, costs of compliance must be necessarily high. As a greater level of defects becomes acceptable, compliance costs fall, but the costs of non-compliance increase. Whilst in theory TQM has zero tolerance of defects, in reality there will normally be an **acceptable level** of defects at which total costs (compliance plus non-compliance) are minimised.

Conclusion

I hope the above information is of assistance ahead of our meeting next week.

71   C1, C2, C3

Text references. Part (a) should be brought forward knowledge but look at the introductory chapter if you need to reread cost controls and techniques. Part (b) can be answered by referring to Chapter 6 on Pricing decisions. Part (c) wants you to explain JIT which is covered in Chapter 9A.

Top tips. In part (a) you are required to calculate the total savings that the company would make as a result of implementing a particular system (JIT).

Easy marks. You could have worked out the total budgeted cost of current operations and the total budgeted cost of JIT operations but it is quicker to consider the incremental changes in costs as we have done. If you took the alternative approach, the total cost of current operations is £1,770,670, the total cost when JIT has been implemented £1,604,110.

You need to tabulate your workings very carefully in part (b). You may have got to your answer in a slightly different way – for example the CIMA model answer calculated set-up costs, material handling costs, inspection costs and machinery costs per car. It was imperative, however, that your decision was based on variable cost and **not** full cost.

Do not make the obvious mistake of writing about JIT in general in part (c).

(a)   <u>Impact of JIT – savings in costs</u>

	£m
Direct labour [£(1,120 + 1,292 + 1,980) × 0.2 × 75,000]	(65.880)
Set-ups	
Variable (£13,000 × 0.3 × 3,500)	13.650
Fixed (£42.66m × 0.3)	12.798
Materials handling	
Variable (£4,000 × 0.3 × 14,600)	17.520
Fixed (£52.89m × 0.3)	15.867
Inspection	
Variable (£18,000 × 0.3 × 3,500)	18.900
Fixed (£59.88m × 0.3)	17.964
Machinery	
Variable (£40 × 0.15 × 4.56m)	27.360
Fixed (£144.54m × 0.15)	21.681
Distribution and warehousing	
Variable (£3,000 × 14,600)	43.800
Fixed	42.900
	166.560

(b)   <u>Savings</u>

<u>Car C1</u>

Price £	Demand Cars	Revenue £m	Direct cost per car (W1) £	Total direct costs £m	Variable overhead cost per car (W2) £	Total variable overhead costs £m	Contribution £m
5,000	75,000	375.00	3,864	289.800	928	69.60	15.60
5,750	65,000	373.75	3,864	251.160	928	60.32	62.27
6,000	50,000	300.00	3,864	193.200	928	46.40	60.40
6,500	35,000	227.50	3,864	135.240	928	32.48	59.78

Therefore, profit-maximising price is £5,750 at output level of 65,000 cars.

<u>Car C2</u>

Price £	Demand Cars	Revenue £m	Direct cost per car (W1) £	Total direct costs £m	Variable overhead cost per car (W3) £	Total variable overhead costs £m	Contribution £m
5,750	75,000	431.25	4,474.4	335.580	1,292	96.90	(1.230)
6,250	60,000	375.00	4,474.4	268.464	1,292	77.52	29.016
6,500	45,000	292.50	4,474.4	201.348	1,292	58.14	33.012
7,500	35,000	262.50	4,474.4	156.604	1,292	45.22	60.676

Therefore, profit-maximising price is £7,500 at output level of 35,000 cars.

<u>Car C3</u>

Price £	Demand Cars	Revenue £m	Direct cost per car (W1) £	Total direct costs £m	Variable overhead cost per car (W4) £	Total variable overhead costs £m	Contribution £m
6,500	75,000	487.50	6,336	475.20	1,405	105.375	(93.075)
6,750	60,000	405.00	6,336	380.16	1,405	84.300	(59.460)
7,750	45,000	348.75	6,336	285.12	1,405	63.225	0.405
8,000	30,000	240.00	6,336	190.08	1,405	42.150	7.770

Therefore, profit-maximising price is £8,000 at output level of 30,000 cars.

Workings

1   Revised direct cost per car

	C1 £	C2 £	C3 £
Direct materials	2,520	2,924.	3,960
Direct labour (× 120%)	1,344	1,550.	2,376
	3,864	4,474.	6,336

2   Revised variable overhead costs for 75,000 C1 cars

	£m
Set-ups (£13,000 × 1,000 × 70%)	9.10
Materials handling (£4,000 × 4,000 × 70%)	11.20
Inspection (£18,000 × 1,000 × 70%)	12.60
Machining (£40 × 1.08m × 85%)	36.72
Distribution and warehousing	–
	69.62

Therefore, cost per car $= \dfrac{£69.62m}{75,000} = £928$

3   Revised variable overhead costs for 75,000 C2 cars

	£m
Set-ups (£13,000 × 1,000 × 70%)	9.1
Materials handling (£4,000 × 5,000 × 70%)	14.0
Inspections (£18,000 × 1,000 × 70%)	12.6
Machining (£40 × 1.8m × 85%)	61.2
Distribution and warehousing	–
	96.9

Therefore, cost per car $= \dfrac{£96.9m}{75,000} = £1,292$

4   Revised variable overhead costs for 75,000 C3 cars

	£m
Set-ups (£13,000 × 1,500 × 70%)	13.65
Materials handling (£4,000 × 5,600 × 70%)	15.68
Inspection (£18,000 × 1,500 × 70%)	18.90
Machining (£40 × 1.68m × 85%)	57.12
Distribution and warehousing	–
	105.35

Therefore, cost per car $= \dfrac{£105.35m}{75,000} = £1,405$

(c)   REPORT

To:	Management of X Ltd
From:	Management accountant
Date:	17 December 20X2
Subject:	Implementation of JIT manufacturing system

1   Introduction

1.1   Set out below are the conditions that are necessary for the successful implementation of a JIT manufacturing system.

2   Suppliers

2.1   Quality raw materials/components

Stocks of raw materials/components, work in progress and finished goods are kept at near zero levels under a JIT system. Raw materials/components must therefore be of **100% quality** as defects stop the production line and, with no buffer stocks available, they could possibly result in failure to meet delivery dates to customers.

2.2 Delivery on time

As well as being responsible for the quality of raw materials/components, suppliers must also guarantee to deliver on time so that there are no production delays.

2.3 Small deliveries

Order sizes should be small to avoid the build up of stocks and the costs associated with this.

2.4 Close relationships

You must therefore establish long-term commitments with a limited number of suppliers with whom you should deal exclusively in their component areas. They guarantee to deliver material of 100% quality on time. In return they are guaranteed demand for their product.

3 Production

3.1 Smooth production flow

The rate of production should be kept as smooth as possible as fluctuations can cause delays and lead to high levels of work in progress.

3.2 Pull system

Production in one process is only carried out when output of that process is needed by the next. Ultimately this means production is entirely based on customer demand for final output.

3.3 Set-ups

Because production runs are short, there are more of them, and set-ups need to be quick and inexpensive.

3.4 Machine maintenance

Routine preventative maintenance will avoid machine downtime.

4 Employees

4.1 Flexible and multi-skilled workers

Workers must be multi-skilled and flexible in order to be able to move between different production lines to maintain output.

4.2 Teamwork

Teamwork will ensure high levels of efficiency and the elimination of non-value added costs.

5 Summary

5.1 If the conditions detailed above were established, the implementation of a JIT manufacturing system within X Ltd is likely to be successful.

5.2 If I can provide any further information, please do not hesitate to contact me.

---

72 MN Ltd

Text references. Read Chapter 9A of your Study Text to give you some pointers for answering this question.

Top tips. You need to begin part (a) by determining the bottleneck resource. And when calculating the cost per factory hour take care to note that labour and variable overheads are given as weekly figures, but fixed production costs are given as an annual figure.

Other ratios that you might have mentioned for part (c) include days' inventory on hand, manufacturing cycle time, cost of quality, customer due date performance and process time to scheduled time. If you found this part difficult because of a lack of knowledge, make a note of the key ratios.

Easy marks. Look at key phrases for the written section, see the bold sections in the answer. This is a time pressured question.

(a) <u>Key resource</u>

	Machine X Output	Machine Y Output	Machine Z Output
Up to 5 hours production time lost per week	$^7/_8 \times \dfrac{180}{4}$		
(= $^1/_8$ of maximum weekly production time)	= 39 TRLS		
Machine Y		52 TRLS	
Machine Z			30 TRLS

Key resource is therefore Machine Z time

	£
Selling price	2,000
Material cost	(600)
	1,400

Time on key resource $\dfrac{40 \text{ hours per week}}{30 \text{ TRLS}}$ = 1.3333 hours per TRL

Return per factory hour $\dfrac{1,400}{1.3333}$ = £1,050

<u>Cost per factory hour</u>

	£
Labour	5,500
Variable overhead	8,000
Fixed production costs $\dfrac{450,000}{48 \text{ weeks}}$	9,375
	22,875

Number of factory hours per week: 40

Cost per factory hour: £571.88

Throughput accounting ratio: $\dfrac{£1,050}{571.88}$ = 1.84

(b) The following **uses** for the throughput accounting ratio have been suggested.

(i) In a throughput environment, production priority must be given to the products best able to generate throughput, that is those products that maximise throughput per unit of key or bottleneck resource. The throughput accounting ratio can be used to **rank products**, the product with the highest value of this ratio being given the highest ranking.

(ii) The throughput accounting ratio compares the rate at which a product earns contribution with the rate at which production costs are incurred. If the ratio is greater than one, contribution is being generated at a rate faster than that at which production costs are being incurred. The opposite is true if the ratio is less than one. The ratio can therefore be used to determine **whether or not a product should be produced**.

(c) Two other ratios which may be used by a company operating throughput accounting

(i) **Schedule adherence**. This will highlight how well production schedules are being adhered to.

(1) Given that products should not be made unless there is a customer waiting for them, it is vital that production is not disrupted otherwise the customer will be kept waiting.

(2) Given that the ideal work in progress level is zero and buffer stocks are not held, it is vital that production schedules are kept to otherwise the entire production process will come to a halt.

(ii) **First-time capability (especially of output from the bottleneck process).** Below quality output at the bottleneck process would use up valuable resource time to transform it into saleable output, thereby reducing throughput capacity and increasing costs.

(d) <u>Contribution in throughput accounting and contribution in marginal costing are based on the same concept.</u>

(i) They are both calculated as the difference between sales revenue and variable costs.

(ii) They are both used to cover an organisation's fixed costs.

In both approaches, the contribution earned can be used **to assess the relative earning capabilities of different products** in order to determine an optimum production mix.

There are **differences** between the approaches, however. For example in marginal costing, material costs, labour costs and variable overheads are classified as variable costs. In throughput accounting, most factory costs, with the exception of materials costs, are classified as fixed costs.

(e) The production manager and the management accountant need to focus on **adherence to production schedules** and **maintenance of low stock levels.**

If machine Z is replaced with machine G and if machine X is overhauled, the existing bottleneck of machine Z time will be removed and the availability of machine X time increased, and so output constraints will be as follows.

Machine X 45 units per week
Machine Y 52 units per week
Machine G 45 units per week

Time on machines X and G will therefore become the **bottleneck resource** during the period from June to October, when demand is estimated to range between 40 and 48 units per week. The changeover to G and the overhaul must therefore be completed and output must be at full capacity by the beginning of June.

First time capability of output from these two machines in particular must be rigorously monitored. The **return per factory hour** given these bottleneck resources and the **throughput ratio** must also be monitored and reported as well as any other indicators that enable the maximisation of throughput.

73 Various cost management techniques

> **Top tips.** Mix and productivity variances for labour are calculated the same way as mix and yield for materials.

(a) Rate variance

	Did pay	Should pay	Difference
Unskilled	12,096	12,960 (W1)	864
Semi-skilled	54,120	52,800 (W1)	(1,320)
Highly skilled	26,840	26,400 (W1)	(440)
Total			(896) (A)

Mix variance

	Actual mix	Std mix	Difference	Std rate	Variance
Unskilled	2,160	2,192 (W2)	32	6	192
Semi-skilled	6,600	6,576 (W2)	(24)	8	(192)
Highly skilled	2,200	2,192 (W2)	(8)	12	(96)
	10,960		0		96 (A)

Yield (productivity) variance

Yield was	380.00
Should be (10,960/30)	365.33
Difference	14.67
Standard rate of std mix	252.00
Variance	3,696.00 (F)

Workings

1   Based on standard rates, ABC should have paid:

		£
Unskilled	2,160 hrs × £6 per hour	12,960
Semi-skilled	6,600 hrs × £8 per hour	52,800
Highly skilled	2,200 hrs × £12 per hour	26,400

> **Top tips**. To find the mix variance you have to find the standard proportions (i.e. standard mix) of the three types of labour that would apply to the actual hours worked.
>
> Do not base this on actual units produced as this would *not* exclude the yield element of the variance.

2

		Hours
Unskilled	10,960 hrs × 6/30	2,192
Semi-skilled	10,960 hrs × 18/30	6,576
Highly skilled	10,960 hrs × 6/30	2,192

(b)

> **Top tips.** Marks for this type of question will normally be awarded for narrative explanations on the principles underlying the numbers as well as for calculations.

(i)   Division A has **spare capacity** and demand for product X is **limited**.

As division A has spare capacity and demand for product X is limited, division A **cannot** supply more of X to the **external market**. Division A therefore needs to provide **incentives** to division B to buy product X from it. Division A therefore needs to consider the **variable costs** of production for product Y. The variable cost for product Y is £70. Division B can buy Y from the external market at £75. The transfer price needs to be £70 or above so that the variable costs of division A are covered, but below £76 so that an incentive is provided to division B to buy from division A.

Therefore, the minimum price that division A would accept would be £70 (the unit variable cost of product Y). As division A has excess capacity and there is limited external demand for product X, there is no opportunity cost associated with the transfer.

The company as a **whole** is better off by £5 for every unit of Y that division A transfers to division B rather than the latter buying it from the external market. One possibility is that this £5 may be split 50:50 between the two divisions. In this case the transfer would be:

	£
Minimum price acceptable to division A	70.00
Add: 50% share of value added to the company	2.50
Transfer price	72.50

However, the 50:50 option is not the only one available and some other basis may be agreed.

(ii)   Division A is operating at full capacity with unsatisfied external demand for product X. Where there is external demand for product X with A operating at full capacity, there is **potential lost revenue** in division A supplying X ie there is an opportunity cost in any transfer of product Y to division B as A will be losing contribution that could be earned by supplying the external market with product X.

For every unit of product Y that division A transfers to B there is a **loss of contribution** of £20 (selling price = £84 – variable costs of £64).

The relevant cost to the company of A supplying product Y to division B is the variable cost of £70 plus the lost contribution of £20 ie £90. It is therefore in the interests of the company as a **whole** if B buys Y **externally** at the cheaper price of £75 per unit. The company can ensure this happens by setting the transfer price for Y above £75 thus encouraging B to buy externally.

SECTION C – BUDGETING AND MANAGEMENT CONTROL

Answers 74 to 91 cover budgeting and management control, the subject of Part C of the BPP Study Text for Paper P2.

74 Preparation question: MPL Ltd

Text reference. Budgets are covered in Chapter 10.

Top tips. The key point to note in the scenario detail is that budgets are issued to the consultants, implying that an imposed system of budgeting is in place.

Easy marks. Remember that presentation is important. You should prepare your report in report format.

REPORT

To: Board of directors of MPL Ltd
From: Management accountant
Subject: <u>Budgeting</u>
Date: 23 April 20X0

1 <u>Overview</u>

1.1 This report considers our present approach to budgeting, including the appropriateness of the format of the opening statement currently prepared.

2 <u>Present approach to budgeting</u>

2.1 Given that the budgets are **'issued to'** consultants, they clearly have very **little or no input to the budget process**. Budgets are **set centrally by senior management** and are **imposed** on consultants without consultants participating in their preparation.

3 <u>Problems of present approach</u>

3.1 Although there are advantages to such an approach (for example, strategic plans are likely to be incorporated into planned activities, there is little input from inexperienced or uninformed employees and the period of time taken to draw up the budgets is shorter), **dissatisfaction, defensiveness and low morale** amongst employees who must work with the budgets is often apparent.

3.2 The budget may be seen as a **punitive device** and **initiative may be stifled.**

3.3 More importantly, however, it is **difficult for people to be motivated to achieve targets that have been set by somebody else.**

(i) **Targets** that are **too difficult** will have a **demotivating** effect because **adverse efficiency variances** will always be reported.

(ii) **Easy targets** are also **demotivating** because there is **no sense of achievement** in attaining them.

(iii) **Targets set at the same levels as have been achieved in the past** will be too low and might **encourage budgetary slack.**

4 <u>Alternative approach</u>

4.1 Academics have argued that each individual has a **personal 'aspiration level'** which the individual undertakes for himself to reach, and so it may be more appropriate to adopt a **participative approach** to budgeting.

4.2 Budgets would be developed by the consultants and would be based on their perceptions of what is achievable and the associated necessary resources.

5 <u>Advantages of alternative approach</u>

5.1 Consultants are more likely to be **motivated** to achieve targets that they have set themselves and overall the budgets are likely to be more **realistic** (as senior management's overview of the business is mixed with operational level details and the expectations of both senior management and the consultants are considered).

6 Disadvantages of alternative approach

6.1 Allowing participation in the budget-setting process is **time consuming**, however, and can produce **budget bias.** It is generally assumed that the bias will operate in one direction only, consultants building **slack** into their budgets so targets are easy to achieve.

6.2 But **bias can work in two directions.** Optimistic forecasts may be made with the intention of pleasing senior management, despite the risk of displeasing them when optimistic targets are not met.

7 Format of the operating statement

7.1 The current format of the operating statement **classifies costs as either fixed or variable** in relation to the number of chargeable consultancy hours and **compares expected costs for the budgeted number of chargeable consultancy hours with actual costs incurred.**

8 Problem with current format

8.1 For **control purposes**, there is little point in comparing costs and revenues for the budgeted numbers of chargeable hours with actual costs and revenues if budgeted and actual hours differ.

9 Alternative format

9.1 An improved format would compare the **costs that should have been incurred given the actual number of chargeable consultancy hours** and **the actual costs incurred.**

9.2 Although fixed costs should be the same regardless of the hours charged, such a comparison requires **variable costs to be flexed** to the actual activity level.

9.3 More appropriate **variances** could then be calculated and denoted as either **adverse or favourable.**

9.4 The report should also **distinguish** between those **costs** which are **controllable** by consultants and those which are **uncontrollable.** Consultants' attention will then be focused on those variances for which they are responsible and which, if significant, require action.

I hope this information has proved useful. If you have any further questions, please do not hesitate to contact me.

Signed: Management accountant

75 Budgeting and budgetary control

(a)

Feedback loop in the control cycle

The term **'feedback control'** refers to the monitoring of outputs achieved against desired or target outputs, making a comparison and taking appropriate action as a result where necessary. In a budgeting context, *feedback control* is exercised by comparing an *ex ante* target (budget) against an *ex post* output (actual performance).

Through this process of comparison, any significant variations are investigated and one of two courses of action taken. Either corrective action is taken to ensure that the target is met by actual performance in future periods or the target is changed if it is concluded that it was not realistically achievable.

The **'feedback loop'** refers to the feedback represented by the loop above whereby corrective action brings actual performance in line with planned results. A criticism of this approach is that it is reactive and backward looking comparing historical costs with planned results. Past events are used as a means of controlling future activity.

The **'feed-forward' control** has been developed to counter this argument. In feed-forward control instead of actual outputs being compared against planned results and taking whatever corrective action is necessary, planned results are compared against predictions or forecasts at any future time. The result is that control is being proactive and forward looking.

(b) Advantages and disadvantages of allowing profit centre managers to participate actively in the setting of the budgets for their units.

Main advantages of participation are as follows:

(i) Acceptance and commitment

If profit centre managers participate in setting the targets they are more likely to accept these and show more commitment towards achieving them

(ii) Narrowing the knowledge and information gap

The detailed knowledge of day to day operations that profit managers have will enable more effective and relevant targets to be set. This process of information sharing will lead to the setting of optimal targets, taking into account both organisational and operational constraints and opportunities and making variance analysis more meaningful

(iii) Motivation and improved performance

Research findings confirm that participation increases job satisfaction, improves work related attitudes and leads to better performance.

Potential disadvantages of participation

(i) Time

The process of participation may be more time consuming in some circumstances participation may lead to less difficult targets or the introduction of budget slack

(ii) People's reaction

Research has shown certain people to react better to an imposed budget.

(c) The controllability principle refers to the degree of influence that a specific manager has over costs, revenue and related items.

The basis for the controllability principle is that managers of responsibility centres should only be held accountable for costs over which they have some influence. Under this principle, a divisional manager would not be held responsible for the allocation of central costs to his department if he has no control over the magnitude or incidence of these costs. It is argued that the benefits derived from responsibility accounting would be reduced and incorrect or sub-optimal judgements made if uncontrollables are not eliminated from the manager's responsibility centre.

Advantages of applying the controllability principle

(i) From a motivation point of view it can be demoralising for a manager to feel that his performance is based on something over which he has no influence.

(ii) It is also important from a control point of view in that reports should ensure that information on costs is reported to the manager who is able to take action to control them.

Disadvantages of the controllability principle

(i) An alternative view argues that holding managers responsible for costs even when they have no control over them can have beneficial effects in two ways.

(ii) It stops managers from viewing some costs as 'free services' and thus discourages overuse.

> **Other disadvantages you may have thought of include:**
>
> Holding managers responsible for costs outside their control may encourage them to become more involved with these costs and as result contribute to their reduction or to the more efficient provision of these services.
>
> It is not always clear cut which costs are controllable or uncontrollable and therefore, following very closely the controllability principle may exclude partially controllable costs from the decision making process.

(d)   (i)   <u>Four perspectives of a balanced scorecard</u>

The balanced scorecard is an approach to performance management that provides information management that provides information on a set of different indicators both financial and non-financial.

The scorecard is referred to as 'balanced' in the sense that managers are required to think in terms of four different perspectives, to prevent improvements being made in one area at the expense of the another. The perspectives are financial, customer, internal business and innovation and learning.

(ii)   For a general insurance company the following are appropriate performance measures for each perspective:

<u>Financial perspective</u>

–   Sales growth compared with previous periods or across the industry
–   Market share (measured quarterly as a %)

<u>Customer perspective</u>

–   New customers acquired on a monthly basis
–   Customer complaints as a % of total customer base

<u>Internal business perspective</u>

–   Speed of producing management information such as details of outstanding claims
–   Despatch time for new policies

<u>Innovation and learning perspective</u>

–   Staff training hours per year
–   Staff turnover (%)

(e)   Circumstances where participation in budget setting is likely to contribute to **poor** performance by managers (only three required)

(i)   Participative budgets can be very time consuming and tend to result in a complex, prolonged and costly budgetary process.

(ii)   Participative budgets may lead to budget slack or budget bias where targets are deliberately set at a lower level so that they can be easily achieved or exceeded. This would lead to lower targets and sub-optimal performance and underachievement disguised as meeting expectations.

(iii)   Budgets may be inappropriate if managers are not qualified to participate.

> **Other points you may have made include:**
>
> (i)   In a stable market environment especially where cost centres are not required to respond to fast moving market conditions participation may result in few or no benefits.
>
> (ii)   Participation may be counterproductive where employees feel they have no real influence but merely a semblance of participation.
>
> (iii)   Some employees respond better to imposed budgets.

76 SFG

> **Text references**. Non-financial performance measures are covered in Chapter 11.
>
> **Top tips**. Make sure you relate performance measures to the scenario ie: the hotel industry in part (b).

(a) Non-financial performance measures are important to companies such as SFG who operate in the service sector.

For instance SFG will want to know how **efficiently** it operates and to measure the **satisfaction** levels of its guests which can directly affect its performance. For example if guests are unsatisfied this could cause bad word of mouth and reduce revenue for the year. By measuring satisfaction levels throughout the year this gives opportunities to rectify the situation rather than waiting until revenue starts falling to realise that there is a problem. For this reason financial indicators are known as "**lagging measures**" but non-financial indicators can be "**leading measures**".

It is also important not to focus on short-term measures to increase current financial performance that may decrease non-financial measures which may lead to lower profit levels in the longer term.

(b) Customer complaints

A non-financial performance measure could be the **number of customer complaints / suggested improvements**. This may highlight poor service or short-cuts from managers that may potentially harm long-run profitability.

Use of hotel facilities

Another potential measure could be the **rate of use of hotel facilities by residents and non-residents**. This may indicate whether guests are making use of the hotel facilities and whether managers are making the range of facilities known to the guests and also whether they are successfully marketing the facilities outside of the hotels.

(c) **Uncontrollable costs** can be included in a performance report of a profit or investment centre so that the managers can be aware of all of the costs of running the business and know whether the centre is **operating at an overall profit**.

However it is unfair to measure a manager's performance on results that include items that are not in their control. Therefore the uncontrollable items should be contained in a **separate section of the report** and the performance of the manager should be based on the **controllable items** only.

77 College

> **Text references**. Participative budgeting is covered in Chapter 10.
>
> **Easy marks**. There are many opportunities to score marks, providing you relate your answer to the scenario.

There are a number of advantages and disadvantages to the college of allowing senior staff to participate in the setting of the budget.

Advantages of participative budgets

The budget will be based on information from staff who are **most familiar** with the department, which is likely to **improve the accuracy** of the budget.

Senior staff may know how to deliver courses more efficiently and effectively as well as how to attract more students to courses and increase profitability.

Furthermore, **staff** are likely to be **more motivated** to achieve any targets as it is 'their' budget.

As a direct result of the above, **morale** amongst senior staff members is likely to improve as they feel that their experience and **opinions are valued**.

Possible disadvantages of participative budgets

Participative budgets may consume **more time** than a top-down budget.

Due to the above, an **earlier start** to the budgeting process could be **required** to ensure that the budget is produced on time.

A participative approach to budgeting could result in senior staff introducing **budgetary slack** and budget bias, thus ensuring that any **targets** set are **easily attainable**.

Involving senior staff in the budget preparation process may lead to **disagreements**. Staff may spend time **arguing** with each other as to how measure the costs and benefits of each course.

78 DW

> **Text references**. Budgeting systems are covered in Chapter 10.
>
> **Top tips**. Remember to address both of the new manager's concerns in part (b).
>
> **Easy marks**. There are easy marks available in part (a) for explaining the differences between the two budgeting systems.

(a)   Rolling budget system

A **rolling budget system** is a system of budgeting that is **continuously updated by adding a further accounting period** (a month or quarter) when the earlier accounting period has expired.

Annual budgeting system

An **annual budgeting system is a system under which budgets are prepared for a 12 month period**, usually running to the end of the financial year of the company.

A key difference between the two systems is that managers using a rolling budget system view it as a **necessary planning and control procedure** that takes place on a regular basis, **not as a separate exercise that is used to monitor and measure their performance**.

Under a **rolling budget system**, there is always a budget which extends for **several months ahead**. For example, if rolling budgets are prepared quarterly there will always be a budget extending for the next 9 to 12 months. This is not the case when fixed annual budgets are used.

(b)   Annual budgets are restrictive

The manager of the Southern Depot is concerned that the current annual budgeting system is **restrictive** and **does not enable managers to make decisions** in response to operational decisions or working practices. For example, budgets for the coming year may not be approved until close to the start of the next year. As a result, managers are likely to find that they **do not have the authority to make decisions relating to next year until the year has almost commenced**.

Under a **rolling budget system**, it is likely that each update to the budget will be approved by the Board of Directors. In this scenario, **managers will have the authority to make decisions in line with the approved budget for the next 12 months or more**.

If DW introduced a system of rolling budgets, it would **enable depot managers to plan ahead and make key decisions in a timely manner**. For example, managers would know how much money is available to recruit new staff within the next 12 month period.

Annual budgets soon become out of date

The new manager also argues that **annual budgets quickly become out of date** as circumstances change. If a rolling budget system employed by DW allows the budget for the remaining part of the current budget year to be revised, it will combat the new manager's argument.

If this is the case, care must be taken to ensure that the system **does not allow managers to eliminate variances caused by actual performance**. Any variances from the approved budget should be **fully investigated**.

79 CW

Marking scheme

		Marks
(a)	Explanation of each problem and its consequence (up to 2 marks each)	Max 4
(b)	Manager motivation issues	2
	Manager's admission of error and its consequences	2
	Removal of costs without agreement of manager	2
		6

(a) If the store managers did overstate their budgeted costs and resource requirements, the following planning and decision-making problems could arise within CW.

Investing in new equipment

Overstating resource requirements may cause CW to **invest in new equipment that is not actually required**. This could reduce the funds available to invest in other areas of the business and could lead to **cash flow problems**.

Borrowing funds

In order to continue to fund the capital investment identified above, CW may need to enter into a loan facility with the bank. Such funding is not required but if used will result in CW incurring financing costs such as interest payments.

Inventory levels

CW may order excess items due to inaccurate budgets. As a result, **inventory holding costs are likely to increase** as products are not sold at the expected rate. Store managers may attempt to prove their budget was accurate by misappropriating items of inventory in the store accounts.

Recruitment of new employees

CW may recruit additional employees in order to meet budgeted resource requirements. This will lead to a **needlessly high headcount**, and increased payroll and training costs. When CW realise headcount is too high, they are likely to make employees redundant which will **reduce morale** within the workforce.

(b) Behavioural issues could arise if excess costs and resources are removed from the store managers' budgets both with and without the permission of the respective store manager.

Excess costs and resources removed with permission of the store manager

Store managers are unlikely to agree that excess can be removed from the budget. By doing this they are effectively **admitting that their original budget was inaccurate** and that the budget was constructed with their own interests in mind at the expense of CW.

Admitting that the budget is inaccurate is likely to give the impression that they do not understand the operations and processes that are key to successfully running the store. As a result their **ability to be a manager may be questioned**.

Excess costs and resources removed without the permission of the store manager

Removal of costs and resources from the budget **without consultation** with the store manager will **damage the relationships** between CW management and the store managers.

Store managers may disown the revised budget and are **unlikely to be motivated** towards achieving it.

There is a risk that store managers will make operational decisions that cause adverse variances when compared to the revised budget in an attempt to **prove that their original budget was more realistic**.

80 Solicitors

Test references. NFPIs and performance evaluation using budgets are covered in Chapter 11.

Top tips. Remember to relate your answer to part (b) to a firm of solicitors.

Easy marks. Explaining 2 NFPIs that that firm could use would score you 4 easy marks.

Examiner's comments. Many candidates ignored the 'discuss' requirement in part (a) and simply gave a description of 'top down', 'bottom up' and 'participative budgets'. A number of candidates answered part (b) in bullet points. This type of answer does not address the requirement to 'explain'.

Marking scheme

		Marks
(a)	Up to 2 marks per point Issues include – wasted time – not being motivated – deliberately setting out to fail – being ignored	
		Max 6
(b)	Explanation of two factors with reference to the scenario (2 marks each)	4
		10

(a) Divisional partners appear to be involved in the budgeting process as they are required to submit a divisional cost budget to the senior partner.

However, the senior partner amends each divisional budget without discussing the amendments and it is evident that the **divisional partners do not have any real involvement** in the process as they are unable to influence the final budget for the respective division.

This is likely to have an **adverse effect on divisional partner motivation**, who will feel that they have wasted their time preparing a budget which has effectively been ignored.

As such, divisional partners are **unlikely to feel personally responsible** for achieving the target costs bestowed upon them. They may even **deliberately fail to achieve the budgeted costs** to prove that their own budget was correct and that the amendments imposed by the senior partner were unrealistic.

(b) The firm could choose to measure **staff experience**. This could be achieved by monitoring staff turnover rate or analysing the qualification levels of newly recruited staff.

Some information could be taken from **internal sources** but much would have to come from colleges or external recruiters. Exit interviews could also be used.

Another NFPI that the firm could measure is **competitiveness**. This could be monitored through the size of **customer base** and **market share** by service or customer group. Regular market surveys drawing on both internal and external sources of information can be used to compile such reports.

81 Budgets for solicitors

Text references. Feedback and feedforward control systems are covered in Chapter 10.

Top tips. Remember to give an example of each type of control system in the context of a firm of solicitors.

Easy marks. Up to 5 marks are available for being able to discuss one advantage and one disadvantage of involving more than one partner in the budget-setting process in part (b).

(a) A feedback control system can be defined as the process of **reporting back control information to management** and the control of information itself. In a business, it is **information produced from within the organisation** (management control reports) with the purpose of helping management and other employees with control decisions.

In a firm of solicitors, a partner may explain that the reason for actual fee income being significantly above budget is due to the win of a new client. As a result of this feedback, the central budget may be updated to take account of the increased fee income going forward.

A feed forward control system is a system which **aims to forecast differences between actual and planned outcomes** and implement action, before the event, to avoid such differences.

An example would be the comparison of the original cash budget (taking the overdraft facility into account) with the target cash balance. Planned expenditure may have to be postponed in order to ensure that the solicitors meet cash targets and stay within the limits of the overdraft facility. In such instance, a second draft of the cash budget will be prepared.

(b) A potentially beneficial consequence of involving the firm's other partners in the budget setting process is **greater transparency** which will help to further partners knowledge of the budgeting system. Each partner will understand exactly which targets they are responsible for and how performance in each area will be measured.

Partners will also understand how **elements of the budget are interdependent**. For example, if actual fee income is significantly below budget, it is unlikely that cash targets will be met.

A potentially adverse consequence of involving the other partners in the budget setting process is that **poor attitudes** or **hostile behaviour** may be shown towards the budgetary control system.

Partners may feel pressured by the draft budget and may complain that it is **not realistic**. They may attempt to **build slack into the budget** to ensure that **targets are more easily achievable** than if the budget was set solely by the managing partner. This could lead to the firm becoming less efficient in the long-term.

82 Budget planning

Text references. Aspects of budgetary planning and control are covered in Chapter 10.

(a) <u>Feedforward control</u>

Feedforward control occurs when mangers **forecast likely outcomes** and then **compare these with the desired outcomes**. **Action can be taken in advance** to correct any adverse situations or to take full advantage of favourable situations.

For example, a cash forecast may show that an organisation is likely to have a negative cash position in November and December, say. Managers can therefore take action now to avoid the situation if necessary. They could, for example, postpone capital expenditure.

Feedforward control means that mangers are **forewarned** of any situation, whether it be good or bad, before it occurs.

Feedback control

Feedback control involves **recording actual results and then comparing them with forecast or budgeted** results. For example, a sales budget can act as a feedback control mechanism if the actual sales figures, are compared with the budgeted sales.

Reasons for differences can be identified and efforts made to ensure that **favourable differences continue to be exploited and adverse differences do not occur in the future**.

(b) Budgets should be realistic to be meaningful. There are several factors in a rapidly changing business environment which may cause the budget to be unrealistic. These include:

- **Political and economic changes**   Changes in interest rates, exchange rates or inflation can mean that future sales and costs are difficult to forecast.

- **Technological changes**   These may mean that the past is not a reliable indication of likely future events. For example new faster machinery may make it difficult to use current output levels as the basis for forecasting future production output.

- **Social changes**   Alterations in taste, fashion and the social acceptability of products can cause forecasting difficulties.

If the budget becomes unrealistic there is little point in using it as a control mechanism.

83 X plc

Text references. Budgeting is covered in Chapter 10.

Top tips. Remember in part (b) that you are comparing the standard cost of actual production with actual cost of actual production. Budgeted production does not come into it at all!

Examiner's comments. The examiner commented that many students seemed poorly prepared for the narrative sections and many failed to make reference to the scenario presented.

Top tips. Read the question carefully. You are being asked to **discuss** the **impact** of material A being in short supply **not just on budget preparation**, but also on **other areas**. Consider **alternative sources** or **substitute products**. Where these are not available X plc will need to start with the production budget as material A will be the principal budget factor. X plc will also need to maximise contribution per unit of limiting factor.

(a) Material A which may be in short supply during the year is referred to as the **principal budget factor, key or limiting budget factor**. It is the factor that limits the activities of the organisation. The scarcity of material A will mean that there is a limit to how many units can be produced.

The company could try to obtain **alternative supplies** or **substitute products**. If this is not possible, the impact this will have is that production will be limited by the supply of material A and therefore, once this has been identified, the production budget has to be prepared before all others. In addition, to make use of limited resources the company will have to concentrate production on the product that **maximises contribution per limiting factor**.

(b)

	Fixed budget	Flexed budget	Actual results	Variance
Production and sales (units)	7,700	7,250	7,250	
	£	£	£	£
Labour				
Skilled	462,000	435,000	568,750	133,750 (A)
Semi-skilled	415,800	391,500	332,400	59,100 (F)
Overheads				
Variable (W)	168,000	158,182	185,000	26,818 (A)
Fixed	112,000	112,000	105,000	7,000 (F)
	1,157,800	1,096,682	1,191,150	94,468 (A)

Working

Annual overheads are £280,000 for budgeted production of 7,700 units. Of these 40% ie, 40% of £280,000 or £112,000 are fixed. The remaining £168,000 vary with total labour hours.

Variable costs of £168,000 would be for budgeted production of 7,700 units. Flexing these to the actual production of 7,250 the variable costs would be:

$$\frac{7,250}{7,700} \times £168,000 = £158,182$$

84 W Limited

Text references. Topics in this question are covered in Chapter 10.

(i) <u>The 'beyond budgeting' approach</u>

The beyond budgeting approach proposes that **traditional budgeting** as most organisations practise it should be **abandoned** in favour of an approach more suited to a **modern business environment** of rapid **technological change** and **market uncertainty**.

Traditional annual plans are often **not responsive** to current situations. Under the beyond budgeting approach managers should plan on **a rolling basis** with a focus on **cash forecasting** rather than purely on cost control.

Emphasis should also be placed on encouraging a culture of **personal responsibility** by delegating decision making and performance accountability to **line managers**.

(ii) W Limited operates in a competitive fast changing industry with uncertain market conditions. Product innovation and a **fast response to industry developments** and relative industry benchmarks is very important for the survival of the company. Traditional budgeting and **long-term planning** may be of **limited value** as it may not be possible for W Limited to **predict** conditions a year in advance.

There are arguments for the 'beyond budgeting' approach which gives local managers the power to make decisions in response to market conditions and customer demand. Performance would be measured against **relative improvements** and **value added**.

It may be necessary to maintain a form of **short term budgeting** provided this is implemented with a degree of **flexibility** in full knowledge and understanding of the dynamic market conditions.

(iii) Standard costing and variance analysis **concentrate on only a narrow range of costs** such as quality and customer satisfaction.

Standard costing systems were developed when the business environment was more stable and less prone to change. The **current business environment** is more **dynamic** and it is not possible to **assume stable conditions**.

Standard costing systems assume that **performance to standard is acceptable**. Today's business environment is more focused on **continuous improvement**.

Alternative suggestions

Many of the variances in a standard costing system focus on the control of short term variable costs. In most modern manufacturing environments, the majority of costs, including direct labour costs, tend to be fixed in the short run.

Most standard costing systems produce control statements weekly or monthly. The manager in the modern business environment needs much more prompt control information to function efficiently in a dynamic business environment.

---

85 M plc

> **Text references.** Fixed and flexible budgets are covered in Chapter 10.
>
> **Top tips.** This question is quite straightforward provided you appreciate that the information as given does not compare like with like. You need to flex the budgets to the actual level of activity to make comparisons appropriate.
>
> In addition, note that the manager's $2,050 fixed salary is erroneously included in the assembly labour costs. This is an inconsistency that will have to be adjusted for, before the data is flexed.
>
> **Easy marks.** In order to get the easy marks in the question you must make sure that you read the requirements carefully and answer the actual question set (rather than what you want the question to ask!)

(a)

	Original budgeted 1	Flexed budgeted 2	Actual costs 3	Variance (3 – 2)
Assembly labour hours	6,400	7,140	7,140	
	$	$	$	$
Variable costs				
Assembly labour (W1, W2, W3)	49,920	55,692	56,177	485 (A)
Furniture packs (W4)	224,000	249,900	205,000	44,900 (F)
Other materials (W5)	23,040	25,704	24,100	1,604 (F)
Variable overheads (W6)	34,560	38,556	76,340	37,784 (A)
	331,520	369,852	361,617	8,235
Fixed costs				
Manager	2,050	2,050	2,050	–
Stepped-fixed cost (W6)	18,500	27,000	27,000	–
Total departmental fixed costs	20,550	29,050	29,050	–
Central costs	9,000	9,000	9,000	–
	361,070	407,902	399,667	8,235 (F)

Workings

1 Both budgeted and actual assembly labour costs given include manager's fixed salary of $2,050 which has to be deducted

$51,970 – $2,050 = $49,920

2 Budgeted assembly labour costs are flexed to reflect actual labour hours by multiplying the cost by:

$$\frac{\text{Actual hours}}{\text{Bugeted hours}}$$

$$\$49,920 \times \frac{7,140 \text{ hours}}{6,400 \text{ hours}} = \$55,692$$

3 We need to deduct the assembly manager's fixed salary of $2,050 from the actual costs of $58,227

$58,227 – $2,050 = $56,177

4 We need to flex the original budget for the cost of furniture packs to reflect the actual labour hours worked.

$$\$224,000 \times \frac{7,140 \text{ hours}}{6,400 \text{ hours}} = \$249,900$$

5 We need to flex the original budget for other materials to reflect the actual labour hours worked

$$\$23,040 \times \frac{7,140 \text{ hours}}{6,400 \text{ hours}} = \$25,704$$

6   The budgeted overheads include a fixed cost of $9,000 and a stepped-fixed cost which we need to work out using the high-low method. The stepped fixed cost changes when the assembly hours exceed 7,000 hours. In order to identify these stepped fixed costs we compare the overhead costs for the two different levels of labour hours at 7,500 and 10,000 hours respectively.

At 7,500 assembly labour hours we have: $a + 7,500 b = \$76,500$

At 10,000 assembly labour hours we have: $a + 10,000 b = \$90,000$

Where, a is defined below as: $a = $ Stepped fixed cost $+ \$9,000$

$a + 10,000 b = \$90,000$ (1)
$a + 7,500 b = \$76,500$ (2)

Subtracting (2) from (1) we get:

$2,500 b = \$13,500$

$$b = \frac{\$13,500}{2,500} = 5.4$$

Substituting the value of b in (1)

$a + 5.4 \times 10,000 = 90,000$
$a = 90,000 - 54,000 = 36,000$
$a = $ stepped fixed costs at 7,000 hours $+ \$9,000 = \$36,000$

Stepped fixed costs at 7,000 hours $= \$36,000 - \$9,000 = \$27,000$

To find the stepped fixed cost component at 5,000 hours, we substitute the value of $b = 5.4$ in the following equation

$a_1 + 5,000 b = \$54,500$

Where a_1 is the stepped fixed cost at 5,000 units (including the central fixed cost of $9,000)

$a_1 + 5,000 \times 5.4 = \$54,500$
$a_1 = \$27,500$

Deducting the central fixed cost of $9,000, the stepped fixed cost for 5,000 units is $27,500 less $9,000 = $18,500.

(b)   (i)   The revised format of the statement is **more helpful** as it has been **flexed** to the actual level of activity and therefore **compares like with like**.

      (ii)   The revised format **separates costs** into variable (and hence **controllable**) costs and fixed costs or central costs (and therefore **uncontrollable**). This will **facilitate analysis**, performance measurement and responsibility accounting.

      (iii)   The format originally submitted has some **inconsistencies** which make **comparison** very **difficult**. In addition to the fact that the format was not comparing like with like, the manager's fixed salary was included in overheads when labour assembly hours related only to the variable labour input.

(c)

> **Top tips.** Whereas bullet points provide a clear way of presentation, the examiner stressed that these should be supplemented by adequate explanatory narrative. Make sure you relate the discussion to the specific entity in question.

Advantages of participative budgets

(i)   They are based on information from employees most familiar with the department
(ii)   Knowledge spread among several levels of management is pulled together
(iii)   Morale and motivation is improved
(iv)   They increase operational managers' commitment to organisational objectives
(v)   In general they are more realistic
(vi)   Co-ordination between units is improved
(vii)   Specific resource requirements are included
(viii)   Senior managers' overview is mixed with operational level details
(ix)   Individual managers' aspiration levels are more likely to be taken into account

The allocation of overheads in M plc is likely to vary considerably depending on the size, complexity and value of the furniture being assembled. It is, therefore, important to involve employees with detailed knowledge of the process. This will not only draw on useful experience but also increase motivation and commitment.

Disadvantages of M plc moving to a system of participative budgeting

(i)   They consume more time
(ii)   An earlier start to the budgeting process may therefore be required
(iii)   They may cause managers to introduce budgetary slack and budget bias
(iv)   Managers may, therefore, set 'easy' budgets to ensure that they are achievable
(v)   They can support 'empire building' by subordinates

In considering the advantages of introducing participative budgeting M plc needs to be aware of the potential disadvantages. The most important potential problem, apart from participative budgets requiring more resource and taking longer to prepare, is the possible introduction of slack.

Negotiated style of budgeting

A **negotiated budget** is a 'budget in which budget allowances are set largely on the basis of negotiations between budget holders and those to whom they report.'

At the two extremes, budgets can be **dictated from** above or simply **emerge from below** but, in practice, different levels of management often agree budgets by a process of **negotiation**. In the **imposed** budget approach, **operational** managers will try to negotiate with senior managers the budget targets which they consider to be **unreasonable** or **unrealistic**. Likewise senior management usually review and revise budgets presented to them under a **participative approach** through a process of **negotiation** with lower level managers. Final budgets are therefore most likely to lie **between** what top management would **really like** and what junior managers believe is **feasible**. The budgeting process is hence a **bargaining process** and it is this bargaining which is of vital importance, determining whether the budget is an effective management tool or simply a clerical device.

(d)   Budgets for planning and budgets for control

Budgets for planning

An organisation planning process can be divided into two sections, **long-term strategic planning** (also known as **corporate planning**) and **short-term planning**.

(1)   Long-term planning

This involves selecting appropriate **strategies** so as to prepare a long-term plan to attain the organisation's **objectives**.

This long-term corporate plan serves as the long-term **framework** for the organisation as a whole but for **operational purposes** it is necessary to convert the corporate plan into a series of **short-term plans (or budgets),** usually covering one year, which relate to sections, functions or departments.

(2)   Short-term planning

The annual process of short-term planning (or **budgeting**) should be seen as **steps** in the progressive fulfilment of the corporate plan as each short-term plan steers the organisation towards its long-term objectives.

The short-term budgets for the various functions of the organisation are **coordinated** and **consolidated** by the budget committee into the **master budget**, which is a summary of organisation-wide plans for the coming period. The master budget is what is known as a **fixed budget**. This does not mean that the budget is kept unchanged. Revisions will be made to it if the situation so demands. It simply means that the budget is prepared on the basis of an estimated volume of production and sales, but no plans are made for the event that actual volumes differ from budgeted volumes.

Budgets for control

Having set the master budget, control processes need to be established. The basic control model involves comparing actual results achieved with what results should have been under the circumstances.

Every business is dynamic, however, and actual volumes of output cannot be expected to conform exactly to the fixed master budget. Comparing actual results directly with the fixed master budget results is meaningless. For useful control information, it is necessary to compare actual results at the actual level of activity achieved with the results that should have been expected at this level of activity, which is shown by a flexible budget.

86   AHW plc

Text references. Budgeting is covered in Chapter 10.

Top tips. This question is straightforward provided you approached it methodically and did not make an arithmetic error. The trick is to work out a budgeted cost per individual processing activity.

Easy marks. Calculation of budgeted costs per processing activity would have gained you the first four marks. Calculation of the actual number of activities was also worth four marks, while the flexed budget and budgetary control statement were worth seven marks.

(a)

	Original budget cost £'000	Flexed budget costs (W) £'000	Actual costs £'000	Variances £'000
Processing activity W	160	159	158	1 (F)
Processing activity X	130	135	139	4 (A)
Processing activity Y	80	78	73	5 (F)
Processing activity Z	200	206	206	–
	570	578	576	2 (F)

Workings

Budgeted number of processing activities

Costs are expected to be variable in relation to the number of processing activities. We therefore need to calculate the budgeted number of activities for each process.

W $(20 \times 4) + (30 \times 5) + (15 \times 2) + (40 \times 3) + (25 \times 1) = 405$
X $(20 \times 3) + (30 \times 2) + (15 \times 5) + (40 \times 1) + (25 \times 4) = 335$
Y $(20 \times 3) + (30 \times 3) + (15 \times 2) + (40 \times 4) + (25 \times 2) = 390$
Z $(20 \times 4) + (30 \times 6) + (15 \times 8) + (40 \times 2) + (25 \times 3) = 535$

Budgeted cost per processing activity

W $\dfrac{£160,000}{405} = £395.06$

X $\dfrac{£130,000}{335} = £388.06$

Y $\dfrac{£80,000}{390} = £205.13$

Z $\dfrac{£200,000}{535} = £373.83$

Actual number of processing activities

W $(18 \times 4) + (33 \times 5) + (16 \times 2) + (35 \times 3) + (28 \times 1) = 402$
X $(18 \times 3) + (33 \times 2) + (16 \times 5) + (35 \times 1) + (28 \times 4) = 347$
Y $(18 \times 3) + (33 \times 3) + (16 \times 2) + (35 \times 4) + (28 \times 2) = 381$
Z $(18 \times 4) + (33 \times 6) + (16 \times 8) + (35 \times 2) + (28 \times 3) = 552$

Budgeted cost for actual number of processing activities

W   £395.06 × 402 = £158,814.12
X   £388.06 × 347 = £134, 656, 82
Y   £205.13 × 381 = £78,154.53
Z   £373.83 × 552 = £206,354.16

(b)   Reasons for managers not to be involved in setting their own budgets

   (i)   Participative budgeting **consumes more time** than a system of imposed budgeting and hence the budgeting process has to **start earlier**.

   (ii)   There may be **dissatisfaction** if senior managers implement changes to budgets drawn up by **lower levels** of management.

   (iii) Budgets may be **unachievable** if managers drawing them up do not have the **necessary skills**, **knowledge** or **expertise**. For example, senior management have an awareness of total resource availability, lower level managers may not.

   (iv)   Participative budgeting gives managers the opportunity to **introduce budgetary slack** and budget bias.

   (v)   A system of allowing managers to participate in the budgeting process can support '**empire building**'.

   (vi)   **Strategic plans** are **less likely** to be successfully **incorporated** into planned activities.

(c)   (i)   There are important **differences between fixed and flexible budgets** at both the budget-setting and performance review stages.

      (1)   Budget setting

          –   **Fixed budgets** are prepared on the basis that a certain volume of activity/production and a certain volume of sales will be achieved (such as 200 units). **No alternatives are given to these levels**.

          –   A **flexible budget** is a budget which is designed to **change** as the **volume of activity changes**. A company may expect to sell 200 units. However it may prepare flexible budgets on the basis that it produces and sells 180 units, or produces 200 units and sells 180 units.

          Thus when preparing flexible budgets it is essential to know **which costs vary with activity levels** and **which costs** are **fixed**. This information is not important when using fixed budgeting because costs are only being budgeted at one level of activity.

      (2)   Performance review

          –   When a period is reviewed, a **fixed budget** would **not be adjusted** for the actual level of activity. Hence budgeted costs at the budgeted level of activity would be compared with actual costs at the actual level of activity; the actual level of activity may well differ from the budgeted level.

          –   **Flexible budgets** at the review stage would be set at the actual level of activity. Thus actual results at the actual level of activity can be compared with the results that should have been achieved at the **actual level of activity**.

      Control of production and non-production costs

      Production costs tend to be **variable** costs and hence **cannot be controlled using fixed budgets** as the budget allowance does not reflect the expected cost at the actual level of production. Control is better achieved using flexible budgets, as the budget cost allowance reflects the cost that should have been achievable given the actual level of production.

      Non-production costs (such as marketing costs) tend to be **unaffected by changes in activity level** and hence can be **controlled by both fixed and flexible budgets**.

   (ii)   Costs that are more appropriately controlled using a fixed budget

      Any fixed cost, and particularly non-production fixed costs, can be controlled using a pre-set expenditure limit, which is a form of fixed budget, because they should be unaffected by changes in activity level (within a certain range). Examples include research costs and advertising costs.

87 DVD and Blu-ray

Text references. Planning and operational variances are covered in the Introduction chapter.

Top tips. Relate your answer to the scenario and clearly label all variance calculations. This is a particularly difficult variance question because you must account for the revised market details. Do not be disheartened if you get this incorrect.

(a) (i) Sales mix profit margin variance

	Actual sales	Revised standard mix *	Difference	Profit per unit	Variance ($)
DVD	3,000	2,800	+200	$25	5,000 (F)
Blu-ray	1,200	1,400	−200	$95	19,000 (A)
	4,200	4,200			14,000 (A)

* The revised standard mix

The revised standard mix is based on the revised budget of 1,500 units of Blu-ray players while DVD sales are unaffected (3,000 units).

DVD = (3,000/4,500) × 4,200 = 2,800

Blu-ray = (1,500/4,500) × 4,200 = 1,400

(ii) Sales volume profit variance

The sales volume profit variance only relates to Blu-ray players as the actual and budgeted sales of DVD players are the same.

The variance is (1,500 − 1,200) × $95 = $28,500 (A)

(b) The sales manager is not responsible for the increase in market size as this was caused by external factors. Therefore the variances relating to changes in market size should be regarded as **planning variances**. The sales manager is responsible for the change in selling price and so any variances attributed to this change should be treated as **operating variances**.

The market size variance compares the original and revised market size. For DVD players the market size is unchanged so there is no variance. For Blu-ray players the variance is:

(1,500 − 1,000) × $95 = $47,500 (F)

This figure is important as it shows the measurement of performance by the sales manager is distorted if the effect of the change in market size is not taken into account. The favourable variance of $19,000 which the sales manager has referred to in his/her e-mail is made up of two parts; the **market size variance** and the **sales volume profit variance** which have both been calculated above.

The overall favourable variance is caused by the change in market size which is a planning variance and outside the control of the manager. Therefore the manager is not responsible for the favourable performance and should not be awarded a bonus as a result.

88 KHL

> **Text references.** Fixed and flexible budgets are covered in Chapter 10. Revision of variance analysis and reconciling profit figures is covered in the Introduction chapter.
>
> **Top tips.** Present your reconciliation statement clearly and show all workings to maximise your score. Remember to calculate cost variances based on production volume, not sales volume.

Calculate the actual production level for February 20X1

Fixed overhead absorbed = $60,000

Absorption rate = $5 per hour × 2 hours per unit = $10 per unit

Therefore production level = 60,000 / 10 = 6,000 units

Reconciliation statement for February 20X1

			$	
Budgeted profit			84,000	
Sales volume variance			4,200	(A)
Standard profit on actual sales			79,800	
Selling price variance			34,200	(A)
			45,600	

	Adverse	Favourable		
Direct material price (W1)		3,720		
Direct material usage (W2)	2,400			
Direct labour rate (W3)	13,800			
Direct labour efficiency (W4)		5,000		
Variable overhead expenditure (W5)	1,150			
Variable overhead efficiency (W6)		2,000		
Fixed overhead expenditure (W7)	7,000			
Fixed overhead volume (W8)		10,000		
Totals	24,350	20,720	3,630	(A)
Actual profit			41,970	

Workings

1   Direct material price variance

	$
18,600kg should have cost (× $4*)	74,400
But did cost	70,680
	3,720 (F)

* $600,000 / 50,000 units / 3kg per unit = $4

2   Direct material usage variance

	Kgs
6,000 units should have used (× 3kg per unit)	18,000
But did use	18,600
Variance in kg	600 (A)
× standard cost per kg	× $4.00
	$2,400 (A)

3   Direct labour rate variance

	$
11,500 hours should have cost (× $10* per hour)	115,000
But did cost	128,800
	13,800 (A)

* $1,000,000 / 50,000 units / 2 = $10

4   Direct labour efficiency variance

	Hrs
6,000 units should have taken (× 2hrs per unit)	12,000
But did take	11,500
Variance in hours	500 (F)
× standard rate per hour	× $10.00
	$5,000 (F)

5   Variable overhead expenditure variance

	$
11,500 hours should have cost (× $4 per hour *)	46,000
But did cost	47,150
	1,150 (A)

* $400,000 / 50,000 units / 2 hours per unit = $4 per hour

6   Variable overhead efficiency variance

	Hrs
6,000 units should have taken (× 2hrs per unit)	12,000
But did take	11,500
Variance in hours	500 (F)
× standard rate per hour	× $4.00
	$2,000 (F)

7   Fixed overhead expenditure variance

	$
Budgeted expenditure	50,000 *
Actual expenditure (60,000 – 3,000)	57,000
	7,000 (A)

* (2hours per unit × $5 per hour × 5,000 units **) = $50,000

** 60,000 units (annual budget) / 12 months (constant monthly rate) = 5,000 units per month.

8   Fixed overhead volume variance

	Units
Actual production	6,000
Budgeted production	5,000
Variance in units	1,000 (F)
× OAR per unit	× $10.00
	$10,000 (F)

89   Direct labour requirements

Text references. Variance analysis is covered in the Introduction Chapter. The learning curve and target costing is covered in Chapter 7.

Top tips. In part (a), remember to calculate the average time per batch for 6 batches assuming a learning curve of 90% to obtain the revised standards. Next, use the revised standards to calculate the planning and operational variances.

Easy marks. If you are familiar with target costing you will pick up a few marks for explaining the concept in part (b).

Examiner's comments. A reasonable attempt was made by most candidates. A worrying number of candidates were not able to calculate the variances required. In part (b), candidates struggled to compare standard costing with target costing.

Marking scheme

		Marks
(a)	Revised standard hours for 6 batches	2
	The planning variance due to the learning effect	2
	The operational variance	2
		6
(b)	Explanation of target costing	1
	Explanation of standard costing	1
	Explanation of the differences	2
		4

(a) <u>Planning variance caused by learning effect</u>

		$
Revised std cost for revised hours for actual output	1,827.816 hours x $7	12,794.71
Original std cost for original hours for actual output	2,400 hours x $7	16,800.00
Planning variance		4,005.29 (F)

<u>Operational efficiency variance</u>

	$
Revised std cost for revised std hours for actual output (1,827.816 hours x $7)	12,794.71
Actual cost	13,650.00
Total **operational** variance	855.29 (A)

Workings

<u>Average time per batch for 6 batches assuming a 90% learning curve</u>

$Y_x = aX^b$

Where
- a = 400 (2,400 budgeted labour hours / 6 batches)
- X^b = 6^b (Cumulative number of batches)

$$b = \frac{\text{Log } 0.90}{\text{Log } 2} = \frac{-0.04576}{0.301} = -0.1520$$

Therefore $6^b = 6^{-0.1520} = 0.76159$ and substituting this into the main formula for the learning curve gives

Y_x = 400 × 0.76159
= 304.636 hours

Revised standard hours for 6 batches = 304.636 hours x 6 = 1,827.816 hours
Original standard = 2,400 hours × $7 = $16,800
Revised standard = 1,827.816 hours × $7 = $12,794.71

(b) <u>Differences between target costing and standard costing</u>

(i) <u>How costs are controlled</u>

With **standard costing**, a standard cost is set at the beginning of a specified period. Costs must be kept within this predetermined standard and variances are calculated to ensure that this is the case.

In a **target costing** system, there are no cost reduction exercises but there is **continual pressure** to ensure that costs are always kept to a minimum.

Cost reduction instead takes place at the **initial design and development stage** to ensure the desired target cost can be met.

(ii) <u>Time frame for cost control</u>

Cost control is a **continuous process** in a target costing system and target costs tend to be revised **monthly**. This ensures that costs are as **up-to-date** as possible.

In a standard costing system, standard costs are revised **annually**, meaning that actual costs are often being compared to **out-of-date** targets.

(iii)   Relationship between product concept, cost and price

With target costing, the product concept is set and then the selling price that customers are likely to be willing to pay is established. **Target cost is determined by deducting the desired profit margin from the selling price**.

The **standard cost is established from the product concept** and the selling price is determined from this cost by adding on a desired profit margin.

(iv)   Link with strategic plans

There is **no link** between standard costs and long-term strategies. The approach is **short-term cost control** through variance analysis.

In a target costing system, the product concept and target profit margin take into account **medium-term strategic plans** by focusing on whether the product can actually be produced for the target cost. If not, the project is abandoned in favour of a more cost-effective alternative.

90 WC

Text references. The areas this question examines are covered in Chapter 10.

Top tips. Part (a) may have made you think about what a sales mix profit variance might be. You may have been able to guess that it is the actual sales at the budgeted mix less the actual sales at the actual mix, multiplied by the budgeted profit. If you didn't guess this then don't worry because it is only a very small part of the question. Part (b) should have been fairly straightforward to set up, even if you couldn't get the profits to reconcile. Don't over-run on time by trying to make the profits reconcile as you will still get marks for your workings. Part (c) specifically asks you to use the statement you prepared in part (b).

Easy marks. In part (b) you must set out your statement clearly so that you get marks for your workings even if the profits don't reconcile.

Examiner's comments. The examiner noted that a common error was failing to provide totals for the company as well as totals for each profit centre. You must read the requirements carefully. You must also label your variances so that the marker can give you the marks that you deserve.

(a)   Sales price variances

	$'000
Kitchens	
Revenue from 2,600 kitchens should have been (× $10,000)	26,000
But was (× $13,000)	33,800
	7,800 (F)
Bathrooms	
Revenue from 2,500 bathrooms should have been (× $7,000)	17,500
But was (× $6,100)	15,250
	2,250 (A)

	$'000
Total sales price variance ($7,800 (F) - $2,250 (A))	5,550 (F)

Sales mix profit variance

Kitchens	
Actual sales at budgeted mix (5,100 × 4/6)	3,400 jobs
Actual sales at actual mix	2,600 jobs
	800 jobs
× budgeted profit per kitchen (× $2,000)	$1,600 (A)

Bathrooms

Actual sales at budgeted mix (5,100 × 2/6)	1,700 jobs
Actual sales at actual mix	2,500 jobs
	800 jobs
× budgeted profit per bathroom (× $1,500)	$1,200 (F)

	$'000
Total sales mix profit variance ($1,600 (A) + $1,200 (F))	400 (A)

Sales quantity profit variance

	Actual qty Std mix	Std qty std mix	Difference in units	X std profit per unit	Variance in $
Kitchens	3,400	4,000	600	2,000	1,200,000 (A)
Bathrooms	1,700	2,000	300	1,500	450,000 (A)
	5,100	6,000			1,650,000 (A)

(b) **Operating statement for the year**

		Kitchens		Bathrooms			Total
	$'000	$'000	$'000	$'000	$'000	$'000	$'000
Budgeted profit			8,000			3,000	11,000
Sales variances	(F)	(A)		(F)	(A)		
Sales price variance	7,800				2,250		5,550
Sales quantity profit variance		1,200			450		(1,650)
Sales mix		1,600		1,200			(400)
			5,000		(1,500)		
Actual sales less standard cost of sales			13,000			1,500	14,500
Cost variances							
Direct cost price (W1)		6,500		750			(5,750)
Central services expenditure (W2)							(2,500)
Central services volume (W3)							(2,250)
			(6,500)			750	
Actual profit/(loss)			6,500			2,250	4,000

Workings

(1) Direct cost variance

	$'000
Kitchens	
Should have cost (2,600 × $5,500)	14,300
But did cost (2,600 × $8,000)	20,800
	6,500 (A)
Bathrooms	
Should have cost (2,500 × $3,000)	7,500
But did cost (2,500 × $2,700)	6,750
	750 (F)

(2) Central services expenditure variance

	$'000
Budgeted expenditure (6,000 jobs x $2,500 recharge per job)	15,000
Actual expenditure	17,500
	2,500 (A)

(3)   Central services volume variance

		Jobs
Budgeted number of jobs (4,000 + 2,000)		6,000
Actual number of jobs (2,600 + 2,500)		5,100
		900 (A)
		$'000
900 jobs x $2,500 (recharge per job)		$2,250

(c)   (i)   The company **budgeted** to make a **profit** of **$8 million on the kitchens and $3 million on the bathrooms**. In fact it only made **$6.5 million on the kitchens and $2.25 million on the bathrooms**.

Kitchens

The company **didn't sell as many kitchens as** it had **budgeted** for (only 2,600 compared to 4,000) and this accounts for the **adverse variance** of $2.8 million shown above.

However, it sold the kitchens at a **higher selling price** ($13,000 per kitchen compared to the budgeted $10,000) and this accounts for the **favourable variance** of $7.8 million shown above.

The **direct cost per kitchen was higher** than the budgeted amount and this led to an **adverse variance** of $6.5 million. The **total central services cost was originally budgeted at $15 million but the actual costs were $17.5 million**. This gave rise to an adverse variance.

Bathrooms

In the case of the bathrooms, the company actually **sold 500 more bathrooms than it had budgeted** to sell, leading to a **favourable variance** of $750,000.

Unfortunately the **average selling price per bathroom was only $6,100** compared to the budget of $7,000. This caused an **adverse variance** of $2.250 million.

The **direct costs per bathroom were $300 less than budgeted** and this caused a **favourable direct cost variance** of $750,000. As explained for the kitchens, the central services cost gave rise to an adverse variance.

(ii)   It seems that the budgeting and reporting process has been **over simplified**. The following changes could be implemented.

Bespoke and off-the-shelf costs

The company installs both **bespoke designs** and **off the shelf designs**. The budgeted revenue and costs for these really need to be **split out** because it is likely that they will be very different. For example the design process for a bespoke kitchen is likely to cost more than an off-the-shelf design.

The operating statement suggests that the budgeted costs are too low but more could be revealed by splitting the costs into bespoke and off-the-shelf.

Materials, labour and other costs

It would also help to split the costs into material, labour and other expenses. This would help to identify areas where variances, for example the $6.5 million on kitchens, have occurred. It should help to pinpoint the **causes** for the over–spending.

Central services costs

The central services costs include design, administration and finance. These costs are charged on the basis of the number of jobs. This does not seem like a very fair way of allocating the costs. For example the administration for a bespoke kitchen would not necessarily be the same as the administration for an off-the-shelf bathroom. It would be worth investigating the **cost drivers** for these costs and allocating them on a fairer basis.

It also seems that there is **no incentive** for the central services departments to keep their costs down as the costs are re-charged to the kitchen and bathroom departments. For controllable costs, the central services should be **held responsible** for these costs and only allowed to re-charge them where it is justified. This should help to encourage **goal congruence** between the departments.

91 Planning & control variances

> **Text references.** Variances are assumed knowledge from Paper P1, and are still examinable in Paper P2. This question offers an opportunity for practising the calculation and interpretation of variances.
>
> **Top tips.** You must make sure that you know how to calculate the various types of variance. This question demonstrates that you also need to be able to discuss variance analysis as well as perform the calculations. This is an important part of the syllabus.
>
> **Easy marks.** Part (b)(i) needed some fairly straightforward calculations. Part (b)(ii) was a gift! Part (c) required you to state the case for and against standard costing as a useful tool for management.

(a) (i)

FA 38,000 units should have used (0.2kg/70%)	10,857.14
FB 25,000 units should have used (0.2kg/70%)	7,142.86
But did use	17,740.00
Variance in kg	260 00 (F)
× standard cost per kg	× $8
	$2,080 (F)

(ii) Content of output = (38,000+25,000) × 0.2kg of C1 = 12,600 kg of C1

Materials input = 17,740 kg of C1

Therefore, actual losses = 5,140 kg of C1

Therefore, actual loss percentage = $\frac{5,140kg}{17,740kg}$ = 29.0%

(b) (i) <u>Planning variance</u>

	$
Revised standard cost (25,000 units × 0.25kg × $14.50)	90,625
Original standard cost (25,000 units × 0.25kg × $12)	75,000
	15,625 (A)

<u>Operational price variance</u>

	$
6,450 should have cost (× $14.50)	93,525
But did cost	94,000
	475 (A)

<u>Operational usage variance</u>

25,000 units should have used (× 0.25kg)	6,250
But did use	6,450
Variance in kg	200 (A)
× revised standard cost per kg	× $14.50
	$2,900 (A)

(ii) One of the problems of planning variances is that it is often difficult even with hindsight to decide what the realistic standard should have been. How is the revised standard set and is the information correct?

Another problem is that it may become too easy to justify all of the variances as being due to bad planning, so no operational variances will be highlighted. There must be a good reason why there was an error in the planning otherwise it could just be an excuse to shift the blame from operations to the planning manager.

(c) <u>The business environment</u>

Variance analysis (and standard costing systems) were **developed** when the **business environment** was more **stable** and **less prone to change**. The current business environment is more dynamic and it is not possible to assume stable conditions. This means that the use of variance analysis for planning and control purposes is not always ideal.

Quality

Modern businesses need to plan for and control quality. Variance analysis concentrates on a **narrow range of costs** only and does not give sufficient attention to issues such as quality and customer satisfaction. Today's business environment is more focused on **continuous improvement** in a **total quality** environment.

Building in continual improvement

Predetermined fixed standards are at odds with the philosophy of **continual improvement** inherent in a total quality management programme, as continual improvements are likely to alter methods of working, prices, quantities of inputs and so on.

Responsibility for variances

Standard costing systems make **individual managers responsible** for the variances relating to their part of the organisation's activities. A TQM programme, on the other hand, aims to make **all personnel** aware of, and responsible for, the importance of supplying the customer with a quality product.

Standard costing – the wrong focus

The use of standard costing in the modern manufacturing environment can make managers **focus their attention on the wrong issues**. For example, **adverse efficiency variances** are meant to be avoided, which means that managers need to prevent idle time and keep up production. In **a just-in-time environment**, however, action to **eliminate idle time** could result in the **manufacture of unwanted products** that would need to be held in store and might eventually be scrapped, which is totally at odds with the aims of JIT.

It could therefore be argued that standard costing and variance analysis are irrelevant in today's manufacturing world.

Standard costing can be relevant

Despite the arguments set out above, standard costing and variance analysis can be relevant in the modern manufacturing environment.

Standard costing and variance analysis can be usefully **employed by modern manufacturing organisations as follows.**

- **Planning**. Even in a TQM environment, budgets will still need to be quantified. For example, the planned level of prevention and appraisal costs needs to be determined. Standards, such as 'returns of a particular product should not exceed 1% of deliveries during a budget period', can be set.

- **Control**. Cost and mix changes from plan will still be relevant in many processing situations.

- **With ABC.** Standard costing can be used to control the costs of unit-level activities (which consume resources in proportion to the number of units produced) and to manage those overhead costs that are fixed in the short term, but variable in the longer term.

> ### SECTION D – CONTROL AND PERFORMANCE MEASUREMENT OF RESPONSIBILITY CENTRES
>
> Answers 92 to 107 cover control and performance measurement of responsibility centres, the subject of Part D of the BPP Study Text for Paper P2.

92 LMN

> **Test references.** Divisional performance statements are covered in Chapter 12. Activity based costing is covered in Chapter 8.
>
> **Top tips.** Remember to apply your answer to part (b) to the scenario. It is very easy to simply list the advantages of activity based costing!
>
> **Easy marks.** Being able to explain the advantages of Activity based costing in part (b) will earn you quick and easy marks.
>
> **Examiner's comments.** Part (a) was generally well answered. A number of candidates failed to score highly in part (b). Whilst it was evident that the majority of candidates had a sound understanding of ABC many failed to 'explain' why it would be better to use ABC, for example to assist in identifying unnecessary costs.

Marking scheme

		Marks
(a)	Up to 2 marks per point Issues include – Responsibility accounting and control – Problems associated with transfer pricing – Control over investments – Problems with head office costs	
		Max 6
(b)	Two factors with reference to the scenario (2 marks each) Advantages include – The method of apportioning costs is fair – Overall cost savings – Divisional external pricing	
		Max $\frac{4}{10}$

(a)   The divisional directors are not happy with the present performance statement and how it is being used to appraise their performance. LMN should consider **involving the directors** at the design stage of the new performance statement.

As well as generating a number of ideas, directors are likely to **buy-in** to the new performance statement if they feel that they are being appraised fairly. This is likely to increase divisional performance.

Currently, inter-divisional trading occurs between divisions with transfer prices being set by Head Office. To continue to ensure that divisions trade with each other and in the best interests of the company, Head Office should ensure that there is **transparency** regarding how the transfer prices are calculated. This will ensure that no division is being favoured over another. The new divisional performance statement should also show the **impact of transfer prices on profitability**.

Currently, Head Office **costs are allocated** to divisions based on four bases including value of shares and capital invested and value of sales. Divisional managers could argue that these bases are unfair and do not allocate costs based on the true trading performance of the business but on an arbitrary basis over which the managers have no control.

LMN may wish to consider introducing **Activity Based Costing** as part of the new divisional performance statement to ensure that costs are allocated to divisions based on transactions rather than volume.

Each of the above factors mean that the divisional directors are not in full control of their own results and it therefore seems unfair to measure their performance in this way.

(b)   Introducing Activity Based Costing (ABC) at Head Office will provide LMN with a **more meaningful analysis of costs**. This should provide a suitable basis for the directors of each division and the Managing Director to make decisions about pricing, product mix, design and production.

ABC recognises the complexity of modern businesses through multiple cost drivers. Identifying **cost drivers** will ensure that costs are allocated from Head Office to LMN divisions fairly and truly reflect the trading performance of each division. LMN could replace its current bases with cost drivers such as number of production runs, number of inspections, number of purchase orders delivered and number of customer orders delivered.

ABC may also assist LMN in cost reduction because it could provide Head Office with an insight into the casual activities of the business. Consequently, the Managing Director may consider **outsourcing particular activities** within the business or even moving to different areas within **the industry value chain**.

Under the current system, it may be difficult to **control** the costs that are allocated to each division from Head Office. An ABC system will provide an insight into the way in which costs are structured and incurred at LMN Head Office. With ABC these costs can be controlled by **effectively managing the activities** which underlie them using a number of key performance measures.

93 C plc

> **Top tips.** Make sure you continue to refer to the scenario when answering this question. It would be easy just write everything you know about transfer pricing, particularly in part (b).

(a)   The senior management of C Plc has stated that the divisions should consider themselves to be independent businesses as far as possible. However, these are highly inter dependent and have **little control** over their business activities. The current policy is bound to have **behavioural implications** and ROI may be inappropriate in terms of the divisions' performance evaluation.

WD selling to PD

As WD sells about two thirds of its output to division PD, the profits of both divisions depend on the transfer price between them. As this is set on a cost plus basis assessing the division on ROI is likely to lead to dysfunctional behaviour and have behavioural implications.

PD buying all timber from WD and selling all output to TD

PD has little control over its business activities and ROI will lead to dysfunctional decision making.

(i)   Short term decisions may be made at the expense of long term improvements, eg replacing machinery may worsen ROI in the short term.

(ii)   No incentive to control or reduce costs

(iii)   No incentive to improve efficiency.

TD selling to outside market

The cost structure of TD is determined by internal transfers, leaving TD with no control over costs. TD may be restricted in sales growth if it cannot have a wider product range.

(b)   The transfer prices more likely to minimise dysfunctional behaviour and sub-optimal decisions are market prices. Where market prices are not reliably available some theories advocate a transfer price as close to the market price as possible.

Transfer from PD to TD

PD has no control over the volume of its output and cannot buy or sell outside C plc. As such it cannot be a profit centre as it has no independence.

It would be more appropriate for PD to be considered as a **cost centre**. As such, there are theoretical arguments for transferring at marginal cost. This of course would be resulting in what appear to be losses for PD. In practice, a **standard cost** may be adopted based on full cost rather than marginal cost basis. The target would be for PD to **break even** as a cost centre. The implication for the receiving division TD is that it may be obtaining products at below market prices. This may be advantageous in that it could lead to higher demand as a result of lower final prices. However, a careful balance must be strictly applied to achieve **profit maximisation**.

94 SK plc (1)

> **Top tip**. Note that part (a) asks for two answers but we have shown all four below.

(a) (i) Marginal cost

With such an approach, variable cost is usually assumed to be equivalent to the marginal cost of the unit being transferred.

Supplying division. A transfer price at marginal cost means that the supplying division does not cover its fixed costs and so makes no contribution on the transfer. The division would therefore have no incentive to provide the service internally.

Receiving division. Provided the variable cost of the service is less than the market price (which it should be if the supplying division is efficient), the receiving division would be keen on such an approach to setting transfer prices.

SK plc. Given that the manager of the supplying division would prefer to transfer externally, head office are likely to have to insist that internal transfers are made.

(ii) Total cost

Supplying division. If the supplying division operates at normal levels of activity, internal transfers at total cost means that the division makes no profit on the transfers. The manager of the division would therefore prefer to transfer externally to earn a profit, regardless of whether or not internal transfers would be in the best interests of SK plc as a whole. If internal transfers cause activity levels above normal levels, however, the division will earn a profit on the transfers. The supplying division will thus make internal transfers provided it has spare capacity.

Receiving division. Provided full cost is less than market price (which it should be if the supplying division is operating efficiently), the receiving division will be better off if it uses internally-provided services.

SK plc. Unless the supplying division has spare capacity, head office is likely to have to force the supplying division to transfer internally.

(iii) Cost plus

Supplying division. The 'plus' acts as an incentive for the division to transfer internally, although external transfers will still be preferable if the 'plus' on external transfers is greater than that on internal transfers.

Receiving division. The 'plus' causes an increase in cost for the receiving division but the division will still prefer internal transfers to external purposes if the cost is less than the market price.

SK plc. Unless the supplying division has spare capacity, it will prefer external transfers to internal transfers if the internal 'plus' is less than the external 'plus', and will transfer less internally. This may or may not be in the best interests of SK plc.

(iv) Opportunity cost

With this approach, the transfer price is set at the standard variable cost per unit in the supplying division plus the opportunity cost to the organisation as a whole of supplying the unit internally instead of externally.

The transfer price will be either the maximum contribution foregone by the supplying division in transferring internally rather than selling externally, or the contribution foregone by not using the same facilities in the supplying division for their next best alternative use.

If there is no external market for the service being transferred and no alternative uses for the supplying division's facilities, the method will give a transfer price of variable (marginal) cost, with its accompanying consequences.

If resources are limited, however:

(1)   The **supplying division** will be indifferent between internal and external sales as the transfer price will be market price.

(2)   The **receiving division** will be indifferent between purchasing internally and eternally (unless internal transfers are accompanied by a far higher level of service).

(3)   The transfer price should ensure that available resources are used in a way which will maximise the benefit to **SK plc** as a whole. An organisational policy will be needed, however, to ensure that internal transfers are accompanied by savings in administration and distribution costs.

(b)   <u>Actual cost versus standard cost</u>

When a transfer price is based on cost, **standard cost** should be used, not actual cost. A transfer at actual cost would give the supplying division **no incentive** to control costs because all of the costs could be passed on to the receiving division. Actual cost plus transfer prices might even encourage the manager of the supplying division to **overspend**, because this would increase divisional profit, even though the organisation as a whole (and the receiving division) suffers.

Standard cost based transfer prices should encourage the supplying division to become more **efficient** as any variances that arise would affect the results of the supplying division (as opposed to being passed on to the receiving division if actual costs were used).

The problem with the approach, however, is that it **penalises** the **supplying division** if the standard cost is **unattainable**, while it penalises the **receiving** division if it is too **easily attainable**.

95 SK plc (2)

(a)   Transfer pricing is used when divisions of an organisation need to charge other divisions of the same organisations for goods and services they provide. The basic object of transfer pricing is that relevant divisions within an organisation are **evaluated effectively** and the transfer price does not **distort** divisional performance **evaluation**.

The level at which a transfer price should be set, however, is **not** a **straightforward** decision for organisations. The situation is even less clear cut for organisations operating in a number of countries, when even more factors need to be taken into consideration. Some of these factors and their impact on the transfer price are set out below. Moreover, the **manipulation** of **profits** through the use of transfer pricing is a common area of confrontation between multinational organisations and host country governments.

(i)   <u>Exchange rate fluctuation</u>

The value of a transfer of goods between profit centres in different countries could depend on fluctuations in the currency exchange rate.

(ii)   <u>Taxation in different countries</u>

If taxation on profits is 20% of profits in Country A and 50% of profits in Country B, a company will presumably try to '**manipulate**' **profits** (by means of raising or lowering transfer prices or by invoicing the subsidiary in the high-tax country for 'services' provided by the subsidiary in the low-tax country) so that profits are maximised for a subsidiary in Country A, by reducing profits for a subsidiary in Country B.

Artificial attempts at reducing tax liabilities could, however, upset a country's tax officials if they discover it and may lead to some form of penalty. Many tax authorities have the power to modify transfer prices in computing tariffs or taxes on profit, although a genuine **arms-length market price** should be accepted.

(iii) <u>Import tariffs/customs duties</u>

Suppose that Country A imposes an import tariff of 20% on the value of goods imported. A multi-national company has a subsidiary in Country A which imports goods from a subsidiary in Country B. In such a situation, the company would minimise costs by keeping the transfer price to a minimum value.

(iv) <u>Exchange controls</u>

If a country imposes restrictions on the transfer of profits from domestic subsidiaries to foreign multinationals, the restrictions on the transfer can be overcome if head office provides some goods or services to the subsidiary and charges **exorbitantly high prices**, **disguising the** '**profits**' as sales revenue, and transferring them from one country to the other. The ethics of such an approach should, of course, be questioned.

(v) <u>Anti-dumping legislation</u>

Governments may take action to protect home industries by preventing companies from transferring goods cheaply into their countries. They may do this, for example, by insisting on the use of a fair market value for the transfer price.

<u>Alternative suggestions</u>

<u>Competitive pressures</u>

Transfer pricing can be used to enable profit centres to match or undercut local competitors.

<u>Repatriation of funds</u>

By inflating transfer prices for goods sold to subsidiaries in countries where inflation is high, the subsidiaries' profits are reduced and funds repatriated, thereby saving their value.

<u>Minority shareholders</u>

Transfer prices can be used to reduce the amount of profit paid to minority shareholders by artificially depressing a subsidiary's profit.

(b) A transfer price based on **marginal cost** is the **theoretically correct transfer price** to encourage total organisational profitability when there is **no external market** for the item being transferred and **no capacity constraints** affecting production (so that there is no opportunity cost associated with the transfer). If there is no external market for the product, marginal cost would be an appropriate transfer price provided that there is no relevant capacity constraints.

A transfer price at marginal cost means that **the supplying division does not cover its fixed costs,** however, and so makes **no contribution on the transfer**, and no profit. There is therefore **no incentive** for the division to make the transfer**. Head office** would therefore be likely to have to **insist** that the transfers were made, thereby **undermining divisional autonomy**.

There are a number of ways in which the **problem of not covering fixed costs can be overcome**, however, such as **dual pricing** and a **two-part tariff system**, although these may also **undermine divisional autonomy**.

96 SWZ

> **Text references.** Measuring performance in divisionalised businesses is covered in Chapter 12.
>
> **Top tips.** Use information provided in the question to illustrate your answer as necessary.

(a)   The performance of S Division over the three year period

The ROI of S Division has increased gradually between 20X8 and 20Y0.

	$'000	ROI
20X8	40/400	10.00%
20X9	56/320	17.50%
20Y0	62/256	24.22%

The gross profit margin has remained steady at 40% for each of the three years.

It appears that sales and cost of sales have remained constant throughout the three year period and the data given has been **adjusted to remove the effects of inflation**. This would indicate there has been **no significant change in trading activity** during the period.

Other operating costs have decreased from $120,000 in 20X8 to $98,000 in 20Y0 which would indicate that S Division has **managed costs effectively during the period through accurate budgeting and control processes**.

However, these **costs include depreciation** which is calculated at the rate of 20% per annum on a reducing balance basis. If the depreciation is excluded, other **operating costs have actually increased** by $4,000 between 20X8 and 20X9 and by $10,000 between 20X9 and 20Y0.

In summary, the improvement in ROI over the three year period is **due to the depreciation policy as opposed to trading performance**.

(b)   Why the manager of S Division is unlikely to go ahead with the investment

The proposed estimate has a **positive NPV of $24,536 and should therefore go ahead in order to benefit the company as a whole**.

If the results in 20Y1 are the same as 20Y0 (ignoring inflation), the ROI for S Division will be higher in 20Y1 if the manager of S Division does <u>not</u> go ahead with the investment (36.5%), compared to if he / she does proceed with the investment (34.3%).

The manager of S Division is **unlikely to go ahead with an investment that will have a negative impact on a key ratio that is used to assess the performance of the division**.

Workings

1   Depreciation charges

	20X8	20X9	20Y0
	$'000	$'000	$'000
Capital invested	400	320	256
Depn charge		400-320 = 80	320 – 256 = 64

We can work out the depreciation charge in 20X8 and in 20Y1 by dividing by 80% and multiplying by 80%.

Depreciation charge in 20X8: 80/80% = $100

Depreciation charge in 20Y1: 64 × 80% = $51.2

2   Other operating costs less depreciation

	20X8	20X9	20Y0
	$'000	$'000	$'000
Other operating costs	120	104	98
Less depn charge	(100)	(80)	(64)
	20	24	34
Increase		4	10

3   Results in 20Y1 if the investment does not go ahead

		$'000
Sales		400
Cost of sales		240
Gross profit		160
Other operating costs	($98 – $64 +$51.2 (W1))	85.2
Pre-tax operating profit		74.8
Capital invested	($256 – $51.2)	204.8
ROI	($74.8 / $204.8)	36.5%

4   Results in 20Y1 if the investment does go ahead

		$'000
Sales		400
Cost of sales	($240,000 × 0.9)	216
Gross profit		184
Other operating costs		97.2 *
Pre-tax operating profit		86.8
Capital invested		252.8 **
ROI	($86.8 / $252.8)	34.3%

* 20Y0 operating costs of $98,000 consists of depreciation ($64,000) and other costs ($34,000). The new depreciation charge for 20Y1 will be $63,200. Assuming other costs remain unchanged, total other operating costs for 20Y1 will be $97,200.

	$'000
** Original NBV	256
Less: NBV of replaced machine	(40)
	216
Cost of new machine	100
	316
Less: Depreciation (20%)	(63.2)
NBV at end of 20Y1	252.8

(c)   The RI calculations below use the figures from part (b).

Without investment		$
Pre-tax operating profits		74,800
Notional capital charge	($204,800 × 8%)	(16,384)
Residual Income		58,416

With investment		$
Pre-tax operating profits		86,800
Notional capital charge	($252,800 × 8%)	(20,224)
Residual Income		66,576

Residual income increases by $8,160 if the company goes ahead with the investment. This is consistent with the company's NPV based decision discussed in part (b).

Alternative solution based on incremental values

		$
Increase in capital	($48,000* × 8%)	(3,840)
Savings in direct costs		24,000
Increase in depreciation	($60,000 × 20%)	(12,000)
Increase in residual income		8,160

* $60,000 - $12,000 depreciation

97 H

> **Test references.** Return on investment (ROI) is covered in Chapter 12. Transfer pricing is covered in Chapter 13.
>
> **Top tips.** There is a load of data to digest in this question. Read the requirements first to ensure you understand what information you need to extract from the scenario.
>
> **Easy marks.** There are 9 marks available in part (c) for discussing the viewpoints of divisional managers in respect of the transfer pricing policy being used.
>
> **Examiner's comments.** Many candidates appeared to struggle with this question. Common errors in part (a) included not annualising the figures and calculating an incorrect asset net book value. Few candidates made comparisons between NPV and ROI in part (b) and instead discussed the advantages and disadvantages of NPV (which the question did not ask for). Part (c) was generally well answered.

Marking scheme

			Marks
(a)	Monthly ROI (1 mark each)	3	
	Annualised ROI	1	
	Discussion of ROI calculations	<u>4</u>	
			8
(b)	ROI if no investment	1	
	If investment is undertaken		
	– Revised sales	1	
	– Revised depreciation	1	
	– ROI	1	
	Discuss NPV vs ROI	<u>4</u>	
			8
(c)	Discussion of process (up to 2 marks per well explained point)	Max	<u>9</u>
			<u>25</u>

(a) (i) ROI is calculated as (profit/capital employed) × 100%.

Process	Profit / (Loss) ($)	Capital value	Month ROI	Annualised ROI
Process B	18,800	$800,000 \times 0.8^5 = \$262,144$	7%	84%
Process C	(15,550)	$500,000 \times 0.8^2 = \$320,000$	(5%)	(60%)
Process D	(5,000)	$300,000 \times 0.8^{10} = \$32,212$	(15%)	(180%)

(ii) Each process division manager is working with equipment that was purchased at different times. As such, the value of the equipment used in ROI calculations is inconsistent across divisions. Equipment bought in different years will have been affected by inflation over different timeframes, whilst the number of years of depreciation charged will also be inconsistent.

Head office costs are allocated to divisions and are beyond the control of the Process Division Manager. It could be considered unfair to manage the performance of process divisions which include such allocated costs.

Process B determines the input volumes of processes C and D. Processes C and D incur fixed costs regardless of the level of output from Process B. As a result, the managers of processes C and D are unable to control the activity levels of their respective divisions, which in turn drive divisional profitability.

The profit or loss of each process is influenced by the transfer prices that are charged between processes. Transfer prices are based on the budgets of the supplier plus a percentage mark-up. Therefore, the customer's performance will be affected by the budget of the supplier. This is unfair as the customer has no control over the supplier's budget.

(b) **(i)** If Process Division C invests in the new equipment, output would increase by 1,500 litres ($20 per litre) = $30,000 as the abnormal loss would be avoided. Income from the scrap sales of the abnormal loss units would be foregone and the depreciation charge would also change, resulting in a profit of $2,367. This would yield an ROI of:

$2,367 (W2) / $1,000,000 = 0.24% - Annualised ROI = 2.88%

If the investment does not go ahead, Process C's monthly loss in 2011 would be $14,484 as a result of the lower depreciation charge. The ROI would be:

($14,484) (W3) / $256,000 = (5.66%) – Annualised ROI = (67.89%)

Workings

W1 – MONTHLY DEPRECIATION CHARGE ON OLD EQUIPMENT

The company depreciates all capital equipment at the rate of 20% per annum on a reducing balance basis.

Original cost in January 20X8 was $500,000.

	Annual depreciation	*Net Book Value c/fwd*
20X8	$100,000	$400,000
20X9	$80,000	$320,000
20Y0	$64,000	$256,000
20Y1	$51,200	

20Y0 Monthly depreciation charge = $64,000 / 12 =	$5,333
20Y1 Monthly depreciation charge = $51,200 / 12 =	$4,267
20Y1 Monthly depreciation charge on new equipment:	
$1,000,000 x 20% / 12 months	$16,666

W2 – IF INVESTMENT DOES GO AHEAD

Loss as shown for 20Y0	($15,550)
Additional sales:	
1,500 litres x ($20 - $0.50)	$29,250
	$13,700
Less: Increase in monthly depreciation charge	
($16,666 - $5,333)	($11,333)
Profit expected for 20Y1	$2,367

W3 – IF INVESTMENT DOES NOT GO AHEAD

Loss as shown for 20Y0	$15,550
Add: Decrease in monthly depreciation charge ($5,333 - $4,267)	$1,066
Loss expected for 20Y1	$14,484

(ii) A **positive NPV** using H's cost of capital would indicate that Process C should **go ahead with plans to invest in the new equipment**.

However, the **low ROI** that can be expected **may discourage the manager of Process C from investing**.

If assets are valued at net book value, **ROI figures generally improve as assets get older**. Thus, as well as discouraging the manager of Process C from investing ROI may encourage the manager to **continue to use out of date equipment**.

Whilst ROI effectively calculates the **efficiency of an investment**, it gives no indication of future cash flows. An investment decision made on the basis of ROI could lead to the company experiencing liquidity problems in the future.

It is important that H introduces a **managerial performance measure that is consistent with the NPV analysis**.

(c) Currently, the transfer price from Process B to processes C and D is based on budgeted costs plus a mark-up of 15%. This policy is successful in **rewarding the manager of process B for any efficiencies** that are achieved as well as **protecting processes C and D against any inefficiencies** of Process B. Managers are able to discuss the basis of apportionment of the joint costs.

Process D is able to buy equivalent material from an external supplier at $7.50 per litre which is significantly cheaper than the $9.20 per litre it pays to Process B under the current arrangement. There is clearly a **conflict of interest** here.

Process B produces two joint products, and it is not possible to produce output for Process C without also producing output for Process D. If Process D were to purchase materials from an external supplier, the **output of D from Process B would have to be scrapped**. There would be no change to the costs of Process B whilst **external costs incurred by H would increase**.

To avoid such a scenario, it is likely that the **transfer price will have to be changed so that Process D is no better off from purchasing materials from an external supplier**. This could be achieved by changing the basis on which the joint costs are allocated or by using $7.50 (market price) as the transfer price. It is likely that these changes will alter the profitability of Process B and Process D and consequently the **ROI of each process would also change**.

A **dual transfer pricing policy** may also me considered. Under this system, different transfer values would be used by both Process B and Process D in respect of the same transfer of materials. Under this method, the performance of Process D would be calculated using the cost value it would have paid had it purchased the materials from an external supplier.

98 Responsibility centres and performance appraisal (1)

(a) <u>Non-financial performance measures (NFPM)</u>

It is argued that management should not focus on a **narrow** range of performance indicators, such as maximising **short-term** profits as this may damage the longer-term objectives of shareholder value maximisation. A full range is required to obtain a **complete picture** of long-term success. In order to achieve the long-term objectives of shareholder value maximisation and profit growth, the company must produce quality goods or services at a price customers are willing to pay. Factors such as quality control, customer satisfaction, innovation, efficiency and staff development are elements that determine long term success.

<u>Advantages</u>

The value of non-financial measures is that they **draw management attention to some of the more strategic issues facing the organisation**. Financial measures tend to make managers more inward looking and may encourage them to focus on short-term performance. Non-financial measures can be selected to encourage managers to think strategically and consider external factors such as competitor actions and customer requirements.

<u>Examples</u>

Examples of non-financial measures could include among others market share and market leadership, innovations, efficiency, productivity, customer satisfaction, service and staff development.

<u>Problems</u>

The problem with implementing these measures is that they may be **difficult to record objectively**. If performance measurement is perceived to be subjective, **this could lead to dysfunctional behaviour**, if management rewards are based on financial performance measures. When introducing NFPM, it is important for management to ensure that the structure of rewards takes these into account.

(b) <u>ROI v RI</u>

<u>ROI</u>

The ROI is a relative performance measure which is calculated as (profit before interest/investment) × 100%.

The ROI can be shown to lead to **sup-optimal decisions** if it is applied too rigidly. For example, an investment may be rejected if it lowers the centre's actual ROI, even though the investment earns more than the company's required return on capital.

RI

The use of RI can **overcome this problem** since it rewards all investments which earn a return which is higher than the company's required return on capital.

RI is calculated as profit before interest minus imputed interest charge on centre investment.

The **imputed interest** is calculated at the rate of the company's required return on capital. The residual income will always increase if an investment earns more than the company's required rate or return.

RI can therefore overcome some of the behavioural problems associated with ROI, but it **suffers from the same problem of profit measurement and asset valuation**.

(i)   **Return on investment (ROI)** is intended to measure the efficiency with which assets are being used, by taking the profit as a proportion of the net assets. **Residual income (RI)** on the other hand, is simply the profit reduced by a financing charge which is based on the net assets. RI is an absolute, not a relative measure.

(ii) **ROI** has the major advantage of taking full account of the size of the business, so that **businesses of different sizes can be compared**. Income, on the other hand, may be **less distorted by inappropriate values for investment**.

99   Responsibility centres and performance appraisal (2)

(a)   Residual income

Residual income (RI) is a **measure** of the **centre's profits** after **deducting a notional or imputed interest cost**.

(i)   The centre's profit is after deducting depreciation on capital equipment.

(ii) The imputed cost of capital might be the organisation's cost of borrowing or its weighted average cost of capital.

Unlike return on investment (ROI) which is a percentage or relative measure, RI is an absolute measure.

Economic value added

Economic value added (EVA) ® is a specific type of residual income (RI) calculated as follows.

EVA® = net operating profit after tax (NOPAT) less capital charge

where the capital charge = weighted average cost of capital x net assets

You can see from the formula that the calculation of EVA is very similar to the calculation of RI. EVA and RI are similar because both result in an **absolute figure** which is calculated by subtracting an imputed interest charge from the profit earned by the investment centre. However, there are differences as follows.

Differences

(i)   The **profit figures are calculated differently**. EVA is based on an 'economic profit' which is derived by making a series of adjustments to the accounting profit, such as adjusting historic accounting depreciation and adding back any 'investment expenditure' such as advertising or R&D.

(ii) The **notional capital charges use different bases** for net assets. The replacement cost of net assets is usually used in the calculation of EVA.

(b)   (i)   **The main features of Economic Value Added** (EVA®) as it would be used to assess the performance of divisions:

EVA like Residual Income (RI) is a **performance measure expressed in absolute terms**. It is based on the concept of net economic profit after tax less a deduction for an imputed interest charge.

The relationship between economic and accounting profit is explained below. The imputed interest charge is based on the company's weighted average cost of capital. The assets are at their replacement cost as explained below. The imputed interest charge is based on the company's weighted average cost of capital.

EVA = net operating economic profit after tax less capital charge where the capital charge = weighted average cost of capital × net assets

The weighted average cost of capital is based on the capital asset pricing model.

(ii) How the use of EVA to assess divisional performance might affect the behaviour of divisional senior executives:

- It is argued that maximisation of the EVA® target will lead to managers maximising wealth for shareholders.

- The adjustments within the calculation of EVA mean that the measure is based on figures closer to cash flows than accounting profits. Hence, EVA is less likely to be distorted by the accounting policies selected.

- EVA like RI is an absolute measure, as compared to a relative one such as ROCE. As such it will not lead to sub-optimal decisions with respect to new investment as it is the absolute increase in shareholder value which is used as a criterion.

- EVA is based on **economic profit** which is derived by making a series of adjustments to **accounting profits**.

- The assets used for the calculation of EVA are valued at their replacement cost and not at their historic accounting cost. They are also increased by any costs that have been capitalised as a result of the above adjustments.

100 Y and Z plc

> **Text references.** Responsibility centres and performance appraisal are covered in Chapter 12.
>
> **Top tips.** A straightforward preparation question but if this were part of an exam question you may have got carried away since it would have been possible to go into great detail in some areas and your time allocation may have gone completely astray. Ensure, therefore, that the points you made were pertinent, brief and concise but that you covered all necessary points.
>
> **Easy marks.** If you are familiar with how profit centres and investment centres work, the marks should be quite easy to obtain.

(a) The following conditions are necessary for the successful introduction of such centres.

(i) The centres must have a **measurable output**. This does not mean that the output must necessarily be sold on the external market. It may be transferred internally for use in another part of the organisation. In this case the 'revenue' generated is determined by the use of a transfer price.

(ii) It must be possible for the **centre manager to exercise control over the level of output.**

(iii) For an **investment centre**, it must be possible for the **centre manager to exercise control over the level of investment in the centre**, and for the **level of investment to be measured objectively**.

(iv) A **reporting system** must be established which provides rapid and accurate feedback to keep centre managers informed about their performance.

(v) **Centre managers** must **accept the change** and must be willing to **accept the extra responsibility** associated with their new role. Provision must be made for adequate **education and training** in the operation of the new responsibility accounting system.

(vi) **Central management** must also fully **understand and accept** the new system, particularly if they are required to delegate authority for decisions which they are accustomed to making themselves.

(b)

> **Top tips.** The question gives the operating statement for one month and requires the calculation of the annualised ROI. This should not throw you, all you need to do is multiply the net income before tax by 12.
>
> This is actually a fairly straightforward question providing plenty of scope for meaningful and relevant discussion.

> Where you are asked to comment on performance (as you often are in this paper) be prepared to pose questions and identify further information that may be required.
>
> Although you are asked to calculate the ROI, your discussion may supplemented with the secondary performance ratios of profit margin and asset turnover.

(i)   Annualised return on investment (ROI)

	Y	Z
Annualised net income before tax	£122,000 × 12 = £1,464,000	£21,000 × 12 = £252,000
ROI	$\frac{1,464,000}{9,760,000} = 15\%$	$\frac{252,000}{1,260,000} = 20\%$

The two divisions Y and Z operate in similar markets. Of the two, Z is the smaller one in terms of both sales and divisional net assets. Z also has the higher ROI of the two, being 20% compared to Y's 15%.

However, what is surprising is the different **proportion** of **variable** costs in relation to sales for the two divisions. Variable costs constitute 38 percent of sales for Y and 56 percent of sales for Z. We need further information to explain the higher variable costs of Z. Could these be related to the lower divisional assets? There is a range of possible explanations here and further **investigation** will be necessary.

It is possible that division Z's assets are old and lead to inefficiency in production. Although Z's overall ROI is **higher**, this may be because its **assets** are **old** and do not reflect the current replacement cost. The results highlight the fundamental problem with using ROI as a single measurement of performance. ROI can lead to **sub-optimal** decisions where a manager is unwilling to undertake further investment which, although giving a positive return, may reduce the current ROI. This may be the case with division Z.

There is no indication that division Z is **outsourcing** part of its production process, which may have been a possible explanation for higher variable costs and lower divisional assets. Further investigation is required.

Looking at the secondary performance ratios of profit margin and asset turnover below, it is easy to see that division Y has the **higher profit margin** and **lower asset turnover**.

Secondary performance ratios

For division Y

$$\text{ROI} = \frac{\text{Divisional profit}}{\text{Divisional sales}} \times \frac{\text{Divisional sales}}{\text{Divisional capital employed}}$$

$$\text{ROI} = \text{Profit margins} \times \text{Asset turnover}$$

$$\frac{122,000 \times 12}{900,000 \times 12} = 13.56\% \times \frac{900,000 \times 12}{9,760,000} \times 1.1\% = 15\%$$

For division Z

$$\text{ROI} = \frac{21,000 \times 12}{555,000 \times 12} = 3.78\% \times \frac{555,000 \times 12}{1,260,000} \times 5.286\% = 20\%$$

We need to look at the relative ages of the assets and their relationship to replacement cost to be able to assess further the divisional performance. We also need further information on the basis for apportioning central costs. If only controllable income is assessed as a proportion of divisional net assets, the returns are even more strikingly different (56.56% for Y and 191% for Z).

(ii) Annualised Residual Income (RI)

Residual income = Accounting profit – Notional interest on capital.

For division Y

RI = (£122,000 × 12) – (12% × £9760,000) = £1,464,000 – £1,171,200 = £292,800

For division Z

RI = (£21,000 × 12) – (12% × £1,260,000) = £252,000 – £151,200 = £100,800

The absolute score RI is **positive** for both divisions. This means that **sufficient** residual income is left for the **shareholders** after an imputed interest charge on divisional assets is deducted from net profit. Whereas the relative measure ROI is higher for division Z, the absolute measure RI is higher for division Y.

RI is a **superior** measure technically but no **single** measure alone is sufficient for a meaningful performance evaluation. As the cost of capital rises, RI will fall. The imputed interest charge should be calculated on the replacement cost of assets. It would appear that here we have assets at historic cost.

(iii) ROI

Advantages

ROI is a relative measure expressed in **percentage terms**. As such it is **easy** to **understand** and can be readily **compared** against a **required benchmark rate**.

Disadvantages

ROI can lead to **sub-optimal decisions**. As the case of divisions Y and Z illustrates, it is not certain whether it is better to have a return of 20% on a £1.2 million investment or a 15% on a £9.8 million investment.

Shareholders may prefer the former in that less of their funds are **tied in the business**. However, the use of ROI may tend to **limit growth** as a manager assessed on ROI alone will be **unwilling** to undertake **further investment providing** a return lower than the current one he is earning.

Residual Income

Advantages

Residual income (RI) requires that a capital charge is imputed on each division's profit.

RI does not suffer from the potential problems of ROI as any **investment** providing a **return** in **excess** of the **required rate** is likely to be **accepted**.

Disadvantages

The imputed capital charge is based on assets at **historic cost**. Divisions with **older assets** may appear to be doing better in the **short term**.

Other methods

Other methods of performance assessment are **Economic Value Added** (EVA®) and profitability measures such as **net profit margin** and **gross profit margin**.

EVA® is similar to RI in that it is an **absolute measure**. However, EVA® is considered an improved variant of RI in that it is based on **economic** and not accounting profit. Moreover, the capital charge is based on the replacement cost of assets.

Net profit margin is measured as a **percentage** of **net profit** to **turnover**. Gross profit is measured as a **percentage** of **gross profit** to **turnover**.

101 The DE Company

> **Text references**. Divisional performance measurement is covered in Chapter 12. Transfer pricing is covered in Chapter 13.
>
> **Top tips**. Pay close attention to the verbs in each question requirement. Part (b) asks for a discussion, <u>not</u> a series of statements showing profit and losses for changes in external demand.
>
> Clearly label all workings in part (c) and refer to them throughout your answer. Part (d) asks for TWO factors. Do not waste your time writing as many as you can think of!
>
> **Easy marks**. Explaining two factors to consider when designing divisional performance measures (part (d)) should be straightforward.

(a) Division E has made internal sales of 70,000 components to Division D at **opportunity cost**. As a result of the transfer, there has been unfulfilled external demand of 42,000 components.

Therefore 42,000 components in the transfer will have been priced at **market value** and the balance of 28,000 will be valued at **variable cost**.

Division E has produced 140,000 components during the year with a total variable cost of $140 million. Therefore **variable cost per unit** is $1,000.

The current **market value selling price** is $1,550 per unit.

	Internal		*External*	*Total*
	Variable cost	Market value		
Components (units)	28,000	42,000	70,000	140,000
	$'000	$'000	$'000	$'000
Variable cost	28,000	42,000	70,000	140,000
Sales value	28,000	65,100	108,500	201,600

(b) Division E has sold 28,000 units to Division D **without making any profit on these units**. The market value of these is $43.4 million which is $15.4 million higher than the **transfer price** (28,000 units × $1,000 per unit = $28.0 million).

Although charging the full market value price may not be appropriate for Division D as the units could not be sold externally, there should be some **reward accruing to Division E** for the supply of the components.

A **transfer price above variable cost** would reduce the profits of Division D and increase the profits of Division E by the same amount. If the transfer price was set at $1,275 per unit (halfway between the variable cost and the market value) then the profit of each division would change by $7.7 million.

An **increase in external demand** would mean more components supplied to Division D would be at **market value** which would further increase the profits of Division E and lower the profits of Division D. The opposite effect would occur if there were a decrease in external demand.

(c) (i) <u>From the perspective of Division E</u>

There are two effects of this investment, an increase in capacity of 10% and a decrease in variable costs of 20%. From the perspective of the manager of Division E these benefits will be diluted by the current transfer pricing policy.

<u>Increased capacity</u>

External annual demand will continue to be 112,000 components. Division E currently sells 70,000 components externally.

If Division E has **10% higher capacity** then it can increase external sales by this 10%. However, in doing this it will increase the number of goods transferred to Division D at **variable cost** as the opportunity cost of the internal transfer will be lower. Therefore the external sales at **market value** will now be [70,000 + (140,000 × 10%)] = 84,000.

The **internal sales at market value** will be lower (28,000 units) as there are now only 28,000 components of unsatisfied external demand. Therefore there are still 112,000 units sold at market value (see part (a)).

As a result the same number of units (112,000 units – 84,000 units) will be sold at market value as before and the rest will generate no profit to Division E. Therefore there is **no benefit for Division E** from the increased capacity.

Reduction in costs

Looking at the reduction in costs, there will be a cost saving to Division E.

Division E currently sells 50% of its components internally and 28/70 of these are transferred at **variable cost** (see part (a)). Therefore the cost savings on these units will be passed on to Division D as a result of the transfer pricing. The **cost saving** relevant to Division E will be limited to the units sold at **market value**.

The variable cost of the items sold at market value is

112,000 units × $1,000 = $112 million

A 20% cost saving would reduce this cost to

$112 million × 0.80 = $89.6 million per annum

Over 5 five years, using the 5 year annuity factor at 8%, this has a present value of

$22.4 million × 3.993 = $89.44 million

This is less than the cost of the investment of $120 million and therefore the investment is **not financially viable** from the perspective of Division E.

(ii) From the perspective of the DE company

Evaluating the investment from the company perspective means taking into account the savings that Division D has made on the items transferred from Division E.

The original cost to Division D of these units was the sales value from Division E

$28 million + $65.1 million = $93.1 million (see part (a)).

Because the proportion of market value units has changed as a result of the investment the new cost is as follows

	$
42,000 components at variable cost ($1,000 × 0.80)	33.6 million
28,000 components at market value of $1,550	43.4 million
	77.0 million

This gives a cost saving to Division D of $93.1 million – $77.0 million = $16.1 million

Added to the savings of Division E this gives total annual savings of

$22.4 (part (i)) + $16.1 = $38.5 million

Over 5 five years, using the 5 year annuity factor at 8%, this has a present value of

$38.5 million × 3.993 = $153.73 million.

Since this exceeds the initial cost of $120 million the investment **is financially viable** from a company point of view.

(d) When designing divisional performance measures a number of factors need to be taken into account.

Simple to calculate and understand.

The measures should be simple to calculate and to understand.

Managers must be able to understand how their performance is measured and be able to see the effect that their decisions will have on the performance measures. If a manager does not understand how a performance measure is calculated they cannot be in a position to judge whether their decisions will improve performance or not.

Control

Performance measures should only include items that are under the control of the manager / division being measured.

Otherwise, the performance measure may be demotivational.

102 PZ Group

> **Text references.** Performance measurement in divisionalised businesses is covered in Chapter 12. Transfer pricing is covered in Chapter 13.
>
> **Top tips.** Maximise your score in part (b) by structuring your answer so that it is easy to mark. Ensure you eliminate the internal transactions from Z Limited's results and calculate the gross profit margin on its external sales.
>
> Once you have compared the margins on internal and external sales, discuss the performance of the two companies considering profitability, gearing and asset values. Remember to show all of your workings.
>
> **Easy marks.** There are 7 marks available for explaining three factors to consider when setting a transfer pricing policy in part (c).

(a)   ROCE = PBIT / Capital employed × 100%

Pre-tax profit % = Pre-tax profit / Sales

Asset turnover = Sales / Capital employed

Company	P Limited	Z Limited
ROCE	10,000/459,600 × 100 = 2.2%	30,000/453,216 × 100 = 6.6%
Pre-tax profit %	10,000/200,000 × 100 = 5.0%	30,000/220,000 × 100 = 13.6%
Asset turnover	200,000/459,600 = 0.435	220,000/453,216 = 0.485

(b)   (i)   The sales value of the intra-group transaction can be identified by comparing the group results against the sum of the individual company results. The sales value is $20,000 (200 + 220 - 400). We are told in note 1 that the cost of these were $10,000. This gives a gross profit margin of 10/20 = 50%.

The gross profit on Z's remaining (external) sales is therefore $50,000 and the revenue from these sales is $200,000. The gross profit margin on these sales is therefore 50/200 = 25%.

(ii)   There is a significant difference between the internal and external margins. If the transaction had not taken place then P would not have had the goods available to sell on. Assuming a constant margin of 15% (30/200) from the figures given, P Ltd would have sold goods costing $20,000 at $23,529 ($20,000 × 100/85). This would be a profit of $3,529 on this sale. Therefore to remove the effect of the transaction, the profit of P should be reduced by $3,529 and the revenue by $23,529. The capital employed will also be reduced by $3,529. Z Limited is assumed not to have sold the goods that were transferred to P Limited.

Company	P Limited	Z Limited
ROCE	6,470/456,071 × 100 = 1.4%	20,000/453,216 × 100 = 4.4%
Pre-tax profit %	6,470/176,470 × 100 = 3.7%	20,000/200,000 × 100 = 10%
Asset turnover	176,470/456,071 = 0.387	200,000/453,216 = 0.441

These calculations show that the performance of each company has changed from the removal of this transaction. Based on the fact that managers' bonuses are based on ROCE this type of manipulation of results needs to be considered.

The difference in performance may be caused, in part, by each of the following factors.

Note the following analysis is carried out on the original calculations rather than the revised ones.

Gearing

P Limited has non-current borrowings of $150,000 and therefore incurs an interest charge on this borrowing. The interest charge is 6.7% (10/150). This is a significant cost in relation to pre-tax profit for P Limited. It is higher than the ROCE using profit before interest and tax of 4.4% (20/459.6).

Non-current asset values

P Limited has non-current assets with an original cost value of two thirds of the level of Z Limited (1 million/1.5 million). However the net book value of non-current assets for P Limited is higher. This is because the non-current assets of P Limited are newer than Z Limited's. This can be seen by the fact that the depreciation policy of both companies is the same (20% per annum on a reducing balance basis). P Limited's assets have depreciated by 59% (590,400/1,000,000) of the original cost whereas Z Limited's assets have depreciated by 73.8% (1,106,784/1,500,000) of their original cost. The higher value of the assets in P Limited will reduce the value of ROCE and asset turnover.

(c)

> **Top tip**. Note that only three factors need to be explained for full marks to this question.

Factors that should be considered when setting a transfer pricing policy are outlined below.

Taxation

If there are any **overseas parts** of the group, the effect(s) of **international taxation** will need to be considered.

Any attempt to **'manipulate' profits** to reduce tax liabilities is likely to **upset the tax authorities** if they discover it and may lead to some form of **penalty**.

Artificial selling price

The transfer price should provide an 'artificial' selling price that enables the **transferring** division to earn a **return for its efforts**, and the **receiving** division to **incur a cost** for benefits received.

Constraints and demand

Transfer prices should reflect capacity constraints and market demand for the item being transferred. The **supplier's opportunity cost** should be reflected in the transfer price.

Goal congruence

The transfer price, if possible, should encourage profit centre managers to agree on the amount of goods and services to be transferred, which will also be at a level that is consistent with the aims of the organisation as a whole such as **maximising company profits**.

The Directors of PZ Group could impose a transfer price, or oversee negotiations between the two companies.

103 The Alpha group

> **Text references.** Performance measures are covered in Chapter 12 and financial performance indicators are covered in Chapter 11.
>
> **Top tips.** Use information provided in the question to illustrate your answer as necessary.
>
> **Examiner's comments.** Answers to this question were extremely poor. Students should remember that transfer pricing is one of the main topics within the P2 syllabus.
>
> In part (a), many candidates failed to recognise the relationship between the three ratios and how a deliberate attempt to improve one ratio can adversely affect one of the other ratios. Part (b) asked candidates to include calculations to support their argument but the majority failed to address this requirement.

Marking scheme

		Marks
(a)	Calculation of each ratio for each business segment (3 x 1 mark)	3
	Comparison of Y Limited and X Limited Production division	
	- Similar ROCE	1
	- Unit profitability and asset turnover	2
	- Different focus for the future	1
	Discussion of the consultancy division	2
		9
(b) (i)	Management friction	1
	Spare capacity	1
	Profit shifting	1
	Loss of orders	1
	Sub optimal decision making	1
(ii)	Market price	1
	Adjusted market price for external factors	1
	Calculations of market price	2
	Variable cost	1
	Calculation of variable cost	2
	Total transfer price	1
		13
(c)	Double taxation	1
	Transactions at arm's length	1
	Different tax rates and profit shifting	1
		3

(a)

(i) $\underline{ROCE}$ = Profit / capital employed × 100%

		$'000	ROCE
X Limited	Production	140/2,000	7%
	Consultancy	210/800	26.25%
Y Limited		370/4,000	9.25%

$\underline{Operating\ profit\ margin}$ = Operating profit / sales × 100%

		$'000	Operating profit
X Limited	Production	140/1,260	11.1%
	Consultancy	210/710	29.6%
Y Limited		370/750	49.3%

$\underline{Asset\ turnover}$ = Sales / capital employed

		$'000	Asset turnover
X Limited	Production	1,260/2,000	0.63
	Consultancy	710/800	0.89
Y Limited		750/4,000	0.19

From the above calculations, it is clear that **all divisions are profitable**. Interestingly, the return on capital employed (ROCE) achieved by the Consultancy division of X (26.25%) is far higher than in other parts of the business.

The nature of **consultancy businesses** means that **profits are often <u>not</u> derived from assets but from investing in high quality staff**. As such, the **level of capital investment** required in consultancy businesses is relatively low.

The ROCE values of the Production division of X Limited (7%) and Y Limited (9.25%) are comparable. Y Limited has **high unit profitability** but the level of capital employed ($4m) is double that of the Production division. In contrast, the Production division is able to generate a **high level of sales relative to its capital employed** but has lower unit profitability.

(b) (i) Allowing the managers of each company or division to **negotiate transfer prices** with each other is likely to have a number of **behavioural implications**.

The current pricing policy **does not benefit the Alpha group as a whole**. X Limited recently missed out on a potentially profitable order due to **high transfer prices** charged by Y Limited. If Y Limited agreed to lower prices for components sold to X, it is likely that X Limited **could pass this on** to customers in the form of **lower prices** and thus **win more orders**.

The current policy also appears to favour Y Limited over X Limited which is likely to **create friction** between the managers of each company.

The manager of Y Limited argues that the prices he charges X Limited are fair because if the **internal sales were not made**, he could **increase external sales**. This is not strictly true since Y Limited would have **spare capacity** if it did not sell to X.

(ii) Market price basis

Unsatisfied external demand for Y Limited is estimated at 20%. As such, it is reasonable that Y limited **supplies some components** to X Limited **at the market price**. X Limited may be able to **negotiate a discount on the market price**, given that selling internally effectively saves Y Limited administration and distribution costs incurred on external sales.

The $400,000 of external sales by Y Limited represent 80% of the external market, so the **unsatisfied demand** equals 20/80 x $400,000 = $100,000. It would be reasonable for Y Limited to sell the components to X Limited for, (say), $95,000. The $5,000 **discount takes account of the cost savings** for Y Limited mentioned above.

Variable cost basis

The remaining supplies to X Limited should be on a **variable cost basis**. X Limited may offer a **slightly higher price as an incentive** for Y to produce the components.

Y Limited's **variable costs** are 60% of $250,000 = $150,000 which is 20% of the total sales value of Y Limited. The remaining $250,000 of internal sales should be sold to X Limited for $250,000 x 20% = $50,000, **plus a small incentive** ($5,000) = $55,000.

In this instance, the total value of internal sales from Y Limited to X Limited would be approximately $150,000.

(c) Different tax rates

If Y Limited is relocated to another country, there is likely to be a **significant difference in tax rates** between the two countries. Alpha group may look to **reduce the level of tax paid** by moving profits from one country to another by way of the **transfer pricing mechanism**.

The tax authorities in each country are likely to have measures that are designed to prevent such events occurring.

Paying tax in both countries

The revised transfer prices outlined in part (b) result in greater amounts of profit being taxed at the higher tax rate, in the current country. However, if Y Limited were to relocate, the revised transfer price is not equal to the external market price and may not be viewed as an arm's length transaction. As a result the Alpha Group may find that it ends up paying tax in both countries.

104 DEF

> **Text references**. Transfer pricing is covered in Chapter 13. Measuring performance in divisionalised businesses is covered in Chapter 12.
>
> **Top tips**. Include examples in parts (a) and (b) using the data from the scenario to add depth to your answers.
>
> **Easy marks**: Being able to explain negotiated transfer pricing in part (b) and dual transfer prices in part (d) will earn you quick and easy marks.

(a)   The performance statement does not show the basis on which capital employed has been calculated for each division. This is likely to be calculated as the original cost of assets less accumulated depreciation. Divisions with older assets are likely to have lower original costs and lower net book values (due to more years of accumulated depreciation). As a result, **comparisons of capital employed between divisions may be distorted**.

The return on capital employed for each division is not included in the performance statement. This is calculated as:

Division D = 2.5%   ($10,000 / $400,000)
Division E = 10%   ($55,000 / $550,000)
Division F = 12%   ($50,000 / $415,000)

From the above calculations, it is evident that **only Division E has met the target return on capital employed** set by Head Office.

Management charges from Head Office are included within administration costs. The management charges are not controllable at a divisional level and should not be included within the division performance summaries.

The performance statement **does not distinguish between internal and external sales**. It is not possible to analyse the performance of each division in the external market.

(b)   A transfer price is **the price at which goods or services are transferred between different divisions of the same company**. Divisional managers are measured on their ability to control internal costs as well as external costs.

Transfer prices are often set by a means of **negotiation**. The agreed price may be finalised from a mixture of accounting arithmetic, politics and compromise.

Negotiated transfer pricing can lead to disputes between division managers who will try to protect their own interests and achieve optimal performance of their own division. Disagreements between divisions are likely to result in **decisions being made** that are **not in the best interests of the company as a whole**.

Inter-divisional trading will affect the performance of each division. Assuming the goods sold between divisions are similar to those sold in the external market, the following analysis can be made:

External sales of Division D were $130,000 for the year ended 30 September 20X9. The variable costs relating to external sales were $32,000, a mark-up of just over 300%. If the same mark-up were applied to the internal sale, profits of Division D would have increased by $52,000 to $62,000 and the profits of Division E would reduce by $52,000.

External sales of Division F were $385,000 for the year ended 30 September 20X9. The variable costs relating to the external sales were $221,000, a mark-up of just under 75%. A mark-up of 67% was added to the internal sale to Division E. The impact on profit reported by Division E and Division F as a result of this transaction is negligible.

(c)

Division	D $'000	E $'000	F $'000
Sales			
– External (net sales)	130	200	385
– Internal (Note 1)	72	0	15
Total sales	202	200	400
Variable production costs			
– External	(50)	(35)	(230)
– Internal (Note 2)		(27)	
– Internal mark-up (Note 2)		(60)	
Fixed production costs	(60)	(50)	(80)
Administration costs	(20)	(17)	(25)
Total costs	(130)	(189)	(335)
Divisional profit	72	11	65
Management charge from Head Office (not controllable at a divisional level)	(10)	(8)	(15)
Profit	62	3	50
Capital employed	400	550	415
ROCE (based on profit)	15.5%	0.5%	12.0%
ROCE (based on divisional profit)	18.0%	2.0%	15.7%

Note 1 – Internal sales are valued at their equivalent external prices by applying the mark-ups calculated in requirement (b).

Note 2 – These balances show the variable cost to the company of the internal transactions and the mark-up that would normally be applied to these transactions.

(d)   Under a dual transfer pricing system, the price recorded by the selling division within DEF **would not be as same as the purchase price recorded by the buying division**.

The buying division would record the costs as the variable cost to the company whilst the selling division would include a value based on external market prices as their sales.

This means that the selling division is able to earn a profit and the receiving division has the correct information in order to make the correct selling decision to maximise the group's profit.

The difference between the two prices will be debited to a **group transfer price adjustment account**. At the end of the accounting period, the profits of the two divisions, and hence of the group, will be overstated to the extent of the price difference. In order to correct this, the total amount in the transfer price adjustment account must be subtracted from the two profits to arrive at the correct profit for the group as a whole.

If dual transfer pricing was applied to the internal transactions within DEF, the "internal mark-up" of $60,000 calculated in requirement (c) would not be disclosed on the divisional performance statement.

The divisional profit of Division E would increase by $60,000 to $71,000, yielding a return on capital employed (based on divisional profit) of 13%.

105 ACF Group

Text reference. Transfer pricing is covered in Chapter 13.

Top tips. We considered the impact of the policies by comparing them to a policy of C being forced to purchase from A at a price based on achieving A's RI.

Easy marks. Part (a) was straightforward and offered some easy marks..

(a) (i) Annual profit = external sales revenue + internal sales revenue − variable costs − fixed costs

Therefore, £564,000 = ((150,000 − 60,000) × £35) + (60,000 × P) − (150,000 × £22) − £1,080,000, where P = transfer price.

Therefore P = £29.90

> Alternative approach
>
> Required profit = £564,000
>
> Expected profit
>
> | | £'000 |
> |---|---|
> | External sales (90,000 × £35) | 3,150 |
> | External costs (150,000 × £22) | (3,300) |
> | Fixed costs | (1,080) |
> | | (1,230) |
> | Plus: transfer revenue (60,000 × transfer price) | X |
> | Required profit | 564 |
>
> X = £(564,000 − 1,230,000)
>   = £(564,000 + 1,230,000) = £1,794,000
>
> Therefore, transfer price = $\dfrac{£1,794,000}{60,000}$ = £29.90

(ii) External sales demand is 110,000 units. Maximum capacity is 150,000 units and so by transferring 60,000 units internally, external sales of 20,000 units are lost.

The **opportunity cost** of these **20,000 units** = variable cost + contribution lost from selling externally = £22 + £13 = **£35 = external selling price**.

The **remaining 40,000 units** can be produced using space capacity and so **opportunity cost = variable cost** = £22.

(b) Current policy

By allowing divisions the freedom to set transfer prices (A sets a price of £29.90) and choose their suppliers, C will not purchase the 60,000 units from A because it can buy them cheaper, externally, from X. C is motivated to take such action to maximise the sole performance measure (RI).

	Situation if C forced to accept transfer price of £29.90 £'000	Situation if C can choose supplier	£'000
A contribution			
external (90,000 × £(35 − 22))	1,170	110,000 × £(35 − 22)	1,430
internal (60,000 × £(29.90 − 22))	474		
	1,644		1,430
C costs			
internal (60,000 × £29.90)	1,794		
External		(60,000 × £28)	1,680

Results

(i) A's external contribution will rise by £260,000 with the current policy.

(ii) Overall A's contribution will fall by £214,000.

(iii)   C's costs will fall by £114,000.

(iv)   Net effect for the group = fall in contribution of £100,000.

(v)   In terms of external transactions:

		£
Increase in external sales	(20,000 × £(35 − 22))	260,000
Increase in external costs	(60,000 × £(28 − 22))	360,000
		(100,000)

Proposed policy

C has two options.

(i)   Purchase 40,000 units from A at £22 per unit
Purchase 20,000 units from Z at £33 per unit
Total cost = £1,540,000

(ii)   Purchase 50,000 units from X at £28 per unit
Purchase 10,000 units from A at £22 per unit
Total cost = £1,620,000

C would choose the first option in order to minimise costs.

Effect on A

	Situation if C forced to accept transfer price of £29.90	*Proposed policy*
A external sales	90,000 × £35	110,000 × £35
A internal sales	40,000 × £29.90	40,000 × £22
	20,000 × £29.90	
	60,000 × £29.90	

Difference on external sales. Proposed policy increases contribution by 20,000 × £35 = £700,000.

Difference on internal sales. Proposed policy reduces contribution by (40,000 × £(29.90 − 22)) + (20,000 × £29.90) = £914,000

Net effect on A. Reduction in contribution of £214,000.

Effect on C. C's costs reduced from £1,794,000 to £1,540,000, a reduction of £254,000.

Effect on group. Net effect, increase in contribution of £40,000.

In terms of external transactions:

	£
Increase in external sales (20,000 × £(35 − 22))	260,000
Increase in external costs (20,000 × £(33 − 22)	220,000
	40,000

Conclusion

(i)   Both policies are flawed in that C can act in its own interests, which might not necessarily be in the interests of the group as a whole.

(ii)   Of the two policies, the proposed policy is the more advantageous to the group.

(iii)   Division C might not have the knowledge to make the correct decision to maximise the group's profit.

(iv)   To maximise group profit, transfers should be made at marginal cost to ensure that C makes the correct decision for the group. This policy has a demotivating effect on the management of A, however, as fixed costs are not covered.

(v)   ACF group should consider introducing a wide range of performance measures and/or qualitative measures to ensure goal congruence and to guard against dysfunctional decision making.

106 FD and TM

> **Text references**. Transfer pricing is covered in Chapter 13.
>
> **Top tips**. This question examines the explanation and demonstration of transfer pricing and the calculation and evaluation of residual income. Note how these two components are from different parts of the syllabus, highlighting the importance of thinking across the syllabus rather than in terms of lots of different sections. Don't compartmentalise your knowledge.

(a)　<u>TM division</u>

Net profit = 15,000 × £24 = £360,000

RI = profit – imputed interest

Therefore, RI = £360,000 – (0.12 × £1.5m) = £180,000

Target RI is £105,000.

The manager is therefore **in line for a bonus** of 5% × £180,000 = £9,000.

<u>FD division</u>

Profit on external sales = £12 × 5,000 = £60,000

Profit on internal transfers = £15,000 × (10% of production cost – fixed admin overhead) = 15,000 × (6 – 4) = £30,000

Therefore, total profit = £90,000

Therefore, RI = £90,000 – (0.12 × £750,000) = £nil

Target RI = £85,000

Therefore, the manager is **not in line for a bonus**.

> **Top tips**. Here is another possible approach. If you are worried about missing out any of the many costs/revenues mentioned in the question scenario and/or like to have a clear audit trail of figures, go for this second (tabular) approach.

Alternative approach

		TM division			*FD division*	
		£'000	£'000		£'000	£'000
Sales						
Internal			–	((£60 × 110%) × 15,000)		990
External	(£500 × 15,000)		7,500	(£80 × 5,000)		400
			7,500			1,390
Less: variable costs						
Production	(£366 × 15,000)	5,490		(£40 × 20,000)	800	
Selling and						
distribution	(£25 × 15,000)	375		(£4 × 5,000)	20	
			5,865			820
			1,635			570
Less: fixed costs						
Production	(£60 × 15,000)	900		(£20 × 20,000)	400	
Administration	(£25 × 15,000)	375		(£4 × 20,000)	80	
			1,275			480
Profit			360			90
Less: imputed interest						
	(0.12 × £1.5m)		(180)	(0.12 × £750,000)		90
Residual income			180			–
Target residual income			105			85
Bonus			9			NIL

Implications of the performance evaluation system

(i)   The manager of TM division will be happy as he has exceeded his target residual income and should receive a bonus of £9,000.

(ii)   The manager of FD division will be unhappy as he has not met his target residual income and will not receive a bonus.

(iii)   The manager of FD division is likely to be demotivated, which could well result in low levels of efficiency and poor quality products. This in turn could lead to high levels of staff turnover, loss of customer goodwill, and so ultimately a negative impact on group profits.

The current performance evaluation system is unacceptable and should be amended.

(b)   (i)   Maximum transfer price manager of TM division would pay

Residual income = net profit – imputed interest

Therefore, to achieve target residual income of £105,000 with imputed interest of 12% × £1.5m = £180,000, net profit must be £285,000 or above.

Net profit per TX = £24 + £66 (current transfer price) – X (revised transfer price)

Total net profit of £285,000 on sales of 15,000 units = 15,000 (£90 – £X)

Therefore, £285,000/£15,000 = £90 – £X

Therefore, £19 = £90 – £X

Therefore, £X = £71

Therefore, the maximum transfer price the manager of TM division would pay is £71.

(ii)   Minimum transfer price manager of FD division would accept

To achieve target residual income of £85,000 with imputed interest of (12% × £750,000) £90,000, net profit must be £175,000 or above.

Net profit on external sales (see (a)) = £60,000.

Net profit on transfers = 15,000 × (revised transfer price X – production costs of £60 per unit – fixed admin overhead of £4 per unit).

= (15,000 × revised transfer price of X) – (£15,000 × £64)

= 15,000 £X – £960,000.

Therefore, to achieve target RI

£175,000 = £60,000 + (15,000 × £X) – £960,000

Therefore, £X = £71.67

Therefore, the minimum transfer price acceptable to the manager of FD division is £71.67.

Top tips. You needed to apply a bit of algebra in this part of the question if you took our approach. You may have got to the correct answers using an alternative method.

(c)

Top tips. There were a wide range of issues to cover in this part of the question and you may have run out of time. Don't be disheartened if you did (but try and plan your time better in future) and don't worry if you didn't come up with four possible solutions to the conflict problems.

Easy marks. Three solutions would have earned you very good marks. It was vital to relate your answer to CTD Ltd to gain these.

REPORT

To: Management of CTD Ltd
From: Management accountant
Date: 21 December 20X2
Subject: Transfer pricing in FD division

1   Introduction

This report **aims** to:

- Explain and recommend the transfer prices which FD division should set in order to maximise group profits

- Consider the implications of actual external customer demand exceeding 5,000 units

- Explain how alternative transfer pricing systems could overcome any possible conflict that may arise as a result of the recommended transfer price

2   Recommended transfer price for FD division

The transfer pricing policy should ensure the **maximisation of CTD Ltd's profits**. This is achieved by the **inclusion** in the transfer price of any **opportunity costs** associated with internal transfer.

Sales of 5,000 units or less to external customers

FD division currently has **spare capacity** of 5,000 units and so production of 15,000 units for TM division has no effect on the ability of FD division to produce 5,000 units for external customers.

There is therefore no opportunity cost associated with internal transfers as they do not cause a reduction in contribution from external sales.

For internal transfers of up to 20,000 units the **transfer price** should therefore be set at **standard variable production cost of £40**.

Given that FD division makes no contribution on transfers at variable production cost, the manager will be **indifferent** between making transfers and producing no output. **Head office intervention** may therefore be required to ensure that transfers take place.

Sales of between 5,000 and 9,999 units to external customers

Up to an external sales level of 9,999 units, FD division would still have spare **capacity** and so the transfer price could remain at £40.

Sales of 10,000 units or more to external customers

Once **external demand exceeds 10,000 units**, however, FD division would be unable to meet both internal and external demand.

For example, if external demand were 12,000 units and FD division continued to supply 15,000 units internally, it would lose the contribution on 2,000 units that could be sold externally. The transfer price must therefore take the opportunity cost of this lost contribution into account.

Recommended transfer pricing system

A **two-tier transfer pricing system** would then be required.

15,000 units would have a transfer price of **variable production cost** of £40 as there would be no external demand for this output.

Once external demand exceeds 10,000, those **units which are transferred internally rather than sold externally** should have a transfer price of **external market price** of £80, **adjusted** for the £4 variable selling and distribution cost (ie £76).

3   Potential conflicts

Theoretically the prices above should **optimise** CTD Ltd's profits.

But the **manager of FD division** will **not accept the transfer price of £40 as it would not allow him to cover his fixed costs and it is below the price of £71.67** required to enable him to earn a bonus. The manager might then **refuse to make internal transfers**. TM division, if it could not source externally, would be unable to make external sales of the TX, which would have a **significant adverse impact on CTD Ltd's profits**.

And the **manager of TM** division will **not accept a transfer price of £80 as it is above £71**, the maximum transfer price that would enable him to earn his bonus. He would prefer to **source externally** at a **price between £40 and £71.67**, but this would **not be in the best interest of CTD Ltd** as **the purchase price would be greater than the marginal cost of making internally.**

There is therefore a **conflict** between the objectives of the two divisions.

4   <u>Alternative transfer pricing systems to overcome the potential conflict</u>

Possible **solutions** which would reward both divisions and eliminate the sub-optimality include the following.

<u>Dual pricing</u>

The **transfer price** would be based on the **variable cost** of £40 per unit and, at the **end of the period**, division FD would be **credited** with a **share of the overall profit** arising from the final sale of the TX. This appears to be a fairer system but the share of profits would need to be determined centrally, thus undermining divisional autonomy.

<u>Variation on dual pricing</u>

Division FD would be **credited** with the **market price** of £80 for transfers made, while **division TM** would be **debited** with the **variable cost** of £40. This would be effective in avoiding dysfunctional behaviour and sub-optimal decisions, but would be **administratively cumbersome.**

<u>Two-part tariff system</u>

Transfer prices would be set at the **variable cost** of £40 and **once a year** there would be a **transfer of a fixed fee to division FD**, representing an allowance for its fixed costs. The fixed fee would be determined centrally, however, **undermining divisional autonomy.**

<u>Negotiated transfer price</u>

It is possible that a transfer price could be agreed based on a mixture of accounting arithmetic, politics and compromise. If such an approach were to be used and the two divisions **could not agree**, the transfer price would have to be set by head office, **undermining divisional autonomy.**

5   <u>Summary</u>

If the two divisions are unable to come to an agreement, the transfer price may need to be **set centrally**, so that the profits of the company as a whole are maximised. This would undermine divisional autonomy and would **demotivate** the managers of divisions TM and FD.

I hope the contents of this report prove useful. If I can provide further information please do not hesitate to contact me.

107   Sports equipment manufacturer

Text references. Transfer pricing is covered in Chapter 13. Performance measures for divisions are covered in Chapter 12.

Top tips. In part (a), don't forget to show the impact on the group as a whole. If you are in doubt about how many sets of wheels the Wheels division is supplying to the Frames division in part (b), state an assumption and complete your calculations based on that assumption. Even if your assumption is incorrect, you will still get marks for technique. In (b)(ii) you have to calculate the total contribution you need to maintain return on assets. You will have to gross up the additional fixed costs by 112.5% (1 + the required return) as part of this calculation. Don't forget to answer the question – that is, determine the minimum price in each case. Part (c) tests your knowledge of the problems associated with transfer pricing and how they could be resolved. Make sure you relate your answer to the scenario and write in report format.

Easy marks. Part (b)(i) needed some fairly straightforward calculations. Part (b)(ii) was a gift! Part (c) required you to state the case for and against standard costing as a useful tool for management.

(a) <u>Wheels division</u>

	$
Additional contribution (5,000 x $300)	1,500,000
Less additional fixed costs	1,000,000
Additional profit earned	500,000

<u>Frames division</u>

Note: it has been assumed that the Wheels division will supply the Frames division with its full requirements of 15,000 sets of wheels, rather than just the spare capacity that the Wheels division has.

Additional purchase cost (15,000 x [$900 – 870]) = $450,000

<u>Group</u>

	$
Additional profits (Wheels)	500,000
Additional costs (Frames)	450,000
Increase in group profit	50,000

(b) (i) The manager of the Wheels division will wish to at least maintain his divisional profit of $1 million.

	$
Additional fixed costs to be covered	1,000,000
Lost contribution from external sales (10,000 x $300)	3,000,000
Contribution required from sales to Frames division	4,000,000

	$
Contribution per unit $\dfrac{\$4\,\text{million}}{15,000}$	266.67
Variable costs per unit	600.00 *
Minimum selling price	866.00

* The Wheels division has agreed to supply wheel sets to the Frames division at a price of $900 per set. This price would earn the same contribution as external sales ($300). Variable costs are therefore $600 per set.

(ii) In order to maintain the return on assets, the Wheels division must cover the **lost contribution** on external sales of $3 million and a **return to cover the additional fixed costs** of $1 million.

Return to cover additional fixed costs = $1 million x 112.5% = $1,125 million

Therefore total contribution required from internal sales = $3 million + $1.125 million
= $4.125 million

	$
Contribution per unit $= \dfrac{\$4.125\,\text{million}}{15,000\ \text{sets of wheels}}$	275
Variable costs per unit	600
Minimum selling price	875

(c) **REPORT**

To:	Managing Director
From:	Management Accountant
Subject:	Transfer pricing issues

This report focuses on the problems that might arise from the directive that the Wheels division must supply the Frames division and the introduction of performance measures. It also offers some possible solutions to these problems.

<u>Loss of divisional autonomy</u>

By issuing the directive that the Wheels division has to supply the Frames division, there is a loss of divisional autonomy. Managers are no longer being given the choice of who to supply (Wheels division) or who to purchase from (Frames division). This could lead to issues regarding the motivation and behaviour of the divisional managers. Frames division is being forced to accept a higher purchase price per unit ($900 rather than $870) which means their profits will be reduced. Whilst Wheels division is able to make use of its spare capacity and earn the same contribution from Frames division as from external sales, they will be losing some external custom. This could lead to problems for remaining external sales if word gets around that they have let customers down.

<u>Maximum and minimum transfer prices</u>

The Group benefits as a whole from the internal transfer of goods from Wheels division to Frames division (profit increases by $50,000). However at the moment there is a problem with the transfer price being charged to Frames division.

The division is paying $30 per unit more for internal transfers which is not acceptable to the management of this division. Profits will be adversely affected and the fact that this price has been imposed may cause ill-feeling between divisions, particularly as Wheels division is enjoying increased profits.

The maximum transfer price that should be charged to Frames division is the lowest market price at which this division could purchase the goods externally, less any internal savings costs in packaging and delivery. The maximum price that Frames division will be willing to pay is the current external price of $870.

The minimum transfer price is the sum of Wheels division's marginal cost and opportunity cost of the item transferred. This has been calculated as $866.67.

The transfer price should therefore be set somewhere between the maximum and minimum prices. The current transfer price is $30 above the maximum price.

<u>Performance measures</u>

The idea behind performance measures is to encourage divisional managers to act in the best interests of the business as a whole whilst at the same time being rewarded for good performance. If such measures are not chosen carefully they may be to the detriment of the organisation as managers start making decisions that are in their own best interests.

The use of 'profit' as a performance measure will enable Wheels division to set a transfer price that will enhance group profits. However the manager of Wheels division may not be keen to supply Frames division at the minimum price of $867 as the division will incur additional fixed costs of $1 million and will be working at maximum capacity.

The price required by Wheels division if 'return on assets' is used as the performance measure does not encourage goal congruence as it is above the market price currently paid by Frames division. The manager of this division will not want to incur higher costs for internally transferred goods.

The problem with both measures is that they are purely financial indicators. Ideally performance measures should reflect both financial and non-financial activities to encourage managers to act in the best interests of the group as a whole.

<u>Potential solutions to the transfer pricing problem</u>

It is not easy to resolve transfer pricing problems as there is a fine line between removing autonomy from divisional managers (by imposing a transfer price) and allowing divisions to settle the transfer prices between themselves (which can lead to negotiation problems).

Divisional managers could be given autonomy to negotiate their own transfer prices. If they failed to reach an agreement then an appointed arbitrator from Head Office could intervene to settle the dispute. In this way managers are being given a chance to reach an agreement by themselves rather than feeling that their positions have been undermined by an imposed price.

Whilst the optimal transfer price should reflect the opportunity costs of both the supplying and receiving divisions, a compromise could be reached by using a 'dual' transfer pricing system. This would involve setting the transfer price at the marginal cost and crediting a fixed fee by way of compensation to the division that is 'losing out'. This could be coupled with an adjustment to the performance measure to reflect the lost contribution or additional costs suffered by this division.

At all times the Group's profit position should be the priority. If disagreement continues between the two divisions and Frames threatens to continue to buy externally, Head Office staff should intervene to avoid the resultant reduction in Group profit.

If you would like to discuss any of these issues further please do not hesitate to contact me.

MOCK EXAMS

254

CIMA
Paper P2 (Management)
Performance Management

Mock Exam 1

Question Paper	
Time allowed	**3 hours**
This paper is divided into two sections	
Section A **Five compulsory questions**	
Section B **Two compulsory questions**	

DO NOT OPEN THIS PAPER UNTIL YOU ARE READY TO START UNDER EXAMINATION CONDITIONS

256

SECTION A – 50 marks

Answer ALL FIVE questions

Question 1

M Ltd has two divisions, X and Y. Division X is a chip manufacturer and Division Y assemble mobile phones.

The budgeted profit and loss statement for Division Y for next year shows the following results.

Mobile phone range	P £'000	Q £'000	R £'000
Sales	10,000	9,500	11,750
Less total costs	7,200	11,700	9,250
Profit/(loss)	2,800	(2,200)	2,500
Fixed costs	2,000	5,400	5,875

Division Y uses a traditional absorption costing system based on labour hours.

The accountant of M Ltd has recently attended a course on activity based costing (ABC) and has recommended that the division should implement an ABC system rather than continue to operate the traditional absorption costing system.

A presenter at the conference stated that 'ABC provides information that is more relevant for decision-making than traditional forms of costing'.

Required

Discuss this statement, using Division Y when appropriate to explain the issues you raise. **(10 marks)**

Question 2

NLM uses a common process to manufacture three joint products: X, Y and Z. The costs of operating the common process total $75,400 each month. This includes $6,800 of apportioned head office costs. The remaining costs are specific to the common process and would be avoided if it were discontinued. Common costs are apportioned to the joint products on the basis of their respective output volumes.

The normal monthly output from the common process is:

X   4,000 litres
Y   5,000 litres
Z   4,500 litres

There are a number of manufacturers of products that are identical to products X, Y and Z and as a result there is a competitive market in which these products can be bought and sold at the following prices.

X $5.00 per litre
Y $4.50 per litre
Z $5.50 per litre

Currently NLM uses the output from the common process as input to three separate processes where X, Y and Z are converted into SX, SY and SZ. The specific costs of these further processes (which are avoidable if the further process is discontinued) are as follows:

X to SX $1.25 per litre plus $1,850 per month
Y to SY $1.80 per litre pus $800 per month
Z to SZ $1.55 per litre plus $2,400 per month

The market selling prices of the further processed products are:

SX $6.75 per litre
SY $7.50 per litre
SZ $7.20 per litre

Required

(a)   Advise NLM as to which (if any) of the further processes should continue to be operated. State any relevant assumptions.   **(6 marks)**

(b)   Advise NLM whether they should continue to operate the common process. State any relevant assumptions.   **(4 marks)**

(Total = 10 marks)

Question 3

(a)   A manufacturing company has developed a new product. The time taken to manufacture the first unit was 24 minutes. It is expected than an 80% learning curve will apply for the first three months of production and that by the end of that period the total number of units produced will have reached 1,024. It is then expected that the time taken for each subsequent unit will be the same as the time taken for the 1,024th unit.

Required

(i)   Calculate the expected time taken for the 8th unit. $y = 24 - 8^{-0.3219}$ **(3 marks)**

(ii)   Explain two reasons why the time taken for the 1,025th unit may be more than expected.   **(2 marks)**

Note: The value of the 80% learning index is –0.3219

(b)   Explain the importance of considering the learning curve when deciding on the terms for a gain sharing arrangement with employees.   **(5 marks)**

(Total = 10 marks)

Question 4

Two of the products that are manufactured by a company use the same machines. The products (P1 and P2) are manufactured using two machines (M1 and M2). During the next period the time available on the machines are 126 hours for M1 and 195 hours for M2.

The company uses throughput accounting.

Unit details of the two products are:

	P1	P2
	$	$
Selling price	36.00	39.00
Materials	14.20	16.75
Labour	6.00	7.50
Variable production overheads	1.00	1.25
Fixed production overheads	2.00	2.50
Profit	12.80	11.00

Any mix of output can be sold at the above prices and there is unlimited demand for each of the products.

The machine time needed to make one unit of the products is:

	P1	P2
M1	0·35 hours	0·40 hours
M2	0·60 hours	0·65 hours

Required

(a) (i) Calculate the maximum production that is possible from each machine for each of the two products and state the bottleneck.

 (ii) Calculate the throughput accounting ratio for each product. **(5 marks)**

(b) Identify, using a throughput approach, the production plan for the next period that would result in the most profitable use of the machines. (All workings must be shown). **(5 marks)**

(Total = 10 marks)

Question 5

You are the Management Accountant of a small engineering company, which is a member of a large engineering group. The Managing Director has recently joined the company and has little experience of the engineering sector. He has recently returned from the group's annual management conference. The Managing Director found the seminars very useful but he is a little confused about one topic.

One of the presentations discussed the use of Target Costing within the group. The Managing Director had previously thought that Target Costing would not be appropriate for an engineering group, because he thought it could only be used in an organisation that manufactured similar products. He now realises that he may be confusing Target Costing and Standard Costing. He seeks your help in explaining Target Costing and how it differs from Standard Costing.

Required

Prepare a report to the Managing Director that explains Target Costing and how it differs from Standard Costing.

(10 marks)

(Total for Section A= 50 marks)

SECTION B – 50 marks

Answer BOTH questions

Question 6

The G Group has a divisionalised structure. One of the divisions manufactures engines and one of the other divisions assembles motor cycles. The performance of the Divisional Managers, and consequently their bonuses, is based on the return on capital employed (ROCE) of their individual divisions. Both of these divisions operate in highly competitive markets.

Motor Cycle Division

A key component in a motor cycle is the engine. Engines are readily available on the open market but the division currently buys 3,600 engines each year internally from the Engines Division for £1,375 per engine. The Manager has just received the following message from the Manager of the Engines Division.

Engine Prices: due to recent cost increases the price per engine will now be £1,600.

On receiving the message the Manager of the Motor Cycle division contacted several external manufacturers and found one that would supply the required engines at £1,375 per engine. However she has since received a directive from the Managing Director of the Group that states that she must buy the engines internally.

Engines Division

Following the recent cost increases, the full absorption cost of a motor cycle engine is £1,450. This includes £400 for fixed production overheads. This type of motor cycle engine is one of many different engines produced by the division.

The Manager of the Engines Division is aware of the competitive external market that he faces and knows that it will be difficult for him to charge external customers more than £1,375 per engine. However, he is also aware that the rising costs will have an impact on his bonus. He is trying to protect his bonus by passing these costs on to the Motor Cycle Division. He is keen to make as much profit as he can from these internal sales because the division is currently working below capacity.

Required

(a) Calculate the impact on the annual profits of each of the two divisions and the G Group as a whole, of the directive that the engines must be purchased internally for £1,600 per engine instead of from the external supplier. **(6 marks)**

(b) Write a report to the Managing Director of the Group that explains the disadvantages and behavioural implications of using ROCE as a divisional performance measure. Your answer must be based on the above scenario and include an explanation of 'responsibility accounting'. **(12 marks)**

(c) The Engines Division has now developed a new 'lean burn' car engine that is sold exclusively to external customers. The production of this engine will utilise the spare capacity of the division and will earn the division a contribution of £40 per machine hour. The demand is so high for the car engines that their production could also use 9,000 machine hours that are currently used to make 1,000 of the motor cycle engines that are transferred to the Motor Cycle Division.

Required

Explain, with supporting calculations, the minimum and maximum transfer prices that could now be charged for the motor cycle engines. **(7 marks)**

(Total = 25 marks)

Question 7

A retail company has a number of individual retail outlets in different towns. Each outlet has its own manager who can make decisions about the individual retail outlet, provided these decisions are within the parameters of the overall company policy. The performance of each individual manager is measured based on the profits of the retail outlet that he or she manages.

Company policy

It is company policy that each of the retail outlets should stock the following categories of items for sale to customers:

• Newspapers and magazines
• Fresh fruit and vegetables
• Tinned food items
• Frozen food items

Company policy also requires that no single category should occupy more than 40% or less than 15% of the total display space available. In addition, at their own discretion, managers are permitted to use up to 10% of the total display space available for other products that meet other localised needs.

The KL Retail Outlet

The following weekly sales and cost data relate to the KL retail outlet, one of the outlets owned by the company:

	Sales $'000	Purchase costs $'000	Display space %
Newspapers and magazines	150	105	25
Fresh fruit and vegetables	130	75	20
Tinned food items	400	240	30
Frozen food items	200	90	15
Other products	150	100	10

The total display space available is 800 square metres.

For each category of items for sale:

• Sales revenue is directly proportional to the floor area occupied
• Purchase costs are directly proportional to sales revenue

In addition to the purchase costs of the items sold the retail outlet incurs other costs that total $280,000 per week.

Required

(a) Demonstrate, using the above information and appropriate calculations, how the manager of the KL retail outlet should allocate the space available between the different categories of items for sale to customers in order to maximise his weekly profit. **(7 marks)**

(b) You have recently joined the retail company as its Assistant Management Accountant and, as your first project, you have been asked to compare the profitability of a number of the retail outlets. One of those within your comparison is the KL retail outlet.

You have visited the KL retail outlet and have investigated the costs that are being incurred in addition to the purchase costs of the items sold. You have confirmed that typically the retail outlet incurs other costs that total $280,000 per week. Further analysis has shown that these include staff salary costs (excluding any profit-related bonus earned by the manager), staff training costs, rent, light & heat, power, equipment depreciation, point of sale software costs, stationery, telephone, inventory storage and handling costs, marketing costs and head office charges.

You have discussed these other costs with the manager of the retail outlet. The manager of the retail outlet does not think that gross profit should be used as the basis for allocating space to items. He has suggested that some of the other costs should be attributed to the product category to which they relate rather than ignored when making the space allocation decision.

Required

Prepare a report, addressed to the manager of the KL retail outlet that explains

(i)   The principles of Direct Product Profitability (DPP);
(ii)   How these principles may be applied to his retail outlet; and
(iii)   How their application may improve the profits of his retail outlet.   **(18 marks)**

(Total = 25 marks)

(Total for Section B= 50 marks)

Answers

DO NOT TURN THIS PAGE UNTIL YOU HAVE COMPLETED THE MOCK EXAM

A PLAN OF ATTACK

We're sure you don't have to be reminded yet again to **take a good look at the paper before diving in to answer questions.** You are obviously going to remember that aren't you?

Which order to do the questions?

Once you have looked through the paper in detail (you have the chance to do this in the 20 minutes' reading time) you can decide in which order you might want to tackle the questions. All the questions are compulsory and obviously have to be attempted at some point in the three hours' writing time but it will help to build your confidence if you can start with a question you feel you can answer well.

The next step

You're probably either thinking that you don't know where to begin or that you could answer the paper in two hours!

Option 1 (Oh dear)

If you're a bit **worried** about the paper, do the **questions in the order of how well you think you can answer them.**

- **Question 1** is a discursive question on ABC and there are a number of easy marks available if you know your stuff on this area.

- **Question 2** on joint costs involves a number of calculations and there are a number of easy marks available.

- **Question 3** covers learning curves – part (c) requires a bit of thought as it relates learning curves to gain sharing arrangements.

- **Question 4** involves throughput accounting calculations and there are some easy marks to be picked up here.

- **Question 5** tests your knowledge of target costing and how it differs from standard costing. A report format is required.

- **Question 6** is one of the two longer questions you have to attempt. This involves a mixture of calculation and narrative on the topic of transfer pricing and responsibility accounting.

- **Question 7** is quite a discursive question covering scarce resources and direct product profitability. The narrative section on DPP can be answered independently of the calculations in part (a) but make sure you relate your answer to the scenario as you are specifically asked to do so.

Option 2 (if you're thinking 'It's a doddle')

Are you sure it is? If you are then that's encouraging but don't forget to do brief answer plans to ensure you don't miss the point of the questions.

- In **question 1**, make sure you relate your answer to the scenario and use headings to separate your answer if you think it will make it clearer.

- Label each step in **question 2** and don't forget to label the axes on the graph.

- Make sure your suggestions in **question 3** are suitable for the company in the scenario. Justify your suggestions.

- In **question 4** make sure you answer the question in part (a)(ii) – that is, remember to state the bottleneck rather than just doing the calculations.

- Don't be tempted to write all you know about budgetary control in **question 5** – relate your answer to the system of standard costing.

- **Question 6** requires a number of calculations so remember to show your workings. Don't forget to use a report format in part (b).

- In **question 7**, remember to relate your answer to the scenario (as mentioned above) and don't forget to use a report format!

And just one more thing...

You must **allocate your time** according to the marks available for the question in total, and for the individual parts of the questions (where applicable). It is essential that you **follow the requirements exactly** – it will be very obvious to the market if you haven't!

Finished with 15 minutes to spare?

Looks like your time allocation went slightly awry. However if you have finished, **don't waste** the last few minutes – go back to **any parts of the questions that you didn't finish** because you ran out of time.

Forget about it!

Forget about what? Excellent, you already have!

SECTION A

Question 1

> **Top tips.** When answering this question it would have been all too easy to write about ABC in general rather than in the context of decision-making, and it was vital to relate your answer to the scenario provided.

Product costs and absorption costing

Division Y **uses a traditional absorption costing** system based on labour hours, which means **overheads** are **absorbed** into product costs on the **basis of the number of direct labour hours** required per product.

Such an absorption basis tends to be used on the **assumption** that the **longer it takes to make a product** (in this case a particular type of mobile phone), the **more overhead is incurred** because of that product.

Such an **assumption may not be correct**, however, as not all overhead costs are incurred in proportion to time. **Product costs** derived on this basis could therefore be **inaccurate**.

ABC product costs

Activity based costing (ABC) is a form of absorption costing which attempts to assign overheads to products using bases that more accurately reflect the way in which the costs are incurred.

In the case of Division Y, for example, the cost of setting up production lines for a particular type of mobile phone is unlikely to be determined by the number of direct labour hours it takes to produce the mobile phone. Instead it is more likely that the cost is determined by the number of production runs.

The **use** of these bases, or **cost drivers**, produces, it is claimed, **more accurate product costs**.

Long-term and short-term variable costs

The **costs of non-volume related support activities** such as setting-up and production scheduling, which assist the efficient manufacture of a range of products, tend to **vary in the long term with the range and complexity of the products** manufactured rather than with some measure of volume of output.

Division Y produces a range of mobile phones. The traditional absorption costing system being used could therefore be allocating too great a proportion of overheads to high volume models (which cause relatively little diversity and hence use fewer support services) and too small a proportion of overheads to low volume models (which cause greater diversity and therefore use more support services).

Again, **an ABC system** would **overcome this problem**. By allocating overheads on the basis of models' usage of activities (by relating overheads to activities and using cost driver rates to allocate overheads to products) more realistic and accurate product costs are produced.

Decision making

Absorption costing product costs are argued as **acceptable in some instances,** such as for financial accounting purposes, stock valuation, some pricing decisions (if the mobile phones were priced at full cost plus, say) and for establishing the profitability of the various types of phone. For the vast majority of **decision-making** purposes, however, absorption costing product costs **should not be used**.

The budgeted profit and loss account for **Division Y** shows that **phone Q** is budgeted to make an **absorption costing loss of £2.2 million,** which could imply that the product should be **discontinued**. The traditional approach to absorption costing is known to be an unreliable source of decision-making information, however, because of the arbitrary nature of the way in which overheads are allocated and the resulting inaccurate and misleading product costs.

Marginal costing can help with decision making in the short term as the effects of minor volume changes are made explicit. The use of marginal costing would show that there would be a **reduction in contribution of £3,200** (sales less (total costs minus fixed costs)) **in the short term if the product were to be discontinued** (assuming all fixed costs are avoidable).

ABC is a form of absorption costing but because overheads are allocated to products on more accurate and realistic bases, the resulting product cost information is a **more valid basis for decisions**.

ABC costs are also **like marginal costs** in that they are variable costs. But they **are long-run variable costs** instead of short-run variable costs as they include all production overheads, not just short-term ones. Because the product costs include long-run as well as short-run variable costs, the **decision** reached **may differ** from that arrived at using marginal costing.

For example, if **phone Q** is particularly **complex**, say, it is likely to consume more resources and therefore **be allocated a higher proportion of (long-term and short-term) variable costs** using ABC. This would **reduce contribution**, possibly to such an extent that the phone Q should be **discontinued**.

Question 2

> **Text references**. Joint costs and further processing decisions are covered in Chapter 1B.
>
> **Top tips**. In part (a) the further processing decision involves comparing the net revenue from further processing with the revenue when no further processing takes place.

(a) <u>Further processing decision</u>

	Revenue without further processing $	Further processing Revenue $	Further costs (W) $	Net $
X	20,000	27,000	(6,850)	20,150
Y	22,500	37,500	(9,800)	27,700
Z	24,750	32,400	(9,375)	23,025

X and Y should be processed further as the net revenue from doing so exceeds the revenue without further processing.

Working

	X $	Y $	Z $
Costs of further processing			
Variable costs	5,000	9,000	6,975
Fixed costs	1,850	800	2,400
Profit/(loss) from further processing	6,850	9,800	9,375

(b) <u>Viability of common process</u>

	$	$
Relevant costs of common process		68,600
Market value of common process outputs:		
X (4,000 litres x $5)	20,000	
Y (5,000 litres x $4.50)	22,500	
Z (4,500 litres x $5.50)	24,750	
		67,250
Deficit		1,350

The process is not viable as the market value of the outputs is less than the relevant costs of the common process. NLM should continue to purchase X, Y and Z externally, provided their availability in the required quantities and the appropriate quality continues.

Question 3

(a) (i) <u>Expected time taken for 8th unit</u>

$Y_x = aX^b$

$b = -0.3219$ (given in the question)

$Y_8 = 24 \times 8^{-0.3219}$

$Y_8 = 12.3$ minutes

Total time for 8 units = 12.3×8 = 98.4 minutes

$Y_7 = 24 \times 7^{-0.3219}$

$Y_7 = 12.83$ minutes

Total time for 7 units = 12.83×7 = 89.8 minutes

Time taken for 8th unit = $98.4 - 89.8$ = 8.6 minutes

(ii) <u>Possible reasons for taking longer by the 1,025th unit</u>

Workers may be getting bored producing the same product over and over again and therefore **motivation** may have declined.

New production processes may have been introduced which workers may take time to get used to.

> **You could also have used the following reasons**:
>
> There may be a **break in production** of the product therefore workers may forget the processes involved and the learning process may begin all over again.
>
> Workers may be switched onto the production of other products and **new workers will have to learn the process** for the first time.

(b) <u>Gain sharing arrangements</u>

Gain sharing arrangements involve the employer and the employee working together on, for example, production issues and sharing the benefits (gains) that result.

Employees often have the **best ideas** of how production processes – and hence efficiency – could be improved as they are working with the processes on a day-to-day basis. Gain sharing arrangements are particularly important in **new production processes** as opportunities for improvements are at their highest. The employees will be **more willing to improve their efficiency** if they have the incentive of sharing in the rewards.

However employers must be aware of **naturally occurring improvements** in efficiency that are not due to improved processes (that is, **the learning curve effect**). Workers will usually improve their efficiency once they get used to a particular process and will therefore work more quickly. There should be a certain element of **expected 'natural' improvement** built into the gain sharing arrangement, or employees will have **no incentive** to increase their production efficiency.

There is a danger of employees suggesting **false improvements** to the processes and then seemingly improving their efficiency in the hope of **sharing in the benefits**, whereas these efficiency improvements could have occurred naturally as employees became more familiar with the existing processes.

Question 4

(a) (i) Product P1

Machine M1: $\dfrac{126 \text{ hours}}{0.35} = 360$ units

Machine M2: $\dfrac{195 \text{ hours}}{0.6} = 325$ units

Product P2

Machine M1: $\dfrac{126 \text{ hours}}{0.4} = 315$ units

Machine M2: $\dfrac{195 \text{ hours}}{0.65} = 300$ units

M2 is the bottleneck (as lowest throughput capacity for both products.)

(ii)

	P1	P2
	$	$
Selling price	36.00	39.00
Materials	(14.20)	(16.75)
Throughput return	21.80	22.25
Conversion costs (lab + prod o/h)	9.00	11.25
Throughput accounting ratio = throughput return/ conversion costs	2.42	1.98

(b)

	P1	P2
Throughput contribution	21.80	22.25
Time on bottleneck	0.60	0.65
Contribution/bottleneck hour	36.33	34.23
Rank	1st	2nd

Profit will be maximised by making as much of product P1 as possible as it has the higher contribution per bottleneck hour.

Maximum production of P1 is 325 units: M1 325 × 0.35 hours = 113.75 hours
M2 325 × 0.6 hours = 195 hours

Question 5

Report to the Managing Director on Target Costing and Standard Costing.

This report has been produced in response to your request for further information on target costing and how it differs from standard costing.

Target costing – what is it?

Target costing is not actually a costing system – it is a **profit planning system** designed to **control costs** and **manage profits** over the life cycle of a product. It seeks to ensure that costs are always kept to a minimum.

The **target cost** is derived through the development of a **product concept** and primary specifications for performance and design. A **price** that customers are likely to be **willing to pay** is then determined and the desired **profit margin** deducted from that price to leave a **total cost** figure. This figure is the target cost. If the product cannot be produced for that cost then it will not be manufactured.

Differences between target costing and standard costing

(i)   How costs are controlled

With **standard costing**, a standard cost is set at the beginning of a specified period. Costs must be kept within this predetermined standard and variances are calculated to ensure that this is the case.

In a **target costing** system, there are no cost reduction exercises but there is **continual pressure** to ensure that costs are always kept to a minimum.

Cost reduction instead takes place at the **initial design and development stage** to ensure the desired target cost can be met.

(ii)   Time frame for cost control

Cost control is a **continuous process** in a target costing system and target costs tend to be revised **monthly**. This ensures that costs are as **up-to-date** as possible.

In a standard costing system, standard costs are revised **annually**, meaning that actual costs are often being compared to **out-of-date** targets.

(iii)   Relationship between product concept, cost and price

With target costing, the product concept is set and then the selling price that customers are likely to be willing to pay is established. **Target cost is determined by deducting the desired profit margin from the selling price**.

The **standard cost is established from the product concept** and the selling price is determined from this cost by adding on a desired profit margin.

(iv)   Link with strategic plans

There is **no link** between standard costs and long-term strategies. The approach is **short-term cost control** through variance analysis.

In a target costing system, the product concept and target profit margin take into account **medium-term strategic plans** by focusing on whether the product can actually be produced for the target cost. If not, the project is abandoned in favour of a more cost-effective alternative.

SECTION B

Question 6

> **Text references.** Responsibility accounting is covered in Chapter 12 and transfer pricing is covered in Chapter 13.
>
> **Top tips.** For part (a) you must lay out your workings so that the marker can clearly see the impact on the profits. Make sure that you show the impact on G Group as a whole as well as on the divisions. Part (b) asks for a report so you must use a report format.
>
> **Easy marks.** There are easy marks in part (b) for an explanation of responsibility accounting and in part (d) for the aims of a transfer pricing system.

(a)   If the engines were purchased **externally** (**Profit summary 1**)

		Motor cycle division £'000	Engine division £'000	Total for G Group £'000
Sales				
Variable costs	(3,600×1,375)	(4,950,000)		(4,950,000)
Profit/(loss)		(4,950,000)		(4,950,000)

If the engines were produced **internally** (**Profit summary 2**)

		Motor cycle division £'000		Engine division £'000	Total for G Group £'000
Sales			(3,600×1,600)	5,760,000	5,760,000
Variable costs	(3,600×1,600)	(5,760,000)	(3,600×1,050)	(3,780,000)	(9,540,000)
Profit/(loss)		(5,760,000)		1,980,000	(3,780,000)

Impact on **annual profit** of purchasing internally: (**Profit summary 2 less profit summary 1**)

	Motor cycle division £'000	Engine division £'000	Total for G Group £'000
Sales		5,760,000	5,760,000
Variable costs	(810,000)	(3,780,000)	(4,590,000)
Profit/(loss)	(810,000)	1,980,000	1,170,000

(b)   <u>REPORT</u>

To: Managing Director of G Group
From: Management accountant
Date: 17 November 20X8
Subject: Using ROCE as a divisional performance measure

<u>Current system of responsibility accounting</u>

G Group currently uses **responsibility accounting** which is the term used to describe **decentralisation** of authority, with the **performance** of the decentralised units (the motor cycle division and the engines division) measured in terms of segregated **accounting results.** To be effective, such a system should only hold divisional managers responsible for those accounting results that they can control.

<u>Investment centres</u>

There are **three types** of responsibility centre: **cost centre**, **profit centre** and **investment centre**. The **motor cycle and engine divisions** are theoretically **investment centres** as the principal performance **measures** for investment centres includes **ROCE.** Managers of investment centres have **control** over controllable costs, sales prices (including transfer prices), output volumes and investment in non-current assets and working capital. Since the manager of the motor cycle division has been told that she **must**

buy engines internally, and the cost of engines is **not a controllable cost**, this goes against the principle of responsibility accounting.

<u>Return on capital employed</u>

The ROCE is the divisional profit expressed as a percentage of the investment in the division. This performance measure has a number of disadvantages and behavioural implications.

<u>Sub-optimal decisions</u>

The ROCE can be shown to lead to sub-optimal decisions if it is applied too rigidly. For example an **investment** may be **rejected** if it lowers the centre's actual ROCE, even though the investment earns **more** than the company's required return on capital.

Even if it not applied as rigidly as just explained, it may still lead to **dysfunctional decisions** by managers as it can **discourage** them from **investing in new assets**. This is because the average divisional ROCE tends to **fall** in the early stages of a new investment.

It is interesting that the engines division is **unable** to produce an engine at the **old price** of £1,375 whereas **external suppliers** continue to sell engines at this price. There may be several reasons for this but it is worth asking whether this is due to **lack of investment by the engines division**? The manager has not explained what the cause of the 'recent cost increases' is. This would be an example of a dysfunctional decision due to the effect on the division's ROCE. The manager does not want to increase investment as he may lose his **bonus**.

<u>Comparing ROCE results</u>

The **activities** of the motor cycle division and the engine division are quite **different**. One assembles and the other manufactures. This means that it is quite **difficult to compare** the percentage ROCE results of the two divisions.

The motor cycle division and the engine division might use **different bases** to **value inventory** and to **calculate depreciation**. **Assets** must be valued **consistently** at historical cost or at replacement cost.

<u>Overcoming sub-optimal decisions</u>

The problem of rejecting an investment if it lowers ROCE, even if it earns more than the company's required rate of return can be overcome by measuring **residual income**. RI rewards all investments which earn a return which is **higher than the company's required rate if return**.

The **RI will always increase** if an investment earns **more** than the **company's required rate of return**.

RI can therefore **overcome** some of the **behavioural problems** associated with ROCE but it suffers from the **same problems** of **profit measurement** and **asset valuation**.

(c)   The minimum transfer price that should be used is the marginal cost plus the opportunity cost to the Engines division (ie any lost contribution due to diverting production work.)

Of the 3,600 engines to be transferred to the Motorcycle division, 2,600 can be made using existing spare capacity and therefore the minimum transfer price for these engines will just be their variable cost of £1,050.

The remaining 1,000 engines to be transferred would require production to be switched from making 'lean burn' engines, so there would be an opportunity cost associated with this. Each motor cycle engine would require nine hours to be diverted, thus losing a contribution of (9 × £40) =£360 per engine. The minimum transfer price for these 1,000 motorcycle engines should therefore be £1,050 plus £360 = £1,410.

The maximum transfer price is £1,375 per engine, being the current external market price.

Question 7

(a) <u>Allocation of space to obtain maximum profit</u>

Limiting factor is display space available therefore space should be allocated according to **contribution per square metre of display space** (subject to company policy constraints).

Category	Display space m²	Total Contribution $'000	Contribution per m² $	Ranking
Newspapers/magazines	200	45	225	5
Fresh fruit and vegetables	160	55	344	4
Tinned food items	240	160	667	2
Frozen food items	120	110	917	1
Other products	80	50	625	3

Company policy requires each of the four main categories to be allocated at least 15% of floor space. This leaves up to 40% of floor space free to be allocated according to the rankings above.

Floor area allocated to **frozen food items** should be **maximised** (that is, 40% of total area). After minimum floor space (15%) has been allocated to the other three main categories, this leaves 15% to be allocated to the **tinned food items** which were ranked second (therefore this category will receive 30% of the total floor area).

The final allocation will be:

Category	Floor space m²	Total profit $'000	
Newspapers/magazines	120	27.00	($225 × 120)
Fresh fruit and vegetables	120	41.28	($344 × 120)
Tinned food items	240	160.08	($667 × 240)
Frozen food items	320	293.44	($917 × 320)
	800	521.80	
Less: Other costs		(280.00)	
		241.80	

(b)   Report on Direct Product Profitability to the manager of the KL retail outlet

Following on from our discussion of 'other' costs and how they might be used to improve the space allocation decision, this report focuses on the principles and potential benefits of **Direct Product Profitability**.

Principles of Direct Product Profitability

Direct Product Profitability (DPP) is a **costing system used by retail businesses** such as the KL retail outlet. Instead of ignoring indirect costs (such as warehouse costs and distribution costs) in the decision-making process, it attributes such costs to each product line. This allows a **net profit** (as opposed to a gross profit) to be calculated which gives a better idea of the **true profitability** of the product line.

This **direct product profit** represents the **contribution made by each product category** to fixed costs and profits.

Costs will not simply be allocated by volume. Whilst warehouse and storage costs can legitimately be allocated in this way (the larger the item the greater the storage space required), other costs such as **insurance and handling costs** depend on different product characteristics. High-value items require greater insurance as do items that carry a greater degree of risk (such as perishable or fragile goods).

Depending on the type of goods there may be a **considerable difference** between gross margin and DPP. Risky goods or bulky goods will be allocated large amounts of insurance or storage space which will **reduce their profitability**. Small goods with a long shelf life will be allocated relatively few additional costs therefore the difference between gross margin and DPP will be smaller.

One of the anomalies of DPP is that **direct product cost** contains part of the **indirect cost** that can be apportioned to the product line.

How DPP can be applied to the KL retail outlet

Based on traditional limiting factor analysis, the majority of the space would be allocated to **frozen food items**. However as noted above such items are **high-risk** and are therefore unlikely to be as profitable as gross profit margins imply. As well as significant insurance costs, the cost of the storage space required for the necessary freezers will **reduce the DPP** of this product category and therefore its attractiveness relative to other categories. However, newspapers and magazines (currently ranked number 5) take up less space and require no special storage or display facilities. As a result, this product category may deserve additional space in the outlet.

'Other products' – the localised category – would receive no space under traditional limiting factor rules, as there would be no space left once minimum and maximum space policies were satisfied. However this may have a **detrimental effect on overall profitability** of the KL retail outlet as customers who would normally pop in for such items might have purchased other goods whilst they were in the store. Depending on the nature of the goods, DPP analysis may have allocated some space to such goods.

As well as giving guidance on the amount of shelf space to be allocated to each product line, DPP can also be used to determine the **positioning of the product lines** within the outlet. Items with high DPP should be positioned near the front of the store as such goods tend to sell more quickly. Stock placed at eye level also sells more quickly therefore if there are particular brands within a category with high DPP these should be given this shelf position.

Improving the profits of the KL retail outlet by applying DPP principles

DPP offers a number of benefits that can contribute towards the improvement of KL's profits.

Detailed information is provided on the **performance** of individual product categories and individual products within each category. This allows management to assess each product's importance to overall profit performance.

DPP also allows **profitable product lines to be identified** and these can be given **more prominent shelf space**. By allocating shelf space and positioning according to DPP analysis, KL is likely to improve its profits as it is focusing customer attention on the most profitable items.

Warehouse space can be allocated to allow **maximum profit-earning potential**. Products with low turnover or low DPP relative to their size can be **downsized or discontinued** to free up more space for more profitable items.

DPP software packages can be purchased to model such variables as rate of sale and inventory holding size. Both variables are critical to the profitability of KL.

Rate of sale should be as fast as possible to minimise storage costs and to avoid loss of consumer interest.

Inventory holding size is critical as the aim is to hold as little as possible without running out of inventory.

<u>Conclusion</u>

Given the analysis above, DPP may be more appropriate for solving the space allocation problem as it could result in higher profits for KL and is particularly suited to the retail line of business.

CIMA
Paper P2 (Management)
Performance Management

Mock Exam 2

Question Paper	
Time allowed	**3 hours**
This paper is divided into two sections	
Section A	**Five compulsory questions**
Section B	**Two compulsory questions**

DO NOT OPEN THIS PAPER UNTIL YOU ARE READY TO START UNDER EXAMINATION CONDITIONS

SECTION A – 50 marks

Answer all FIVE questions

Question 1

HZ is reviewing the selling price of one of its products. The current selling price of the product is $45 per unit and annual demand is forecast to be 130,000 units at this price. Market research shows that the level of demand would be affected by any change in the selling price. Detailed analysis of this research shows that for every $1 increase in selling price, annual demand would reduce by 10,000 units and that for every $1 decrease in selling price, annual demand would increase by 10,000 units.

A forecast of the costs that would be incurred by HZ in respect of this product at differing activity levels is as follows:

Annual production and sales (units)	100,000	160,000	200,000
	$000	$000	$000
Direct materials	280	448	560
Direct labour	780	1,248	1,560
Variable overhead	815	1,304	1,630
Fixed overhead	360	360	360

The company seeks your help in determining the optimum selling price to maximise its profits.

Required

(a) Calculate the optimum forecast annual profit from the product. **(6 marks)**

(b) Explain the effect on the optimal price and quantity sold of independent changes to:

    (i)   the direct material cost per unit; **(2 marks)**

    (ii)   the annual fixed overhead cost. **(2 marks)**

Note: If Price (P) = a – bx then Marginal Revenue = a – 2bx

(Total = 10 marks)

Question 2

DTG is a management accounting consultancy that specialises in providing services to small businesses that do not have in-house expertise in management accounting techniques. Its clients vary in size and operate in many different sectors including manufacturing, retail and service industries. Although they are different, all clients require similar services most of which are provided by DTG's team of employed accountants and support staff. Occasionally DTG will engage the services of specialists on a one-off contract basis to help to solve the problem faced by a particular client.

Before accepting clients, DTG will meet with them to discuss their requirements and to agree the basis of their fees.

DTG has an ongoing relationship with many of its clients. This level of involvement within the client's business enables DTG to foresee potential problems for the client and offer further services. This works well for the clients and particularly well for DTG who gain a considerable number of new assignments in this way.

New clients tend to be initially for "one-off" assignments. Working with new clients requires time and effort to be invested to become familiar with the client's business and procedures. DTG hopes to form a relationship and attract more assignments and referrals from each client it works with.

Required

Explain how Customer Life Cycle costing could be used by DTG. **(10 marks)**

Question 3

In order to compete globally many companies have adopted Kaizen Costing. Consequently they are changing their performance measurement systems and are abandoning standard costing systems as they think traditional standard costing and variance analysis is of little use in the modern environment.

Required

Discuss why Kaizen Costing could be more useful for performance measurement than standard costing and variance analysis in such companies. **(10 marks)**

Question 4

GRV is a chemical processing company that produces sprays used by farmers to protect their crops. One of these sprays is made by mixing three chemicals. The standard material cost details for 1 litre of this spray is as follows:

	$
0.4 litres of chemical A @ $30 per litre	12.00
0.3 litres of chemical B @ $20 per litre	6.00
0.5 litres of chemical C @ $15 per litre	7.50
Standard material cost of 1 litre of spray	25.50

During August GRV produced 1,000 litres of this spray using the following chemicals:

600 litres of chemical A costing $18,000
250 litres of chemical B costing $8,000
500 litres of chemical C costing $8,500

You are the Management Accountant of GRV and the Production Manager has sent you the following e-mail:

I was advised by our purchasing department that the worldwide price of chemical B had risen by 50%. As a result, I used an increased proportion of chemical A than is prescribed in the standard mix so that our costs were less affected by this price change.

Required

(a) Calculate the following operational variances:

    (i)   direct material mix and; **(3 marks)**
    (ii)   direct material yield **(2 marks)**

(b) Discuss the decision taken by the Production Manager. **(5 marks)**

(Total = 10 marks)

Question 5

ZJET is an airline company that operates both domestically and internationally using a fleet of 20 aircraft. Passengers book flights using the internet or by telephone and pay for their flights at the time of booking using a debit or credit card.

The airline has also entered into profit sharing arrangements with hotels and local car hire companies that allow rooms and cars to be booked by the airline's passengers through the airline's web site.

ZJET currently measures its performance using financial ratios. The new Managing Director has suggested that other measures are equally important as financial measures and has suggested using the Balanced Scorecard.

Required

(a)   Discuss how the Balanced Scorecard differs from traditional financial performance measurement.

(4 marks)

(b)   Explain THREE non-financial performance measures (ONE from EACH of THREE different perspectives of the Balanced Scorecard) that ZJET could use as part of its performance measurement process.

(6 marks)

(Total = 10 marks)

(Total for Section A = 50 marks)

Section B – 50 marks

Answer BOTH questions

Question 6

WTL manufactures and sells four products: W, X, Y, and Z from a single factory. Each of the products is manufactured in batches of 100 units using a just-in-time manufacturing process and consequently there is no inventory of any product. This batch size of 100 units cannot be altered without significant cost implications. Although the products are manufactured in batches of 100 units, they are sold as single units at the market price. WTL has a significant number of competitors and is forced to accept the market price for each of its products. It is currently reviewing the profit it makes from each product, and for the business as a whole, and has produced the following statement for the latest period:

Product	W	X	Y	Z	Total
Number of:					
units sold	100,000	130,000	80,000	150,000	
Machine hours	200,000	195,000	80,000	300,000	775,000
Direct labour hours	50,000	130,000	80,000	75,000	335,000
	$	$	$	$	$
Sales	1,300,000	2,260,000	2,120,000	1,600,000	7,280,000
Direct materials	300,000	910,000	940,000	500,000	2,650,000
Direct labour	400,000	1,040,000	640,000	600,000	2,680,000
Overhead costs	400,000	390,000	160,000	600,000	1,550,000
Profit /(Loss)	200,000	(80,000)	380,000	(100,000)	400,000

WTL is concerned that two of its products are loss making and has carried out an analysis of its products and costs. This analysis shows:

1   The sales of each product are completely independent of each other.

2   The overhead costs have been absorbed into the above product costs using an absorption rate of $2 per machine hour.

3   Further analysis of the overhead cost shows that some of it is caused by the number of machine hours used, some is caused by the number of batches produced and some of the costs are product specific fixed overheads that would be avoided if the product were discontinued. Other general fixed overhead costs would be avoided only by the closure of the factory. Details of this analysis are as follows:

	$000	$000
Machine hour related		310
Batch related		230
Product specific fixed overhead:		
Product W	500	
Product X	50	
Product Y	100	
Product Z	50	700
General fixed overhead		310
		1,550

Required

(a)   Prepare a columnar statement that is more useful for decision making than the profit statement prepared by WTL. Your statement should also show the current total profit for the business.   **(8 marks)**

(b)   Prepare a report to the Board of WTL that:

   (i)   Explains why your statement is suitable for decision making;   **(4 marks)**

   (ii)   Advises WTL which, if any, of its four products should be discontinued in order to maximise its company profits.   **(4 marks)**

(c)   Calculate the break even volume (in batches) for Product W.   **(4 marks)**

(d)   Explain how WTL could use Value Analysis to improve its profits.   **(5 marks)**

(Total = 25 marks)

Question 7

TY comprises two trading divisions. Both divisions use the same accounting policies. The following statement shows the performance of each division for the year ended 31 August:

Division	T	Y
	$000	$000
Sales	3,600,000	3,840,000
Variable Cost	1,440,000	1,536,000
Contribution	2,160,000	2,304,000
Fixed Costs	1,830,000	1,950,000
Operating Profit	330,000	354,000
Capital Employed	3,167,500	5,500,000

Division Y manufactures a single component which it sells to Division T and to external customers. During the year to 31 August Division Y operated at 80% capacity and produced 200,000 components. 25% of the components were sold to Division T at a transfer price of $15,360 per component. Division T manufactures a single product. It uses one of the components that it buys from Division Y in each unit of its finished product, which it sells to an external market.

Investment by Division T

Division T is currently operating at its full capacity of 50,000 units per year and is considering investing in new equipment which would increase its present capacity by 25%. The machine has a useful life of three years. This would enable Division T to expand its business into new markets. However, to achieve this it would have to sell these additional units of its product at a discounted price of $60,000 per unit. The capital cost of the investment is $1.35bn and the equipment can be sold for $400m at the end of three years.

Division T believes that there would be no changes to its cost structure as a result of the expansion and that it would be able to sell all of the products that it could produce from the extra capacity. It is company policy of TY that all divisions use a 10% cost of capital to evaluate investments.

Required

(a)   Prepare an analysis of the sales made by Division Y for the year ended 31 August to show the contribution earned from external sales and from internal sales.   **(3 marks)**

(b)   Assuming that the current transfer pricing policy continues,

   (i)   Evaluate, using NPV, the investment in the new equipment from the perspective of Division T;   **(8 marks)**

   (ii)   Evaluate, using NPV, the investment in the new equipment from the perspective of TY.

   Ignore taxation and inflation.   **(4 marks)**

(c)   Discuss the appropriateness of the current transfer pricing policy from the perspective of EACH of the divisional managers AND the company as a whole.   **(10 marks)**

(Total = 25 marks)

(Total for Section B = 50 marks)

Answers

**DO NOT TURN THIS PAGE UNTIL YOU HAVE
COMPLETED THE MOCK EXAM**

A PLAN OF ATTACK

We're sure you don't have to be reminded yet again to **take a good look at the paper before diving in to answer questions.** You are obviously going to remember that aren't you?

Which order to do the questions?

Once you have looked through the paper in detail (you have the chance to do this in the 20 minutes' reading time) you can decide in which order you might want to tackle the questions. All the questions are compulsory and obviously have to be attempted at some point in the three hours' writing time but it will help to build your confidence if you can start with a question you feel you can answer well.

The next step

You're probably either thinking that you don't know where to begin or that you could answer the paper in two hours!

Option 1 (Oh dear)

If you're a bit **worried** about the paper, do the **questions in the order of how well you think you can answer them.**

Question 1 is about the calculation of a sales price and sales quantity that will result in maximum profit. To do this you need to establish a formula for marginal revenue and you also need to identify the marginal cost. You are then required to comment on how the profit-maximising price and sales quantity would change if there is a change in the direct material unit cost or in fixed costs. There is a lot to do for just 10 marks, so you need to know the technique well.

Question 2 is on customer life cycle costing, but it requires you to apply your knowledge of the topic to a specific consultancy company and explain how this company could make use of the technique. Applying the theory of a technique to a particular business or situation calls for some careful thinking and clear explanation.

Question 3 involves a comparison of Kaizen costing and standard costing in performance measurement. This might seem fairly straightforward as a discursive question so if you like written questions, this might be the one to start with. However, you need to remember that the question asks you to discuss these two approaches to cost management from the specific angle of performance measurement. Your answer should not simply provide a general explanation of the two approaches to costing.

Question 4 is a question on standard costing mix and yield variances, but with half the marks awarded for an analysis of the variances and the decision taken by the production manager. The variance calculations may seem fairly straightforward, but part (b) must be answered well to obtain good marks.

Question 5 tests your knowledge of the balanced scorecard for performance measurement. Like Question 2, the challenge in this question is to apply theoretical knowledge about the balanced scorecard to a particular business, which in this case is an airline company. It is only a 10-mark question, so you need to think quickly to get an answer together.

Question 6 is the first of the long questions. Most of the question is about the analysis of product profitability and the most appropriate way of presenting information for management. A large part of the question involves re-arranging the figures so that they are more useful for decision-making, but there is a tricky break-even calculation in part (c). Part (d) brings in a different topic, value analysis, which you should apply to the situation of the company in the question.

Question 7 deals with the problems of transfer pricing, and the problem that transfer pricing policy can lead to sub-optimal decision making within a divisionalised organisation. The question does this by introducing a proposed capital investment and asking for the investment to be appraised using DCF from the perspective of one of the divisions and the company as a whole. You are then required to discuss the appropriateness of the transfer pricing policy – which is quite a lot to do within the time available.

Option 2 (if you're thinking 'It's a doddle')

Are you sure it is? If you are then that's encouraging but don't forget to do brief answer plans to ensure you don't miss the point of the questions.

Make sure you present your workings to **question 1** clearly and remember to make your explanations in part (b) clear and comprehensible.

Remember to show that you know what customer life cycle costing is in your answer to **question 2**, but you must also apply your knowledge to the 'case study' in the question.

In **question 3**, demonstrate that you know how both Kaizen costing and standard costing are used for performance measurement and compare the two approaches. You are asked why Kaizen costing could be more useful than standard costing, so remember to deal with this point in your answer.

In **question 4** present your computations of mix and yield variances clearly. Note that half the marks are available for an analysis of the production manager's decision and what the variances indicate.

Question 5 asks for a brief discussion of the balanced scorecard approach, but it may be a good idea to think about suitable non-financial measures for the airline before starting to write an answer to part (b).

With **question 6** make sure that you present the figures in a useful way to assist decision-making. The question gives you a strong hint that the revised presentation should help management with decisions about discontinuing any of the four products. Don't spend too long on the breakeven calculation in part (c); it is more complex than it might first seem. In part (d) make sure that you give a clear explanation of what value analysis is, as well as applying the technique to the 'case study' in the question.

A problem with **question 7** is that you need to get each part of the question correct in order to make a good answer to the next part of the question. It is difficult to answer part b(i) well if your answer to part (a) is incorrect, and a good answer to part (b)(ii) depends on your correct approach to part (b)(i). Although part (c) is about the general problem of sub-optimal decision making in an organisation with profit centres and transfer pricing, it is difficult to answer part (c) well unless your answer to part (b) is reasonably accurate.

And just one more thing...

You must **allocate your time** according to the marks available for the question in total, and for the individual parts of the questions (where applicable). It is essential that you **follow the requirements exactly** – it will be very obvious to the marker if you haven't!

Finished with 15 minutes to spare?

Looks like your time allocation went slightly awry. However if you have finished, **don't waste** the last few minutes – go back to **any parts of the questions that you didn't finish** because you ran out of time.

Forget about it!

Forget about what? Excellent, you already have!

SECTION A

Question 1

Text references. The MR = MC approach to calculating profit-maximising sales price and quantity is covered in Chapter 6.

Top tips. Ensure that you clearly show all workings to part (a) to maximise your mark and remember to calculate the profit, not just the sales price and sales quantity.

Easy marks. The question is straightforward only if you can work out the formula for the demand 'curve' but at least the marginal cost per unit should not be a problem.

Examiner's comments. Many candidates were clearly aware of the formula for establishing the selling price that would maximise the profit of the company, but made basic mathematical errors when applying it. A number of answers to part (b) were general in nature and did not specifically relate to the question.

Marking scheme

			Marks
(a)	Variable cost per unit		1
	Price at which demand is zero		1
	Elasticity of demand		1
	Optimum quantity and selling price		2
	Profit		<u>1</u>
			<u>6</u>
(b)(i)	1 mark per valid point	Max	2
(ii)	1 mark per valid point	Max	2

(a) <u>Optimum forecast annual profit</u>

Profit is maximised where MR = MC.

Production / sales ('000s)	Total variable cost ($'000)	Variable cost per unit ($)
100	1,875	18.75
160	3,000	18.75
200	3,750	18.75

Marginal cost (MC) is assumed to be the variable cost per unit = $18.75 at all volumes of output and sales.

P = a – bx   where

P = the selling price

x = the quantity demanded at that price

a = the price at which demand will be zero

b = the change in price required to change demand by one unit (change in price / change in quantity)

<u>Find 'b'</u>

b = 1 / 10,000 = 0.0001

Find 'a'

The price at which demand will be zero is calculated as follows.

$$a = \$ \text{ (current price)} + \left(\frac{\text{Current quantity at current price}}{\text{Change in quantity when price changed by } \$b} \times \$b \right)$$

$45 + ([130,000/10,000] \times \$1) = \$58

The demand curve is therefore $P = 58 - 0.0001x$

Marginal revenue (MR)

$MR = a - 2bx$

$MR = 58 - 2(0.0001)x$

$MR = 58 - 0.0002x$

MR = MC

Profit is maximised when $58 - 0.0002x = 18.75$

Therefore $0.0002x = 39.25$

$x = 196,250$

$P = 58 - (0.0001 \times 196,250) = \$38.375$

At a price of $38.375, the unit contribution is $(38.375 - 18.75) = $19.625.

Annual profit

	$
Total contribution (196,250 × 19.625)	3,851,406.25
Fixed costs	360,000.00
Annual profit	3,491,406.25

(b) (i) Changes to the direct material cost per unit

A change in the material cost per unit will change the marginal cost (MC) per unit. Profit is maximised where MR = MC. In this case, $58 - 0.0002x$ = MC. If MC rises, the profit-maximising quantity 'x' will be lower.

The sales price is $58 - 0.0001x$, so if 'x' is lower, the sales price P at the profit-maximising output will be higher.

The opposite will happen if MC falls. The profit-maximising output will be higher, and the sales price P lower.

(ii) Changes to the annual fixed overhead cost

A change in the annual fixed overhead cost will not affect the marginal cost per unit, therefore the optimal price and sales quantity will not be affected.

Question 2

Text references. Customer life cycle costing is covered in Chapter 7.

Top tips. Remember to relate your answer to the scenario.

Easy marks. Explaining what customer life cycle costing is will score you quick and easy marks.

Examiner's comments. The majority of answers were extremely poor. Many candidates simply wrote all they knew about product life cycle costing. Customer life cycle costing has a number of unique characteristics.

Marking scheme

		Marks
Up to 2 marks per well explained point	Max	10

Life cycle costing

Life cycle costing involves planning and recording the costs of an item over their **entire life cycle**. This approach to costing can be used for products, but also for **customers**. The purpose of this costing method is to try to ensure that the product or customer provides a profit for the organisation over its full life cycle. In the case of a product, the life cycle begins with product development and introduction and ends with the withdrawal of the product from the market. With customers, the **life cycle begins with the first meeting** with the customer and the cost of efforts to **win the customer's business**, and it ends when the relationship with the customer finally comes to an end.

Life cycle costing system

To establish a **customer life cycle costing system**, DTG will need to have an accounting system in which all costs that are incurred in relation to individual clients are recorded as a **cost of that client**. This will include costs incurred on activities that do not earn fees, such as the cost of initial meetings with a client. For established clients there will be further administrative costs (and time) for which fees are not charged, such as costs of sending out invoices and chasing the client for payment. These should be recorded, as well as costs incurred in fee-earning activities, so that the **full costs incurred** on the client are recorded.

New clients

Although DTG's **new clients** tend to be for 'one-off' assignments, costs incurred on these clients should be identified and recorded as a client cost.

If a new client asks for a one-off assignment, the fee that is negotiated for the work should be **sufficient to cover all expected costs to be incurred**, including the costs of **non-chargeable** time. This means that the charging rate per hour should be sufficient to cover these costs (and an appropriate amount for overheads), as well as the expected costs of any external specialists who may be used and the costs of carrying out the assignment.

Established clients

For established clients, the fee rate that is agreed should also be sufficient to cover expected costs of non-chargeable time plus overheads. A **lower rate per hour** may be possible, because the cost of preparing for a new job for an existing client should be **less than the costs of negotiating with a new client**, whose business will not yet be familiar to DTG.

By establishing a customer life cycle costing system, DTG will be able to monitor the **profitability of each client**, and the information should also help with identifying **which types of client are more profitable than others**.

Question 3

Marking scheme

		Marks
Up to 1 mark per valid point	Max	10

Kaizen costing

Kaizen costing is a costing system based on the principle of **continuous improvement**. There should be continual small improvements in operations, with the aim of **reducing costs (or improving quality)**. The approach to identifying small improvements involves the **participation of all workers**. Many of the ideas for improvement come from the workers, and they are not imposed from above by management.

Kaizen costing and performance measurement

Kaizen costing can be used for performance measurement. A target for improvement (reduction in cost) can be set for the year, and workers should be **encouraged to find improvements** through the course of the year that will result in the **target cost** being achieved. Performance throughout the year is monitored by comparing the current cost with the target. If continuous improvement is achieved, the **gap between actual and target will be reduced** over the course of the year. Even if the target is achieved before the end of the year, further improvements should be looked for.

Standard costing and performance measurement

Traditional standard costing takes a different approach to performance measurement. A **standard cost is established**, typically once a year, and the costs may be calculated on the basis of **current operating methods and current costs**. An element of improvement may be included in the standard, but the standard is constructed on the basis of existing methods and procedures of operating. Differences between actual and standard are **reported each month as variances**, which may be **favourable** or **adverse**.

Kaizen costing v standard costing

Kaizen costing may be more useful for performance measurement than traditional standard costing in a company that has to **compete globally**. This is because when competition is fierce, **companies need to innovate** and improve all the time to succeed and **remain competitive**. Small improvements may involve changes in ways of operating, so that 'standard' procedures have to be altered. Whereas standard costing **focuses on existing procedures**, Kaizen costing recognises that **improvements may require changes in procedures**, and that methods of operating should **not become fixed**. In summary, Kaizen costing is more compatible with operating in a competitive market than traditional standard costing.

Question 4

Text references. Mix and yield variances are covered in the Introduction chapter.

Top tips. Remember to analyse the decision of the Production Manager by interpreting the mix and yield variances that you have calculated. The question refers to mix and yield **operational** variances, so you also need to recognise that the variances should be calculated using an ex-post (revised) standard cost based on the new higher price of chemical B.

Easy marks. There are easy marks for calculating mix and yield variances, although for full marks you need to use the new higher price for chemical B.

Examiner's comments. Attempts at this question were extremely poor. Students often struggle with variance questions despite it being one of the main items within the Management Accounting pillar.

Marking scheme

			Marks
(a)(i)	Mix variance		3
(ii)	Output shortfall & valuation		2
(b)	Up to 2 marks per well developed point	Max	5

(a) The mix and yield variances will be calculated using the revised standard price of $20 × 150% = $30 per litre for chemical B.

Standard mix of actual output

Chemical A	0.4/1.2	×	1,350 litres	=	450	litres
Chemical B	0.3/1.2	×	1,350 litres	=	337.5	litres
Chemical C	0.5/1.2	×	1,350 litres	=	562.5	litres
					1,350	litres

Direct material mix variance

Chemical	Should mix Actual qty Std mix	Did mix Actual qty Actual mix	Difference		Standard price per litre	Mix variance	
	litres	litres	litres		$	$	
A	450.0	600	150.0	(A)	30	4,500.0	(A)
B	337.5	250	87.5	(F)	30	2,625.0	(F)
C	562.5	500	62.5	(F)	15	937.5	(F)
	1,350.0	1,350				937.5	(A)

Direct material yield variance

Operational standard cost per litre of output = (0.4 × $30) + (0.3 × $30) + (0.5 × $15) = $28.50

Therefore, each 1.2 litres of input should produce 1 litre of output.

	Output litres	
1,350 litres of input should produce (/1.2)	1,125	
1,350 litres did produce	1,000	
Yield variance	125	(A)
× standard cost per litre	$28.50	
	$3,562.50	(A)

(b)   The Production Manager responded to the higher cost of chemical B by **increasing the proportion of chemical A** in the product mix, but chemical A has the **same standard price** as the revised standard price for chemical B. This change did nothing to make the materials mix cheaper. On the contrary, by increasing the proportion of chemical A and reducing the proportion of the cheapest chemical, chemical C, the production manager **made the mix more expensive**.

The change in the materials mix may also have had an adverse effect on the yield from the process. Instead of requiring 1,200 litres of input to make 1,000 litres of spray, the process used 1,350 litres of input.

The production manager has therefore made a decision that resulted in an **adverse mix** and an **adverse yield variance**, with a total adverse variance of **$4,500**. This decision seems to have been a bad one, taken without consulting anyone else. The effect of changing the materials mix may well have **altered the quality of the end product**, the chemical spray, and the changes should not have been made without consulting GRV's **product designers**.

If the production manager had consulted the purchasing department, the mistake of increasing the proportion of chemical A in the mix would probably have been **recognised and avoided**.

Question 5

Text references. The balanced scorecard is covered in Chapter 11.

Top tips. In part (b) explain the purpose and value of the non-financial performance indicators you have chosen. The suggested solution below suggests just one for each non-financial perspective of performance. Other performance indicators could be used instead, but your answer must indicate <u>why</u> you have selected them.

Easy marks. Part (a) asks for an explanation of the main features of the balanced scorecard approach, and a simple explanation should earn useful marks.

Examiner's comments. Part (a) was poorly answered. Candidates were required to 'discuss'. Simply describing the four perspectives or drawing up a table did not meet the question requirements. Part (b) was generally well answered.

Marking scheme

		Marks
(a)	Four perspectives of the balanced scorecard	1
	FPIs do not identify causes of performance	1
	Non-financial success can lead to financial success	2
		4
(b)	Measures relevant to the airline company (1 mark per measure)	3
	Explanation of each measure (1 mark per measure)	3
		6

(a)   The balance scorecard approach

Traditional financial performance measurement measures performance in **financial terms only**.

A **balanced scorecard** sets objectives and measures performance from **four perspectives**, a **financial** perspective, a **customer** perspective, an **internal business** perspective and an **innovation and learning** perspective. It is recognised that in a commercial business, the main objective is a financial one, but in order to achieve financial objectives over the long term, **non-financial aspects of performance must not be ignored**. Unless non-financial standards of performance are achieved, financial objectives will not be met.

For example, a successful business must recognise the importance of satisfying the customer. To **maintain competitiveness** it will be important to achieve **operational standards**, to be **innovative** and to improve the **skills** and **knowledge** of the work force.

Using financial performance indicators alone, **management will not give sufficient attention to all these factors** on which financial performance depends, particularly over the longer term.

(b)   Customer perspective

An important aspect of customer service seems to be an efficient **online and telephone booking system**. Success in selling tickets depends on providing an efficient and effective service. For telephone bookings, an important non-financial performance indicator may be the **proportion of customer calls that result in a successful sale** (as compared with the proportion of unsuccessful calls, for example where the customer terminates the call because waiting time has been too long). A similar performance measure could be applied to online bookings – the **proportion of bookings initiated** by customers online that **result in a successful completion of a ticket sale**.

Internal business perspective

The airline needs to provide an efficient service to customers. An important aspect of **operational efficiency** may be the success of the telephone sales service and on-line booking system in persuading customers to buy hotel accommodation and car hire as well as airline tickets. A suitable measure of performance may be the **proportion of airline bookings that also have an additional hotel or car hire booking**.

Innovation and learning perspective

ZJET has had some success in arranging for hotels and car hire firms to sell their services through the airline. There may be considerable scope for increasing the number of hotels and car hire firms in different parts of the world that have an association with ZJET. There may also be **opportunities for selling other add-ons**, such as tickets to tourist sites, taxis, or tickets to theatres or sporting events. A measure of performance may therefore be the **number of new arrangements** with other organisations for selling their services through the ZJET booking system.

SECTION B

Question 6

Text references. Decisions on discontinuing an operation are covered in Chapter 1B. Breakeven analysis is covered in Chapter 5, and value analysis in chapter 7.

Top tips. Set out your statement in part (a) clearly. This should make a clear distinction between variable costs, directly attributable fixed costs and general overhead costs. Your statement should therefore identify the contribution from each product, and the net profit or loss after deducting directly attributable fixed costs from contribution. Part (b) asks you to prepare a report so remember to present your answer in a report format.

Examiner's comments. Though most candidates obtained a pass for this question, many marks could not be awarded in part (a) due to poorly presented statements. Part (b) was generally well answered.

Answers to part (c) were extremely poor, indicating that many candidates had not studied or revised breakeven analysis. Part (d) was also poorly answered with a number of candidates believing that value analysis was simply another name for the value chain.

Marking scheme

			Marks
(a)	Machine hour related overhead per product		2
	Batch-related overhead per product		2
	Directly attributable fixed costs		1
	Contribution per product		1
	General fixed costs		1
	Overall profit		$\underline{1}$
			$\underline{8}$
(b)(i)	The causes of overhead costs can be identified		2
	Statement shows the costs that can be avoided in different scenarios		2
(ii)	Advise product(s) to be discontinued		2
	Reasons for the above		$\underline{2}$
			$\underline{8}$
(c)	Directly attributable fixed cost		1
	Contribution per unit		1
	Breakeven level (units)		1
	Breakeven level (batches)		$\underline{1}$
			$\underline{4}$
(d)	Up to 2 marks per well explained point	Max	5

(a)   <u>Columnar statement for WTL</u>

	W	X	Y	Z	Total
	$'000	$'000	$'000	$'000	$'000
Sales	1,300	2,260	2,120	1,600	7,280
Variable costs:					
Direct materials	(300)	(910)	(940)	(500)	(2,650)
Direct labour	(400)	(1,040)	(640)	(600)	(2,680)
Overheads:					
Machine-hour-related overhead (W1)	(80)	(78)	(32)	(120)	(310)
Batch-related overhead (W2)	(50)	(65)	(40)	(75)	(230)
Gross contribution	470	167	468	305	1,410
Directly attributable fixed costs	(500)	(50)	(100)	(50)	(700)
Net contribution	(30)	117	368	255	710
General fixed costs					(310)
Overall profit					400

Workings

(1)   <u>Machine-hour-related overhead</u>
The variable cost of overheads per machine hour is $310,000 / 775,000 machine hours = $0.40 per machine hour.

	W	X	Y	Z
Total machine hours	200,000	195,000	80,000	300,000
× $0.40 per machine hour	$80,000	$78,000	$32,000	$120,000

(2)   <u>Batch-related overhead</u>
Total production was 460,000 units, so the cost per batch is $230,000 / 4,600 batches = $50 per batch.

	W	X	Y	Z
Sales (units)	100,000	130,000	80,000	150,000
Number of batches (100 units per batch)	1,000	1,300	800	1,500
× $50 per batch	$50,000	$65,000	$40,000	$75,000

(b)   To: Board of WTL

From: Management accountant

Date: XX/XX/XX

Subject: Profitability statement

Please find enclosed the results for the latest financial period, presented in a way that will be more useful for decision-making by the board.

(i) <u>Why the statement is suitable for decision making</u>

When considering the financial implications of any decision, it is important to recognise the **relevant costs** that would be affected by a decision. Relevant costs are costs that will be incurred or saved as a direct result of the decision under consideration.

Whilst showing costs and revenues for each product, the profit statement produced by WTL prior to this report makes and uses **assumptions to attribute overheads to each product**. There is no distinction between **general overhead costs** and **product-specific overhead costs** that would be avoided if the product were to be discontinued.

The profit in the statement attached to this report identifies the sales revenue, variable costs, contribution and directly attributable fixed costs **for each product**. This provides information that can **assist with decision-making**, both for normal **operational purposes** and also to assist with decisions about the **continuation or discontinuation of individual products**.

(ii) <u>Recommendation about discontinuation of products</u>

The statement shows that **all four products make a positive contribution** towards fixed overhead costs and profit. It also shows the financial effect that discontinuing each of the products would have on profit. This is shown by the total contribution earned by each products minus the fixed overhead costs that are **directly attributable to the product**.

The profits of WTL would fall if any of products X, Y or Z were discontinued, but profits would have been **higher by $30,000** in the period if **product W** had not been made and sold.

By **discontinuing production of product W**, WTL may therefore be able to **increase profits** in future periods. Ending production of product W would mean that there will be **spare machine hour capacity** and it may be possible to increase profits further by using this capacity to **increase output of the other products**.

(c)   Directly attributable **fixed costs** of Product W are $500,000.

The **variable cost per unit** of W is $830,000/100,000 units = $8.30.

The **contribution per unit** is $13 – $8.30 = $4.70.

This suggests that the breakeven **level of production and sales** is $500,000/$4.70 = 106,383 units.

Production is in batches of 100 units, indicating that 106,400 units would have to be produced in order to sell 106,383 units.

This means that the breakeven point is not 106,383 units, because the **additional variable cost** of making 106,400 units would be (106,400 – 106,383) × $8.30 = $141.10.

To break even, more than 106,383 units must be sold. For each additional unit above 106,383 that is sold, additional contribution will be the sales revenue, $13 per unit. To break even we therefore need to sell an additional $141.10/$13 = 10.85 = 11 units.

Breakeven sales volume = 106,383 + 11 = 106,394 units (1,064 batches).

(d)   Value analysis is an approach to cost management where the aim is to identify ways of **reducing costs without reducing value to the customer**. Value to the customer is represented by the **quality** and **reliability** of the product that the customer buys. Therefore value analysis seeks to reduce costs without reducing product quality or reliability.

Alternatively, value analysis can be used as a way of trying to improve the value to the customer without increasing costs. Value would be improved by better quality or reliability.

WTL could use value analysis to improve its profits by **investigating the value** that is given to customers by the various aspects and features of the products that it sells, and the **processes** that are used in their manufacture. Features or **processes that do not add value can be deleted**, and cheaper ways of achieving the same end result should also be considered.

For WTL, it may be possible to find **ways of making the product more efficiently**, so that the total contribution is higher than the directly attributable fixed costs. **Simplification of production procedures**, for example, may provide **savings in labour time and costs**, and also some savings in directly attributable fixed costs, without any loss in value to the customer.

Question 7

Text references. Transfer pricing is covered in Chapter 13.

Top tips. Show your workings to parts (a) and (b) to maximise your score. Remember to discuss the transfer pricing policy from the perspective of both divisions and the company as a whole in part (c).

Examiner's comments. Part (a) was well answered. Attempts at part (b) were extremely poor and demonstrated that many candidates do not understand investment appraisal.

Many answers to part (c) did not relate to the scenario in the question. The figures in part (a) allowed candidates to easily calculate the transfer price, the external market price and the variable cost of production for Division Y. Most of the answers were general in nature and only gained a few marks.

Marking scheme

		Marks
(a)	Units	1
	Sales value	1
	Variable cost	_1_
		_3_
(b)(i)	No capacity constraints in Division Y	2
	Contribution from sales with new equipment	1
	Present value of contribution	2
	Present value of resale value	1
	Initial investment	1
	Negative NPV so manager of Division T will reject	1
(ii)	Additional contribution	2
	Present value of additional contribution	1
	Overall company NPV	_1_
		_12_
(c)	Current transfer price	1
	Transfer price v total cost v market price	2
	Division T & Division Y perspective	4
	Company perspective	_3_
		_10_

(a) Analysis of Division Y sales

	Internal sales (25%)	External sales	Total
Units	50,000	150,000	200,000
	$'000	$'000	$'000
Revenue	768,000	3,072,000	3,840,000
Variable costs	384,000	1,152,000	1,536,000
Contribution	384,000	1,920,000	2,034,000

Note: The figures for external sales are calculated as the difference between the total for Division Y and the internal transfers to Division T.

The variable cost per unit in Division Y is $7,680 ($1,536 million / 200,000 units).

(b) (i) Division T

Division T is paying $15,360 per unit for transfers from Division Y, and the **total variable cost per unit** is $1,440,000,000/50,000 = $28,800, including the **transfer cost**. The additional variable cost per unit incurred in Division T is therefore $(28,800 – 15,360) = $13,440.

The new machine would **increase the capacity** of Division T by 12,500 units per year. Since Division Y has spare capacity of 50,000 units, there would be **no capacity constraints** in Division Y.

The selling price for the additional 12,500 units would be $60,000, giving a unit contribution for Division T of $60,000 – $28,800 = $31,200. Total contribution from sales with the new equipment each year would be 12,500 × $31,200 = $390,000,000.

Year		Cash flow	Discount factor at 10%	Present value
		$'000		$'000
0	Equipment	(1,350,000)	1.000	(1,350,000)
1 - 3	Annual contribution	390,000	2.487	969,930
3	Resale value	400,000	0.751	300,400
	Net present value			(79,670)

From the **perspective of Division T**, the investment would have a **negative net present value** and the divisional manager **would not want to invest in the equipment**.

(ii) The company (TY)

From the perspective of the company as a whole, the variable cost of making and selling each unit would be the variable cost in Division Y plus the variable cost in Division T (excluding the transfer price). This is $13,440 + $7,680 (part (a)) = $21,120.

From the company perspective, the additional contribution per unit from the new equipment would be $(60,000 – 21,120) = $38,880. Total annual contribution from selling 12,500 units would be 12,500 × $38,880 = $486,000,000.

Year		Cash flow	Discount factor at 10%	Present value
		$'000		$'000
0	Equipment	(1,350,000)	1.000	(1,350,000)
1 - 3	Annual contribution	486,000	2.487	1,208,682
3	Resale value	400,000	0.751	300,400
	Net present value			159,082

From the **company perspective**, the investment would have a **positive net present value** of over $159 million, and the company management **would want Division T to make the investment**.

(c) Division Y

Division Y is operating below 100% capacity, which indicates that it cannot sell more units in the **external market**, and Division T (without the new equipment) is operating at **full capacity**. The variable cost per unit produced in Division Y is $7,680 ($1,536,000/200,000 units).

The **transfer price** of $15,360 per unit is giving Division Y a contribution of $7,680 per unit, indicating that the transfer price has been set at **variable cost plus 100%**.

The manager of Division Y might argue that the **transfer price is too low**, because the **external sales price** is $20,480 ($3,072,000,000/150,000). However, since Division Y cannot sell any more units at this price, the external market price is **not a reasonable basis for setting the transfer price**.

Any transfer price in excess of $7,680 per unit would provide Division Y with positive contribution.

If the new equipment were purchased by Division T, a transfer price for the additional 12,500 units in excess of $7,680 per unit (creating a two-tier transfer pricing arrangement) would add to the contribution of Division Y.

Division T

Division T is currently paying a **transfer price** for units from Division Y that is **above variable cost** but **below the external market price**. Before taking into consideration the opportunity to buy the new equipment, this arrangement seems reasonable.

However Division T will not purchase the new equipment because of the size of the transfer price from Y. The manager of division T could argue, correctly, that any transfer price for the additional 12,500 units **in excess of the opportunity cost** would increase profits in Division Y and so would not be fair. As indicated above, this is a valid argument. The opportunity cost of transferring additional units for Division Y is $7,680, the **variable cost per unit**.

Company perspective

From the company perspective, an arrangement is required that would **motivate the manager of Division T** to **invest in the equipment** and the **manager of Division Y** to **provide the 12,500 additional units**. A **two-tier transfer pricing structure** might be agreed. The transfer price for the additional 12,500 units should be a price that would provide a DCF return for Division T in excess of 10%, but be higher than the variable cost of $7,680.

The management at head office should encourage the managers of the two divisions to **enter into negotiations** over this issue, with the objective of **negotiating a transfer price** that would benefit both of them.

CIMA
Paper P2 (Management)
Performance Management

Mock Exam 3

Question Paper	
Time allowed	**3 hours**
This paper is divided into two sections	
Section A	**Five compulsory questions**
Section B	**Two compulsory questions**

DO NOT OPEN THIS PAPER UNTIL YOU ARE READY TO START UNDER EXAMINATION CONDITIONS

SECTION A – 50 MARKS

[You are advised to spend no longer than 18 minutes on each question in this section.]

ANSWER *ALL* FIVE QUESTIONS IN THIS SECTION. EACH QUESTION IS WORTH 10 MARKS. YOU SHOULD SHOW YOUR WORKINGS AS MARKS ARE AVAILABLE FOR THE METHOD YOU USE.

Question One

A company has developed a new product. Details are as follows:

Selling price and product life cycle
The product will have a life cycle of 10,000 units. It is estimated that the first 9,000 units will be sold for $124 each and then the product will enter the "decline" stage of its life cycle. It is difficult to forecast the selling price for the 1,000 units that will be sold during this stage.

Costs
Labour will be paid at $12 per hour. Other variable costs will be $38 per unit. Fixed costs will total $80,000 over the life cycle of the product. The labour rate and both of these costs will not change throughout the product's life cycle.

Learning curve
The first batch of 100 units will take 1,500 labour hours to produce. There will be an 85% learning curve that will continue until 6,400 units have been produced. Batches after this level will each take the same amount of time as the 64th batch. The batch size will always be 100 units.

> *Required:*
>
> **Calculate**
>
> *(a)* the cumulative average time per batch for the first 64 batches
>
> *(2 marks)*
>
> *(b)* the time taken for the 64th batch
>
> *(3 marks)*
>
> *(c)* the average selling price of the final 1,000 units that will allow the company to earn a total profit of $100,000 from the product
>
> *(5 marks)*
>
> *(Total for Question One = 10 marks)*
>
> Note: The learning index for an 85% learning curve is -0.2345
>
> Ignore the time value of money.

Question Two

SF manufactures and sells a limited range of flat pack furniture. Due to the standardisation of its products, SF uses a standard costing system to monitor its performance. At the start of each financial year the company directors agree a set of standard costs for each of the company's products. Monthly variance reports are discussed at each monthly board meeting.

A few months ago the Production Director attended a conference on World Class Manufacturing and was very interested in a presentation on Kaizen Costing. The presenter illustrated how the use of Kaizen Costing had enabled her company to reduce its unit manufacturing costs by 20%.

Required:

(a) **Explain** the principles of Kaizen Costing.

(4 marks)

(b) **Discuss** how Kaizen Costing conflicts with SF's current performance reporting procedures.

(6 marks)

(Total for Question Two = 10 marks)

Question Three

LCG was established in 1998 and manufactures a range of garden tables and chairs which it makes from timber purchased from a number of suppliers.

The recently appointed Managing Director has expressed increasing concern about the trends in falling sales volumes, rising costs and hence declining profits over the last two years. There is general agreement amongst the managers of LCG that these trends are the result of the increased intense competition that has emerged over the last two years. LCG continues to have a reputation for high quality but this quality is now being matched by the competition.

The competitors are taking LCG's share of the market by selling equivalent products at lower prices. It is thought that in order to offer such low prices the production costs of the competitors must be lower than LCG's.

Required:

Discuss how LCG could improve its sales volumes, costs and profits by using (i) value analysis and (ii) functional cost analysis.

(Total for Question Three = 10 marks)

Question Four

WX, a consultancy company, is preparing its budgets for the year to 31 December 2012. The directors of the company have stated that they would like to reduce the company's overdraft to zero by 30 June 2012 and to have a positive cash balance of $145,000 by the end of the year. In addition, the directors would like to achieve a 20% growth in sales revenue compared to 2011 and a pre-tax profit of $180,000 for the year.

Required:

Illustrate the differences between feedforward control and feedback control using the above information about WX's cash budget.

(Total for Question Four = 10 marks)

Question Five

An airline company has operated short haul passenger and cargo flights to various destinations from a busy airport for several years. Its competitive advantage has been the fact that it offers low ticket prices to passengers. It now faces increased competition on a number of its routes.

The company currently monitors its performance using financial measures. These financial measures have served it well in the past, but a new director has suggested that non-financial measures may also be used to provide a better indication of overall performance. She has suggested that the company should consider using the Balanced Scorecard.

Required:

(a)   **Explain** the concepts of the Balanced Scorecard and how it could be used by the airline company.

(6 marks)

(b)   **Explain** TWO non-financial measures that the airline company could use to monitor its performance.

(4 marks)

(Total for Question Five = 10 marks)

(Total for Section A = 50 marks)

SECTION B – 50 MARKS

[You are advised to spend no longer than 45 minutes on each question in this section.]

ANSWER *BOTH* QUESTIONS IN THIS SECTION. EACH QUESTION IS WORTH 25 MARKS.   YOU SHOULD SHOW YOUR WORKINGS AS MARKS ARE AVAILABLE FOR THE METHOD YOU USE.

Question Six

RFT, an engineering company, has been asked to provide a quotation for a contract to build a new engine. The potential customer is not a current customer of RFT, but the directors of RFT are keen to try and win the contract as they believe that this may lead to more contracts in the future. As a result they intend pricing the contract using relevant costs.

The following information has been obtained from a two-hour meeting that the Production Director of RFT had with the potential customer. The Production Director is paid an annual salary equivalent to $1,200 per 8-hour day.

110 square metres of material A will be required. This is a material that is regularly used by RFT and there are 200 square metres currently in inventory. These were bought at a cost of $12 per square metre. They have a resale value of $10.50 per square metre and their current replacement cost is $12.50 per square metre.

30 litres of material B will be required. This material will have to be purchased for the contract because it is not otherwise used by RFT. The minimum order quantity from the supplier is 40 litres at a cost of $9 per litre. RFT does not expect to have any use for any of this material that remains after this contract is completed.

60 components will be required. These will be purchased from HY. The purchase price is $50 per component.

A total of 235 direct labour hours will be required. The current wage rate for the appropriate grade of direct labour is $11 per hour. Currently RFT has 75 direct labour hours of spare capacity at this grade that is being paid under a guaranteed wage agreement. The additional hours would need to be obtained by either (i) overtime at a total cost of $14 per hour; or (ii) recruiting temporary staff at a cost of $12 per hour. However, if temporary staff are used they will not be as experienced as RFT's existing workers and will require 10 hours supervision by an existing supervisor who would be paid overtime at a cost of $18 per hour for this work.

25 machine hours will be required. The machine to be used is already leased for a weekly leasing cost of $600. It has a capacity of 40 hours per week. The machine has sufficient available capacity for the contract to be completed. The variable running cost of the machine is $7 per hour.

The company absorbs its fixed overhead costs using an absorption rate of $20 per direct labour hour.

Required:

(a) **Calculate** the relevant cost of building the new engine.

You should present your answer in a schedule that clearly shows the relevant cost value for each of the items identified above. You should also explain each relevant cost value you have included in your schedule and why the values you have excluded are not relevant.

(13 marks)

(b) HY, the company that is to supply RFT with the components that are required for this contract, is another company in the same group as RFT. Each component is being transferred to RFT taking account of HY's opportunity cost of the component. The variable cost that will be incurred by HY is $28 per component.

Discuss the factors that would be considered by HY to determine the opportunity cost of the component.

(5 marks)

(c) When there is no external market for the item being supplied between divisions of a company the transfer price is often based on the supplying division's cost.

(i) **Illustrate**, using a numerical example, the performance measurement problem that can arise when using a transfer price based on actual cost.

(3 marks)

(ii) **Explain** how using standard costs rather than actual costs as the basis of the transfer price would solve the problem identified in (i) above.

(4 marks)

(Total for Question Six = 25 marks)

Question Seven

SHG manufactures and installs heating systems for commercial customers. SHG commenced trading in 1990. At first, all operations were confined to the northern region but since 2006 SHG has expanded its operations into the southern region. In May 2009 the directors of SHG decided to adopt a divisionalised structure in order to facilitate better management control of SHG's operations. SHG created two divisions, the Northern division and the Southern division.

The following information is available:

1. Net assets of SHG as at 31 May were as follows:

Division	2011 Northern $m	2011 Southern $m	2010 Northern $m	2010 Southern $m	2009 Northern $m	2009 Southern $m
Non-current assets (net book value)	78.75	146.25	72.45	134.55	70.00	130.00
Net current assets	47.25	87.75	46.55	86.45	42.00	78.00
Net assets	126.00	234.00	119.00	221.00	112.00	208.00
Non-current assets acquired in year	15.05	27.95	10.50	19.50		

Notes:

There were no disposals of non-current assets during the above periods.

Depreciation is charged at 10% per annum on a reducing balance basis in respect of all non-current assets held at the end of the year.

2. For the years ended 31 May 2010 and 2011, turnover and operating cashflows were as follows:

Division	2011 $m	2010 $m
Turnover:		
Northern	168	148
Southern	240	220
Operating cash flows:		
Northern	42	37
Southern	60	55

3. Each division has a target return on capital employed (ROCE) of 20% on average capital employed throughout each year. The managers of both divisions are entitled to receive an annual bonus under a management incentive scheme if the target rate of ROCE is achieved for their division.

NOTE: Ignore Taxation and Inflation

Required:

(a)

(i)   **Calculate** the Return on Capital Employed (ROCE) (using average capital employed) achieved by each division during the years ended 31 May 2010 and 31 May 2011.

(7 marks)

(ii)   **Calculate** (1) the asset turnover and (2) the profit/sales % achieved by each division during the years ended 31 May 2010 and 31 May 2011.

(4 marks)

(iii)   **Discuss** the relative performances of the two divisions.

(4 marks)

(b)   SHG realises that its present performance reporting system does not highlight quality costs. The reports contain the information below, but the directors require this to be reported in an appropriate format.

The following information is available in respect of the year ended 31 May 2011:

1. Production data:

Units requiring rework	1,500
Units requiring warranty repair service	1,800
Design engineering hours	66,000
Inspection hours (manufacturing)	216,000

2. Cost data:

	$
Design engineering cost per hour	75
Inspection cost per hour (manufacturing)	40
Rework cost per heating system unit reworked (manufacturing)	3,000
Customer support cost per repaired unit (marketing)	200
Transportation costs per repaired unit (distribution)	240
Warranty repair costs per repaired unit	3,200

3. Staff training costs amounted to $150,000 and additional product testing costs were $49,000.

4. The marketing director has estimated that sales of 1,400 units were lost as a result of bad publicity in trade journals. The average contribution per heating system unit is estimated at $6,000.

Required:

Prepare a cost of quality report for SHG that shows its costs of quality (using appropriate headings) for the year ended 31 May 2011.

(10 marks)
(Total for Question Seven = 25 marks)

(Total for Section B = 50 marks)

Answers

**DO NOT TURN THIS PAGE UNTIL YOU HAVE
COMPLETED THE MOCK EXAM**

A PLAN OF ATTACK

We're sure you don't have to be reminded yet again to **take a good look at the paper before diving in to answer questions.** You are obviously going to remember that aren't you?

Which order to do the questions?

Once you have looked through the paper in detail (you have the chance to do this in the 20 minutes' reading time) you can decide in which order you might want to tackle the questions. All the questions are compulsory and obviously have to be attempted at some point in the three hours' writing time but it will help to build your confidence if you can start with a question you feel you can answer well.

The next step

You're probably either thinking that you don't know where to begin or that you could answer the paper in two hours!

Option 1 (Oh dear)

If you're a bit **worried** about the paper, do the **questions in the order of how well you think you can answer them.** Only question 1 of the first five questions is computational in nature; the other four are discursive 'written' questions.

Question 1 covers the learning curve and then asks for a selling price to achieve a target profit. This final part of the question combines the learning curve with marginal costing/cost-volume-profit analysis.

Question 2 is about Kaizen Costing and how it differs from traditional standard costing.

Question 3 is about the use of value analysis and functional cost analysis to improve sales volumes, costs and profits.

Question 4 is about the differences between feedback and feedforward control, with particular reference to a cash budget.

Question 5 tests your knowledge of the Balanced Scorecard, and asks for two non-financial measures that an airline company could use to monitor performance.

Question 6 is the first of the long questions. The first two parts of the question are about relevant costs, including opportunity costs, and the final part of the question is about transfer pricing at cost.

Question 7 is in two parts. The first part is a mainly computational question to calculate the ROCE, asset turnover and profit/sales ratio for two divisions (investment centres), together with a discussion of the performance of the two divisions. The second part of the question asks for the presentation of a quality cost report from numerical data provided.

Option 2 (if you're thinking 'It's a doddle')

Are you sure it is? If you are then that's encouraging but don't forget to do brief answer plans to ensure you don't miss the point of the questions.

Make sure you present your workings to **question 1** clearly and remember to include all the costs in your calculations for the final part of the question.

In **question 2**, present your explanation in part (a) and discussion in part (b) clearly. Written questions call for intelligible explanations, and an important challenge is to communicate your ideas well. Remember to answer the question and discuss the conflict with standard costing in part (b).

In **question 3**, demonstrate your understanding of value analysis and functional cost analysis, but remember to relate your points to the specific question – improving sales volumes, costs and profits.

Question 4 asks you to illustrate the differences between feedforward and feedback control using information about a cash budget for your illustration. Make sure that you deal with this specific requirement in relation to a cash budget.

Question 5 asks about the concepts of the Balanced Scorecard but then asks for two non-financial measures that could be used for the company in the question. There is no unique answer to this question, but you may need to think before you decide what your two appropriate performance measures should be.

For part (a) of **question 6** make sure that you present a clear schedule and a clear explanation of relevant and non-relevant costs. The other two parts of the question require clear explanations, so think a bit before starting to write an answer.

Calculating the ratios is the easy part of **question 7** part (a), but there are a lot of calculations and you need to present your calculations clearly, including your figures for the depreciation charges.

For part (b) you need to identify the quality costs that should be presented within each of the four component elements of quality costs. The calculations themselves are quite straightforward. This question is about organisation and presentation.

And just one more thing…

You must **allocate your time** according to the marks available for the question in total, and for the individual parts of the questions (where applicable). It is essential that you **follow the requirements exactly** – it will be very obvious to the marker if you haven't!

Finished with 15 minutes to spare?

Looks like your time allocation went slightly awry. However if you have finished, **don't waste** the last few minutes – go back to **any parts of the questions that you didn't finish** because you ran out of time.

Forget about it!

Forget about what? Excellent, you already have!

SECTION A

Question 1

Text references. The learning curve is covered in Chapter 7.

Top tips. Ensure that you clearly show all workings to part (a) to maximise your mark. In particular, demonstrate clearly how you reach your solutions in parts (b) and (c). Don't worry about the number of decimal places you use in your calculations, just as long as the techniques in your answer are correct. Your answer may differ a bit from the one shown below because of rounding differences.

Easy marks. Using your calculator to answer part (a) should earn you easy marks, provided that you know the learning curve formula. If you are struggling with parts (b) and (c), remember that some of the figures to present in the answer to (c) should be straightforward and should be worth some marks.

(a) <u>Cumulative average time per batch for the first 64 batches</u>

$Y_x = aX^b$

Where Y_x = Cumulative average time per unit to produce X units

a = The time required to produce the first unit of output

X = The cumulative number of units

b = The learning coefficient (log of the learning rate / log of 2)

The cumulative average time per batch, with a learning curve of 85% is therefore

$Y_x = aX^{-0.2345}$

where a = the time for the first batch (1,500 hours) and X is the number of the batch. For the 64th batch, X = 64.

$Y_x = 1,500 \times 64^{-0.2345}$

$= 1,500 \times 0.37709 = 565.6.$

The cumulative average time per batch for the first 64 batches is 565.6 hours.

(b) <u>Time taken for the 64th batch</u>

The cumulative average time per batch for the first 63 batches is

$Y_x = 1,500 \times 63^{-0.2345}$

$= 1,500 \times 0.37849 = 567.7.$

	Hours
Total time for 1st 64 batches (64 × 565.6)	36,198.4
Total time for 1st 63 batches (63 × 567.7)	35,765.1
Time for the 64th batch	433.3

(c) The question states that the average time per batch will be the same for all batches after the 64th batch. The time for the 64th batch was 433.3 hours (part (b)).

		$
Labour cost for the first 6,400 units (64 batches)	(36,198.4 × $12)	434,381
Labour cost for the next 3,600 units (36 batches)	(36 × 433.3 × $12)	187,186
Other variable costs	(10,000 × $38)	380,000
Incremental fixed costs		80,000
Total costs		1,081,567
Required profit		100,000
Required sales revenue		1,181,567
Less: Revenue from first 9,000 units sold	(9,000 × $124)	(1,116,000)
Revenue required from next 1,000 units		65,567

Selling price required for the final 1,000 units = $65,567/1,000 = $65.57 per unit – say **$66 per unit**.

Question 2

> **Text references**. Kaizen Costing is covered in Chapter 9A.
>
> **Top tips**. Remember to make your points clearly, but keep an eye on the time. Don't write everything you know and so write too much.
>
> **Easy marks**. If you know what Kaizen Costing is, there should be some easy marks to gain in part (a) – but remember to make your points clearly.

(a) Kaizen costing

Kaizen means 'continuous improvement' and Kaizen Costing is concerned with **reducing the costs of an item through continuous improvements**.

For each product item the actual unit cost achieved in one year becomes **the starting point for further cost reductions** in the next year. At the beginning of each year (or perhaps more frequently, say every month) a Kaizen cost goal is set. This goal is a cost **lower than the cost at the start** of the period. The aim is then to work towards the Kaizen cost goal in the period.

When a Kaizen cost goal is achieved, it becomes the starting point for targeting further cost reductions with a **new Kaizen cost goal**.

This is a continuous process. Improvements may typically be achieved by eliminating waste and idle time, and finding more efficient ways of doing something.

Another important principle of Kaizen costing is **participation** by everyone in the work team. Employees are empowered to devise **new methods** and **new ways of operating**, in order to reduce costs.

(b) The principles of Kaizen Costing differ from those that apply in standard costing. A **standard cost** is the **expected cost** of an item, analysed in detail (quantities of materials and prices per unit, hours of labour and rates per hour, and so on). SF reviews its standard costs annually, and these are likely to be based on expected or current standards of performance. **Regular (monthly) control reports** compare actual costs with the standard costs and report differences as **favourable** or **adverse** variances.

With Kaizen Costing, **target** or 'standard' **costs are not established** in any detail, and it does not matter how the Kaizen target cost is achieved. Actual costs are compared regularly with the Kaizen target cost, and the **differences indicate** how much **further progress** is needed to achieve the target. There are no adverse variances as such, and favourable variances are inconsistent with Kaizen costing principles.

It may therefore be stated that whereas **standard costing** is concerned with **cost control** and avoiding **excessive variances**, Kaizen costing is **focused on cost reduction**. Standard costs assume that **constant operating conditions** will apply throughout the financial year, whereas Kaizen costing assumes **continuous change**, and so changes in operating conditions and practices, and a **dynamic work environment**.

SF applies its standard costs for one year. With Kaizen costing, if the Kaizen cost target is achieved before the year end, a **new cost target is established**, so that the process of **continuous improvement** can be sustained.

The standard costs are set each year by the directors of SF and variances are discussed at board level. This is a **top-down management philosophy**, based on the concept of strict management control. This is inconsistent with the **participative philosophy** on which Kaizen is based, and the principles of empowerment of the work force.

Differences between current costs and the Kaizen target should provide **motivation for improvement**. In contrast, investigating reasons for adverse variances and making individuals responsible for these variances would be inconsistent with the philosophy of Kaizen.

Question 3

Text references. Value analysis and functional cost analysis are covered in Chapter 7.

Top tips. Demonstrate that you know what value analysis and functional cost analysis are, but make sure too that you answer the question and relate these techniques or methods to increasing sales volume, reducing costs and increasing profits. An answer structure that divides into part (i) value analysis and (ii) functional cost analysis seems suitable.

Easy marks. You should be able to pick up a few marks by explaining what the two techniques or methods are.

Value analysis

Value analysis is a **planned approach to cost reduction** which reviews the material composition of a product and production design so that **modifications and improvements** can be made which do not reduce the value of the product to the consumer or the user.

Value analysis is an inter-disciplinary exercise, and the full co-operation of all functions within the organisation will be required to **find ways of enhancing value**. Costs can be reduced by eliminating activities that do not add value, by finding ways to **economise** or improve the **efficiency** or **effectiveness** of activities.

Typical considerations

LCG should investigate the possibility of **using cheaper substitute materials**, which are as good, if not better than the material currently used to manufacture the garden tables and chairs.

LCG should also consider whether it is possible to use **standardised components** or **reduce the number of components used**. For example, could a garden table be assembled safely with a smaller number of screws?

How value analysis can benefit LCG

If ways can be found to deliver the **same value at a lower cost**, cost reductions can be achieved **without damaging customer satisfaction**. Lower costs will mean higher profits.

LCG may be able to lower its prices to the level of competitors' prices because of the extra cost savings. The lower selling price may lead to greater sales volumes and increased profits.

Alternatively, LCG may decide to offer greater value **without changing the price of products**. This would help to **re-establish LCG's reputation** for manufacturing high quality goods at an affordable price thus yielding a source of **competitive advantage** over its rivals and increased demand for (and therefore increased sales volumes of) LCG products.

Functional cost analysis

Functional cost analysis is concerned with **improving profits by attempting to reduce costs** and / or by **improving products** by adding new features in a cost-effective way. Functional analysis is typically used prior to the **production of new products**.

Typical considerations

A new product (or service) is analysed into its **component parts**, and the function of each separate component is specified in short and simple terms (typically by a verb and noun). The function of a component may be classified as **primary** (essential to the performance of the product) or **secondary** (needed to support a basic function). Components that do not fulfil a primary or secondary function may be unnecessary. The cost of each component is also **measured or estimated**.

LCG should start by assessing the value provided by each component part of the product. Deciding value can be subjective, but it can be based on **market research**. The **value created** by each component is then **compared** with the **value it will provide** to the customer.

Alternative ways of creating the same value with **cheaper components**, or **creating more value** without adding to cost, are then considered. For example, ways may be identified to reduce the number of components in the product, reduce packaging, remove unnecessary components, create a simpler product design, use standardised instead of specialised components, allow more relaxed tolerances in product specifications, use less expensive materials or different methods of transportation.

Where **better design alternative are found**, they should be adopted.

How functional cost analysis can benefit LCG

Functional cost analysis could help LCG to **reduce costs of new products**. If new products can be produced at a lower cost and sold at a market price, the lower costs will lead to higher profits. Lower product costs will create an opportunity to sell products at a lower price, and this should result in higher sales volumes.

If more value can be built into a new product within a target unit cost, **customer demand** for the product at a given price **should be stronger**, and LCG may be able to sell the product at a higher price, or a larger volume at a lower price.

The biggest value gains and financial benefits are often achieved at the **design stage** of a product's life cycle, and the potential benefits from functional cost analysis are therefore substantial.

Question 4

Text references. Feedforward control and feedback control are covered in Chapter 10.

Top tips. Remember to use WX's cash budget as an illustration. The solution given here begins with feedback control and goes on to describe feedforward control before illustrating the differences, but they could just as easily be discussed the other way round.

Easy marks. There should be easy marks available for explaining the difference between the two types of control.

Feedback control

Feedback control (or more strictly, single loop feedback control) is the **traditional system for management control reporting**. 'Feedback' as a term is used to describe both the **control information** and the **control system**. In a feedback control system, **actual performance** is compared periodically with a **budget** or **target** (such as a standard cost) and differences between the actual results and the budget or target are reported as **negative** or **positive** differences or **variances**.

Where the **variances** are large, they are **investigated** to establish the cause. Where appropriate, **control action** is then taken to **correct the cause** of an adverse variance or, possibly, exploit a favourable variance further.

Feedback control systems are therefore **backward-looking**, in the sense that they report on **historical results** and do not directly consider the implications of actual performance for the future.

Feedforward control

Feedforward control is a control system, but is **forward-looking**. Control reports within a feedforward control system compare the **current forecast** of what will happen with the **original budget** or **target**. Differences are therefore the amount by which actual performance should be expected to differ from the original budget by the **end of the financial period**, unless control measures are taken.

Actual performance is not irrelevant, because a current forecast of what will happen in the period includes **actual results to date** as well as the forecast of what will happen in the remainder of the financial period. The forecast for the remainder of the period **may also be based on actual results to date**, projected into the future.

Feedforward control systems, by providing a comparison between planned outcomes and current expectations, provides management with information about **what needs to be done to eliminate the differences**, by taking control action 'before the event'. (With feedback systems, control action is 'after the event' and is not directly concerned with taking action to achieve the budget or target.)

The differences between feedforward and feedback control

Feedback control can provide information to indicate situations where actual results have differed from the plan by a significant amount, and where control action may be necessary to **improve performance in the future**. It is commonly used in budgetary control systems to compare actual sales, costs and profit with the **original budget**.

Cash flow is a different problem. If actual cash flows and cash balances differ from the **cash budget**, there may be **several reasons for the difference**, not just insufficient sales or excessive costs. The timing of receipts and payments may **differ from the assumptions in the budget**, for example because a **large payment from a customer is delayed**. Investigating reasons for the differences between actual cash flows and the budget would be time-consuming and is **unlikely to provide much more useful information** than comparisons of actual costs and revenues with the budget would provide.

The main concern with cash flow for WX should be whether the company will have **sufficient cash or access to borrowings** (such as an overdraft facility) to meet its payment obligations. If there may be insufficient cash, measures can be taken to deal with the problem, such as **delaying some large payments, chasing customers for payment of overdue amounts, or negotiating short-term borrowing from the bank**. The risk of having insufficient cash to make payments can be financial collapse due to illiquidity. Measures can be taken to manage cash flows, but only if **management is aware** that there is a cash flow problem and **how much the cash shortfall might be**.

The directors of WX want to eliminate the overdraft balance by June and to have a positive cash balance of $145,000 by the end of the year. To achieve these targets successfully, management need to be kept informed about **expected cash flows**. **Feedforward information**, comparing the current forecast with the target, provides this information whereas **feedback on historical cash flows would not**.

Question 5

(a) An organisation may have a primary objective. For commercial organisations, this objective is usually financial and may be expressed in terms of a target for growth in earnings or return on capital. However when an organisation focuses on a single objective, there is a risk that **decisions that are made to improve performance in the short term could have damaging or unfavourable consequences in the longer term**.

The balanced scorecard

The concept of the balanced scorecard is that in order to achieve its primary objective over the long term, an organisation must also achieve standards of performance in other aspects of the business. For commercial organisations, unless performance is satisfactory in non-financial aspects of operations, they will not achieve satisfactory financial performance in the long term.

With the balanced scorecard, the **non-financial aspects of performance** are grouped into three categories: performance from a **customer perspective**, from an **internal efficiency perspective** and from an **innovation and learning perspective**. There is also a **financial perspective**; therefore performance is considered from **four perspectives**.

For each perspective of performance, **critical success factors are identified** and **performance targets** are established for each critical success factor. There may be several critical success factors for each perspective, but each of them is considered essential to the long-term success of the organisation. The key performance targets for each perspective of performance together make up a balanced scorecard of performance targets and measurements. Actual performance is monitored against all the targets, **non-financial as well as financial**.

A hierarchy of balanced scorecards can be established, from senior management at the top down to lower management, and the performance targets must all be consistent with each other.

How the balanced scorecard could be used by the airline company

The **airline company in the question** has pursued a **low-price strategy** for competitive advantage, but there are now indications that this strategy is no longer as successful as in the past, and other competitors are taking business away. A balanced scorecard approach could be used to identify the main aspects of non-financial performance that the company needs to improve in order to remain successful and competitive.

If the company intends to maintain its low-price strategy, for example, it may be essential to achieve a **higher level of internal operating efficiency** in order to minimise costs. It may also be considered important **to raise levels of customer satisfaction** with aspects of the airline's services, such as on-board services or convenience of the ticketing system. The airline's problems may also be related to its **failure to innovate** by offering flights to different destinations. By identifying non-financial aspects of performance that are critical to commercial success, the airline company can build up a balanced scorecard and use this balanced set of critical success factors to set targets of performance and monitor actual performance.

(b) Customer satisfaction is probably a critical factor for the success of an airline's passenger services. Low price may be a major consideration, but other factors may be important for customers too, and may help to explain why rival airlines are winning business.

Customer satisfaction

A suitable non-financial measure of performance may be the **number of tickets sold**, and a target for performance may be **growth in ticket sales**. Alternatively, if reliable market research information can be obtained, **customer satisfaction surveys** could be used and a target set for a minimum customer satisfaction rating.

Operating efficiency

To be able to offer low prices, it is essential to be a **low-cost operator**. Aspects of internal efficiency that will affect cost are therefore critically important. The **proportion of seats that are occupied** on flights is a key element of operating efficiency and a target may be established for this.

***

Top tip. A range of different non-financial performance indicators could be used in the answer to part (b). For example the airline carries cargo and a key aspect of the cargo service for customers may be **speed and timeliness of deliveries**. If so, targets for the average time for delivery or for the percentage of deliveries made on time could be used.

From an innovation perspective, it may be argued that the airline is losing competitiveness because it is not introducing enough new flights or cargo services. Targets could therefore be set for the **proportion of total revenue obtained from services introduced in the past two or three years**.

Your answer needs to identify just two non-financial aspects of performance, but you should explain why you consider them to be critical success factors. It would also be useful to indicate the perspective of performance in the balanced scorecard to which your selected performance measurements belong.

SECTION B

Question 6

> **Text references.** Relevant costs are covered in Chapter 1A and transfer pricing is covered in Chapter 13.
>
> **Top tips.** For part (a) set out your relevant costs clearly in a schedule, but the key to a good answer is to explain how you arrived at your figures for relevant costs and why other costs mentioned in the question are not relevant. Part (b) and part (c) also require clear explanations using examples from the scenario.
>
> **Easy marks.** Easy marks can be earned by calculating relevant costs correctly in part (a).

(a)   Relevant cost of building the new engine

The relevant cost of building the new engine is the net incremental cash outflow that will be incurred if the contract is undertaken. Any price in excess of this relevant cost will provide marginal profit for the company.

Cost item	Note	$
Production Director's time	1	Nil
Material A	2	1,375
Material B	3	360
Components from HY	4	3,000
Direct labour	5	2,100
Machine costs	6	175
Fixed overheads	7	Nil
Total relevant cost		7,010

Notes

1   Production Director's time

The cost of the Production Director's time is not relevant for two reasons. The Director is paid a fixed annual salary, and no additional cash expenditure is incurred. The Director's time has already been used, and costs incurred in the past cannot be relevant costs, even if they had resulted in extra cash spending.

Relevant cost = $Nil

2   Material A

If 110 square metres are used from existing inventory, this will lead to additional purchases being required, because the material is in regular use. Therefore, the relevant cost is the current replacement cost.

Relevant cost = 110 square metres × $12.50 = $1,375

3   Material B

Although only 30 litres of material B are required, the minimum order quantity is 40 litres. The surplus quantity would have no other use and so would presumably be disposed of (a zero cost of disposal is assumed.)

Relevant cost = 40 litres × $9 = $360

4   Components

The purchase cost is a relevant cost.

Relevant cost = 60 components × $50 = $3,000

5   Direct labour

235 direct labour hours are required. The first 75 hours of direct labour can be obtained at no extra cost, because there is spare capacity for this amount of time, and the employees will be paid anyway under the guaranteed wage agreement.

Only 160 hours will have to be paid for. These hours can be obtained by getting employees to work overtime, and the incremental cost would be 160 hours × $14 = $2,240. Alternatively temporary staff could be used with supervision and the incremental cost would be (160 hours × $12) + (10 hours × $18) = $2,100. The supervisor's time is an incremental cost because it would be overtime work.

Using temporary staff would cost less, and it is assumed that the cheaper option will be selected.

Relevant cost = $2,100

6   Machine costs

The lease cost is a committed cost that will be incurred anyway – it is not a relevant cost. The relevant cost is the incremental cost of using the machine.

Relevant cost = 25 hours × $7 = $175

7   Fixed overheads

Absorbed fixed overheads are not an incremental cost. It is assumed that there will be no incremental fixed costs as a consequence of performing the contract.

Relevant cost = $Nil

(b)   Opportunity cost

Opportunity cost is the **benefit forgone** by using a resource for one purpose instead of using it for its most profitable alternative purpose. HY will transfer components to RFT for $50 each and the variable cost of making each unit will be $28. This suggests that the opportunity cost that HY will cover in the transfer price is $22 per unit.

The following factors should be considered by HY to determine the opportunity cost of the component.

External market sales

It is not clear as to whether there is an **external market** for the components manufactured by HY. HY may be **unable to meet any external market demand** as a result of supplying RFT with components. Furthermore, the external market price may be significantly higher than the current transfer price of $50.

If this is the case, the opportunity cost for HJ would be the **maximum contribution forgone** as a result of transferring internally rather than selling goods externally.

Raw materials

An opportunity cost can also arise when resources are in short supply.

The shortage of resources in HY may be the **raw materials** that are used to make the components. If so, making components for RFT would mean producing lower quantities of other components or products, and the opportunity cost would be the **contribution forgone** from the lost sales of the other items.

Labour time

Similarly, the shortage of resources in HY may be **labour time**. If labour is in limited supply, producing components for RFT would mean that fewer units of other products or components could be made, and the opportunity cost for HY would be the **contribution forgone** from lost sales of the other items.

(c)   (i) <u>Transfer pricing at actual cost</u>

When there is **no external market** for an item that is transferred between two divisions, the transfer price cannot be market-based and will probably be based on cost. 'Based on cost' should mean that the transfer price is at cost **plus a margin for profit**, otherwise the transferring division makes no profit from the transfer. If the company wants each division to be a profit centre, a transferring division should be able to earn profit from its transfers.

However if the transferring division is a cost centre rather than a profit centre, transfers will be at cost without a mark-up for profit.

For example, suppose that an item is transferred between two divisions at actual cost. If the item costs $80, say, the receiving division will be charged $80. However if the transferring division is **inefficient** or **incurs excessive costs**, the item may cost $100 rather than $80. If so, when the item is transferred at actual cost, $100, the receiving division **effectively pays for the lack of economy** or the inefficiency in the transferring division. The transferring division has **no incentive to control costs**. The receiving division can do nothing to control the cost of the items that it is receiving from the other division, but its performance will be judged partly on the cost of the items that it 'buys' internally.

This means that the main problem with using actual cost as the basis for a transfer price is that **responsibility for poor cost control is not properly attributed** and **control** is therefore **not properly exercised** over costs.

(ii) <u>Transfer pricing at standard cost</u>

A different situation will apply if items are transferred at a **budgeted** or **standard** cost. When standard cost is used, responsibility for any favourable or adverse variances in the transferring division is attributed to the **transferring division, not the receiving division**.

For example suppose that the standard cost of a transferred item is $80 but the actual cost is $100. The receiving division would be charged $80 for the item, and an **adverse variance of $20** would be attributed to the **transferring division**. The manager of the transferring division would be responsible for the excessive cost and would be expected to take control measures to deal with the problem.

The manager of the receiving division, by paying the standard cost of $80, **would not be held responsible** for the excess spending in the other division, and would be held responsible only for those items of cost and revenue that are **within the divisional manager's control**.

The manager of the transferring division would also be credited with favourable variances, and it may be possible to establish a **bonus payment system** related to the amount of favourable variances in each period. If so, this may **provide some motivation** for the management of the **transferring division** to achieve favourable variances by **keeping actual costs below standard**.

Question 7

Text references. Financial ratios are covered in Chapter 11 and investment centres and ROI are covered in Chapter 12. Quality costs are covered in Chapter 9A.

Top tips. There are lot of calculations required for each part of this question, and clear presentation of the figures is important. In part (a) it is important to identify the method of calculating depreciation. In part (b) the challenge is to organise the quality costs into their four categories for presentation in the cost of quality report.

(a)   (i) <u>Return on capital employed</u>

	North		South	
	2010	2011	2010	2011
Return on capital employed	25.1%	27.1%	18.7%	19.2%
(Profit (W3) / Average net assets (W2) × 100)				

(ii) <u>Asset turnover and profit/sales %</u>

	North		South	
	2010	2011	2010	2011
Asset turnover	1.28	1.37	1.03	1.05
(Sales (W3) /Average net assets (W2))				
Profit/sales %	19.6%	19.8%	18.2%	18.2%
Profit (W3) / Sales (W2) × 100				

(iii) <u>Relative performance</u>

North Division **exceeded the target ROCE** in both 2010 and 2011, and ROCE in 2011 was higher than in 2010. The improvement in 2011 is attributable mainly to an improvement in the **asset turnover ratio** from 1.28 to 1.37, but there was also some increase in the profit/sales ratio. North Division therefore appears to have **performed well**.

South Division's performance does not seem to be as good. The division **did not achieve the target ROCE** of 20% in either year, although ROCE was better in 2011 than in 2010 and was close to 20% in 2011. The improvement in ROCE is attributable to better asset turnover; there was no change in the **profit margin** between 2010 and 2011.

The company only recently established operations in the south. It is possible that the lower ROCE is attributable to **newer** (and so more expensive) **non-current assets**, as well as to a need to sell at **lower prices to win customers** in a new region. So although South Division has not performed as well as North Division, there may well be acceptable reasons.

Workings

1   <u>Depreciation</u>

	North	South
	$m	$m
2010 Opening non-current assets	70.00	130.00
Purchases	10.50	19.50
	80.50	149.50
Depreciation 2010 (10%)	8.05	14.95
2011 Opening non-current assets	72.45	134.55
Purchases	15.05	27.95
	87.50	162.50
Depreciation 2011 (10%)	8.75	16.25
2011 Closing non-current assets	78.75	146.25

2 Average net assets

	North 2010 $m	North 2011 $m	South 2010 $m	South 2011 $m
Opening non-current assets	70.00		130.00	
Opening net current assets	42.00		78.00	
Opening net assets	112.00	119.00	208.00	221.00
Closing non-current assets	72.45	78.75	134.55	146.25
Closing net current assets	46.55	47.25	86.45	87.75
Closing net assets	119.00	126.00	221.00	234.00
Average net assets	115.50	122.50	214.50	227.50

3 Profit

	North 2010 $m	North 2011 $m	South 2010 $m	South 2011 $m
Sales	148.00	168.00	220.00	240.00
Operating cash flow	37.00	42.00	55.00	60.00
Depreciation (W1)	8.05	8.75	14.95	16.25
Profit	28.95	33.25	40.05	43.75

(b) To: The Directors

From: Management Accountant

Date: XX/XX/XX

Subject: Cost of quality report for the year ended 31 May 2011

This quality cost report analyses quality costs into four categories: costs of **prevention**, costs of **appraisal**, costs of **internal failure** and costs of **external failure**.

Costs of prevention are costs incurred to **prevent quality failures** from happening, and for SHG these consist of the costs of product design engineering and also staff training in quality issues.

Costs of appraisal are the costs of **inspection** and **associated testing**.

Costs of internal failure are the costs of correcting errors or failures that are **detected and corrected** before the products are delivered to customers. These consist of the costs of **re-working faulty items**.

Costs of external failure are costs incurred due to **quality failures** after the products have been **delivered to customers.** They consist of the costs of **repairs under warranty** and also the contribution/profit lost as a result of bad **publicity and lost sales**.

Cost of quality: Year ended 31 May 2011

	$	$
Costs of prevention:		
Design engineering costs: (66,000 hours × $75)	4,950,000	
Staff training costs	150,000	
		5,100,000
Costs of appraisal:		
Inspection costs (manufacturing): (216,000 hours × $40)	8,640,000	
Additional product testing costs	49,000	
		8,689,000

Costs of internal failure:

Rework costs (manufacturing): (1,500 units × $3,000)   4,500,000

Costs of external failure:

Warranty repair costs: (1,800 units × $3,200)   5,760,000

Customer support costs (marketing): (1,800 units × $200)   360,000

Transportation costs (distribution): (1,800 units × $240)   432,000

Lost contribution due to lost sales: (1,400 units× $6,000)   8,400,000

                                                                                                                                       14,952,000

Total quality costs   33,241,000

MATHEMATICAL TABLES
AND EXAM FORMULAE

MATHS TABLES AND FORMULAE

Present value table

Present value of 1 unit of currency, that is $(1 + r)^{-n}$ where r = interest rate; n = number of periods until payment or receipt.

Periods (n)	\multicolumn{10}{c}{Interest rates (r)}
	1%	2%	3%	4%	5%	6%	7%	8%	9%	10%
1	0.990	0.980	0.971	0.962	0.952	0.943	0.935	0.926	0.917	0.909
2	0.980	0.961	0.943	0.925	0.907	0.890	0.873	0.857	0.842	0.826
3	0.971	0.942	0.915	0.889	0.864	0.840	0.816	0.794	0.772	0.751
4	0.961	0.924	0.888	0.855	0.823	0.792	0.763	0.735	0.708	0.683
5	0.951	0.906	0.863	0.822	0.784	0.747	0.713	0.681	0.650	0.621
6	0.942	0.888	0.837	0.790	0.746	0.705	0.666	0.630	0.596	0.564
7	0.933	0.871	0.813	0.760	0.711	0.665	0.623	0.583	0.547	0.513
8	0.923	0.853	0.789	0.731	0.677	0.627	0.582	0.540	0.502	0.467
9	0.914	0.837	0.766	0.703	0.645	0.592	0.544	0.500	0.460	0.424
10	0.905	0.820	0.744	0.676	0.614	0.558	0.508	0.463	0.422	0.386
11	0.896	0.804	0.722	0.650	0.585	0.527	0.475	0.429	0.388	0.350
12	0.887	0.788	0.701	0.625	0.557	0.497	0.444	0.397	0.356	0.319
13	0.879	0.773	0.681	0.601	0.530	0.469	0.415	0.368	0.326	0.290
14	0.870	0.758	0.661	0.577	0.505	0.442	0.388	0.340	0.299	0.263
15	0.861	0.743	0.642	0.555	0.481	0.417	0.362	0.315	0.275	0.239
16	0.853	0.728	0.623	0.534	0.458	0.394	0.339	0.292	0.252	0.218
17	0.844	0.714	0.605	0.513	0.436	0.371	0.317	0.270	0.231	0.198
18	0.836	0.700	0.587	0.494	0.416	0.350	0.296	0.250	0.212	0.180
19	0.828	0.686	0.570	0.475	0.396	0.331	0.277	0.232	0.194	0.164
20	0.820	0.673	0.554	0.456	0.377	0.312	0.258	0.215	0.178	0.149

Periods (n)	\multicolumn{10}{c}{Interest rates (r)}
	11%	12%	13%	14%	15%	16%	17%	18%	19%	20%
1	0.901	0.893	0.885	0.877	0.870	0.862	0.855	0.847	0.840	0.833
2	0.812	0.797	0.783	0.769	0.756	0.743	0.731	0.718	0.706	0.694
3	0.731	0.712	0.693	0.675	0.658	0.641	0.624	0.609	0.593	0.579
4	0.659	0.636	0.613	0.592	0.572	0.552	0.534	0.516	0.499	0.482
5	0.593	0.567	0.543	0.519	0.497	0.476	0.456	0.437	0.419	0.402
6	0.535	0.507	0.480	0.456	0.432	0.410	0.390	0.370	0.352	0.335
7	0.482	0.452	0.425	0.400	0.376	0.354	0.333	0.314	0.296	0.279
8	0.434	0.404	0.376	0.351	0.327	0.305	0.285	0.266	0.249	0.233
9	0.391	0.361	0.333	0.308	0.284	0.263	0.243	0.225	0.209	0.194
10	0.352	0.322	0.295	0.270	0.247	0.227	0.208	0.191	0.176	0.162
11	0.317	0.287	0.261	0.237	0.215	0.195	0.178	0.162	0.148	0.135
12	0.286	0.257	0.231	0.208	0.187	0.168	0.152	0.137	0.124	0.112
13	0.258	0.229	0.204	0.182	0.163	0.145	0.130	0.116	0.104	0.093
14	0.232	0.205	0.181	0.160	0.141	0.125	0.111	0.099	0.088	0.078
15	0.209	0.183	0.160	0.140	0.123	0.108	0.095	0.084	0.074	0.065
16	0.188	0.163	0.141	0.123	0.107	0.093	0.081	0.071	0.062	0.054
17	0.170	0.146	0.125	0.108	0.093	0.080	0.069	0.060	0.052	0.045
18	0.153	0.130	0.111	0.095	0.081	0.069	0.059	0.051	0.044	0.038
19	0.138	0.116	0.098	0.083	0.070	0.060	0.051	0.043	0.037	0.031
20	0.124	0.104	0.087	0.073	0.061	0.051	0.043	0.037	0.031	0.026

Cumulative present value of 1 unit of currency per annum, Receivable or Payable at the end of each year for:

n years $\dfrac{1-(1+r)-n}{r}$

Periods					Interest rates (r)					
(n)	1%	2%	3%	4%	5%	6%	7%	8%	9%	10%
1	0.990	0.980	0.971	0.962	0.952	0.943	0.935	0.926	0.917	0.909
2	1.970	1.942	1.913	1.886	1.859	1.833	1.808	1.783	1.759	1.736
3	2.941	2.884	2.829	2.775	2.723	2.673	2.624	2.577	2.531	2.487
4	3.902	3.808	3.717	3.630	3.546	3.465	3.387	3.312	3.240	3.170
5	4.853	4.713	4.580	4.452	4.329	4.212	4.100	3.993	3.890	3.791
6	5.795	5.601	5.417	5.242	5.076	4.917	4.767	4.623	4.486	4.355
7	6.728	6.472	6.230	6.002	5.786	5.582	5.389	5.206	5.033	4.868
8	7.652	7.325	7.020	6.733	6.463	6.210	5.971	5.747	5.535	5.335
9	8.566	8.162	7.786	7.435	7.108	6.802	6.515	6.247	5.995	5.759
10	9.471	8.983	8.530	8.111	7.722	7.360	7.024	6.710	6.418	6.145
11	10.368	9.787	9.253	8.760	8.306	7.887	7.499	7.139	6.805	6.495
12	11.255	10.575	9.954	9.385	8.863	8.384	7.943	7.536	7.161	6.814
13	12.134	11.348	10.635	9.986	9.394	8.853	8.358	7.904	7.487	7.103
14	13.004	12.106	11.296	10.563	9.899	9.295	8.745	8.244	7.786	7.367
15	13.865	12.849	11.938	11.118	10.380	9.712	9.108	8.559	8.061	7.606
16	14.718	13.578	12.561	11.652	10.838	10.106	9.447	8.851	8.313	7.824
17	15.562	14.292	13.166	12.166	11.274	10.477	9.763	9.122	8.544	8.022
18	16.398	14.992	13.754	12.659	11.690	10.828	10.059	9.372	8.756	8.201
19	17.226	15.679	14.324	13.134	12.085	11.158	10.336	9.604	8.950	8.365
20	18.046	16.351	14.878	13.590	12.462	11.470	10.594	9.818	9.129	8.514

Periods					Interest rates (r)					
(n)	11%	12%	13%	14%	15%	16%	17%	18%	19%	20%
1	0.901	0.893	0.885	0.877	0.870	0.862	0.855	0.847	0.840	0.833
2	1.713	1.690	1.668	1.647	1.626	1.605	1.585	1.566	1.547	1.528
3	2.444	2.402	2.361	2.322	2.283	2.246	2.210	2.174	2.140	2.106
4	3.102	3.037	2.974	2.914	2.855	2.798	2.743	2.690	2.639	2.589
5	3.696	3.605	3.517	3.433	3.352	3.274	3.199	3.127	3.058	2.991
6	4.231	4.111	3.998	3.889	3.784	3.685	3.589	3.498	3.410	3.326
7	4.712	4.564	4.423	4.288	4.160	4.039	3.922	3.812	3.706	3.605
8	5.146	4.968	4.799	4.639	4.487	4.344	4.207	4.078	3.954	3.837
9	5.537	5.328	5.132	4.946	4.772	4.607	4.451	4.303	4.163	4.031
10	5.889	5.650	5.426	5.216	5.019	4.833	4.659	4.494	4.339	4.192
11	6.207	5.938	5.687	5.453	5.234	5.029	4.836	4.656	4.486	4.327
12	6.492	6.194	5.918	5.660	5.421	5.197	4.988	4.793	4.611	4.439
13	6.750	6.424	6.122	5.842	5.583	5.342	5.118	4.910	4.715	4.533
14	6.982	6.628	6.302	6.002	5.724	5.468	5.229	5.008	4.802	4.611
15	7.191	6.811	6.462	6.142	5.847	5.575	5.324	5.092	4.876	4.675
16	7.379	6.974	6.604	6.265	5.954	5.668	5.405	5.162	4.938	4.730
17	7.549	7.120	6.729	6.373	6.047	5.749	5.475	5.222	4.990	4.775
18	7.702	7.250	6.840	6.467	6.128	5.818	5.534	5.273	5.033	4.812
19	7.839	7.366	6.938	6.550	6.198	5.877	5.584	5.316	5.070	4.843
20	7.963	7.469	7.025	6.623	6.259	5.929	5.628	5.353	5.101	4.870

Formulae

FORMULAE

PROBABILITY

$A \cup B$ = **A or B**. $A \cap B$ = **A and B** (overlap).
$P(B \mid A)$ = probability of B, **given** A.

Rules of Addition
If A and B are mutually exclusive: $P(A \cup B) = P(A) + P(B)$
If A and B are not mutually exclusive: $P(A \cup B) = P(A) + P(B) - P(A \cap B)$

Rules of Multiplication
If A and B are *independent*:: $P(A \cap B) = P(A) * P(B)$
If A and B are **not** *independent*: $P(A \cap B) = P(A) * P(B \mid A)$

$E(X) = \sum$ (probability * payoff)

DESCRIPTIVE STATISTICS

Arithmetic Mean

$$\bar{x} = \frac{\sum x}{n} \qquad \bar{x} = \frac{\sum fx}{\sum f} \quad \text{(frequency distribution)}$$

Standard Deviation

$$SD = \sqrt{\frac{\sum(x - \bar{x})^2}{n}} \qquad SD = \sqrt{\frac{\sum fx^2}{\sum f} - \bar{x}^2} \quad \text{(frequency distribution)}$$

INDEX NUMBERS

Price relative = $100 * P_1/P_0$ Quantity relative = $100 * Q_1/Q_0$

Price: $$\frac{\sum w * \left(\dfrac{P_1}{P_o}\right)}{\sum w} \times 100$$

Quantity: $$\frac{\sum w * \left(\dfrac{Q_1}{Q_o}\right)}{\sum w} \times 100$$

TIME SERIES

Additive Model

Series = Trend + Seasonal + Random

Multiplicative Model

Series = Trend * Seasonal * Random

FINANCIAL MATHEMATICS

Compound Interest (Values and Sums)

Future Value S, of a sum of X, invested for n periods, compounded at $r\%$ interest

$$S = X[1 + r]^n$$

Annuity

Present value of an annuity of £1 per annum receivable or payable for n years, commencing in one year, discounted at $r\%$ per annum:

$$PV = \frac{1}{r}\left[1 - \frac{1}{[1+r]^n}\right]$$

Perpetuity

Present value of £1 per annum, payable or receivable in perpetuity, commencing in one year, discounted at $r\%$ per annum:

$$PV = \frac{1}{r}$$

LEARNING CURVE

$$Y_x = aX^b$$

where:

Y_x = the cumulative average time per unit to produce X units;
a = the time required to produce the first unit of output;
X = the cumulative number of units;
b = the index of learning.

The exponent b is defined as the log of the learning curve improvement rate divided by log 2.

INVENTORY MANAGEMENT

Economic Order Quantity

$$EOQ = \sqrt{\frac{2C_o D}{C_h}}$$

where: C_o = cost of placing an order
C_h = cost of holding one unit in inventory for one year
D = annual demand

Review Form – Paper P2 Performance Management (01/12)

Name: _____   Address: _____
                                            _____
                                            _____

How have you used this Kit?
(Tick one box only)

☐ Home study (book only)
☐ On a course: college _____
☐ With 'correspondence' package
☐ Other _____

Why did you decide to purchase this Kit?
(Tick one box only)

☐ Have used the complementary Study text
☐ Have used other BPP products in the past
☐ Recommendation by friend/colleague
☐ Recommendation by a lecturer at college
☐ Saw advertising
☐ Other _____

During the past six months do you recall seeing/receiving any of the following?
(Tick as many boxes as are relevant)

☐ Our advertisement in *Student Accountant*
☐ Our advertisement in *Pass*
☐ Our advertisement in *PQ*
☐ Our brochure with a letter through the post
☐ Our website www.bpp.com

Which (if any) aspects of our advertising do you find useful?
(Tick as many boxes as are relevant)

☐ Prices and publication dates of new editions
☐ Information on product content
☐ Facility to order books off-the-page
☐ None of the above

Which BPP products have you used?

Text	☐	*Success CD*	☐	*Interactive Passcards*	☐
Kit	☑	*i-Pass*	☐	*Home Study Package*	☐
Passcard	☐	*Learn Online*	☐	*Home Study PLUS*	☐

Your ratings, comments and suggestions would be appreciated on the following areas.

	Very useful	Useful	Not useful
Passing P2	☐	☐	☐
Planning your question practice	☐	☐	☐
Questions	☐	☐	☐
Top Tips etc in answers	☐	☐	☐
Content and structure of answers	☐	☐	☐
'Plan of attack' in mock exams	☐	☐	☐
Mock exam answers	☐	☐	☐

Overall opinion of this Kit   Excellent ☐   Good ☐   Adequate ☐   Poor ☐

Do you intend to continue using BPP products?   Yes ☐   No ☐

The BPP author of this edition can be e-mailed at: ianblackmore@bpp.com

Please return this form to: Stephen Osborne, CIMA Publishing Manager, BPP Learning Media, FREEPOST, London, W12 8BR

Review Form (continued)

TELL US WHAT YOU THINK

Please note any further comments and suggestions/errors below.